AQA PSYCHOLOGY

FOR A LEVEL

YEAR 2

Cara Flanagan

Michael Griffin

Jo Haycock

Rob Liddle

Arwa Mohamedbhai

Revision Guide

Illuminate Publishing

Published in 2017 by Illuminate Publishing Ltd,
P.O. Box 1160, Cheltenham, Gloucestershire GL50 9RW

Orders: Please visit www.illuminatepublishing.com
or email sales@illuminatepublishing.com

British Library Cataloguing in Publication Data

A catalogue record for this book is available from the
British Library

ISBN 978-1-908682-45-1

Printed by Barley Print, Cuffley, Herts

2nd impression 04.17

The publisher's policy is to use papers that are natural,
renewable and recyclable products made from
wood grown in sustainable forests. The logging and
manufacturing processes are expected to conform to the
environmental regulations of the country of origin.

Every effort has been made to contact copyright holders
of material produced in this book. If notified, the publisher
will be pleased to rectify any errors or omissions at the
earliest opportunity.

Editor: Nic Watson, Haremi
Cover design: Nigel Harriss
Text design: Nigel Harriss and John Dickinson
Layout: John Dickinson
Front cover photographer: Julia Trotti
Model: Madeline Rae Mason
Makeup: Lidija Jevremovic
Stylist: Jessie McNaught

Unsung heroes

This wonderful little book is the work of a cast of
thousands – well slightly fewer than that but we do have a
large support team to thank.

We owe a considerable debt of gratitude to our writing
partners who worked on the textbook and the Revision
App: Matt Jarvis and Anna Horwitz. This book is entirely
an adaptation of these works.

We have enormous appreciation for those who manage
the whole production – first of all our friend, mentor
and publisher, Rick Jackman and his wonderful team at
Illuminate (Clare Jackman, Peter Burton, Saskia Santos and
Vikki Mann). They really are unique and wonderful.

Finally there is the very special team who design and
check the product you see before you. We owe thanks to
the Nigemeister – Nigel Harriss, supreme designer who is
responsible for the unique and spectacular original design.
This design and layout of the book has been adapted,
refined and applied with enormous care by John Dickinson.
This is no mean feat and it is extraordinary that each page
is a thing of beauty.

And finally a thank you to the meticulous and thoughtful
Nic Watson, a perfectionist who dots all the I's and a lot
more in ensuring the clarity of our words.

Thank you all.

About the authors

Cara is author of many books for A level and GCSE Psychology students and a
conference organiser and speaker; she is also senior editor of *Psychology Review*.
She is looking forward to one day spending more time lying on a beach or
climbing mountains but does manage it occasionally.

Mike is a teacher of psychology, Assistant Headteacher and previous Head of
Sixth Form. He is an author of resources for the delivery of psychology lessons
and provides CPD for other psychology teachers. He is enjoying being a Dad and
still loving, ahem, changing nappies and early mornings.

Jo is Head of Psychology and Head of Sixth Form at Newport Girls' High
School. She set up the Shropshire Psychology Teacher's network and has taught
psychology at A level and undergraduate level as well as completing a range of
practitioner-based research projects. She contributes to whole school training on
study skills and growth mindset. She is passionate about psychology generally,
football and cycling between vineyards.

Rob was an A level psychology teacher for more than 20 years, before turning
to writing. He ventured back into teaching again recently and would like to give
a big shout-out to his ex-colleagues at Winstanley College. He has finally come
to terms with never seeing *Frozen*, despite having two granddaughters.

Arwa is Head of Year 12 at Bacup and Rawtenstall Grammar School, Lancashire.
She delights in making interactive teaching resources to spice up her lessons and
is a popular and enthusiastic psychology teacher. She enjoys dining out, playing
netball and her husband thinks she may have a shopping addiction.

CONTENTS

Introduction

Exam advice

AO stands for 'assessment objective'.

Apply it

The 'Apply it' questions throughout this book aim to help you practise AO2 skills; 30% of the marks in the exam are AO2.

In the A level exam there are three papers:

Paper 1
A: Social influence (24 marks)
B: Memory (24 marks)
C: Attachment (24 marks)
D: Psychopathology (24 marks)

Paper 2
A: Approaches in Psychology (24 marks)
B: Biopsychology (24 marks)
C: Research methods (48 marks)

Paper 3
A: Issues and debates in Psychology (24 marks)
B: Relationships OR Gender OR Cognition and development (24 marks)
C: Schizophrenia OR Eating behaviour OR Stress (24 marks)
D: Aggression OR Forensic Psychology OR Addiction (24 marks)

On all sections of the exam the type of question is unpredictable. You might have an essay question and/or there may be research methods questions and/or an application question.

Research methods questions will be in every section in addition to the Research methods section on Paper 2.

25%

At least 25% of the marks for your A level exam will come from questions on research methods.

Type of exam questions

AO1	Identify, define, outline, describe, explain	Identify **one** emotional characteristic of depression. (*1 mark*)
		Outline the multi-store model of memory. (*4 marks*)
		Explain what is meant by 'reductionism'. Briefly explain why the biological approach is considered to be an example of reductionism in psychology. (*4 marks*)
AO2	Application	[Stem] Siddik was in a car accident and since then he has had difficulty producing speech fluently. He speaks very slowly and it takes a lot of effort to produce sentences, which often lack fluency.
		[Question] Using your knowledge of localisation of function suggest which area of Siddik's brain was damaged in the car accident. Explain your answer. (*3 marks*)
AO3	One criticism	Explain **one** criticism of Milgram's research on obedience. (*3 marks*)
	Evaluation	Evaluate humanistic psychology. (*10 marks*)
AO1 + AO3	Mini-essays	Outline and evaluate research into **one** biological rhythm. (*8 marks*)
	Extended writing	Discuss gender bias in psychological research. (*16 marks*)
AO1 + AO2 + AO3	Extended writing + applications	[Stem] Billy's wife, Cheryl, was adopted as a child. Billy has read about attachment and wonders if Cheryl's early experiences will affect her relationships with their children. However, she was adopted very early and had a close relationship with her adoptive parents.
		[Question] Discuss the influence of early attachment on childhood and adult relationships. Refer to Billy's concerns in your answer. (*16 marks*)

Research methods questions

AO1	Explain	Explain what is meant by a 'critical value' when using inferential statistics. (*2 marks*)
AO2	Application	[Stem] In a study on memory the researcher wanted to ensure that the memory abilities of participants would not act as an extraneous variable.
		[Question] Explain how a matched pairs design could have been used in this experiment. (*2 marks*)
AO3	Evaluate	Explain **one** limitation of qualitative data. (*2 marks*)
		Below are five statements about the limitations of questionnaires compared with interviews. Which **two** statements are correct?
		A. Answers may be inaccurate because people portray themselves in a good light.
		B. People who cannot read will be unable to take part.
		C. It is difficult to get a large number of people to respond.
		D. There are only closed questions.
		E. People may misunderstand a question and can't ask for help. (*2 marks*)

What to do for a Grade A

Top class AO1	Top class AO1 … includes details and specialist terms. For example: • This is good → Siffre (in the 1960s) described how his circadian rhythms changed … • This isn't good → One study found that people's daily rhythms became different … You don't need to write *more*, you just need to include specific *bits* of information such as specialist terms, researcher's names, percentages and so on.
Top class AO2	Top class AO2 … uses text or quotes from the stem of the question. For example (answer to the question about Cheryl on the facing page): • This is good → Cheryl may have developed a secure attachment with her adoptive parents as she was adopted early, before the end of the sensitive period for attachment development. • This isn't good → Strong attachments are most likely to form during a sensitive period in development which may be true in early adoptions, like Cheryl. It's not enough to just mention a few key words – you must really *engage* with the stem. This is a skill that needs practice.

Top class AO3	Top class AO3 … is elaborated and therefore effective. For example:
	
	❶ *Beginner* level: State your point: One criticism is … This theory is supported by … One strength is ….
	
	❷ *Intermediate* level: Add some *context*.
	
	  • This is good → One limitation is that artificial materials were used. The study by the Petersons used consonant syllables.
	
	  • This isn't good → One limitation is that artificial materials were used. This doesn't tell us about everyday life.
	
	  The second example is *generic* – it could be used anywhere.
	
	  Context is king.
	
	❸ *Expert* level: Add further explanation to make the point *thorough* + finish 'This shows that …'
	
	  Read the criticisms throughout this book as examples of expert level. We have provided further elaboration and a conclusion for each one.
	
	If you find expert level difficult then just do intermediate. In an extended writing essay for A level do five or six intermediate criticisms and that should get you the full 10 marks. Do four expert level criticisms and that should be sufficient.
	
	Whatever you do AVOID a list of beginner level criticisms with no context.

Top class A level essays	Make it organised – it helps the examiner see the separate elements of your answer. Use paragraphs. There is more advice on essay (extended writing) questions on the next page …

Describe **FEWER** studies but describe them in detail.

Identify **FEWER** critical points, but explain each one thoroughly.

List-like is bad.

It's actually quite easy to list lots of points – explaining them is challenging.

Context is king

Good evaluation points must contain evidence.

Your point may be well-elaborated but, if the same elaborated point can be placed in many different essays then it is too **EASY**.

Good evaluation points must have **CONTEXT**.

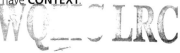

Exam advice

The term 'research' refers to theories, explanations or studies.

KNOWLEDGE CHECK

The questions throughout this book should help you identify all the different ways that questions can be asked.

Each A level paper has 96 marks and it is a 2 hour exam (120 minutes) which gives you 1¼ minutes for each mark.

Just because you have written lots doesn't mean you will get high marks.

Students who write long answers often do poorly.

- Such answers tend to ramble and may not answer the question.
- Spending too much time on one question means less time elsewhere.
- Your answer may lack detail – lists of studies and lists of critical points don't get high marks.
- Long essays are often very descriptive and there are never more than 6 marks for description.

Download suggested answers to the Knowledge Check questions from **www.illuminatepublishing.com/psychrganswers2**

More information if you can bear it

There are lots of little rules

One or more Two or more	*Discuss **one or more** explanations of obedience.* (16 marks)
	Means you can potentially gain full marks for just one explanation (gives you time to describe and evaluate it fully, which is important to show detail).
	Or you can elect to do more explanations – but too many explanations is not good because your answer becomes list-like (no details).
Difference between	*Explain the difference between electroencephalograms (EEGs) and event-related potentials (ERPs).* (4 marks)
	The danger is that you will simply describe each item. You must find a way to contrast them both, for example considering the data produced by each one.
Questions with extra information	*Describe and evaluate the cognitive approach. Refer to **one** other approach in your answer.* (16 marks)
	*Describe **one** animal study of attachment. Include details of what the researcher(s) did and what they found.* (4 marks)
	Make sure you satisfy the demands of ALL parts of the question.

How much should I write?

In general 25–30 words per mark is a good rule – as long as the answer is focused on the topic.

For an A level essay of 16 marks you might therefore write:

AO1 150–200 words   AO3 250–300 words

Here are two ways to produce top class A level essays:

Route 1	Route 2
6 marks AO1	*6 marks AO1*
Six paragraphs/points, write about 150 words.	*Six* paragraphs/points, write about 150 words.
10 marks AO3	*10 marks AO3*
Five or *six* paragraphs/criticisms at *intermediate* level.	*Three* or *four* paragraphs/criticisms at *expert* level (with plenty of discussion).
	Doing just four gives you time to elaborate more and produce more of a discussion (offering a contrasting view).

Effective revision

Create revision cards	For the **description** the amount you need is about 150–200 words. • Identify 6–8 points on the topic. • Record a trigger phrase in the left-hand column. • Record about 25–30 words in the right-hand column. For example, for a description of the psychodynamic approach:

AO1 trigger phrase	Description
Unconscious	We are aware of our conscious mind, we can be aware of pre-conscious thinking in dreams and the unconscious is beyond awareness. It stores biological drives and instincts.
Tripartite	The id is the primitive part driven by the pleasure principle. The ego mediates between the id and the superego, driven by the reality principle. The superego is driven by the morality principle.
Psychosexual stages	Each stage is marked by a different conflict that the child must resolve to move on to the next stage. Unresolved conflicts lead to fixations.

… and reduce your cards to the minimum for revision:

AO1 trigger phrase	Description
Unconscious	Conscious, pre-conscious (e.g. dreams), unconscious (beyond awareness).
Tripartite	Id (primitive, pleasure principle), ego (mediator, reality), superego (morality).
Psychosexual stages	Each stage has conflict to resolve or leads to fixations.

For the **evaluation** the amount you need is about 250–350 words.
- Identify 4–6 critical points.
- Record a trigger phrase in the left-hand column.
- Record evidence or explanation in the next column.
- If you are doing expert level, add elaboration and end with a conclusion (link back).
- A well-elaborated critical point should be about 60 words.

For example, for criticisms of the psychodynamic approach, read what is in this book…

Trigger phrase	Context	Elaboration	Conclusion
One strength is that the psychodynamic approach has explanatory power.	Although Freud's theory is controversial and often bizarre, it has had huge influence on Western contemporary thought.	It has been used to explain a wide range of behaviours (moral, mental disorders) and drew attention to the influence of childhood on adult personality.	Alongside **behaviourism**, it was the dominant approach in psychology for the first half of the twentieth century.

… and reduce your cards to the minimum for revision:

Trigger phrase	Context	Elaboration	Conclusion
Explanatory power.	Influence on Western thought.	Wide range of behaviours (moral, mental disorders), influence of childhood.	Dominant approach in psychology.

Rehearse the trigger phrases	Cover up all columns except the left-hand one and try to recall what is there using the trigger phrase.
Rehearse the content	When you are standing at a bus stop, see if you can remember all the trigger phrases for one topic.
Practise writing timed answers	Write an essay answer with your trigger phrases in front of you. Give yourself 20 minutes for a 16-mark answer.

If you learn too much you will just try to squeeze it into the exam and you don't have time.

Focus on fewer points and make sure you *explain* them in detail. That's where the marks are.

In this book we have aimed to provide six points of AO1 for each topic, consisting of a trigger phrase and explanations. For example, on page 20 you will find the following AO1 (descriptive) content for the psychodynamic approach:

Key assumptions of the psychodynamic approach	
The *unconscious mind* has an important influence on behaviour.	Sigmund Freud suggested the mind is made up of: • Conscious – what we are aware of. • Pre-conscious – memories and thoughts we are not currently aware of but can be accessed. • Unconscious – we are unaware of the contents of the unconscious. It is a vast storehouse of biological drives and instincts that influence our behaviour.
Tripartite structure of personality. Dynamic interaction between the three parts determines behaviour.	Freud saw personality as having three parts: • *Id* – primitive part of the personality operates on the *pleasure principle*, demands instant gratification. • *Ego* – works on the *reality principle* and is the mediator between the id and superego. • *Superego* – internalised sense of right and wrong, based on the *morality principle*. Punishes the ego through guilt.

On the facing page (page 21) there are five evaluation points. The trigger phrase is across the top and there are three boxes below with suggested elaboration.

No athlete would dream of running a race without doing many practice runs of the right distance and within a set time.

Understanding marking

AO1 question: Outline the cognitive approach to psychology. *(4 marks)*

Answer The cognitive approach is one of a number of approaches that psychologists use. It focuses especially on the mind and internal thought processes. Cognitive basically means thinking.

Computer-processing models are used to look at these as it is believed that information processing within the mind works much like a computer does. One example of this is Atkinson and Shiffrin's multi-store model of memory which shows how the brain processes memory step-by-step in a similar way to how a computer works. It uses the ideas of input and output like a computer does   (93 words)

AO2 question: [Stem] Asif is studying psychology and tells his mother about biological rhythms: 'We learned about a part of the brain that sets a constant rhythm for the body so you wake and fall asleep at about the same time every day. It's so cool.'

His mother is interested and responds: 'That doesn't explain why I wake up a lot earlier in summer when it gets light at 5am. If there is a constant rhythm why would this change?'

[Question] With reference to the conversation above, explain how the sleep/wake cycle is controlled by biological factors. *(6 marks)*

Answer Your sleep/wake cycle is the phrase that is used to describe when you go to sleep and when you wake up. All people all over the world go to sleep and wake up and so do animals. It is very important for their well-being. Well, what is it that determines when you go to sleep? There is a small part of your brain that sets a constant rhythm. This is the biological pacemaker. It sets the pace for the processes in your body and makes everything work in tune. This is what Asif was talking about.

However, Asif's mother is right too because this is reset by light. The biological rhythms in your body are tuned into biological factors and also the world outside. It is important for both of these to be in tune.   (135 words)

AO3 question: Discuss one **criticism of the behaviourist approach in psychology.** *(4 marks)*

Answer A strength of the behaviourist approach is that it focused on observable behaviour and therefore was an objective approach. This objectivity gave psychology scientific credibility. Behaviourists made careful measurements in controlled lab settings. The controlled settings meant they could replicate the research and demonstrate that their findings were valid. However, it might be pointed out that the validity might not extend to humans, nevertheless the scientific approach did increase the status of psychology in the eyes of other scientists.   (79 words)

Examiner comments

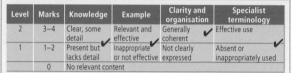

Level	Marks	Knowledge	Example	Clarity and organisation	Specialist terminology
2	3–4	Clear, some detail	Relevant and effective ✓	Generally coherent ✓	Effective use
1	1–2	Present but lacks detail	Inappropriate or not effective ✓	Not clearly expressed	Absent or inappropriately used ✓
	0	No relevant content			

Comments The length of this answer (93 words) is a little short for 4 marks. A 4-mark question probably requires two aspects, each with some detail – which means there should be four 'things' in the answer (aspect 1 + detail, aspect 2 + detail). In this answer, aspect 1 (thinking) lacks detail. The answer fits the descriptors of Level 2 but, as overall detail is lacking, we are tempted by the level below = 3 marks. Note that 2 out of 4 marks would be 50% (probably a fail) whereas 3 out of 4 marks would be 75% (probably a Grade B answer).

Level	Marks	Knowledge	Application	Focus	Organisation	Specialist terminology
3	5–6	Clear and appropriate	Mostly effective	Clear focus		Mostly used effectively
2	3–4	Apparent and mostly appropriate ✓	Partly effective		Lacks clarity and organisation in places ✓	Used inappropriately on occasions
1	1–2	Some explanation	Limited or absent	Poorly focused	Lacks clarity, poorly organised	Often inappropriately used
	0	No relevant content		✓		

Comments There is good and bad in this answer. There is some engagement with the stem, for example, 'This is what Asif was talking about', and the answer addresses some specific aspects of the stem, e.g. 'constant rhythm'. However, the answer reads more like a prepared answer than an answer to Asif's mother's question.

There are a number of missed opportunities for specialist terms, for example, 'biological pacemaker' should be 'endogenous pacemaker', and there is no link between light and exogenous zeitgebers.

The answer is Level 2 but clearly we would be tempted to the band below, so 3 out of 6 marks.

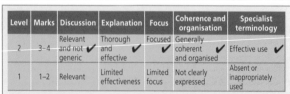

Level	Marks	Discussion	Explanation	Focus	Coherence and organisation	Specialist terminology
2	3–4	Relevant and not generic ✓	Thorough and effective ✓	Focused ✓	Generally coherent and organised ✓	Effective use ✓
1	1–2	Relevant	Limited effectiveness	Limited focus	Not clearly expressed	Absent or inappropriately used

Comments For the most part critical points are embedded in essays rather than a stand-alone question requiring only one criticism. However, it is good to practise these as a way of developing your skills of effective evaluation. This answer fulfils all of the top level criteria and, as we are not tempted by any Level 1 criteria, it is worth 4 out of 4 marks. Notice also the *discussion* – a counterpoint is introduced. It's not all one criticism.

Understanding marking

Examiner comments

AO1 + AO3 question: **Discuss reductionism in psychology.**
(16 marks)

Answer Reductionism is the attempt to reduce concepts and explanations to simpler components so that it is easier to understand behaviour. It also refers to reducing things to the simplest level – the physical basis for behaviour. Psychological and social explanations are at higher levels. Biological and chemical explanations are at lower levels.

Psychologists who are reductionists, such as behaviourists, think that reductionism enables us to better understand behaviour. Psychologists conduct experiments, such as pigeons learning in a Skinner box, and assume that this can be used as the basic unit of all human behaviour. However, other research has shown that in the real world there are many other factors that influence the learning process, such as motivation and teacher styles. Reducing human behaviour to that of animals has provided some useful insights into behaviour (because conditioning can explain behaviour) but is not that useful.

Another example of reductionism in psychology is the biological approach, where behaviour is reduced to the activity of the nervous system and hormones. An example of this is schizophrenia where dopamine levels increase the chance of some people developing the disorder. The treatment arising from this approach (drugs) is also very reductionist and has been quite successful. This approach means that psychologists have been able to explore the causes of behaviour.

In contrast with the reductionist approach in psychology the holistic approach suggests that reductionism represents complex systems too simply. Gestalt psychologists took a holistic perspective and suggested that the whole thing does not equal the sum of the parts. An example of the holistic approach is humanistic psychologists who saw successful therapy as bringing together all aspects of the 'whole person'. The problem with holistic explanations is they tend not to lend themselves to rigorous scientific testing. For example, humanistic psychology, tends to be criticised for its lack of empirical evidence, and is instead seen as a rather loose set of concepts.

One solution would be to combine holistic and reductionist approaches. However, if you do that, for example when trying to explain depression, it becomes difficult to establish which one to use as a basis for therapy. This suggests, when it comes to finding solutions for real-world problems, lower level explanations may be more appropriate.

The reductionist approach has strengths and weaknesses. Its strengths are that many successful approaches in psychology have conducted reductionist research and provided reductionist theories. Without this research we would know far less. On the other hand some psychologists question whether such research really does give us any useful insights. (418 words)

The introduction starts with a lengthy definition, which was not required by the question. It is scene-setting but not an especially good use of time.

A useful AO1 example of reductionism in psychology followed by a reasonably effective counterpoint about why reductionism doesn't work. In contrast with the first paragraph, the second paragraph *is* focused on reductionism *in psychology*, as required by the question.

There is a second example of reductionism (the biological approach) which is described in detail and extended to drug therapies, using some specialist terminology and examples from across the specification. The paragraph ends with a brief evaluation (AO3) point.

The holistic approach is described – however, that is not the subject of the essay. This is largely a wasted paragraph as a description and evaluation of holism is largely irrelevant. A mistake like this is all too easy to make without careful planning. If the same material had been phrased as an evaluation of reductionism then it would have been creditworthy.

This penultimate paragraph *is* using holism as a commentary on reductionism (AO3).

The final paragraph appears to be intended as a conclusion but in fact is little more than a summary of points already made and therefore does not add much.

Overall comments

The marking grid on the left shows in red the criteria that are unique to A level essays.
Knowledge: well-detailed.
Accuracy: accurate.
Discussion: some effective points but limited in quantity and quality.
Focus: lacks focus on the demands of the question. If we consider the creditworthy material only then there is more description. Loss of focus at the beginning and end of the essay.
Clarity and organisation: mostly clear and organised.
Specialist terminology: mostly used appropriately but not extensive use of specialist terms.
Overall the level that best describes this answer is Level 3 but we are tempted lower, making this 9 or 10 marks, probably Grade C/D.

Level	Marks	Knowledge	Accuracy	Evaluation	Focus	Clarity and organisation	Specialist terminology
4	13–16	Generally well-detailed ✔	Accurate ✔	Thorough Effective	Focused	Clear and coherent	Used effectively (minor flaws)
3	9–12	Evident	Occasional inaccuracies / omissions	Mostly effective	Occasionally lacking	Mostly clear and organised ✔	Mostly used appropriately ✔
2	5–8	Limited knowledge is present	Lacks accuracy in places	Some but limited ✔ effectiveness	Mainly descriptive ✔	Lacks clarity and organisation in places	Used inappropriately on occasions
1	1–4	Very limited	Many inaccuracies	Limited or absent	Poorly focused	Lacks clarity, poorly organised	Absent or inappropriately used
	0	No relevant content					

Origins of psychology

Spec spotlight

Origins of psychology: Wundt, introspection and the emergence of psychology as a science.

If you're not sure what is meant by 'introspection', you need to take a long hard look at yourself.

Apply it

Two students are discussing whether or not psychology can really be considered a science. Tara thinks it can and argues that Wundt made a significant contribution to the development of psychology as a science. Max accepts that behaviourism is quite scientific but reckons that many approaches in psychology are not scientific at all.

Can psychology be regarded as a science? Explain your answer, referring to Tara's and Max's views.

Wundt and introspection

Wilhelm Wundt established the first psychology lab.	Opened in Leipzig, Germany in 1879. The aim was to describe the nature of human consciousness (the 'mind') in a carefully controlled and scientific environment – a lab.
Wundt pioneered the method of introspection.	Introspection was the first systematic **experimental** attempt to study the mind by breaking up conscious awareness into basic structures of thoughts, images and sensations. Isolating the structure of consciousness in this way is called *structuralism*.
Standardised procedures.	The same standardised instructions were given to all participants. Procedures could be repeated (**replicated**). For instance, participants were given a ticking metronome (to pace their responses) and they would report their thoughts, images and sensations, which were then recorded.
Significance of Wundt's work.	Although Wundt's early attempt to study the mind would be seen today as naïve, his work was significant as it marked the separation of modern scientific psychology from its broader philosophical roots.

Emergence of psychology as a science

1900s Early **behaviourists** rejected introspection.	John B. Watson (1913) argued that introspection was subjective, in that it varied from person to person. According to the behaviourist approach, 'scientific' psychology should only study phenomena that can be observed and measured.
1930s behaviourist scientific approach dominated psychology.	B.F. Skinner (1953) brought the language and rigour of the natural sciences into psychology. The behaviourists' focus on learning, and the use of carefully controlled lab studies, would dominate psychology for the next few decades.
1950s **cognitive** approach used scientific procedures to study mental processes.	Following the cognitive revolution of the 1960s, the study of mental processes was seen as legitimate within psychology. Although mental processes remain 'private', cognitive psychologists are able to make *inferences* about how these work on the basis of tests conducted in a controlled environment (lab).
1990s The **biological approach** introduced technological advances.	Biological psychologists have taken advantage of recent advances in technology, including recording brain activity, using scanning techniques such as **fMRI** and **EEG**, and advanced genetic research.

One strength is some of Wundt's methods are scientific.

For instance, he recorded the introspections within a controlled lab environment.

He also standardised his procedures so that all participants received the same information and were tested in the same way.

For this reason, Wundt's research can be considered a forerunner to the later scientific approaches in psychology that were to come.

One limitation is that some aspects of the research are not scientific.

Wundt relied on participants self-reporting their 'private' mental processes. Such data is subjective and participants may not have wanted to reveal some of the thoughts they were having.

Participants would also not have had exactly the same thoughts every time, so establishing general principles would not have been possible. General laws are useful to predict future behaviour, one of the aims of science.

Wundt's early efforts to study the mind were naïve and would not meet the criteria of scientific enquiry.

One strength is that research in modern psychology can claim to be scientific.

Psychology has the same aims as the natural sciences – to describe, understand, predict and control our world.

The learning approaches, cognitive approach and biological approach all rely on the use of scientific methods – for example, lab studies to investigate theories in a controlled and unbiased way.

Throughout the 20th century and beyond, psychology has established itself as a scientific discipline.

One limitation with psychology is that not all approaches use objective methods.

The **humanistic approach** is anti-scientific and does not attempt to formulate general laws of behaviour. It is concerned only with documenting unique subjective experience.

The **psychodynamic** approach makes use of the **case study** method. This is based on interview techniques which are open to bias, and no attempt is made to gather a representative sample of the population.

For this reason, many claim that a scientific approach to the study of human thought and experience is not possible, nor is it desirable, as there are important differences between the subject matter of psychology and the natural sciences.

REVISION BOOSTER

An essay on Wundt's work alone is perhaps less likely than other areas in the Approaches section. One possibility is that you might be asked to 'outline and briefly evaluate the work of Wundt' or 'briefly discuss the contribution of Wundt to the emergence of psychology as a science'. In both of these questions evaluative points would be required so these are included here.

Similarly, it is debatable whether an essay would be set on the *emergence of psychology as a science*, but for evaluation, you could consider which approaches in psychology would meet scientific criteria and which would not.

A 16-mark essay on the origins of psychology is unlikely so we have just covered two points for each of the separate topics.

I ♥ PSYCHOLOGY

Yes of course you do – but the question of whether psychology is a science is not one that has a straightforward answer...

KNOWLEDGE CHECK

1. Explain what Wundt meant by 'introspection'. *(3 marks)*
2. Outline and briefly evaluate the work of Wundt. *(8 marks)*
3. Briefly discuss the emergence of psychology as a science. *(6 marks)*

The learning approach: Behaviourism

Spec spotlight

Learning approaches: The basic assumptions of the behaviourist approach, including classical conditioning and Pavlov's research, operant conditioning, types of reinforcement and Skinner's research.

'Conditioning' means 'learning'.

'Have you heard of a bloke called Ivan Pavlov?'

'I must admit, the name rings a bell.'

Apply it

Joel is addicted to online fruit machine gambling. He spends a lot of time and money on this and other forms of online gambling.

Explain Joel's gambling addiction in terms of operant conditioning. Use the concepts of positive and negative reinforcement in your explanation. Explain a feature of operant conditioning that might lead to a reduction in his gambling behaviour.

Key assumptions of the behaviourist approach

Focus on *observable* behaviour only.	The **behaviourist** approach is only concerned with studying behaviour that can be observed and measured. It is not concerned with mental processes of the mind. *Introspection* was rejected by behaviourists as its concepts were vague and difficult to measure.
Controlled lab studies.	Behaviourists tried to maintain more control and objectivity within their research and relied on lab studies to achieve this.
Use of non-human animals.	Behaviourists suggest the processes that govern learning are the same in all species, so animals (e.g. rats, cats, dogs and pigeons) can replace humans as **experimental** subjects.

Classical conditioning Pavlov's research.	Learning through association.	**Pavlov's research** – conditioning dogs to salivate when a bell rings: *Before conditioning*:
	$UCS \rightarrow UCR$ $NS \rightarrow$ no response	UCS = food, UCR = salivation, NS = bell
	$NS + UCS$	*During conditioning* Bell and food occur at same time.
	$CS \rightarrow CR$	*After conditioning* CS = bell, CR = salivation
	(See examples on pages 138 and 234.)	Pavlov showed how a neutral stimulus (bell) can come to elicit a new learned response (conditioned response) through association.

Operant conditioning Skinner's research	Learning is an active process whereby humans and animals *operate* on their environment. Behaviour is shaped and maintained by its *consequences*.	**Skinner's research** – rats and pigeons, in specially designed cages (Skinner boxes). When a rat activated a lever (or a pigeon pecked a disc) it was *rewarded* with a food pellet. A desirable consequence led to behaviour being repeated. If pressing a lever meant an animal avoided an electric shock, the behaviour would also be repeated.

Three types of *consequences* of behaviour.	**Positive reinforcement** – receiving a reward when behaviour is performed. **Negative reinforcement** – when an animal or human produces behaviour that avoids something unpleasant. **Punishment** – an unpleasant consequence of behaviour. Positive reinforcement and negative reinforcement increase the likelihood that behaviour will be repeated. Punishment decreases it.

One strength of behaviourism is that it gave psychology scientific credibility.

The approach focused on the careful measurement of observable behaviour within controlled lab settings.

Behaviourists emphasised the importance of scientific processes such as objectivity and **replication**.

This brought the language and methods of the natural sciences into psychology, giving the subject greater credibility and status.

One strength is the laws developed by behaviourists have real-life application.

The principles of conditioning have been applied to a broad range of real-world behaviours and problems.

Token economy systems reward appropriate behaviour with tokens that are exchanged for privileges (operant conditioning). These systems are successfully used in prisons and psychiatric wards.

Treatments like these are suitable for patients who lack 'insight' into their condition and are not capable of talking about their problems.

One limitation is the behaviourist approach portrays a mechanistic view.

Animals and humans are seen as passive and machine-like responders to the environment, with little conscious insight into their behaviour.

Other approaches, such as **social learning theory** and the **cognitive** approach, have placed much more emphasis on the mental events that occur during learning.

The processes that mediate between stimulus and response suggest that humans play a much more active role in their own learning.

Another limitation is behaviourism is a form of environmental determinism.

The approach sees all behaviour as determined by past experiences that have been conditioned and ignores any influence that **free will** may have on behaviour.

Skinner suggested that free will was an illusion. When something happens we impose a sense of having made the decision but our past conditioning determined the outcome.

This is an extreme position and ignores the influence of conscious decision-making processes on behaviour (as suggested by the cognitive approach).

A final limitation is that animal research has ethical and practical issues.

Although experimental procedures such as the Skinner box allowed behaviourists to maintain a high degree of control over their research subjects, critics have drawn attention to the ethical issues involved.

The animals were exposed to stressful and aversive conditions and this may have affected how they reacted to the experimental situation.

This means the **validity** of the findings from these studies might be questioned because the observed behaviour was not 'normal'.

REVISION BOOSTER

When writing critical points it is desirable to explain them thoroughly.

- Always start with a statement of your point (P).
- Provide further explanation (E) using examples (E) and/or evidence (E).
- If you can, end your criticism with a conclusion / link (L) back to the point you were making (= PEEL).

CRAIG SWANSON © WWW.PERSPICUITY.COM

A former participant in the Skinner box studies struggles to find work.

KNOWLEDGE CHECK

1. Explain **two** assumptions of the behaviourist approach.
   (4 marks)
2. Outline Skinner's research into operant conditioning.
   (3 marks)
3. Explain how **two** types of reinforcement could be used by a parent to encourage their child to come home by 9pm on a school night.
   (4 marks)
4. Describe and evaluate the behaviourist approach in psychology. Refer to both Pavlov's and Skinner's research in your answer.
   (16 marks)

The learning approach: Social learning theory

Spec spotlight

Learning approaches: The basic assumptions of the social learning theory including imitation, identification, modelling, vicarious reinforcement, the role of mediational processes and Bandura's research.

Imitation – the sincerest form of flattery, apparently.

Apply it

Barney is an 8-year-old boy. Although he has never been bullied at his primary school, several times he has seen an older boy bullying other children. The older boy is physically aggressive, sometimes to get money or sweets, or just to show everyone who's boss.

Explain the social learning processes which may lead to Barney becoming a bully himself. Refer in your explanation to the roles of imitation, identification, modelling and vicarious reinforcement.

*In terms of mediational processes, explain **three** ways in which Barney is unlikely to become a bully.*

Note that modelling is a named term on the specification that can be used in two subtly different ways. From the observer's perspective, 'modelling' is imitating the behaviour of a role model. From the role model's perspective, it is demonstrating behaviour that may be imitated.

Key assumptions of social learning theory (SLT)

Learning that occurs *indirectly*.	Albert Bandura agreed with the **behaviourist** approach that learning occurs through experience. However, he also proposed that learning takes place in a social context through *observation* and *imitation* of others' behaviour.
Learning related to consequences of behaviour – *vicarious reinforcement*.	Children (and adults) observe other people's behaviour and take note of its consequences. Behaviour that is seen to be rewarded (reinforced) is much more likely to be copied than behaviour that is punished. Bandura called this vicarious reinforcement.
Mediational **(cognitive)** *processes* play a crucial role in learning.	There are four mediational processes in learning: 1. *Attention* – whether behaviour is noticed. 2. *Retention* – whether behaviour is remembered. 3. *Motor reproduction* – being able to do it. 4. *Motivation* – the will to perform the behaviour. The first two relate to the learning of behaviour, the last two to the performance of behaviour (so, unlike behaviourism, learning and performance do not have to occur together).
Identification with role models is important.	Children are more likely to imitate the behaviour of people with whom they identify. Such role models are similar to the observer, tend to be attractive and have high status.

Imitation of aggression Bandura's research	**Bandura's research 1 –** children watched an adult either: • Behaving aggressively towards a Bobo doll. • Behaving non-aggressively towards a Bobo doll. When given their own doll to play with, the children who had seen aggression were much more aggressive towards the doll.	**Bandura's research 2 –** children saw an adult who was either: • Rewarded. • Punished. • Neither rewarded nor punished. When given their own doll to play with, the children who saw the aggression rewarded were much more aggressive themselves.

Children *model* aggressive behaviour	The Bobo doll studies suggest that children are likely to imitate (model) acts of violence if they observe these in an adult role model. It is also the case that **modelling** aggressive behaviour is more likely if such behaviour is seen to be rewarded (vicarious reinforcement).

One strength is SLT emphasises the importance of cognitive factors in learning.

Neither **classical conditioning** nor **operant conditioning** can offer a comprehensive account of human learning on their own because cognitive factors are omitted.

Humans and animals store information about the behaviour of others and use this to make judgements about when it is appropriate to perform certain actions.

SLT provides a more complete explanation of human learning than the behaviourist approach by recognising the role of mediational processes.

One limitation is SLT relies too heavily on evidence from lab studies.

Many of Bandura's ideas were developed through observation of children's behaviour in lab settings and this raises the problem of **demand characteristics**.

The main purpose of a Bobo doll is to hit it. So the children in those studies may have been behaving as they thought was expected.

Thus the research may tell us little about how children actually learn aggression in everyday life.

Another limitation is SLT underestimates the influence of biological factors.

A consistent finding in the Bobo doll **experiments** was that boys showed more aggression than girls, regardless of the specifics of the **experimental condition**.

This may be explained by differences in the levels of **testosterone**, which is present in greater quantities in boys and is linked to aggression.

This means that Bandura may have underplayed the important influence of biological factors on social learning.

Another strength is SLT can account for cultural differences in behaviour.

Social learning principles can account for how children learn from other people around them, as well as through the media, and this can explain how cultural norms are transmitted.

This has proved useful in understanding a range of behaviours such as how children come to understand their gender role by imitating role models.

In contrast, the **biological approach** can only explain universal behaviours because human biological processes do not change with culture.

A final strength is SLT is less **determinist** than the behaviourist approach.

Bandura emphasised *reciprocal determinism* – we are influenced by our environment, but we also exert an influence upon it through the behaviours we choose to perform.

This element of choice suggests that there is some **free will** in the way we behave.

This is a more realistic and flexible position than is suggested by the behaviourist approach as it recognises the role we play in shaping our own environment.

The word 'bobo' is Spanish for 'clown'. The word 'doll' is English for 'doll'.

The specification includes the terms: imitation, identification, modelling, vicarious reinforcement, the role of mediational processes and Bandura's research.

This means that exam questions may include any of these.

KNOWLEDGE CHECK

1. Using an example, explain what is meant by 'identification' in social learning theory. *(3 marks)*
2. Outline Bandura's research into social learning. *(3 marks)*
3. With reference to mediational processes in social learning, explain how a child might learn to bake a cake by watching his mother. *(6 marks)*
4. Describe and evaluate the social learning approach in psychology. *(16 marks)*

The cognitive approach

Spec spotlight

The cognitive approach: The basic assumptions of the approach, the study of internal mental processes, the role of schema, the use of theoretical and computer models to explain and make inferences about mental processes. The emergence of cognitive neuroscience.

REVISION BOOSTER

Note the difference between a theoretical model and a computer model. Both are named on the specification so you need to be able to provide an explanation and an example of each.

Also note the other terms that you can be examined on: internal mental processes, schema, inferences and the emergence of cognitive neuroscience.

PARIS
IN THE
THE SPRING

Did you spot the second 'the'? If not, that'll be your schema then.

Key assumptions of the cognitive approach

The scientific study of mental processes.	In direct contrast to the **behaviourist** approach, the **cognitive** approach argues that mental processes should be studied, e.g. studying perception and memory.
The role of *inference* in the study of mental processes.	Mental processes are 'private' and cannot be observed, so cognitive psychologists study them indirectly by making inferences (assumptions) about what is going on inside people's heads on the basis of their behaviour.
The use of *theoretical models* when describing and explaining mental processes.	The information processing approach suggests that information flows through a sequence of stages that include input, storage and retrieval, as in the *multi-store model* (part of your Year 1 studies).
The use of *computer models* when describing and explaining mental processes.	Computer models refer to programmes that can be run on a computer to imitate the human mind. By running such a programme psychologists can test whether their ideas about information processing are correct.
The idea of **schema** is central to the cognitive approach.	• Schema are packages of information developed through experience. • They act as a 'mental framework' for the interpretation of incoming information received by the cognitive system. • Babies are born with simple motor schema for innate behaviours such as sucking and grasping. • As we get older, our schema become more detailed and sophisticated.
The emergence of *cognitive neuroscience*.	• Cognitive neuroscience is the scientific study of the influence of brain structures (neuro) on mental processes (cognition). • With advances in brain scanning technology in the last twenty years, scientists have been able to describe the neurological basis of mental processing. • This includes research in memory that has linked *episodic* and *semantic memories* to opposite sides of the prefrontal cortex in the brain. • Scanning techniques have also proved useful in establishing the neurological basis of some disorders, e.g. the *parahippocampal gyrus* and OCD.

One strength is the approach uses scientific and objective methods.

Cognitive psychologists have always employed controlled and rigorous methods of study, e.g. lab studies, in order to infer cognitive processes at work.

This has enabled the two fields of biology and cognitive psychology to come together (cognitive neuroscience).

This means that the study of the mind has established a credible, scientific basis.

One limitation is that the approach is based on machine reductionism.

Although there are similarities between the operations of the human mind and a computer (inputs and outputs, central processor, storage systems), the computer analogy has been criticised.

For instance, human emotion and motivation have been shown to influence accuracy of recall, e.g. in eyewitness accounts. These factors are not considered within the information-processing model.

Therefore, the cognitive approach oversimplifies human cognitive processing and ignores important aspects that influence performance.

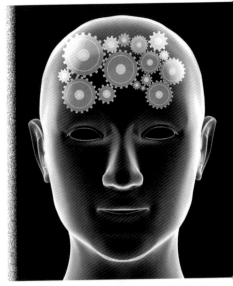

Probably why they call it 'cog psychology'.

Another limitation is research on the approach lacks external validity.

Cognitive psychologists are only able to infer mental processes from the behaviour they observe, so the approach sometimes suffers from being too abstract and theoretical.

Also, research is often carried out using artificial stimuli, such as recall of word lists in studies of memory which may not represent everyday experience.

Therefore, research into cognitive processes may lack external validity.

One strength of the approach is the application to everyday life.

The cognitive approach is dominant in psychology today and has been applied to a wide range of practical and theoretical contexts.

For instance, the approach has made an important contribution to the field of *artificial intelligence* (AI) and the development of robots.

These exciting advances are likely to revolutionise how we live in the future.

Another strength is the approach is less determinist than other approaches.

The cognitive approach is based on **soft determinism**, recognising that our cognitive system can only operate within certain limits, but that we are free to think before responding to a stimulus.

This is in contrast to the behaviourist approach which suggests that we are passive 'slaves' to the environment and lack free choice in our behaviour.

The cognitive approach takes a more reasonable and flexible middle-ground position in the **free will**-determinism debate and is more in line with our subjective sense of free will.

Apply it

Amber is 2 years old. Her parents have noticed that her play behaviour is not random, but seems to demonstrate certain patterns. For example, she is obsessed with Russian dolls and loves to get adults to remove each doll one at a time, then replace them over and over again. She really enjoys putting smaller objects inside larger ones and making dens and sitting in them.

Explain how the concept of a schema can help us understand such patterns of play.

KNOWLEDGE CHECK

1. Using an example, outline what cognitive psychologists mean by the word 'schema'. *(3 marks)*
2. Briefly explain how theoretical models are used in cognitive psychology to make inferences about mental processes. *(4 marks)*
3. Outline the emergence of cognitive neuroscience in psychology. *(6 marks)*
4. Briefly discuss the cognitive approach. *(8 marks)*
5. Describe and evaluate the cognitive approach in psychology. *(16 marks)*

The biological approach

Spec spotlight

The biological approach: The basic assumptions of the approach, the influence of genes, biological structures and neurochemistry on behaviour. Genotype and phenotype, genetic basis of behaviour, evolution and behaviour.

Yeah they look cute now but wait until they wake up.

Wilson's disease is a rare genetic disorder which can affect several of the body's systems, including the brain. This results in symptoms such as clumsiness, speech problems, difficulty in concentrating, depression and anxiety. It is caused by the body storing too much copper, a mineral which we need in just tiny amounts. There is no cure. But the disorder can be managed by reducing the amount of copper in the diet, and carefully monitoring blood and urine, so the individual can develop normally.

Using Wilson's disease as an example, explain the difference between genotype and phenotype.

Key assumptions of the biological approach

Everything psychological is at first biological.	If we want to fully understand human behaviour we must look to biological structures and processes within the body, such as *genes*, *neurochemistry* and the *nervous system*.
Behaviour has a *genetic* and *neurochemical* basis.	Behaviours are inherited in the same way as physical characteristics such as height or eye colour. For example, the 5HT1-D beta gene implicated in OCD. Neurochemistry also explains behaviour, for example low levels of **serotonin** in OCD.
The mind and body are one and the same.	From a biological perspective, the mind lives in the brain – meaning that all thoughts, feelings and behaviour ultimately have a physical basis. This is in contrast to the **cognitive** approach which sees the mind as separate from the brain.
Twin studies are used to investigate the genetic basis of behaviour.	**Concordance rates** between twins are calculated – the extent to which twins share the same characteristic. Higher concordance rates among identical (monozygotic, **MZ**) twins than non-identical (dizygotic, **DZ**) twins is evidence of a genetic basis. For example, 68% of MZ twins both have OCD compared with 31% of DZ twins (Nestadt *et al.* 2010).
The difference between *genotype* and *phenotype*.	<ul><li>A person's genotype is their actual genetic make-up.</li><li>Phenotype is the way that genes are expressed through physical, behavioural and psychological characteristics.</li><li>The expression of genotype (phenotype) is influenced by environmental factors.</li><li>For example, *phenylketonuria (PKU)* is a genetic disorder that can be prevented by a restricted diet.</li><li>This suggests that much of human behaviour depends on the interaction of **nature and nurture**.</li></ul>
The *theory of* **evolution** is used by the **biological approach** to explain many aspects of behaviour.	<ul><li>Charles Darwin (1859) proposed the theory of natural selection.</li><li>Any genetically determined behaviour that enhances survival *and* reproduction will be passed on to future generations.</li><li>Such genes are described as **adaptive** and give the possessor and their offspring advantages.</li><li>For instance, attachment behaviours in newborns promote survival and are therefore adaptive and naturally selected.</li></ul>

One strength of the approach is its use of scientific methods of investigation.

In order to investigate the genetic and biological basis of behaviour, the biological approach makes use of a range of precise and highly scientific methods.

These include scanning techniques (e.g. **fMRIs**) and drug trials. It is possible to accurately measure biological and neural processes in ways that are not open to bias.

This means that the biological approach is based on reliable data.

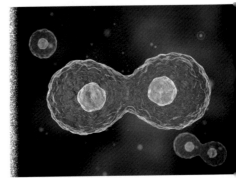

Biology is the only science in which multiplication is the same thing as division.

Another strength is the biological approach has real-life application.

Increased understanding of biochemical processes in the brain has led to the development of psychoactive drugs that treat serious mental disorders, such as depression.

Although these drugs are not effective for all patients, they have revolutionised treatment for many.

This is a strength of the approach because it means that sufferers are able to live a relatively normal life, rather than in hospital.

A limitation is difficulty establishing cause and effect with neurotransmitters.

The role of neurotransmitters in mental illness comes from studies that show a particular drug reduces symptoms of the disorder by changing levels of neurotransmitter. It is assumed that the neurotransmitter is the cause.

This is a bit like assuming that the cause of a headache is lack of paracetamol simply because paracetamol is effective in relieving symptoms of a headache.

This is a limitation because the biological approach is claiming to have discovered causes where only an association exists.

Apply it

Biological psychologists believe that behaviours have evolved because they provide some advantage, in terms of allowing us to adapt to our environments. Examples from your Year 1 studies include: (1) conforming to the behaviour of other members of a group; (2) having both long-term and short-term memories; (3) suffering from depression (which many psychologists believe has a genetic basis).

For each of these examples, explain what the adaptive advantages could be.

Another limitation is the approach is based on a determinist view of behaviour.

The biological approach is determinist in that it sees human behaviour as governed by internal, biological causes over which we have no control.

However, this is at odds with the legal system which sees offenders as responsible for their actions. The discovery of a 'criminal gene' may complicate this principle.

Such research may have (possibly negative) implications for wider society as criminals may be able to excuse their behaviour.

A final limitation is the difficulty of separating nature and nurture.

Identical twins, non-identical twins and members of the same family all have genetic similarities, so any similarity in the way they behave must be genetic from a biological perspective.

However, the fact that family members are exposed to similar environmental conditions is an important **confounding variable**.

This is a problem for the biological approach because findings could be just as easily interpreted as supporting nurture rather than nature.

KNOWLEDGE CHECK

1. Outline **two** key features of the biological approach in psychology.   *(6 marks)*
2. Using an example, distinguish between 'genotype' and 'phenotype'.   *(3 marks)*
3. Explain what is meant by 'evolution and behaviour'. Illustrate your answer with an example of a human **or** non-human behaviour.   *(3 marks)*
4. Describe and evaluate the biological approach in psychology.   *(16 marks)*

The psychodynamic approach

Spec spotlight

The psychodynamic approach: The basic assumptions of the approach, the role of the unconscious, the structure of personality, that is id, ego and superego, defence mechanisms including repression, denial and displacement, psychosexual stages.

Id. A handy word to know if you're running out of tiles in Scrabble.

REVISION BOOSTER

The psychodynamic approach is complex and wide-ranging. It would be easy to overdo the AO1 content in an essay on this approach. Keep description of things like Freud's psychosexual stages to a minimum and only select a few examples.

Apply it

Gregory got his girlfriend's and his mum's names mixed up the other day. Felix is only interested in satisfying his own desires. Lisbeth feels guilty all the time over the smallest things. Heathcliffe's parents are having trouble getting him potty-trained. Alanis is 5 years old and wants to marry her daddy when she grows up. There are holes in Donald's bedroom door where he punches it when he comes in from work.

Identify the psychodynamic concepts on this page that could apply to these people. Explain your choices.

Key assumptions of the psychodynamic approach

The *unconscious mind* has an important influence on behaviour.	Sigmund Freud's psychoanalytic theory is an example of the **psychodynamic** approach. He suggested that the mind is made up of: • Conscious – what we are aware of. • Pre-conscious – memories and thoughts we are not currently aware of but can be accessed. • Unconscious – we are unaware of the contents of the unconscious. It is a vast storehouse of biological drives and instincts that influence our behaviour.
Tripartite structure of personality. Dynamic interaction between the three parts determines behaviour.	Freud saw personality as having three parts: • *Id* – primitive part of the personality operates on the *pleasure principle*, demands instant gratification. • *Ego* – works on the *reality principle* and is the mediator between the id and superego. • *Superego* – internalised sense of right and wrong, based on the *morality principle*. Punishes the ego through guilt.
Five *psychosexual stages* that determine adult personality.	Each stage is marked by a different conflict that the child must resolve to move on to the next. Any conflict that is unresolved leads to fixation where the child becomes 'stuck' and carries behaviours associated with that stage through to adult life.
The sequence of stages is fixed.	*Oral* (0–1 years) – pleasure focus = mouth, the mother's breast is the object of desire. *Anal* (1–3 years) – pleasure focus = anus, the child gains pleasure from withholding and eliminating faeces. *Phallic* (3–5 years) – pleasure focus = genital area. *Latency* – earlier conflicts are repressed. *Genital* (puberty) – sexual desires become conscious.
The *Oedipus complex* is an important psychosexual conflict occurring at the phallic stage.	In the phallic stage, little boys develop incestuous feelings towards their mother and a murderous hatred for their father. Later, boys repress their feelings for their mother and identify with their father, taking on his gender role and moral values. Girls of the same age experience penis envy.
Defence mechanisms are used by the ego to keep the id 'in check' and reduce anxiety.	Unconscious strategies used by the ego, for example: • *Repression* – forcing a distressing memory out of the conscious mind. • *Denial* – refusing to acknowledge reality. • *Displacement* – transferring feelings from their true source onto a substitute target.

One strength is that the psychodynamic approach has explanatory power.

Although Freud's theory is controversial and often bizarre, it has had huge influence on Western contemporary thought.

It has been used to explain a wide range of behaviours (moral, mental disorders) and drew attention to the influence of childhood on adult personality.

Alongside **behaviourism**, it was the dominant approach in psychology for the first half of the twentieth century.

REVISION BOOSTER

A useful way to evaluate any approach is to make comparisons with one of the other approaches. However, be sure to stick to making comparisons rather than simply providing a description of another approach.

One limitation is the case study method that Freud relied on has been criticised.

Freud's ideas were developed using a small number of case studies, e.g. Little Hans, Dora and the Rat Man. Critics have suggested that it is not possible to make universal claims about human nature based on such a limited sample.

Although Freud's observations were detailed and carefully recorded, his interpretations were highly subjective and it is unlikely that any other researcher would have drawn the same conclusions.

In comparison with other approaches, Freud's methods lacked scientific rigour.

Another limitation is the approach includes lots of untestable concepts.

Karl Popper (philosopher of science) argued that the psychodynamic approach does not meet the scientific criterion of *falsification*, in the sense that it cannot be proved or disproved.

Many of Freud's concepts, such as the id or the Oedipus complex, occur at an unconscious level making them difficult, if not impossible, to test.

This affords psychodynamic theory the status of pseudoscience ('fake' science) rather than real science.

Freudian slip joke: Sigmund Freud walked into a bra...

A further strength is the approach has practical application in the real world.

Freud introduced a new form of therapy: *psychoanalysis*. The therapy is designed to access the unconscious mind using a range of techniques such as dream analysis.

Psychoanalysis is most suitable for individuals suffering from mild neuroses but has been criticised as inappropriate for people with severe mental disorders such as schizophrenia.

That said, psychoanalysis is the forerunner to many modern-day psychotherapies and 'talking cures' that have since been established.

A final limitation is the approach is based on psychic determinism.

The psychodynamic approach explains all behaviour as determined by unconscious conflicts that are rooted in childhood.

Even something as apparently random as a 'slip of the tongue' is driven by unconscious forces and has deep symbolic meaning.

This is an extreme determinist stance and suggests that **free will** may have no influence on behaviour.

KNOWLEDGE CHECK

1. The psychodynamic approach places emphasis on the role of the unconscious in behaviour. Using an example, explain the role of the unconscious in behaviour. *(4 marks)*

2. Explain how **one** defence mechanism might help someone cope with the anxiety of losing their job. *(3 marks)*

3. Name and explain **one** of Freud's psychosexual stages of development. *(3 marks)*.

4. Describe and evaluate the psychodynamic approach in psychology. *(16 marks)*

The humanistic approach

Spec spotlight

Humanistic psychology: The basic assumptions of the approach, free will, self-actualisation and Maslow's hierarchy of needs, focus on the self, congruence, the role of conditions of worth. The influence of counselling psychology.

Humanistic psychologists believe we have 'free will' – a philosophical position which suggests we are able to reject internal and external influences. Not to be confused with 'Free Willy', which is a film about a whale.

Apply it

Anika feels depressed because she feels that her life is empty and worthless. There were so many things she wanted to do and be but now sees that it's too late. She sees a person-centred therapist for counselling.

Referring to both Maslow's hierarchy of needs and Rogers' concept of congruence, explain how Anika could be helped to recover from depression.

Key assumptions of the humanistic approach

The concept of **free will** is central.	The **humanistic approach** rejects attempts to establish scientific principles of human behaviour.
	We are all unique, and psychology should concern itself with the study of subjective experience rather than general laws – a person-centred approach.
Maslow's *hierarchy of needs* has *self-actualisation* at the top.	Self-actualisation refers to the innate tendency that each of us has to want to achieve our full potential and become the best we can possibly be.
	In Abraham Maslow's hierarchy of needs the four lower levels (deficiency needs) must be met before the individual can work towards self-actualisation – a growth need.
Focus on the self.	The self refers to the ideas and values that characterise 'I' and 'me' and includes perception of 'what I am' and 'what I can do'.
The aim of therapy is to establish *congruence* between the self-concept and the ideal self.	Carl Rogers argued that personal growth requires an individual's concept of self to be congruent with their ideal self (the person they want to be).
	If the gap is too big, the person will experience a state of incongruence and self-actualisation isn't possible.
Parents who impose *conditions of worth* may prevent personal growth.	Issues such as worthlessness and low self-esteem have their roots in childhood and are due to a lack of *unconditional positive regard* from our parents.
	A parent who sets boundaries on their love for their child (conditions of worth) by claiming 'I will only love you if...' is storing up psychological problems for that child in future.
The humanistic approach has had a lasting influence on *counselling psychology.*	In Rogers' client-centred therapy an effective therapist should provide the client with three things: • Genuineness. • Empathy. • Unconditional positive regard. The aim is to increase feelings of self-worth and reduce incongruence between the self-concept and the ideal self. Rogers' work transformed psychotherapy. 'Non-directive' counselling techniques are practised not only in clinical settings but throughout education, health, social work and industry.

One strength is humanistic psychology is anti-reductionist.

Humanistic psychologists reject any attempt to break up behaviour and experience into smaller components.

They advocate **holism** – the idea that subjective experience can only be understood by considering the whole person (their relationships, past, present and future, etc.).

This approach may have more **validity** than its alternatives by considering meaningful human behaviour within its real-life context.

One limitation is the approach has limited application in the real world.

It is true that Rogerian therapy has revolutionised counselling techniques and Maslow's hierarchy of needs has been used to explain motivation, particularly in the workplace.

However, compared to other approaches, humanistic psychology has had limited impact within psychology as a whole – perhaps because it lacks a sound evidence base.

As a result, the approach has been described not as a comprehensive theory but as a rather loose set of abstract concepts.

Another strength is the approach is a positive one.

Humanistic psychologists have been praised for promoting a positive image of the human condition – seeing people as in control of their lives and having the freedom to change.

Freud saw human beings as slaves to their past and claimed all of us existed somewhere between 'common unhappiness and absolute despair'.

Humanistic psychology offers a refreshing and optimistic alternative.

Another limitation is that the approach includes untestable concepts.

Humanistic psychology includes a number of vague ideas that are abstract and difficult to test, such as 'self-actualisation' and 'congruence'.

Rogers did attempt to introduce more rigour into his work by developing the *Q-sort* – an objective measure of progress in therapy.

As would be expected of an approach that is 'anti-scientific', humanistic psychology is short on empirical evidence.

A final limitation is the approach may have a Western cultural bias.

Many of the ideas that are central to humanistic psychology, such as individual freedom, autonomy and personal growth, would be more readily associated with **individualist** cultures in the Western world such as the US.

Collectivist cultures such as India, which emphasise the needs of the group and interdependence, may not identify so easily with the ideals and values of humanistic psychology.

Therefore, it is possible that the approach would not travel well and is a product of the cultural context within which it was developed.

Ella Fitzgerald famously said, 'It isn't where you've come from, it's where you're going that counts'. Unlike psychoanalysis, Rogerian therapy looks forward not back.

Comparison of approaches

Spec spotlight

Comparison of approaches.

Comparing apples is somewhat easier than comparing psychological approaches...

REVISION BOOSTER

Comparing approaches is a good way of getting AO3 evaluation marks in an essay – as long as you make it clear how the comparison highlights a strength or limitation of the approach you have been asked about.

Apply it

This spread presents several important issues in psychology. The various approaches have unique perspectives on each one, for example nature versus nurture.

Which approach do you think most emphasises nature, and which most emphasises nurture? Explain how these approaches differ.

*Now choose **two** approaches which take a similar line on this issue (i.e. both nature or both nurture). How are they similar?*

(You could answer the same questions for the other debates, such as determinism and reductionism.)

Approach	Behaviourist	Social learning	Cognitive
Views on development	The processes that underpin learning are continuous, occurring at any age.	Same as behaviourism.	Stage theories of child development, particularly the idea of concept formation (**schema**) as child gets older.
Nature versus nurture	Babies are 'blank slates' at birth. All behaviour comes about through learned associations and reinforcements.	As for behaviourism with additional processes of observation and imitation.	Recognises that many of our information-processing abilities are innate, but are constantly refined by experience.
Reductionism	Reduces complex learning into stimulus-response units for ease of testing in a controlled lab environment.	Recognises how cognitive factors interact with the external environment.	Machine reductionism: use of the information-processing analogy and the fact that it ignores human emotion.
Determinism	All behaviour is environmentally determined by external forces that we cannot control.	We are influenced by our environment and also exert some influence upon it (*reciprocal determinism*).	Suggests we are the 'choosers' of our own behaviour, but only within the limits of what we know (**soft determinism**).
Explanation and treatment of abnormal/ atypical behaviour	Abnormality arises from maladaptive or faulty learning. Behavioural therapies take a symptom-based approach to the unlearning of behaviour.	Principles such as **modelling** have been used to explain the development of aggressive behaviour.	Led to cognitive therapies such as **cognitive behaviour therapy** (**CBT**) in the treatment of depression, which aims to eradicate faulty thinking.

Biological	Psychodynamic	Humanistic
Genetically determined maturational changes influence behaviour, e.g. cognitive/intellectual development.	The most coherent theory of development, tying concepts and processes to age-related stages.	The development of the self is ongoing throughout life.
'Anatomy is destiny': behaviour stems from the genetic blueprint we inherit from our parents.	Suggests that much of our behaviour is driven by biological drives and instincts, but also sees the child's relationships with its parents as crucial.	Regards parents, friends and wider society as having a critical impact on the person's self-concept.
Reduces and explains human behaviour at the level of the gene or neuron.	Reduces behaviour to the influence of biological drives and instincts, although also sees personality as a dynamic, **holistic** interaction.	Anti-reductionist, based on holistic investigation of all aspects of the individual.
A form of genetic determinism, much of our behaviour is directed by innate influences.	Unconscious forces drive our behaviour (psychic determinism) and these are rationalised by our conscious minds.	Human beings have **free will** and are active agents who determine their own development.
Psychoactive drugs that regulate chemical imbalances in the brain have revolutionised the treatment of mental disorders.	Anxiety disorders emerge from unconscious conflicts and overuse of defence mechanisms. Psychoanalysis aims to put people in touch with their unconscious thoughts.	Humanistic therapy, or counselling, is based on the idea that reducing incongruence will stimulate personal growth.

The TV usually does what we tell it to – but to what extent are we in control of our thoughts and behaviour?

Eclecticism

It's worth noting that most modern psychologists would take an eclectic (multidisciplinary) approach to the study of human behaviour. Very few researchers work entirely within one approach.

Eclecticism refers to the combining of several approaches and/ or methods to provide a more comprehensive account.

For example, the diathesis–stress model suggests that many mental disorders are a complex interaction of genetic predisposition and environmental triggers.

Another example of an eclectic approach is combining treatment options from several different perspectives, e.g. drugs, cognitive therapy, family therapy, has led to more effective outcomes for patients and lower relapse rates.

KNOWLEDGE CHECK

1. Outline **one** way in which the psychodynamic approach and humanistic psychology overlap. *(3 marks)*
2. Briefly discuss **one** difference between the social learning approach and the behaviourist approach. *(4 marks)*
3. Outline and briefly compare the biological approach and the cognitive approach. *(10 marks)*

The nervous system

Spec spotlight

The divisions of the nervous system: central and peripheral (somatic and autonomic).

The function of the endocrine system: glands and hormones.

The fight or flight response, including the role of adrenaline.

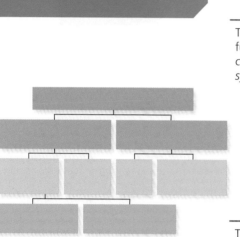

You might have to label a diagram in the exam. Nervous..? Did you get the joke?

Apply it

Leah is being interviewed for a job. It's really important to her and everything is going fine, until one interviewer asks her a question and she suddenly realises she doesn't know the answer. She tries hard to remember the information she needs but can't concentrate. She can hear her heart beating faster, her face is reddening, her hands are shaking and she feels sick.

Explain the roles of (1) the CNS, (2) the ANS, and (3) the endocrine system in Leah's behaviour.

The nervous system

The key features of the *nervous system*.	The nervous system is a specialised network of cells and our primary communication system. It has two main functions: 1. To collect, process and respond to information in the environment. 2. To coordinate the working of different organs and cells in the body. It is divided into the central nervous system and the peripheral nervous system.
The structure and function of the *central nervous system* (CNS)	• The CNS is made up of the *brain* and the *spinal cord*. • The brain is the centre of all conscious awareness. • The outer layer of the brain, the cerebral cortex, is highly developed in humans and is what distinguishes our higher mental functions from those of animals. • The spinal cord is an extension of the brain and is responsible for reflex actions. • It passes messages to and from the brain and connects nerves to the PNS.
The structure and function of the *peripheral nervous system* (PNS)	• The PNS transmits messages, via millions of neurons, to and from the nervous system. • The PNS is further sub-divided into the **autonomic nervous system** (ANS) and the **somatic nervous system** (SNS). • The ANS governs vital functions in the body such as breathing, heart rate, digestion, sexual arousal and stress responses. • The SNS controls muscle movement and receives information from sensory receptors.

```
                Human Nervous System
                 /                \
    Peripheral                        Central
  Nervous System                   Nervous System
    /        \                      /         \
Autonomic   Somatic            Brain      Spinal Cord
Nervous     Nervous
System      System
  /    \
Sympathetic    Parasympathetic
Nervous System  Nervous System
```

The major sub-divisions of the human nervous system.

The endocrine system

The key features of the *endocrine system*.	The endocrine system works alongside the nervous system to control vital functions in the body through the action of hormones. It works much more slowly than the nervous system but has widespread and powerful effects.
Glands	Glands are organs in the body that produce hormones. The major endocrine gland is the *pituitary gland*, located in the brain. It is called the 'master gland' because it controls the release of hormones from all the other endocrine glands in the body.
Hormones	Hormones are secreted in the bloodstream and affect any cell in the body that has a receptor for that particular hormone. For example, *thyroxine* produced by the thyroid gland affects cells in the heart and also cells throughout the body which increase metabolic rates. This in turn affects growth rates.
The endocrine system and the ANS work together. For example, the *fight or flight response*.	Often the endocrine system and the ANS work in parallel, for instance during a *stressful event*. • When a stressor is perceived, the *hypothalamus* triggers activity in the **sympathetic branch** of the ANS. The ANS changes from its normal resting state (the *parasympathetic state*) to the physiologically aroused sympathetic state. • The stress hormone *adrenaline* is released from the *adrenal medulla* into the bloodstream. • Adrenaline triggers physiological changes in target organs in the body and causes, for example, increased heart rate, dilation of the pupils, decreased production of saliva. This is called the fight or flight response. • Once the threat has passed, the **parasympathetic nervous system** returns the body to its resting state (sometimes referred to as the 'rest and digest' response). This acts as a 'brake' and reduces the activities of the body that were increased by the actions of the sympathetic branch.

© Mike Baldwin / Cornered

REVISION BOOSTER

Questions on this spread (and the next spread) are likely to be either description (AO1) or application (AO2).

Sympathetic state	Parasympathetic state
Increases heart rate	Decreases heart rate
Increases breathing rate	Decreases breathing rate
Dilates pupils	Constricts pupils
Inhibits digestion	Stimulates digestion
Inhibits saliva production	Stimulates saliva production
Contracts rectum	Relaxes rectum

KNOWLEDGE CHECK

1. Using an example, explain what is meant by the 'fight or flight response'. *(4 marks)*
2. Identify and outline **two** divisions of the peripheral nervous system. *(4 marks)*
3. Identify and describe **two** glands of the endocrine system. *(4 marks)*
4. Explain the difference between the nervous system and the endocrine system. *(3 marks)*

The structure and function of neurons

Spec spotlight

The structure and function of sensory, relay and motor neurons.

The process of synaptic transmission, including reference to neurotransmitters, excitation and inhibition.

REVISION BOOSTER

It is important that you can describe the structure and function of each of the three types of neuron as these are specifically named on the spec.

cell body
sensory neuron
direction of conduction
nodes of Ranvier
myelin sheath
dendrites
relay neuron
axon
cell body
axon
motor neuron

Yeah, my heart stood still, a neuron ron yeah a neuron ron.

Ask your parents... Or possibly your grandparents...

The structure and function of neurons

Types and function of *neurons*.

There are 100 billion nerve cells (neurons) in the human nervous system, 80% of which are located in the brain.

By transmitting signals *electrically* and *chemically*, these provide the nervous system with its primary means of communication.

There are three types of neuron:

1. *Motor neurons* connect the CNS to effectors such as muscles and glands. They have short dendrites and long axons.

2. *Sensory neurons* carry messages from the PNS to the CNS. They have long dendrites and short axons.

3. *Relay neurons* connect sensory neurons to motor or other relay neurons. They have short dendrites and short axons.

The structure of a neuron.

Neurons vary in size but all share the same basic structure:

- *Cell body* (or soma) – includes a nucleus which contains the genetic material of the cell.

- *Dendrites* – branch-like structures that protrude from the cell body. These carry nerve impulses from neighbouring neurons towards the cell body.

- *Axon* – carries the electrical impulse away from the cell body down the length of the neuron.

   o It is covered in a fatty layer of *myelin sheath* that protects the axon.

   o Gaps in the axon called *nodes of Ranvier* speed up the transmission of the impulse.

- *Terminal buttons* at the end of the axon communicate with the next neuron in the chain across a gap called the *synapse*.

Electric transmission.

The firing of a neuron.

When a neuron is in a resting state the inside of the cell is *negatively charged* compared to the outside.

When a neuron is activated, the inside of the cell becomes *positively charged* for a split second causing an *action potential* to occur.

This creates an electrical impulse that travels down the axon towards the end of the neuron.

Synaptic transmission

A *synapse*	Each neuron is separated from the next by a tiny gap called the synapse.
Chemical transmission. The events that occur at the synapse	Signals within neurons are transmitted electrically; however, signals between neurons are transmitted chemically across the synapse. When the electrical impulse reaches the end of the neuron (the *presynaptic terminal*) it triggers the release of *neurotransmitter* from tiny sacs called *synaptic vesicles*. Once the neurotransmitter crosses the gap, it is taken up by the *postsynaptic receptor* site on the next neuron. The chemical message is converted back into an electrical impulse and the process of electric transmission begins.
Neurotransmitters.	Neurotransmitters are chemicals that diffuse across the synapse to the next neuron in the chain. Several dozen neurotransmitters have been identified. Each has its own specific molecular structure that fits perfectly into a postsynaptic receptor site, like a lock and key. Each has specific functions. For example: • *Acetylcholine* (ACh) found where a motor neuron meets a muscle, causing muscles to contract. • **Serotonin** affects mood and social behaviour (among other things) which is why it has been implicated as a cause of depression.
Excitation and inhibition.	Neurotransmitters generally have either an excitatory or inhibitory effect on the neighbouring neuron. • *Adrenaline* – generally excitatory, increasing the positive charge of the postsynaptic neuron, making it more likely the neuron will fire. • *Serotonin* – generally inhibitory, increasing the negative charge of the postsynaptic neuron, making it less likely the neuron will fire. • **Dopamine** is an unusual neurotransmitter as it is equally likely to have excitatory or inhibitory effects on the next neuron in the chain.
Summation	Excitatory and inhibitory influences are summed and must reach a certain threshold in order for the action potential of the postsynaptic neuron to be triggered. If the net effect of the neurotransmitters is inhibitory then the postsynaptic neuron is less likely to fire. It is more likely to fire if the net effect is excitatory.

Synapse

My friend just burst into my room and asked me what an electrical synapse in the human body was.

The nerve.

Apply it

Sabiha loves chocolate. She eats it all the time and really believes that it gives her a 'boost' and makes her feel happier. Her friend Bev tells her that's probably because chocolate contains chemicals that have a real effect on the neurotransmitters of the nervous system.

Use your knowledge of synaptic transmission to explain what is happening at Sabiha's synapses.

KNOWLEDGE CHECK

1. Explain the difference between a motor neuron **and** a relay neuron. *(2 marks)*
2. Briefly describe the structure of a neuron. *(3 marks)*
3. With reference to neurotransmitters, explain what is meant by 'excitation' and 'inhibition'. *(4 marks)*
4. Briefly explain the sequence of events that take place at the synapse. *(4 marks)*

Spec spotlight

Localisation of function in the brain: motor, somatosensory, visual, auditory and language centres; Broca's and Wernicke's areas.

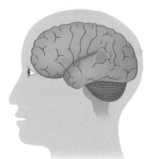

The person who came up with the name 'brain' for the brain must have used their brain to come up with it. So what that means, if you think about it, is that the brain named itself. Spooky.

Apply it

Melvin had a stroke (a burst blood vessel caused damage to part of his brain). He has problems walking because his right arm and leg are partly paralysed. He experiences numbness down his right side and also has trouble speaking, although he can understand what people are saying to him.

Use your knowledge of localisation of brain function to explain Melvin's experience and symptoms.

REVISION BOOSTER

You will improve your marks if you use specialist terms wherever possible.

Localisation of function in the brain

Holistic theory replaced by *localisation theory* in recent years.	Scientists in the early 19th century supported the holistic theory that all parts of the brain were involved in processing thought and action.
	But specific areas of the brain were later linked with specific physical and psychological functions (localisation theory).
	If an area of the brain is damaged through illness or injury, the function associated with that area is also affected.
Brain is divided into two *hemispheres* and *lateralised*.	Brain is divided into two halves – left and right hemispheres.
	Lateralisation: some physical and psychological functions are controlled by a particular hemisphere.
	Generally, the left side of the body is controlled by the right hemisphere; the right side of the body by the left hemisphere.
Outer layer of brain is called the *cerebral cortex*.	The cerebral cortex is like a 'tea cosy' covering the inner parts of the brain. It is about 3 mm thick and is what separates us from lower animals as it is highly developed.
	The cortex appears grey due to the location of cell bodies – hence the phrase 'grey matter'.
Cortex of both hemispheres is divided into *four lobes* (frontal, parietal, occipital and temporal).	*Motor area*: at the back of the frontal lobe (both hemispheres). Controls voluntary movement. Damage may result in loss of control over fine motor movements.
	Somatosensory area: at the front of the parietal lobes. Processes sensory information from the skin (touch, heat, pressure, etc.). The amount of somatosensory area devoted to a particular body part denotes its sensitivity.
	Visual area: in the occipital lobe at the back of the brain. Each eye sends information from the right visual field to the left visual cortex, and from the left visual field to the right visual cortex. So damage to the left hemisphere, for example, can produce blindness in the right visual field of both eyes.
	Auditory area: in the temporal lobe. Analyses speech-based information. Damage may produce partial hearing loss – the more extensive the damage, the more serious the loss.
Broca's area: Speech production.	Identified by Broca in the 1880s, in the left frontal lobe.
	Damage to this area causes Broca's aphasia which is characterised by speech that is slow, laborious and lacking in fluency. Broca's patients may have difficulty finding words and naming certain objects.
	Patients with Broca's aphasia have difficulty with prepositions and conjunctions (e.g. 'a', 'the', 'and').
Wernicke's area: Language comprehension.	Identified by Wernicke in the 1880s, in the back of the temporal lobe.
	Patients produce language but have problems understanding it, so they produce fluent but meaningless speech.
	Patients with Wernicke's aphasia will often produce nonsense words (neologisms) as part of the content of their speech.

One strength of localisation theory is there is brain scan evidence to support it.

Petersen *et al.* (1988) used brain scans to show activity in Wernicke's area during a listening task and in Broca's area during a reading task, suggesting these areas of the brain have different functions.

Also, a study of long-term memory by Tulving *et al.* (1994) revealed semantic and episodic memories are located in different parts of the frontal cortex.

There now exists a number of sophisticated and objective methods for measuring activity in the brain, providing sound scientific evidence of localisation of function.

Another strength of localisation theory is support from neurological evidence.

Surgically removing or destroying areas of the brain to control aspects of behaviour was developed in the 1950s by Walter Freeman – though these early attempts were brutal and imprecise.

Dougherty *et al.* (2002) reported on 44 OCD patients who had had a *cingulotomy* (lesioning the cingulate gyrus). At a 32-week follow-up, one-third met the criteria for successful response to surgery and 14 per cent for partial response.

The success of such procedures strongly suggests that symptoms and behaviours associated with serious mental disorders are localised.

A further strength of localisation theory is support from case studies.

Unique cases of neurological damage support localisation theory, such as the case of Phineas Gage who received serious brain damage in an accident.

Gage survived but the damage to his brain affected his personality – he went from someone who was calm and reserved to someone quick-tempered, rude and 'no longer Gage'.

The change in Gage's temperament following the accident suggests the frontal lobe may be responsible for regulating mood.

A limitation of localisation theory is the existence of contradictory research.

The work of Lashley (1950) suggests higher **cognitive** functions (e.g. learning processes) are not localised but distributed in a more holistic way in the brain.

Lashley removed between 10% and 50% of the cortex in rats learning a maze. No one area was more important than any other in terms of the rats' ability to learn the maze.

As learning required every part of the cortex rather than just particular areas, this suggests learning is too complex to be localised and involves the whole of the brain.

Another limitation is that neural plasticity is a challenge to localisation theory.

When the brain has become damaged (e.g. through illness or accident) and a function has been compromised or lost, the rest of the brain is able to reorganise itself to recover the function.

Lashley called this the *law of equipotentiality* – what happens is that other areas of the brain 'chip in' so the same neurological action can be achieved.

Although this does not happen every time, there are several documented case studies of stroke victims recovering abilities seemingly lost as a result of the illness.

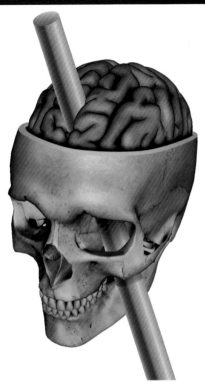

Phineas Gage was working on a railroad when a tamping iron shot through his cheek taking a chunk of his frontal lobe with it. Now we've all had some bad days, but that takes the biscuit.

KNOWLEDGE CHECK

1. Select **three** specific areas of the brain that you have studied and briefly outline the functions of each.
   (2 marks + 2 marks + 2 marks)

2. Outline research into localisation of function in the brain. *(6 marks)*

3. Discuss **two** criticisms of research into localisation of function in the brain.
   (3 marks + 3 marks)

4. A clinical psychologist's report on a patient who suffered a brain injury concludes that the patient had damage to the motor, somatosensory and language centres of her brain.

   Discuss localisation of function in the brain. Refer to the **three** brain areas mentioned in the psychologist's report. *(16 marks)*

Plasticity and functional recovery of the brain

Spec spotlight

Plasticity and functional recovery of the brain after trauma.

The brain is plastic, not rubber.

Apply it

Michael Schumacher won the world Formula One racing championship seven times. In 2013 he suffered a serious head injury during a skiing accident. He was in a medically-induced coma for several months. Schumacher's condition slowly improved and he showed some signs of recovery. He began to learn to walk and speak again, but continued to have memory problems.

Using Michael Schumacher's experience as an example, explain what psychologists have discovered about plasticity of the brain and its functional recovery after trauma.

REVISION BOOSTER

On these AO1 pages, there are nearly always six key points for each topic. This easily covers the descriptive content you would need for any essay – because description is worth 6 marks. Don't be tempted to over-describe.

Brain plasticity

The brain is *'plastic'* – synaptic connections form and are pruned.	During infancy, the brain experiences a rapid growth in synaptic connections, peaking at about 15,000 at age 2–3 years (Gopnik *et al.* 1999). As we age, rarely used connections are deleted and frequently used connections are strengthened – *synaptic pruning*. It was once thought these changes were limited to childhood. But recent research suggests neural connections can change or be formed at any time, due to learning and experience.
The concept of plasticity is supported by studies.	Maguire *et al.* (2000) found significantly more volume of grey matter in the posterior hippocampus in London taxi drivers than in a matched **control group**. This part of the brain is linked with the development of spatial and navigational skills. As part of their training, London cabbies take a complex test called 'The Knowledge' to assess their recall of city streets and possible routes. This learning experience appears to alter the structure of the taxi drivers' brains! The longer they had been in the job, the more pronounced was the structural difference.
Plasticity is also supported by other research.	Draganski *et al.* (2006) imaged the brains of medical students three months before and after final exams. Learning-induced changes were seen in the posterior hippocampus and the parietal cortex, presumably as a result of the exam.

Functional recovery of the brain after trauma

Following trauma unaffected areas of the brain take over *lost functions*.	Functional recovery of the brain after trauma is an important example of neural plasticity – healthy brain areas take over functions of areas damaged, destroyed or even missing. Neuroscientists suggest this process occurs quickly after trauma (spontaneous recovery) and then slows down – at which point the person may require rehabilitative therapy.
The brain 'rewires' itself by forming new synaptic connections.	The brain is able to rewire and reorganise itself by forming new synaptic connections close to the area of damage. *Secondary neural pathways* that would not typically be used to carry out certain functions are activated or 'unmasked' to enable functioning to continue.
Structural changes in the brain (e.g. *axonal sprouting*).	Further structural changes may include: • *Axonal sprouting* – growth of new nerve endings which connect with other undamaged cells to form new neuronal pathways. • *Reformation of blood vessels.* • *Recruitment of homologous (similar) areas* on the opposite side of the brain to perform specific tasks.

One strength of plasticity and recovery research is its practical application.

Understanding processes involved in plasticity has contributed to the field of *neurorehabilitation*.

Techniques include movement therapy and electrical stimulation of the brain to counter deficits to **cognitive** functioning experienced following a stroke.

This shows that although the brain may have the capacity to 'fix itself' to a point, this process requires further intervention if it is to be successful.

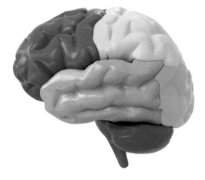

Not that kind of plastic. And not those colours either.

One limitation of neural plasticity is potential negative consequences.

The brain's ability to rewire itself can have maladaptive behavioural consequences. For example, prolonged drug use can result in poorer cognitive functioning and increased risk of dementia (Medina *et al.* 2007).

Also, 60–80% of amputees develop *phantom limb syndrome* – continued experience of sensations in the missing limb (as if it were still there), usually painful and thought to be due to reorganisation in the somatosensory cortex (Ramachandran and Hirstein 1998).

Such evidence suggests the structural and physical processes involved in functional recovery may not always be beneficial.

Funny word, plastic

Here's a definition of the word plastic: materials easily shaped or moulded.

Another limitation is that the relationship between age and plasticity is complex.

Functional plasticity tends to reduce with age. The brain has a greater propensity for reorganisation in childhood as it constantly adapts to new experiences and learning.

However, Bezzola *et al.* (2012) demonstrated how 40 years of golf training produced changes in the neural representation of movement in participants aged 40–60.

This shows that neural plasticity does continue throughout our lifespan.

REVISION BOOSTER

Have you checked out our revision advice on pages 4 to 9?

One strength is further support for neural plasticity from animal studies.

Hubel and Wiesel (1963) sewed one eye of a kitten shut and analysed the brain's cortical responses.

The area of the visual cortex associated with the shut eye was not idle but continued to process information from the open eye.

This pioneering study demonstrates how loss of function leads to compensatory activity in the brain – evidence of neural plasticity.

KNOWLEDGE CHECK

1. Explain what is meant by the term 'plasticity' in relation to the brain. *(2 marks)*
2. Outline research into functional recovery of the brain after trauma. *(6 marks)*
3. Evaluate research into functional recovery of the brain after trauma. *(6 marks)*
4. A newspaper recently carried the following headline and story: 'Knowledge changes the brain, claim psychologists. Brain scans show that taxi drivers who have to learn hundreds of London routes have bigger brain areas than the rest of us.'

   Describe and evaluate research into plasticity of the brain. Refer to the newspaper report in your answer. *(16 marks)*

One limitation is neural plasticity may be related to cognitive reserve.

Evidence suggests a person's educational attainment may influence how well the brain functionally adapts after injury.

Schneider *et al.* (2014) found the more time brain injury patients had spent in education (an indication of their *cognitive reserve*), the greater their chances of a disability-free recovery.

This suggests that cognitive reserve is a crucial factor in determining how well the brain adapts after trauma.

Split-brain research into hemispheric lateralisation

Spec spotlight

Hemispheric lateralisation: split-brain research.

The next time you describe yourself as having a 'splitting headache', spare a thought for Sperry's patients.

Getting it right (or left)

RVF = right visual field.
LVF = left visual field.
RH = right hemisphere.
LH = left hemisphere.

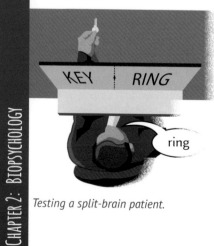

Testing a split-brain patient.

Split-brain research

Hemispheric lateralisation.	Concerns behaviours controlled by just one hemisphere.
	Language is an example of hemispheric lateralisation (usually controlled by the left hemisphere).
Split-brain studies involved a unique group of individuals.	Sperry (1968) sought to demonstrate that the two hemispheres were specialised for certain functions and could perform tasks independently of one another.
	Normally the hemispheres are connected by the *corpus callosum* and a few other structures. A *commissurotomy* is an operation to cut the corpus callosum and is sometimes performed to control epileptic seizures.
	Sperry studied a group of epileptics who had the operation.
Sperry devised a *unique procedure* to test his split-brain patients.	An image or word is projected to a patient's RVF (processed by LH) and another image to the LVF (processed by RH).
	In the normal brain, the corpus callosum 'shares' information between both hemispheres. In the split brain, the information cannot be conveyed from the chosen hemisphere to the other.
Describing what was seen.	Object shown to:
	• RVF → patient easily describes what is seen.
	• LVF → patient says 'there's nothing there'.
	Can't describe objects in LVF because RH usually lacks language centres. Messages received by RH are normally relayed via the corpus callosum to language centres in LH.
Recognition by touch.	Objects shown to LVF:
	• Could not name them but could select a matching object using left hand (connected to RH receiving information from LVF).
	• Left hand could also select an object that was associated with image presented to the LVF (e.g. ashtray selected in response to a picture of a cigarette).
	In each case, the person could not *verbally* identify what they had seen (because the LH is needed for this) but could 'understand' what the object was (using the RH) and select the corresponding object.
Composite words and matching faces.	Two words presented on either side of the visual field (e.g. 'key' presented to the left and 'ring' to the right). Patient:
	• Selects a key with their left hand (LVF goes to RH linked to left hand).
	• Says the word 'ring' (RVF linked to LH with speech centres).
	Composite picture made up of two different halves of a face was presented (one half to each hemisphere):
	• LH dominated the verbal description.
	• RH dominated the selection of a matching picture.

One strength of split-brain research is it shows lateralised brain functions.

The left hemisphere is analytical and verbal ('the analyser') and the right is adept at spatial tasks and music (the 'synthesiser').

The right hemisphere can only produce basic words and phrases but contributes emotional content to language.

Recent research suggests this distinction may be too simplified and several tasks associated with one hemisphere can also be carried out by the other.

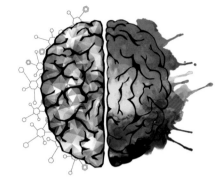

If we're talking hemispheres of the brain, it would seem that opposites attract.

Another strength is the methodology that Sperry used.

Sperry's carefully **standardised procedure** of presenting visual information to one hemispheric field at a time was quite ingenious.

Participants stared at a fixed point with one eye. An image was flashed up for 0.1 seconds, so the patient had no time to move their eyes over the image and spread the information across both sides of the visual field or both sides of the brain.

This allowed Sperry to vary aspects of the basic procedure and ensure only one hemisphere received information at a time – a very useful and well-controlled procedure.

A further strength is Sperry's work started a debate about the nature of the brain.

Sperry's work triggered a theoretical and philosophical debate about the nature of consciousness and the degree of communication between the two hemispheres in everyday functioning.

Pucetti (1977) suggested the hemispheres are so functionally different they represent a form of duality in the brain (we are effectively two minds). Others argued the two hemispheres are highly integrated and work together in most tasks.

The value of Sperry's work is in prompting this complex debate.

Apply it

Daisy had a split-brain operation to treat her severe epilepsy. Most of the time it doesn't seem to affect her everyday life. But some psychologists have asked her to take part in experiments to test her visual and language abilities. She knows you are studying psychology, so has asked you to explain what she can expect.

Use your knowledge of split-brain research to outline what Daisy might expect.

One limitation is issues with generalisation in relation to Sperry's work.

Many researchers have said these findings cannot be widely accepted, as split-brain patients are such an unusual sample of people.

Only 11 patients took part in all variations and all had a history of seizures. This may have caused unique changes in the brain that influenced the findings.

This limits the extent to which the findings can be generalised to normal brains, reducing the **validity** of the conclusions.

KNOWLEDGE CHECK

1. Outline research into hemispheric lateralisation. *(6 marks)*

2. Describe **one** split-brain study. In your answer explain what the researcher(s) did and what they found. *(6 marks)*

3. Discuss **one** strength and **one** limitation of research into hemispheric lateralisation. *(3 marks + 3 marks)*

4. Describe and evaluate split-brain research. *(16 marks)*

A further limitation is differences in hemispheric functions may be overstated.

A legacy of Sperry's work is a growing body of pop-psychological literature that oversimplifies and overstates the difference in function between the two hemispheres.

Modern neuroscientists argue these distinctions are not at all clear-cut. Many behaviours that are typically associated with one hemisphere can be performed by the other when situations require.

The apparent flexibility of the two hemispheres suggests some of the conclusions drawn by Sperry may be too simplistic.

Ways of studying the brain

Spec spotlight

Ways of studying the brain: scanning techniques, including functional magnetic resonance imaging (fMRI); electroencephalograms (EEGs) and event-related potentials (ERPs); post-mortem examinations.

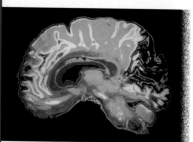

Even though your brain is only about 2% of your weight, it uses 20–30% of the calories you consume. So go on, have that dessert... your brain needs it.

Psychology and fMRI

Psychologists typically study brain activity by getting participants to have their brains scanned while they perform a task involving mental processing (e.g. memory, language). The assumption is that brain areas active during the task must be correlated with that mental process.

Apply it

Danny is a friend of yours who has frequent seizures. It appears he may have epilepsy and is going to have some tests to diagnose the disorder. He has been told he will have an EEG and an fMRI scan.

Referring to Danny's case, explain what is involved in these **two** ways of studying the brain, and what they tell us about brain functioning.

Scanning and other techniques

Psychologists use *medical techniques* to investigate brain localisation.	Techniques for investigating the brain are often used for medical purposes in the diagnosis of illness.
	The purpose of scanning in psychological research is often to investigate localisation – to determine which parts of the brain do what.
fMRI: Highlights active areas of the brain.	Functional magnetic resonance imaging (**fMRI**) detects changes in blood oxygenation and flow that occur due to neural activity in specific brain areas.
	When a brain area is more active it consumes more oxygen and blood flow is directed to the active area (*haemodynamic response*).
	fMRI produces a 3D image showing which parts of the brain are active and therefore must be involved in particular mental processes.
EEG: Shows overall electrical activity.	Electroencephalogram (**EEG**) measures electrical activity within the brain via electrodes using a skull cap (looks a bit like a swimming cap with the electrodes attached).
	The scan recording represents the brainwave patterns generated from millions of neurons. This shows overall brain activity.
	EEG is often used as a diagnostic tool. For example unusual arrhythmic patterns of brain activity may indicate abnormalities such as epilepsy, tumours or sleep disorders.
ERPs: Brainwaves related to particular events.	Event-related potentials (ERPs) are what is left when all extraneous brain activity from an EEG recording is filtered out.
	This is done using a statistical technique, leaving only those responses that relate to the presentation of a specific stimulus or performance of a certain task (for example).
	ERPs are types of brainwave that are triggered by particular events.
	Research has revealed many different forms of ERP and how these are linked to **cognitive** processes (e.g. perception and attention).
Post-mortem examinations.	A technique involving the analysis of a person's brain following their death.
	Areas of the brain are examined to establish the likely cause of a deficit or disorder that the person suffered in life.
	This may also involve comparison with a neurotypical brain in order to assess the extent of the difference.

A strength of fMRI is that it is non-invasive.

Unlike other scanning techniques (e.g. PET), fMRI does not rely on the use of radiation and is safe.

Another strength is it produces images with high spatial resolution, showing detail by the millimetre.

This means fMRI can provide a clear picture of how brain activity is localised.

A limitation of fMRI is that it is expensive.

fMRI is expensive compared to other techniques and can only capture a clear image if the person stays still.

Another limitation is it has poor temporal resolution because of 5-second lag between initial neural activity and image.

This means fMRI may not truly represent moment-to-moment brain activity.

A strength of EEG is it is invaluable in diagnosing conditions such as epilepsy.

EEG has also contributed to our understanding of the stages of sleep.

Another strength is that EEG has extremely high temporal resolution.

EEGs can detect brain activity at a resolution of a single millisecond.

A limitation of EEG is information is received from many thousands of neurons.

The EEG produces a generalised signal from thousands of neurons.

Another limitation is it's difficult to know the exact source of neural activity.

EEG can't distinguish the activity of different but adjacent neurons.

A strength of ERPs is very specific measurement of neural processes.

ERPs are more specific than can be achieved using raw EEG data.

Another strength is that, like EEGs, ERPs have excellent temporal resolution.

This is especially so compared to fMRI, for example.

A limitation of ERPs is lack of standardisation in methodology between studies.

This makes it difficult to confirm findings in studies involving ERPs.

Another limitation is that background noise and extraneous material must be completely eliminated.

This may not always be easy to achieve.

A strength is post-mortems provided the foundation for understanding the brain.

Broca and Wernicke both relied on post-mortem studies.

Another strength is post-mortem studies improve medical knowledge.

They help generate hypotheses for further study.

A limitation of post-mortems is that causation may be an issue.

Observed damage in the brain may not be linked to the deficits under review but to some other related trauma or decay.

Another limitation is post-mortem studies raise ethical issues of consent from the patient before death.

Patients may not be able to provide **informed consent** (e.g. patient HM).

The skull cap. Part of the Lady Gaga summer collection.

REVISION BOOSTER

On this page we have identified EIGHT evaluation points. For each of these, we have included THREE levels of elaboration. As evaluation is worth up to 10 marks, this amount of expansion is just what you need to produce great answers.

KNOWLEDGE CHECK

1. Explain **two** differences between functional magnetic resonance imaging (fMRI) and post-mortem examinations as ways of studying the brain. *(2 marks + 2 marks)*
2. Briefly outline electroencephalograms (EEGs) **and** event-related potentials (ERPs) as ways of studying the brain. *(6 marks)*
3. Discuss **two** criticisms of any **one** way of studying the brain. *(3 marks + 3 marks)*
4. Discuss **two or more** ways psychologists study the brain. *(16 marks)*

Biological rhythms: Circadian rhythms

Spec spotlight

Biological rhythms: circadian rhythms.

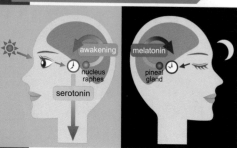

Day or night, you're a 'slave to the rhythm'.

Biorhythms are not the same as biological rhythms. Biorhythms are a pseudoscientific idea that we perform better when certain biological cycles are aligned – 'pseudoscientific' because there is no valid evidence to support the idea.

Apply it

Tameka is a nurse who works in the accident and emergency department of a large hospital. She works different shifts over a period of time. Whenever her shift changes she feels tired and less alert than usual. Tameka feels anxious and worries that she could make a mistake at work. She is also worried about her health.

Explain what psychologists have discovered about circadian rhythms. Refer to Tameka's experience in your answer.

REVISION BOOSTER

Evidence is key in psychology. But whether its description (AO1) or evaluation (AO3) depends on how you use it. The studies here are descriptive – so focus on procedures and findings, and what they tell us about circadian rhythms.

Circadian rhythms

Biological rhythms governed by *endogenous pacemakers* and *exogenous zeitgebers*.	Biological rhythms are periodic activity, governed by: 1. Internal biological 'clocks' (endogenous pacemakers). 2. External changes in the environment (exogenous zeitgebers). Some of these rhythms occur many times a day (*ultradian rhythms*); others take less than a day to complete (*infradian rhythms*) and in some cases much longer (*circannual rhythms*).
The *circadian rhythm* lasts for about 24 hours.	*Circa* meaning 'about' and *diem* meaning 'day'. There are several important types of circadian rhythm such as the sleep/wake cycle.
Sleep/wake cycle governed by internal and external mechanisms.	Exogenous zeitgebers – the fact we feel drowsy when it's night-time and alert during the day shows the effect of daylight. Endogenous pacemakers – a biological clock 'left to its own devices' without the influence of external stimuli (e.g. light) is called 'free-running'. There is a basic rhythm governed by the *suprachiasmatic nucleus* (SCN), which lies just above the optic chiasm and receives information about light directly from this structure. The exogenous zeitgeber (light) can reset the SCN.
Siffre demonstrated a free-running circadian rhythm of about 25 hours.	French caver Siffre spent long periods in dark caves to examine the effects of free-running biological rhythms – two months (in 1962) in the caves of the Southern Alps and six months (in the 1970s) in a Texan cave (when he was 60). In each **case study**, Siffre's free-running circadian rhythm settled down to just above the usual 24 hours (about 25 hours). Importantly, he did have a regular sleep/wake cycle.
Aschoff and Wever also found a similar circadian rhythm.	A group of participants spent four weeks in a World War 2 bunker deprived of natural light (Aschoff and Wever 1976). All but one (whose sleep/wake cycle extended to 29 hours) displayed a circadian rhythm between 24 and 25 hours. Siffre's experience and the bunker study suggest that the 'natural' sleep/wake cycle may be slightly longer than 24 hours but is entrained by exogenous zeitgebers associated with our 24-hour day (e.g. number of daylight hours, typical mealtimes, etc.).
Endogenous pacemakers may have stronger influence than *exogenous zeitgebers*.	Folkard *et al.* (1985) studied a group of 12 people who lived in a dark cave for three weeks, going to bed when the clock said 11.45pm and waking when it said 7.45am. The researchers gradually speeded up the clock (unbeknown to the participants) so an apparent 24-hour day eventually lasted only 22 hours. Only one participant comfortably adjusted to the new regime. This suggests the existence of a strong free-running circadian rhythm that cannot easily be overridden by changes in the external environment.

One strength of circadian rhythm research is practical application to shift work.

Boivin *et al.* (1996) found shift workers experience a lapse of concentration around 6am (a *circadian trough*) so mistakes and accidents are more likely.

Research also suggests a link between shift work and poor health, with shift workers three times more likely to develop heart disease (Knutsson 2003).

Thus, research into the sleep/wake cycle may have economic implications in terms of how best to manage worker productivity.

Another strength is practical application to drug treatments.

Circadian rhythms coordinate the body's basic processes (e.g. heart rate, hormone levels) with implications for *pharmacokinetics* (action of drugs on the body and how well they are absorbed and distributed).

Research shows there are times during the day or night when drugs are more effective. Guidelines have been developed for the timing of dosing for a range of drugs including treatments for cancer and epilepsy (Baraldo 2008).

Thus research into circadian rhythms may have real-life medical benefits.

One limitation is the use of case studies and small samples in studies.

Studies of the sleep/wake cycle often use small groups of participants (e.g. Aschoff and Wever), or even single individuals (e.g. Siffre).

Participants may not be representative of the wider population and this limits making meaningful **generalisations**. Siffre observed that his internal clock ticked much more slowly at 60 than when he was younger.

This suggests that, even when the same person is involved, there are factors that may prevent general conclusions being drawn.

Another limitation is the poor control in research studies.

Participants deprived of natural light still had access to artificial light (e.g. Siffre had a lamp turned on from when he woke up until he went to bed). Artificial light was assumed to have no effect on free-running rhythms.

But Czeisler *et al.* (1999) adjusted participants' circadian rhythms from 22 to 28 hours using dim lighting. Using artificial light may be like taking a drug that resets participants' biological clocks.

This suggests that researchers may have ignored an important **confounding variable** in circadian rhythm research.

A further limitation is that individual differences may be an influence on results.

An issue complicating the generalisation of findings from studies of the sleep/wake cycle is that individual cycles can vary from 13 to 65 hours (Czeisler *et al.* 1999).

Also, Duffy *et al.* (2001) found some people display a natural preference for sleeping and rising early ('larks') but others prefer the opposite ('owls'). There are also age differences in sleep/wake patterns.

This means that findings from sleep/wake cycle studies may not fully represent individual differences within the population.

Owls like to stay up late and sleep during the day. Very much the teenagers of the bird world.

Getting it right

Confused about exogenous and endogenous? Try this: the prefix 'exo' means 'external'. The first two letters tell you everything you need to remember.

KNOWLEDGE CHECK

1. Using an example, explain what is meant by the term 'circadian rhythms'. *(3 marks)*
2. Describe **one** study into circadian rhythms. In your answer explain what the researcher(s) did and what they found. *(6 marks)*
3. Evaluate research into circadian rhythms. *(6 marks)*
4. Discuss research into circadian rhythms. In your answer refer to research evidence. *(16 marks)*

Biological rhythms: Infradian and ultradian rhythms

Spec spotlight

Biological rhythms: infradian and ultradian rhythms.

The Stern and McClintock study; it's the pits.

Apply it

Naga and Claudia are talking about their university days back in the 1980s. They remember living in female-only halls of residence. Naga says, 'All of us on the same corridor used to have the same menstrual cycles.' Claudia agrees, 'Yes, when we first arrived we all had different cycles, but it didn't take long for us to synchronise.'

Outline what psychologists have discovered about infradian rhythms. Address the issues in Naga's and Claudia's conversation in your answer.

SAD and melatonin

The relationship is this: when the sun goes down, your melatonin comes up.

REVISION BOOSTER

Write very brief essay plans for each possible essay and then practise writing the essay out in full from these. Time yourself – 20 minutes for a 16-mark essay.

Infradian rhythms

The *female menstrual cycle* is an infradian rhythm.	The human female menstrual cycle is about 28 days (i.e. less than one cycle in 24 hours – *infra diem* meaning 'below' a day). Rising levels of **oestrogen** cause the ovary to develop and release an egg (ovulation). Then *progesterone* helps the womb lining to thicken, readying the body for pregnancy. If pregnancy does not occur, the egg is absorbed into the body and the womb lining comes away and leaves the body (menstrual flow).
Exogenous zeitgebers may synchronise menstrual cycles.	Stern and McClintock (1998) studied 29 women with irregular periods. Pheromones were taken from some at different stages of their cycles, via a cotton pad under their armpits. These pads were cleaned with alcohol and later rubbed on the upper lips of the other participants. 68% of women experienced changes to their cycle which brought them closer to the cycle of their 'odour donor'.
SAD is another infradian rhythm.	Seasonal affective disorder (SAD) is a depressive disorder (low mood, lack of activity) with a seasonal pattern. Often called the 'winter blues' because the symptoms are triggered during the winter months when the number of daylight hours becomes shorter. SAD is an infradian rhythm called a circannual (yearly) cycle.
SAD may be caused by the hormone *melatonin*.	During the night, the pineal gland secretes melatonin until dawn when there is an increase in light. During winter, the lack of light in the morning means secretion goes on for longer. This has a knock-on effect on the production of **serotonin** in the brain (low serotonin is linked to depressive symptoms).

Ultradian rhythms

Stages of sleep are an ultradian rhythm.	Sleep pattern occurs in 90-minute periods (i.e. more than one cycle in 24 hours – *ultra diem* meaning 'beyond' a day). Divided into five stages, each characterised by a different level of brainwave activity (monitored using **EEG**).
Five stages of sleep have been identified.	Stages 1 and 2: light sleep. Person may be easily woken. Brainwaves become slower and more rhythmic (alpha waves), slowing further as sleep becomes deeper (beta waves). Stages 3 and 4: difficult to rouse someone. Deep sleep or slow wave sleep characterised by delta waves which are slower still and have a greater amplitude. Stage 5: REM (rapid eye movement) sleep. Fast, jerky activity of eyes. Body paralysed yet brain activity speeds up.

One strength is research on the menstrual cycle shows its evolutionary value.

It may have been advantageous for our ancestor females to menstruate together and become pregnant around the same time, so offspring could be cared for collectively, increasing their chances of survival.

However, Schank (2004) questions the **validity** of this perspective – too many females cycling together within a social group would produce competition for highest quality males (lowering the fitness of potential offspring).

From this point of view, the *avoidance* of synchrony would appear to be the most **adaptive evolutionary** strategy and therefore the one that would be naturally selected.

How's my tan looking? What, it's for depression? Oh right.

One limitation is the methodology used in synchronisation studies.

Commentators argue that there are many factors that may change a woman's menstrual cycle and act as **confounding variables** in research (e.g. stress, changes in diet).

So any pattern of synchronisation (e.g. in Stern and McClintock's study) is what we would expect to occur by chance. Also, research involves small samples of women and relies on them self-reporting onset of their own cycle (may be inaccurate).

This suggests that important aspects of synchronisation studies may lack validity.

One strength is evidence supports qualitatively different stages in sleep.

A landmark study by Dement and Kleitman (1957) monitored the sleep patterns of nine participants in a sleep lab and found evidence for stages of sleep, specifically REM sleep.

REM activity during sleep correlated with dreaming; brain activity varied according to how vivid dreams were; participants woken during dreaming reported accurate recall of their dreams.

The study suggests that REM (dreaming) sleep is a distinct ultradian rhythm and an important component of the ultradian sleep cycle.

One limitation of research in this area is the use of animal studies.

The role of pheromones in animal sexual behaviour is well-documented and is the basis for most of our knowledge.

For example, sea urchins release pheromones into the surrounding water so other urchins eject their sex cells simultaneously.

In contrast, evidence for the effects of pheromones on human behaviour remains speculative and inconclusive.

One strength of research into SAD is its practical application.

An effective treatment for SAD is *phototherapy*, a lightbox that simulates strong light in the morning and evening (thought to reset melatonin levels).

This relieves symptoms in up to 60% of sufferers (Eastman *et al.* 1998). But the same study recorded a **placebo** effect of 30% using a 'sham negative-ion generator'.

This casts doubt on the real value of phototherapy, which may only be effective because of expectations.

Endogenous pacemakers and exogenous zeitgebers

Spec spotlight

The effect of endogenous pacemakers and exogenous zeitgebers on the sleep/wake cycle.

Even though the SCN connections have been destroyed in my brain, a milky drink before bedtime and I'm out like a light.

Apply it

Will is a teenager with a sleep problem. He finds it very hard to get to sleep at night and wakes after a short time, getting only about two hours sleep each night. He feels very tired during the day and his college work and health are suffering. Will has a chaotic lifestyle with no regular routines. He has irregular mealtimes and goes to bed at different times. He spends a lot of time before sleeping working on his tablet.

Using Will's experience as an example, explain the effects of both endogenous pacemakers and exogenous zeitgebers on the sleep/wake cycle.

SCN goes to Hollywood

Who remembers the film 'Mary Poppins'? You must remember that great song about endogenous pacemakers and the sleep/wake cycle. All together now: Superchiasmaticnucleusexpialidocious...

Endogenous pacemakers and the sleep/wake cycle

SCN is a primary endogenous pacemaker.	The suprachiasmatic nucleus (SCN) is a tiny bundle of nerve cells in the hypothalamus which helps maintain circadian rhythms (e.g. sleep/wake cycle). Nerve fibres from the eye cross at the *optic chiasm* on their way to the visual cortex. The SCN lies just above the optic chiasm and receives information about light from this structure.
Influence of SCN on the sleep/wake cycle demonstrated with chipmunks and hamsters.	DeCoursey *et al.* (2000) destroyed SCN connections in the brains of 30 chipmunks which were returned to their natural habitat and observed for 80 days. Their sleep/wake cycle disappeared and many were killed by predators. Ralph *et al.* (1990) bred 'mutant' hamsters with a 20-hour sleep/wake cycle. SCN cells were transplanted from the foetal tissue of these hamsters into the brains of normal hamsters, which then developed cycles of 20 hours.
Pineal gland and melatonin are endogenous mechanisms.	The SCN passes information on day length to the pineal gland which increases production of melatonin during the night. Melatonin is a hormone that induces sleep and is inhibited during periods of wakefulness. It has also been suggested as a causal factor in seasonal affective disorder.

Exogenous zeitgebers and the sleep/wake cycle

External environmental factors that reset biological clocks.	The German word *zeitgeber* means 'time giver'. Resetting biological clocks is a process known as *entrainment*. Without external cues, the free-running biological clock continues to 'tick' in a cyclical pattern. Zeitgebers reset the sleep/wake cycle: an interaction of internal and external factors.
Light is a key exogeneous zeitgeber that influences the sleep/wake cycle.	Light can reset the body's main endogenous pacemaker (SCN), and also has an indirect influence on key processes in the body controlling hormone secretion, blood circulation, etc. Campbell and Murphy (1998) woke 15 participants at various times and shone a light on the backs of their knees – producing a deviation in the sleep/wake cycle of up to three hours. Light is a powerful exogenous zeitgeber detected by skin receptor sites and does not necessarily rely on the eyes to influence the SCN.
Social cues also have an important influence on the sleep/wake cycle.	The sleep/wake cycle is fairly random in human newborns, but most babies are entrained by about six weeks. Schedules imposed by parents are a key influence, including adult-determined mealtimes and bedtimes. Research also shows adapting to local times for eating and sleeping (not responding to one's own feelings of hunger and fatigue) entrains circadian rhythms and tackles jet lag.

One limitation of research into the SCN is that it may obscure other body clocks.

Body clocks (*peripheral oscillators*) are found in many organs and cells (e.g. lungs, liver, skin, pancreas). They are highly influenced by the actions of the SCN but can act independently.

Damiola *et al.* (2000) showed how changing feeding patterns in mice altered circadian rhythms of cells in the liver for up to 12 hours, leaving the rhythm of the SCN unaffected.

This suggests there may be many other complex influences on the sleep/wake cycle, aside from the master clock (SCN).

'Oh how embarrassing, being caught without my nightshirt on...'

Another limitation is the use of animals.

There is an issue in **generalising** findings from research into the sleep/wake cycle from animal studies because **cognitive** factors may be more significant in humans.

A more disturbing issue (e.g. in the DeCoursey *et al.* study) is the ethics of such research – animals were exposed to great harm and potential risk when returned to their natural habitat.

Whether what we learn from investigations on biological rhythms justifies the aversive procedures involved is a matter of debate.

A further limitation is the influence of exogenous zeitgebers may be overstated.

Miles *et al.* (1977) note the case of a man blind from birth with a circadian rhythm of 24.9 hours. His sleep/wake cycle could not adjust to social cues so he took sedatives at night and stimulants in the morning to align with the 24-hour world.

Similarly, studies of individuals who live in Arctic regions (where the sun does not set during the summer months) show normal sleep patterns despite prolonged exposure to light.

Both these examples suggest there are occasions when exogenous zeitgebers may have little bearing on our internal rhythms.

REVISION BOOSTER

In an exam everyone feels some measure of anxiety – when you are anxious, you forget those things which are not well learned or well practised. So practise, practise, practise!

Another limitation is methodological issues in exogenous zeitgebers research.

Campbell and Murphy's study has yet to be **replicated** and is criticised because there may have been some light exposure to participants' eyes – a major **confounding variable**.

Also, isolating one exogenous zeitgeber (light) in this way does not give insight into the many other zeitgebers that influence the sleep/wake cycle.

This suggests that some studies may have ignored or underplayed the way in which different exogenous zeitgebers interact.

KNOWLEDGE CHECK

1. Outline what is meant by the terms 'endogenous pacemakers' and 'exogenous zeitgebers'. *(2 marks + 2 marks)*

2. Describe **one** study into the effect of endogenous pacemakers on the sleep/wake cycle. *(6 marks)*

3. Outline research into the effect of exogenous zeitgebers on the sleep/wake cycle. *(6 marks)*

4. Describe and evaluate research into the effects of endogenous pacemakers **and** exogenous zeitgebers on the sleep/wake cycle. *(16 marks)*

A final limitation is endogenous pacemakers and exogenous zeitgebers interact.

Only in exceptional circumstances do endogenous pacemakers free-run unaffected by exogenous zeitgebers.

Total isolation experiences (e.g. Siffre's study) are extremely rare and present an unrealistic view of how the system works.

Endogenous pacemakers and exogenous zeitgebers interact in real life – it makes no sense to separate them just for research purposes.

Spec spotlight

The AS/Year 1 specification is listed in the table below right.

Remember

Overall, at least 25% of the marks in assessments for A level Psychology will be based on assessment of research methods.

On Paper 2 at A level there is a section of the exam on research methods – worth 48 marks (that's a lot of questions).

But research methods are also assessed on any other topic on any other paper!

It's not what you do... it's the way that you do it.

KNOWLEDGE CHECK

1. Distinguish between an aim and a hypothesis. *(2 marks)*
2. Explain what is meant by the term 'quasi-experiment'. Give an example in your answer. *(3 marks)*
3. Explain **one** strength and **one** limitation of using a repeated measures design. *(2 marks + 2 marks)*
4. Explain how a psychologist could select a stratified sample of participants. *(3 marks)*
5. Explain the difference between a naturalistic and controlled observation. *(3 marks)*
6. Briefly discuss the use of **one** self-report technique in psychology. *(4 marks)*

AS and Year 1 – Specification content

The A level exam includes all you have learned already in Year 1. The list below indicates what that is!

Tick off what you already know and would feel confident answering questions on in the exam. Revisit concepts if necessary.

Aims: stating aims, the differences between aims and hypotheses.	☐
Hypotheses: directional and non-directional. Variables and control.	☐
Types of experiment, laboratory and field experiments; natural and quasi-experiments. Experimental designs: repeated measures, independent groups, matched pairs.	☐
Sampling: the difference between population and sample; sampling techniques including: random, systematic, stratified, opportunity and volunteer; implications of sampling techniques, including bias and generalisation.	☐
Ethics, including the role of the British Psychological Society's code of ethics; ethical issues in the design and conduct of psychological studies; dealing with ethical issues in research.	☐
Observational techniques. Types of observation: naturalistic and controlled observation; covert and overt observation; participant and non-participant observation. Observational design: behavioural categories, event sampling, time sampling.	☐
Self-report techniques. Questionnaires; interviews, structured and unstructured. Questionnaire construction, including use of open and closed questions; design of interviews.	☐
Correlations. Analysis of the relationship between co-variables. The difference between correlations and experiments. Positive, negative and zero correlations.	☐
Quantitative and qualitative data; the distinction between qualitative and quantitative data collection techniques. Primary and secondary data, including meta-analysis.	☐
Descriptive statistics: measures of central tendency: mean, median, mode; calculation of mean, median and mode; measures of dispersion: range and standard deviation; calculation of range.	☐
Mathematical content: calculation of percentages, converting a percentage to a decimal, converting a decimal to a fraction, using ratios, mathematical symbols, probability, significant figures.	☐
Introduction to statistical testing: the sign test.	☐
Presentation and display of quantitative data: graphs, tables, scattergrams, bar charts, histograms. Distributions: normal and skewed distributions; characteristics of normal and skewed distributions.	☐
Pilot studies and the aims of piloting.	☐
The role of peer review in the scientific process.	☐
The implications of psychological research for the economy.	☐

Analysis and interpretation of correlations

An association between two *co-variables*.	**Correlation** refers to a mathematical technique which measures the relationship or association between two continuous variables (co-variables). These are plotted on a scattergram where each axis represents one of the variables being investigated.
Correlation coefficient represents the strength of the correlation.	Statistical tests of correlation produce a numerical value somewhere between −1 and +1. This is the correlation coefficient. This value tells us the strength of the relationship between the two variables. The closer the coefficient is to 1 (+1 or −1), the stronger the relationship between the co-variables. The closer to zero, the weaker the relationship is. However, it should be noted that coefficients that appear to indicate weak correlations (e.g. .30) can still be statistically significant – it depends on the size of the data set.
Correlation coefficient represents the direction of the correlation.	Value of +1 represents a perfect positive correlation. Value of −1 represents a perfect negative correlation. Note that a correlation coefficient of +.50 is as strong as −.50. The sign just informs us of the direction. Correlation coefficients are calculated using an inferential test, such as Pearson's (for interval level data) or Spearman's.

Scattergrams showing various correlation coefficients

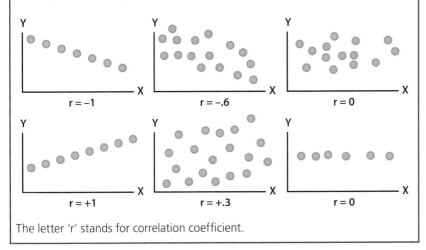

The letter 'r' stands for correlation coefficient.

Spec spotlight

Analysis and interpretation of correlation, including correlation coefficients.

An understanding of correlation as a method of research is covered in the Year 1 book, including the strengths and limitations. The A level specification adds a bit more on this topic.

Correlations are all about how two (or more) things are related.

KNOWLEDGE CHECK

A psychologist measured the correlation between accuracy of memory recall and age. He found a significant negative correlation of −.72.

1. Identify and sketch an appropriate graph that approximately represents this finding. Label your graph carefully. *(4 marks)*
2. Describe the nature of the relationship between memory and age. *(4 marks)*
3. Explain what is meant by the term 'correlation coefficient'. *(2 marks)*

Case studies

Spec spotlight

Case studies.

Gavin had taken his psychology teacher's suggestion that he should 'study a case' a little too literally.

Case study versus case history

A case history is the record of information that is collected about a person or group. It is something that a doctor or social worker might prepare but it also is an important component of a case study.

The term 'case study' refers to the research methods used to collect information about the case being studied – observation, interviews, psychological tests. It is the methods that are used for data collection and analysis.

Apply it

A cognitive psychologist investigates a patient (RL) with severe amnesia. She interviews RL about his distant past, recent past and present to find out how much he can and cannot remember. She also observes RL's day-to-day behaviour and asks family members to complete questionnaires. She does this over a period of one year to detect any changes in his amnesia.

Explain **two** strengths and **two** limitations of this case study as an investigation into amnesia.

Case studies

Detailed, in-depth and longitudinal.	To study a 'case' in psychology is to provide a detailed and in-depth analysis of an individual, group, institution or event. **Case studies** tend to take place over a long period of time (**longitudinal**) and may involve gathering data from family and friends of the individual as well as the person themselves.	
Unusual and also *typical* cases.	Case studies often involve analysis of unusual individuals or events, such as a person with a rare disorder or the sequence of events that led to the 2011 London riots. Case studies may also concentrate on more 'typical' cases, such as an elderly person's recollections of their childhood.	
Usually involve *qualitative* data.	Researchers will construct a case history of the individual or event concerned, perhaps using interviews, observations, questionnaires or a combination of all of these. The data collected is mainly qualitative. Psychological tests may also be used to assess, for example, intelligence or personality. These are likely to produce quantitative data.	
⊕ Rich, detailed insight.	Preferred to the more 'superficial' forms of data that might be collected (e.g. from an **experiment** assessing one aspect of behaviour at one moment in time).	Such detail is likely to increase the **validity** of the data collected.
⊕ Enables study of unusual behaviour.	Some behaviours/ conditions are very rare (e.g. HM) and cannot be studied using other methods.	In addition some cases can help understanding of 'normal' functioning.
⊖ Prone to **researcher bias**.	Conclusions are based on the subjective interpretation of the researcher.	This may reduce the validity of the study.
⊖ Participants' accounts may be biased.	Personal accounts (from participants and family) may be prone to inaccuracy/memory decay.	Therefore evidence provided may be low in validity.

Content analysis

People are studied *indirectly* through their communications.	Content analysis is a type of observational research. People are studied indirectly via the communications they have produced. This may include: • Spoken interaction (e.g. a speech or conversation). • Written forms (e.g. texts or email). • Examples from the media (e.g. books, magazines, TV).	
Coding may produce quantitative data.	Coding is the first stage of content analysis. Some data sets may be extremely large (such as the transcripts of several dozen lengthy interviews). So information needs to be categorised into meaningful units. This may involve counting up the number of times a particular word or phrase appears in the text to produce quantitative data. For instance, newspaper reports may be analysed for the number of times derogatory terms for the mentally ill are used, such as 'crazy' or 'mad'.	
Thematic analysis produces qualitative data.	A theme in content analysis refers to any idea that is recurrent, i.e. it keeps 'cropping up' in the communication being studied. These themes are more descriptive than the coding units. For instance, the mentally ill may be represented in newspapers as a 'threat to our children' or as a 'drain on the NHS'. Such themes may then be developed into broader categories, such as 'control' or 'stereotyping' of the mentally ill.	
⊕ Many ethical issues may not apply.	The material to study (e.g. TV adverts, films, etc.) may already be in the public domain.	So there are no issues with obtaining consent, for example.
⊕ A flexible method.	Content analysis can be adapted to produce both quantitative and qualitative data as required.	This means it is a flexible approach that can be adapted to suit the aims of the research.
⊖ Communication is studied out of context.	The researcher may attribute motivations to the speaker or writer that were not intended.	This is likely to reduce the validity of the conclusions drawn.
⊖ May lack objectivity.	Content analysis may lack objectivity, especially when more descriptive forms of thematic analysis are used.	Such bias may threaten the validity of the findings and conclusions. However, *reflexivity* is a method of addressing the lack of objectivity. Personal viewpoints are seen as an important part of the data collected.

Spec spotlight

Content analysis and coding. Thematic analysis.

The content of some communication doesn't need that much analysis.

A researcher investigates the degree of aggression exhibited in online communications. She has to collect examples of online communication and decides to use content analysis to test her hypothesis.

Bearing in mind the aim of the study, explain how the researcher could code her data.

KNOWLEDGE CHECK

1. A researcher intends to investigate one father's role in parenting. Explain how the researcher might conduct this case study. *(4 marks)*
2. Explain the difference between content analysis and thematic analysis. *(3 marks)*

Reliability across all methods of investigation

Spec spotlight

Reliability across all methods of investigation. Ways of assessing reliability: test-retest and inter-observer; improving reliability.

'What do I love about him?' mused Duck. 'It's his reliability I suppose. He doesn't say much and he never buys me flowers – but no matter where I go, and however long I go for, he'll never be far from where I left him.'

Reliability: it ain't great unless it's …

+.8

Statisticians don't write correlations with a leading zero and in reality they always write it as two decimal places but +.80 kinda spoils the rhyme!

A clinical psychologist constructed a questionnaire to measure the amount of stress experienced by sixth-form students.

a. She decided to check the reliability of her questionnaire. Explain how she could have done this.

b. Using this method, the psychologist discovered that the reliability of her questionnaire was low. Explain **one** way in which she could have improved the reliability of the questionnaire.

Reliability

Reliability is a measure of *consistency*.	If a particular measurement is repeated and the same result is obtained then that measurement is described as being reliable. Reliability = consistency.

Assessing reliability

Test-retest: Test the same person twice.	The same test or questionnaire is given to the same person (or people) on two or more different occasions. If the test or questionnaire is reliable the results should be the same (or very similar) each time it is administered.
Inter-observer: Compares observations from different observers	In an observation, two or more observers compare their data by conducting a *pilot study* – a small-scale trial run of the observation to check that observers are applying behavioural categories in the same way. Observers should watch the same event, or sequence of events, but record their data independently.
Reliability is measured using a *correlation*.	In test-retest and inter-observer reliability, the two sets of scores are correlated. The correlation coefficient should exceed +.80 for reliability.

Improving reliability

Questionnaires – rewrite questions.	A questionnaire that produces low test-retest reliability may need some items to be deselected or rewritten. The researcher may replace some open questions (which can be misinterpreted) with closed, fixed choice alternatives which may be less ambiguous.
Interviews – improved training.	The best way of ensuring reliability in an interview is to use the same interviewer each time. If this is not possible, all interviewers must be trained (e.g. so they avoid questions that are leading or ambiguous).
Experiments – **standardised procedures**.	Lab experiments are often described as being reliable because of the strict control over many aspects of the procedure, such as the instructions that the participants receive and the conditions within which they are tested.
Observations – **operationalisation** of behavioural categories.	Behavioural categories should be measurable (e.g. 'pushing' is less open to interpretation than 'aggression'). Categories should not overlap (e.g. 'hugging' and 'cuddling') and all possible behaviours should be included. If categories are overlapping or absent, different observers have to use their own judgement in deciding what to record and where, and may end up with inconsistent records.

Validity

Validity = is the result *legitimate*?	In other words, whether an observed effect is genuine and represents what is actually 'out there' in the real world.
Data can be reliable but not valid.	For instance, a test that claims to measure intelligence (IQ test) may produce the same result every time when the same people are tested but not measure what it is designed to.
Ecological validity Do findings generalise to other settings	Ecological validity refers to whether findings can be **generalised** from one setting to another, most particularly generalised to everyday life. This may not be related to the setting (e.g. a lab) but more to the task that participants are asked to perform.
Temporal validity Do findings remain true over time?	Findings should be consistent over time. For example Asch's study may lack temporal validity because it was conducted during a conformist era in American history.

Assessing validity

Face validity Whether a test looks like it measures what it should.	A basic method to assess validity – does the test measure what it's supposed to measure 'on the face of it'? This is achieved by simply 'eyeballing' the measuring instrument or by passing it to an expert to check.
Concurrent validity Whether findings are similar to those on a well-established test.	A new intelligence test, for instance, may be administered to a group of participants. Their scores are then compared with performance on a well-established test (correlation should exceed +.80 for validity).

Improving validity

Experiments – control group and standardisation.	A **control group** means that the researcher is more confident that changes in the DV were due to the effect of the IV. Standardised procedures minimise the impact of participant reactivity and investigator effects.
Questionnaires – lie scale and confidentiality.	Lie scales control for the effects of **social desirability bias**. Respondents are assured that all data submitted is confidential.
Observations – good categories.	Behavioural categories that are well-defined, thoroughly operationalised and not ambiguous or overlapping.
Qualitative research – interpretive validity and triangulation.	Interpretive validity demonstrated through the coherence of the reporting and the inclusion of direct quotes from participants. Triangulation involves using a number of different sources as evidence (e.g. interview data, personal diaries, etc.).

Spec spotlight

Types of validity across all methods of investigation: face validity, concurrent validity, ecological validity and temporal validity. Assessment of validity. Improving validity.

Does it do what it says on the tin? If the answer's yes, then it's got validity.

KNOWLEDGE CHECK

1. In the context of any research method, distinguish between reliability and validity. *(3 marks)*
2. Two psychologists conducted an observational study of behaviour at a pedestrian crossing. Explain how inter-observer reliability could be established and what could be done to improve it if it was low. *(4 marks)*
3. A psychologist conducted an experiment in which he measured attachment behaviour in young children. Explain **two** ways in which he could have assessed the validity of this experiment.
(3 marks + 3 marks)

Statistical testing

Spec spotlight

Spec spotlight

Factors affecting the choice of statistical test, including level of measurement and experimental design. When to use the following tests: Spearman's rho, Pearson's r, Wilcoxon, Mann–Whitney, related t-test, unrelated t-test and Chi-Squared test.

Luck is when people take probability personally.

KNOWLEDGE CHECK

1. A psychologist investigated whether older people (over 50) or younger people (under 30) were more likely to binge drink alcohol. Which statistical test should the psychologist use to analyse the data? Give **three** reasons for your choice.
   (1 mark + 3 marks)

2. Give **three** reasons why a researcher would use a Wilcoxon test to analyse data from a research study. *(3 marks)*

3. A psychologist compared the number of people working day shifts and night shifts who reported being depressed or happy. Which statistical test should the psychologist use to analyse the data? Give **three** reasons for your choice.
   (1 mark + 3 marks)

Choice of statistical test

Statistical tests are used to see if results are due to *chance*.

A statistical test is used to determine whether a difference or association/**correlation** found in a particular investigation is statistically significant (i.e. whether the result could have occurred by chance or there is a real effect).

Choosing a statistical test

Three criteria.

1. Looking for a difference or a correlation/association?
2. Is **experimental** design related (repeated measures/ matched pairs) or unrelated (independent groups)?
3. What is the level of measurement?

Choosing a statistical test

	Test of Difference		Test of association or correlation
	Unrelated design	Related design	
Nominal data	Chi-Squared	Sign test	Chi-Squared
Ordinal data	Mann–Whitney	Wilcoxon	Spearman's rho
Interval data	Unrelated *t*-test	Related *t*-test	Pearson's r

Note that Chi-Squared is a test of both difference and association/correlation. Data items must be unrelated.

Also note that the three tests on the blue background are parametric tests (the two forms of *t*-test and Pearson's r).

Statistical tests and their conditions for use

Nominal data:
Categories.

Each item can only appear in one category. There is no order.

For example, people naming their favourite football team.

Ordinal data:
Placed in order, intervals are subjective.

Data is collected on a numerical, ordered scale but intervals are variable, so that a score of 8 is not twice as much as a score of 4.

Ordinal data lacks precision because it is based on subjective opinion rather than objective measures.

For example, asking someone to rate how much they like psychology on a scale of 1 to 10 where 1 is 'do not like psychology at all' and 10 is 'absolutely love psychology'.

Interval data:
Units of equal size.

Interval data is based on numerical scales that include units of equal, precisely defined size.

This includes counting observations in an observational study (8 tallies is twice as much as 4 tallies) or any 'public' unit of measurement (e.g. time, temperature, length).

Interval data is 'better' than ordinal data because more detail is preserved as the scores are not converted to ranks.

Probability and significance

If the statistical test is not significant the *null hypothesis* is accepted.	The null hypothesis states there is 'no difference' or 'no correlation' between the conditions. The statistical test determines which hypothesis (null or alternative) is 'true' and thus which we accept and reject.
The null hypothesis is accepted or rejected at a particular level of *probability*.	*Probability* is a measure of the likelihood that a particular event will occur, where 0 is a statistical impossibility and 1 a statistical certainty. There are no statistical certainties in psychology but there is a *significance level* – the point at which the null hypothesis is accepted or rejected.

Using statistical tests

The usual *level of significance* is 0.05 (or 5%).	This means the probability that the observed effect (the result) occurred by chance is equal to or less than 5%. This is a compromise between too lenient (10%) or too stringent (1%).
The *calculated* and *critical* values.	To check for statistical significance the calculated value (result of the statistical test) is compared with a critical value in a table of critical values based on probabilities.
Using *tables of critical values*.	To find the correct critical value, there are three criteria: • Hypothesis one-tailed (directional) or two-tailed (non-directional). • Number (*N*) of participants or degrees of freedom (*df*). • Level of significance (or *p* value).

Type I and Type II errors

Type I error.	The null hypothesis is rejected and the alternative hypothesis is accepted when the null hypothesis is 'true'. This is an optimistic error or false positive as a significant difference or correlation is found when one does not exist.
Type II error.	The null hypothesis is accepted but, in reality, the alternative hypothesis is 'true'. This is a pessimistic error or false negative.
What makes each error more likely?	A Type I error is more likely to be made if the significance level is too lenient (too high, e.g. 0.1 or 10%). A Type II error is more likely if the significance level is too stringent (too low, e.g. 0.01 or 1%), as potentially significant values may be missed.

There are 7.5 billion people on the planet. So even if you are one in a million, there are still 7,500 people like you. Sobering thought.

The rule of R

In the exam you will be provided with a table of critical values to determine if a particular calculated value is significant.

Some statistical tests require the calculated value to be equal to or more than the critical value for statistical significance; for other tests, the calculated value must be equal to or less than the critical value.

The rule of R can help with this. Those statistical tests with a letter 'R' in their name are those where the calculated value must be equal to or more than the critical value (note that there is also an 'r' in 'more' which is a further clue!).

KNOWLEDGE CHECK

1. A psychologist collected data in a study and analysed it with a statistical test. The result of the test was significant at p<0.05. What is meant by the phrase 'the result of the test was significant at p<0.05'? *(2 marks)*

2. In relation to statistical testing, explain what is meant by the term 'probability'. *(2 marks)*

3. In relation to statistical testing, explain the difference between a Type I and Type II error. *(3 marks)*

Inferential tests and testing

Spec spotlight

Students should demonstrate knowledge and understanding of inferential testing and be familiar with the use of inferential tests.

An 'inferential test' is another term for a statistical test. In Year 1 of the course you learned to use a statistical test of difference – the sign test. You may be asked to calculate this in an exam.

In addition it is expected that you will be familiar with the use of the other inferential tests named in the specification.

On this spread we recap the key points of calculating the inferential tests.

Apply it

A researcher uses the Wilcoxon test to analyse his data. The results are shown in the table below. Fill in the column 'Rank' by ranking the differences.

Participant	Difference between condition A and B	Rank
1	6	
2	3	
3	16	
4	6	
5	4	
6	19	
7	12	
8	6	
9	4	

In all cases, after you have worked out the calculated value, this is then compared with values in the table of critical values, and a statement made about whether the null hypothesis must be accepted or can be rejected. You should also state the probability level (e.g. p<0.05).

Inferential testing

Chi-Squared

Step 1 Input observed values (O) in a contingency table. For example:

	5-year-olds	8-year-olds	Total
Decentre	6 (cell A)	28 (cell B)	34
Could not decentre	27 (cell C)	9 (cell D)	36
Total	33	37	70

Step 2 Calculate expected frequencies (E) for each cell
= row total x column total / overall total

Σ means 'sum of'.

Step 3 Work out the calculated value of χ^2.
$$\chi^2 = \Sigma(O - E)^2 / E$$

Sign test

Step 1 Convert the data to nominal data if necessary.

Step 2 Work out how many pluses and how many minuses.

Step 3 S = the number of the less frequent sign.

Mann–Whitney

Step 1 Rank all data.

To rank items you need to list all the data from lowest to highest (see data table bottom left). The lowest number has a rank of 1. In the case where two data items are the same you add up the ranks they would get and give the mean for those ranks.

Where there are a lot of multiple ranks it may help to use a frequency table.

Group A participant no.	Interview rating	Rank	Group B participant no.	Interview rating	Rank
1	12	8.5	11	16	15
2	10	3.5	12	12	8.5
3	13	11	13	14	12
4	8	1	14	15	13.5
5	12	8.5	15	18	18
6	10	3.5	16	17	16.5
7	11	5.5	17	11	5.5
8	15	13.5	18	17	16.5
9	9	2			
10	12	8.5			
		$R_A =$ 65.5			$R_B =$ 105.5

Step 2 Work out the calculated value of *U*.
Use the smaller value of *U*.
For the data above it is Group A because R_A is smaller.
Therefore the value of *U* is now called U_A.
N_A is the number of participants in group A.
$$U_A = R_A - [N_A(N_A + 1)] / 2$$

Using the data above:
$$U_A = 65.5 - [10 \times (10 + 1)] / 2 = 10.5$$

Inferential testing

Wilcoxon

Step 1 Calculate the differences between each pair of data.

Rank the difference (ignoring the signs and ignoring no differences).

Participant	Anger score before treatment	Anger score after treatment	Difference	Rank of difference
1	39	30	+9	7.5
2	42	44	−2	1
3	28	25	+3	3
4	35	32	+3	3
5	32	32	−	−
6	40	30	+10	9
7	50	44	+6	6
8	46	50	−4	5
9	29	20	+9	7.5
10	44	29	+15	10
11	25	28	−3	3
12	38	38	−	−

Step 2 Work out the calculated value of T.

T is the sum of the less frequent sign.

Using the data above, the less frequent sign is *minus*, so the sum of the ranks of the minus values is 1+5+3.

$T = 9$.

Spearman's rho

Work out the calculated value of *rho*…

$$rho = 1 - \frac{6\Sigma d^2}{N(N^2 - 1)}$$

Where $\Sigma d^2 = 43$ and $N = 14$

$rho = 1 - [(6 \times 43) / (14 \times (14 \times 14 - 1))]$

$\quad = 1 - [258 / 2730] = .91$ (answer to 2 decimal places)

Pearson's r

Unrelated and related t-test

The formula for these tests is very complex and very unlikely to be used in an exam.

You might be required to calculate the degrees of freedom (*df*):

Pearson's r $\quad\quad df = N - 2$

Related *t*-test $\quad\quad df = N - 1$

Unrelated *t*-test $\quad\quad df = N_A + N_B - 2$

(N_A is the number of participants in condition A and N_B is the number of participants in condition B).

NO to FORMULA

You do NOT have to learn any formula given here.

The mathematical skills section says 'Substitute numerical values into algebraic equations using appropriate units for physical quantities. Solve simple algebraic equations.'

A possible YES to substitution

So you MIGHT be asked to substitute values in a formula but would be given the formula. You just need to be familiar with the abbreviations.

KNOWLEDGE CHECK

1. A psychologist uses an unrelated *t*-test. Group A has 12 participants. Group B has 16 participants. Calculate the degrees of freedom (*df*) using this formula:
   $df = N_A + N_B - 2$ *(2 marks)*

2. A correlational study has ordinal data so Spearman's *rho* is used to analyse the results. The formula for this statistic is:

   $$1 - \frac{6\Sigma d^2}{N(N^2 - 1)}$$

   The researcher works out that $\Sigma d^2 = 3090$ and $N = 20$.

   Calculate the value of *rho* to 2 decimal places. *(3 marks)*

3. State whether your result is significant at the 2.5%, 5% or 10% level of significance, assuming that the hypothesis was directional. *(2 marks)*

Level of significance for a one-tailed test	0.05	0.025
Level of significance for a two-tailed test	0.10	0.05
$N = 20$	.380	.447

Reporting psychological investigations

Spec spotlight

Reporting psychological investigations. Sections of a scientific report: abstract, introduction, method, results, discussion and referencing.

Experimental psychologist's Valentine's poem:

Roses are red,
Violets are blue,
If you were a null hypothesis,
I would fail to reject you.

Apply it

A researcher conducted an experiment, collected and analysed data and drew conclusions. He now has to write a report of the experiment.

a. Identify **six** sections that he should include.

b. Choose **one** of these sections and briefly explain what information he should include.

KNOWLEDGE CHECK

1. In relation to reporting psychological investigations, explain what is meant by the 'abstract'. *(2 marks)*

2. Identify **two** sections of a report of a psychological investigation. *(2 marks)*

3. Explain what information should be included in the method section of a report of a psychological investigation. *(4 marks)*

Reporting psychological investigations

Abstract A summary of the study.	A short summary (about 150–200 words in length) that includes all the major elements: the aims and hypotheses, method/procedure, results and conclusions.
Introduction A literature review.	A look at relevant theories, concepts and studies that are related to the current study. The research review should follow a logical progression – beginning broadly and becoming more specific until the aims and hypotheses are presented.
Method Detailed enough for replication.	The method should include sufficient detail so that other researchers are able to **replicate** the study: • Design (e.g. independent groups, naturalistic observation, etc.), and reasons/justification given for the choice. • Sample – how many participants, biographical/demographic information (as long as this does not compromise anonymity), the sampling method and target population. • Apparatus/materials – detail of any assessment instruments used and other relevant materials. • Procedure – a 'recipe-style' list of everything that happened in the investigation. This includes a verbatim record of everything that was said to participants: briefing, **standardised instructions** and debriefing. • Ethics – how these were addressed within the study.
Results Descriptive and inferential statistics.	A summary of key findings from the investigation. • Descriptive statistics such as tables, graphs and charts, measures of central tendency and measures of dispersion. • Inferential statistics including reference to the choice of statistical test, calculated and critical values, the level of significance and the final outcome (i.e. which hypothesis was rejected and which retained). • Any raw data that was collected and any calculations appear in an appendix rather than the main body of the report.
Discussion Summary, relationship to previous research, limitations and implications.	There are several elements: • Summary of findings in verbal, rather than statistical, form. • Relationship of the results to previous research (this research may have been presented in the introduction). • Consideration of the limitations of the study, plus suggestions of how these might be addressed in a future study. • Wider real-world implications of the research are considered.
Referencing.	Referencing may include journal articles, books, websites, etc. For example: Flanagan, C. (2016) Experiments in psychology. *Psychology Review*, 23(2), 23–25. Flanagan, C. and Berry, D. (2016) *A Level Psychology*, Cheltenham: Illuminate Publishing.

Features of science

Paradigms and *paradigm shifts.*	Kuhn (1962) said that what distinguishes scientific disciplines from non-scientific disciplines is a shared set of assumptions and methods – a paradigm. Kuhn argued that social sciences (including psychology) lack a universally accepted paradigm and are best seen as 'pre-science', unlike natural sciences such as biology. Paradigm shifts occur, according to Kuhn, when there is a scientific revolution. A handful of researchers begin to question the accepted paradigm when there is too much contradictory evidence to ignore.
Theory construction.	A theory is a set of general laws or principles that have the ability to explain particular events or behaviours. Testing a theory depends on being able to make clear and precise predictions on the basis of the theory (i.e. to state a number of possible hypotheses). A hypothesis can then be tested using scientific methods to determine whether it will be supported or refuted. The process of deriving a new hypothesis from an existing theory is known as deduction.
Falsifiability Proof is not possible.	Popper (1934) argued that the key criterion of a scientific theory is its falsifiability. Genuine scientific theories should hold themselves up for hypothesis testing and the possibility of being proved false. Popper distinguished between theories which can be challenged, and what he called 'pseudosciences' which couldn't be falsified. He believed that even when a scientific principle had been successfully and repeatedly tested, it was not necessarily true. Instead it had simply not been proved false – yet!
Replicability Testing the **validity** of research results.	If a scientific theory is to be 'trusted', the findings from it must be shown to be repeatable across a number of different contexts. By repeating a study, as Popper suggested, we can see the extent to which the findings can be **generalised**.
Objectivity To reduce bias in research.	Scientific researchers must keep a 'critical distance' during research. They must not allow their personal opinions or biases to 'discolour' the data or influence the behaviour of participants. As a general rule, those methods in psychology that are associated with the greatest level of control (such as lab **experiments**) tend to be the most objective.
Empirical method Direct experience.	The word *empiricism* is derived from the Greek for 'experience'. Empirical methods emphasise the importance of data collection based on direct, sensory experience. The experimental method and the observational method are good examples of the empirical method in psychology. Early empiricists such as John Locke saw knowledge as determined only by experience and sense perception. A theory cannot claim to be scientific unless it has been empirically tested.

Spec spotlight

Features of science: objectivity and the empirical method; replicability and falsifiability; theory construction and hypothesis testing; paradigms and paradigm shifts.

Falsification is about never having to say you're right.

KNOWLEDGE CHECK

1. Outline **two** features of science. *(2 marks + 2 marks)*
2. Explain the importance of the empirical method in science. *(4 marks)*
3. In relation to features of science, explain what is meant by 'hypothesis testing' and 'paradigm shifts'. *(2 marks + 2 marks)*
4. Distinguish between replicability and falsifiability in relation to features of science. *(3 marks)*

Gender and culture in psychology: Gender bias

Spec spotlight

Gender and culture in psychology – universality and bias. Gender bias including androcentrism and alpha and beta bias.

The burden of gender bias may have hampered the progress of women in psychology in the past. It's certainly not helping here...

Apply it

Two psychology students were discussing the issue of gender bias. Ed says, 'I think a lot of psychological theories suggest males are superior to females.' Louise replies, 'That's funny, because I think psychological research assumes males and females are basically the same.'

Referring to Ed and Louise's points of view, explain how gender bias might operate in psychology.

Links across the specification

In this chapter on issues and debates it is expected that you will draw on examples from your own studies of psychology. We have provided some examples but you should constantly be thinking of others as you read through this chapter.

Gender bias

Psychologists seek *universality* but *bias* may be inevitable.	Psychologists possess beliefs and values influenced by the social and historical context within which they live. This may undermine psychologists' claims to discover *facts* about human behaviour that are objective, value-free and consistent across time and culture (universality). One form of bias is **gender bias**: psychological theory and research may not accurately represent the experience and behaviour of men and women.
Alpha bias exaggerates differences.	Differences between the sexes are usually presented as real, enduring, fixed and inevitable. These differences occasionally heighten the value of women, but are more likely to devalue females in relation to males.
An example of alpha bias is the *sociobiological theory of relationship formation*.	Wilson (1975) explained human sexual attraction through 'survival efficiency' – it is in a male's interests to try and impregnate as many females as possible to increase the chances of his genes being passed on to the next generation. The female's best chance to preserve her genes is to ensure the survival of the relatively few offspring she may produce. Sexual promiscuity in males is naturally selected and genetically determined but females who engage in the same behaviour are seen as going against their 'nature' – an exaggeration of the difference between the sexes (alpha bias).
Beta bias minimises differences.	Ignoring or underestimating differences between men and women often occurs when female participants are not included in the research process and it is assumed that research findings apply equally to both sexes.
An example of beta bias is the *fight or flight response*.	Early research into fight or flight was based exclusively on male animals (preferred for research because female hormones fluctuate). The fight or flight response was assumed to be a universal response to a threatening situation. Taylor *et al.* (2000) suggest female biology has evolved to inhibit the fight or flight response, shifting attention towards caring for offspring (tending) and forming defensive networks with other females (befriending). Females exhibit a *tend and befriend* response governed by the hormone **oxytocin**.
One consequence of beta bias is **androcentrism**.	If our understanding of 'normal' behaviour comes from research involving all-male samples, then any behaviour that deviates from this standard is judged as 'abnormal' or 'inferior'. This leads to female behaviour being misunderstood and even pathologised (taken as a sign of illness). For example, many feminists object to the category of pre-menstrual syndrome (PMS) because it medicalises female emotions (e.g. anger) by explaining these in hormonal terms. But male anger is often seen as a rational response to external pressures (Brescoll and Uhlman 2008).

One limitation is problems of gender bias in psychological research.

Gender-biased research may create misleading assumptions about female behaviour and **validate** discriminatory practices.

It may provide a scientific justification to deny women opportunities within the workplace or in wider society (e.g. because of PMS).

Gender bias in research is not just a methodological problem but may have damaging consequences which affect the lives and prospects of real women.

Another limitation is that gender bias promotes sexism in the research process.

A lack of women at senior research level means female concerns may not be reflected in research questions asked. Male researchers are more likely to have work published.

Also, female participants in lab studies are in an inequitable relationship with a (usually male) researcher who has the power to label them irrational and unable to complete complex tasks.

This means psychology may be guilty of supporting a form of institutional sexism that creates bias in theory and research.

One strength is that an understanding of gender bias leads to reflexivity.

Researchers recognise the effect of their values on their work (reflexivity). They embrace bias as an important aspect of the research process rather than see it as a problem threatening the objective status of their work.

In their study of the lack of women in executive positions in accountancy firms, Dambrin and Lambert (2008) include reflection on how their gender-related experiences influence their understanding of events.

Such reflexivity is an important development in psychology and may lead to greater awareness of the role of personal bias in shaping future research.

Is there a 'glass ceiling' in psychology, denying women opportunities at senior research level?

A limitation is essentialist arguments are common in gender-biased research.

Many gender differences reported by psychologists are based on an essentialist perspective – that gender difference is inevitable (essential) and fixed in nature.

Walkerdine (1990) reports how 'scientific' research in the 1930s showed that intellectual activity (e.g. attending university) shrivelled a woman's ovaries and harmed her chances of giving birth!

Essentialist accounts are often politically motivated arguments disguised as biological 'facts'. This can create a 'double-standard' in how the same behaviour is viewed from a male and female perspective.

A strength is feminist psychologists propose how gender bias can be avoided.

Worell and Remer (1992) suggest criteria researchers can follow to avoid gender bias. Women should be studied within meaningful real-life contexts, and genuinely participate in research instead of being objects of study.

Also, diversity in groups of women should be studied, rather than comparisons made between women and men. Finally, there should be a greater emphasis on collaborative research methods that collect qualitative data.

This way of doing research may be preferable, and less gender-biased, than laboratory-based research.

KNOWLEDGE CHECK

1. Explain what is meant by the terms 'universality' and 'bias' in relation to gender.
   (2 marks + 2 marks)

2. Outline gender bias in psychology. Include in your answer reference to androcentrism. *(6 marks)*

3. In relation to gender bias in psychology, evaluate the roles of alpha bias **and** beta bias.
   (6 marks)

4. A news website carried this item: 'It's official! Men and women are different. Men really are better at maths and women really are better at talking, psychologists claimed yesterday.'

   With reference to this item, describe and evaluate the role of gender bias in psychology. *(16 marks)*

Gender and culture in psychology: Cultural bias

Spec spotlight

Gender and culture in psychology – universality and bias. Cultural bias, including ethnocentrism and cultural relativism.

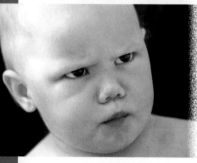

This is Norm. People don't mess with Norm. Over the years, the norms of psychology may have created cultural bias.

Apply it

Lesley is a psychologist who replicates Milgram's obedience study in Japan. She finds that the levels of obedience are higher than in Milgram's study. She concludes that people are generally more obedient than Milgram believed.

Explain how Lesley's research and conclusion might display cultural bias.

REVISION BOOSTER

A word of warning about over-describing and not sticking to the topic. By all means use (for example) conformity studies but the key word here is 'use'. Remember that the question you are answering is about cultural bias, not conformity as such.

So don't be sidetracked into describing Asch's conformity studies (which you will probably know a lot about, so it's tempting). Keep your focus on cultural bias.

Cultural bias

Psychologists seek *universality* but *bias* may be inevitable.	Many critics argue that although psychology may claim to have unearthed truths about people all over the world (universality), in reality findings from studies only apply to the particular groups of people who were studied (i.e. show **cultural bias**).
Universality assumed for results of Western research.	Researchers have wrongly assumed that findings from studies in Western cultures can be applied all over the world. For example, studies of conformity (Asch) and obedience (Milgram) revealed very different results when they were **replicated** in parts of the world outside the US. If the norm or standard for a particular behaviour is judged only from the standpoint of one particular culture, then any cultural differences in behaviour will inevitably be seen as 'abnormal', 'inferior' or 'unusual' (cultural bias).
Ethnocentrism results in a view that other behaviours are deficient.	Ethnocentrism is the belief in the superiority of one's own cultural group. In psychological research this may be communicated through a view that any behaviour that does not conform to the (usually Western) model is somehow deficient or underdeveloped.
One notable example of ethnocentric research is the *Strange Situation*.	Ainsworth (1970) has been criticised as reflecting only the norms and values of American culture in attachment research. She identified the key defining variable of attachment type as the child's experience of anxiety on separation. She suggested the ideal (or secure) attachment was the infant showing moderate distress when left alone by the mother figure. This led to misinterpretation of child-rearing practices in other countries which deviated from the American norm. For example, German mothers were seen as cold and rejecting rather than encouraging independence in their children. Thus the Strange Situation was revealed as an inappropriate measure of attachment type for non-US children.
Respecting *cultural relativism* helps to avoid cultural bias.	The 'facts' and 'things' that psychologists discover may only make sense from the perspective of the culture within which they were discovered. Being able to recognise this is one way of avoiding cultural bias in research.
Etic and *emic* approaches are universal or culture-specific respectively.	Berry (1969) argues that: • An etic approach looks at behaviour from outside a given culture and identifies behaviours that are universal. • An emic approach functions from within certain cultures and identifies behaviours that are specific to that culture. Ainsworth's research illustrates an imposed etic – she studied behaviours within a single culture (America) and then assumed her ideal attachment type could be applied universally.

One limitation is the distinction between individualism and collectivism.

Psychologists have often referred to culture in the context of individualism versus collectivism. Individualist cultures (e.g. the US) value the individual and independence. Collectivist cultures (e.g. India) value the group and interdependence.

Critics argue this is a lazy and simplistic distinction that no longer applies. Takano and Osaka (1999) found 14 out of 15 studies comparing the US and Japan found no evidence of a distinction between the two types of culture.

This could suggest that this form of cultural bias (seeing the world as individualist versus collectivist) is less of an issue than it once was.

One strength is the recognition of both cultural relativism and universals.

The 'imposed etic' shows the culturally-specific nature of psychology. But we should not assume all psychology is culturally relative and that there is no such thing as universal human behaviour.

Ekman (1989) suggests basic facial expressions for emotions are the same all over the human and animal world. Some features of human attachment (e.g. imitation and interactional synchrony) are universal.

A full understanding of human behaviour requires the study of both universals and variation among individuals and groups.

Evidence suggests that some emotions, such as disgust, are universal in the way they are expressed. I'm no expert but I reckon this lass isn't a huge broccoli fan...

Another limitation is cross-cultural research prone to demand characteristics.

When conducting research in Western culture the participants' familiarity with the general aims and objectives of scientific enquiry is assumed.

In cultures without historical experience of research local populations may be more affected by demand characteristics than Western participants.

This is a particular form of cultural bias where unfamiliarity with the research tradition threatens the **validity** of the outcome.

A further limitation is difficulties with the interpretation of variables.

Another issue with conducting research in different cultures is that the variables under review may not be experienced in the same way by all participants.

Emotions may give rise to different behaviours within an indigenous population compared to the West (e.g. invasion of personal space is normal in China, but threatening in the West).

Issues like these may affect interactions between the researcher and participants in cross-cultural studies and this may reduce the validity of the findings.

KNOWLEDGE CHECK

1. In relation to culture in psychology, explain what is meant by the terms 'bias' and 'universality'. *(2 marks + 2 marks)*

2. Using an example, outline the role of cultural bias in psychology. *(6 marks)*

3. Evaluate the role of cultural bias in psychology. *(6 marks)*

4. Some psychological research has been criticised for studying behaviour in one culture and assuming the findings apply to all cultures.

   Discuss cultural bias in psychology. Refer in your answer to ethnocentrism and cultural relativism. *(16 marks)*

Another strength is cross-cultural research challenges Western assumptions.

One of the great benefits of conducting cross-cultural research is that it may challenge our typically Western ways of thinking and viewing the world.

Understanding that the knowledge and concepts we take for granted are not shared by others may promote greater sensitivity to individual differences and cultural relativism.

This means the conclusions psychologists draw are likely to have more validity if they recognise the role of culture in bringing them about.

Free will and determinism

Spec spotlight

Free will and determinism: hard determinism and soft determinism; biological, environmental and psychic determinism. The scientific emphasis on causal explanations.

Not everyone succumbs to environmental determinism.

Apply it

Greg has schizophrenia. His dad and other members of his family also have the disorder. Greg suffered a great deal of trauma and stress as he was growing up. He spent little time at school and eventually turned to crime and drugs.

Using Greg's experience as an example, explain what is meant by determinism. Refer to **three** types of determinism in your answer.

REVISION BOOSTER

There are some things you just have to remember. Quite a lot of things, actually. So try this. Once you've thoroughly familiarised yourself with what's on a page, close the book. But wait, there's more. Then, write down everything you can remember about what you've just read. Organise it, structure it, focus on headings and key words. Start with the 'big picture'. Then fill in the details.

Free will and determinism

Free will is the idea that we are self-determining.	The notion of free will suggests human beings are free to choose their thoughts and actions.
	There are biological and environmental influences on our behaviour – but free will implies we can reject them.
	This is the view of the **humanistic approach**.
Hard and soft determinism.	**Hard determinism** (*fatalism*): all human action has a cause – it should be possible to identify these causes. This is compatible with the aims of science which assume that what we do is dictated by internal or external forces that we cannot control.
	Soft determinism: all human action has a cause but people have conscious mental control over behaviour. James (1890) thought scientists should explain the determining forces acting upon us, but we still have freedom to make choices.
Biological determinism = control from physiological, genetic and hormonal processes.	The **biological approach**:
	• Physiological processes are not under conscious control, (e.g. influence of **autonomic nervous system** on anxiety).
	• Genetic factors may determine many behaviours and characteristics (e.g. mental disorders).
	• Hormones may determine behaviour (e.g. the role of **testosterone** in aggressive behaviour).
Environmental determinism = we are determined by conditioning.	The **behaviourist** approach popularised the idea of environmental determinism – Skinner said free will is 'an illusion' and argued all behaviour is the result of conditioning.
	Our experience of 'choice' is just the sum total of reinforcement contingencies that have acted upon us throughout our lives.
	We might think we are acting independently, but our behaviour has been shaped by environmental events and agents of socialisation (parents, teachers, institutions, etc.).
Psychic determinism = we are directed by unconscious conflicts.	Like Skinner, Freud thought free will is an illusion but placed emphasis on biological drives and instincts underpinning psychological responses rather than conditioning.
	Freud's psychic determinism sees behaviour as determined and directed by unconscious conflicts repressed in childhood.
	For example, even a seemingly random 'slip of the tongue' is determined by the unconscious.
Science seeks to find causal explanations where one thing is *determined* by another.	A basic principle of science is that every event has a cause and these can be explained with general laws. Knowledge of these allows scientists to predict and control events.
	In chemistry, adding a chemical (X) to a chemical (Y) results in a reaction (Z) within the controlled environment of the test tube. In other words the behaviour of Z is *determined* by X and Y.
	In psychology, the laboratory **experiment** lets researchers simulate the conditions of the test tube and remove all other **extraneous variables** to demonstrate a causal effect.

One strength of determinism is that it is consistent with the aims of science.

The notion that human behaviour is orderly and obeys laws places psychology on equal footing with other more established sciences, increasing its credibility.

Another strength is that the prediction and control of human behaviour has led to the development of treatments and therapies (e.g. drug treatments to manage schizophrenia).

The experience of schizophrenia (loss of control over thoughts and behaviour) suggests some behaviours are determined (no one 'chooses' to have schizophrenia).

One limitation is hard determinism is not consistent with the legal system.

Offenders are morally accountable for their actions in law. Only in extreme circumstances are juries instructed to act with leniency (e.g. when the *Law of Diminished Responsibility* is applied in cases of mental illness).

Another limitation is that determinism as an approach to scientific enquiry is not falsifiable. It is based on the idea that causes of behaviour will always exist, even though they may not yet have been found.

As a basic principle this is impossible to disprove! This suggests that the determinist approach may not be as scientific as it first appears.

One strength of free will is that we often make choices in everyday life.

Everyday experience 'gives the impression' that we are constantly making choices on any given day. This gives **face validity** to the idea of free will (i.e. it makes sense).

Another strength is that, even if we do not have free will, the fact that we think we do may have a positive impact on mind and behaviour.

Roberts *et al.* (2000) showed that adolescents with a strong belief in fatalism (that their lives were 'decided' by events outside their control) were more at risk of depression.

One limitation of free will is that it is not supported by neurological evidence.

Brain studies of decision-making have revealed evidence against free will – and slightly disturbing evidence at that!

Libet (1985) and Soon (2008) found that the brain activity related to the decision to press a button with the left or right hand occurs up to 10 seconds *before* participants report being consciously aware of making such a decision.

This shows that even our most basic experiences of free will are decided and determined by our brain before we become aware of them. Scary thought…

One strength is a compromise in the middle-ground position.

Approaches in psychology that have a **cognitive** element (e.g. **social learning theory**) are those which tend to adopt a soft determinist position.

Bandura argued that although environmental factors in learning are key, we are free to choose who or what to attend to and when to perform certain behaviours.

This middle-ground approach is helpful in understanding aspects of human behaviour which are not a straightforward choice between free will and determinism (e.g. learning).

'I cannot be held responsible for this crime, your Honour. A combination of psychic, biological and environmental determinism made me do it.'

Dave's carefully researched defence was starting to fall apart.

Herr Professor Sigismund Schlomo Freud

KNOWLEDGE CHECK

1. Distinguish between hard determinism and soft determinism. **(4 marks)**
2. Briefly outline **three** types of determinism. **(2 marks + 2 marks + 2 marks)**
3. Briefly discuss the strengths and/or limitations of taking a determinist approach in psychology. **(6 marks)**
4. Discuss free will and determinism in psychology. **(16 marks)**

The nature–nurture debate

Spec spotlight

The nature–nurture debate: the relative importance of heredity and environment in determining behaviour; the interactionist approach.

Heritability

The **heritability coefficient** is a number from 0 to 1 which indicates the extent to which a characteristic has a genetic basis (a value of 1 means it is entirely genetically determined).

'It says in here that genetic similarity may cause people to behave, think and dress in the same way,' said Len. 'Sounds like baloney to me,' replied Ken.

Twin studies

MZ twins share 100% of genes but DZ twins only 50% (on average) – so we would expect a greater likelihood of both MZ twins developing a behaviour if it is mostly genetic.

This is because both MZ and DZ twins are raised together in the same environment, but MZ twins have a greater degree of genetic similarity than DZs.

REVISION BOOSTER

IQ is mentioned as an example on these pages. But lots of other characteristics, such as schizophrenia or depression, have a heritability coefficient around 50%. So all of them are good examples to use to illustrate an interactionist approach to the nature–nurture debate.

The nature–nurture debate

Nature: innate and genetic influences, usually 0.5 heritability.	Early nativists (e.g. Descartes) argued that human characteristics are innate – the result of heredity. The general figure for heritability of IQ is around .50 (Plomin 1984). The fact this is not 1.0 (100%) suggests that genetics and the environment are both important factors in IQ.
Nurture: environmental influences (e.g. learning and experience pre- and postnatal).	Empiricists (e.g. Locke) argued the mind is a blank slate at birth upon which experience writes – the **behaviourist** approach. Lerner (1986) has identified different levels of the environment: • Defined in narrow prenatal terms (e.g. the mother's physical and psychological state during pregnancy). • Defined more generally though postnatal experiences (e.g. the social conditions the child grows up in).
The relative importance of nature and nurture.	The **nature–nurture debate** is impossible to answer because environmental influences in a child's life begin as soon as it is conceived (perhaps even earlier). Practically and theoretically it makes little sense to try to separate nature and nurture (e.g. in twin studies it is difficult to tell whether high **concordance rates** are more the result of shared genetics or shared upbringing).
Interactionism (e.g. attachment).	The focus of the debate is now on the relative contribution of each influence. For example, the interactionist approach to attachment sees the bond between infant and parent as a 'two-way street': • The child's innate temperament influences how the parent behaves towards them. • The parent's responses in turn affect the child's behaviour (Belsky and Rovine 1987).
Interactionism in mental illness: the **diathesis-stress model**.	The diathesis-stress model suggests mental disorder is caused by a biological vulnerability (diathesis) which is only expressed when coupled with an environmental trigger (stressor). For example, Tienari *et al.* (2004) studied a group of Finnish adoptees and found that those most likely to develop schizophrenia had biological relatives with a history of the disorder (the vulnerability) and had relationships with their adoptive families defined as 'dysfunctional' (the trigger).
Interactionism: *epigenetics*, the third element.	Epigenetics is a change in genetic activity without changing the genetic code. Lifestyle and events we encounter (e.g. smoking, diet, pollution, poverty) leave epigenetic 'marks' on our DNA – these marks tell our bodies which genes to ignore and which to use, and may influence the genetic code of our children. So epigenetics introduces a third element into the nature–nurture debate – the life experience of previous generations.

One strength is understanding the interaction may have real-world implications.

Extreme beliefs in the influence of nature or nurture may have negative implications for how we view human behaviour.

Nativists suggest genes determine behaviour and characteristics ('anatomy is destiny'). This has led to controversy (e.g. linking race to eugenics policies, and advocating a model of society that manipulates its citizens).

Recognising that human behaviour is both nature and nurture is a more reasonable way to approach the study and 'management' of human behaviour.

Father passing on his love of 'music' to his daughter. Hmmm... those wigs look familiar...

One limitation is the confounding factor of unshared environments.

Research that tries to 'tease out' environmental influences is complicated by the fact that even siblings raised within the same family will not have identical upbringings – there are *shared* and *unshared* environments.

Dunn and Plomin (1990) suggest individual differences mean siblings may experience life events differently (e.g. age and/or temperament leads to a life event such as parental divorce having a different meaning to each sibling).

This would explain the finding that even MZ twins reared together do not show perfect concordance rates.

Apply it

Most psychologists agree that both heredity and environment play a role in determining behaviour. But they disagree on how important their contributions are.

Choose a specific behaviour that is familiar to you from your AS studies (e.g. OCD). Use your knowledge of the nature–nurture debate to explain how heredity and environment determine the behaviour. Outline how the interactionist approach tries to resolve the debate.

Another strength is gene–environment interactions explained by constructivism.

People create their own nurture by actively selecting environments appropriate for their nature. This two-way interaction between nature and nurture is known as constructivism.

A naturally aggressive child is more comfortable around similar children and 'chooses' their environment accordingly. This environment then affects their development. Plomin (1994) calls this *niche-picking* and *niche-building*.

Constructivism shows it is impossible and illogical to try to separate nature and nurture influences on a child's behaviour.

KNOWLEDGE CHECK

1. Using an example, explain what is meant by the 'nature–nurture debate'. *(4 marks)*

2. Briefly discuss the relative importance of heredity and environment in determining behaviour. *(6 marks)*

3. In relation to the nature–nurture debate, briefly evaluate the interactionist approach. *(4 marks)*

A further strength is evidence for the gene–environment interaction.

Scarr and McCartney (1983) outlined three types of gene–environment interaction: passive, evocative and active.

The interaction is different for each type – e.g. in *passive interaction* parent's genes influence how they treat their children (musically-gifted parents play to their children and encourage love of music).

Again, this points to a complex and multi-layered relationship between nature and nurture.

4. This article appeared on a magazine's website: 'The way we behave comes down to a combination of factors. People are shaped by their experiences, families and upbringing. But they are also born with characteristics that contribute to who they are.'

With reference to the issues raised above, discuss the nature–nurture debate in psychology. *(16 marks)*

Another strength is understanding nature–nurture relates to the other debates.

A strong commitment to either a nature or nurture position corresponds to a belief in **hard determinism**.

The nativist perspective suggests 'anatomy is destiny' whilst empiricists argue that interaction with the environment is all.

These equate to **biological determinism** and **environmental determinism**, showing how nature–nurture links to other debates.

Holism and reductionism

Spec spotlight

Holism and reductionism: levels of explanation in psychology. Biological reductionism and environmental (stimulus-response) reductionism.

'The whole is greater than the sum of its parts.' Where cake is concerned, she's inclined to agree.

Apply it

Brendan and Stacey both have obsessive-compulsive disorder (OCD) and have been learning more about their condition. Brendan says, 'I think it's a psychological thing really because it's mainly about the obsessive thoughts.' But Stacey disagrees: 'For me it's more to do with biological factors because I find that medication helps.'

Explain the role of reductionism in psychology. Address both Brendan's and Stacey's arguments in your answer.

REVISION BOOSTER

Reductionism – it can be a tricky one. Students often misunderstand it and therefore misuse the concept in exam answers. Examiners frequently read that a reductionist approach is one that 'ignores other factors'. Try to avoid this very general point. Instead, consider that reductionism is more to do with explaining particular behaviours or phenomena at the simplest level possible. Oh, and don't forget about holism.

Holism and reductionism

Holism
People and behaviour should be studied as a whole system.

Gestalt psychologists (Germany in 1920s and 30s) claimed that 'the whole is greater than the sum of its parts'. Breaking up behaviour and experience is inappropriate as these can only be understood by analysing the person or behaviour as a whole.

This view is shared by **humanistic** psychologists who see successful therapy as bringing together all aspects of the whole person.

Reductionism
Breaking down behaviour into constituent parts.

Reductionist approaches analyse behaviour by breaking it down into smaller units.

This is based on the scientific principle of *parsimony* – all phenomena should be explained using the most basic, lowest level and simplest principles (e.g. behaviour of individual cells).

Levels of explanation from socio-cultural to neurochemical.

The notion of levels of explanation suggests there are different ways of viewing the same phenomena in psychology – some are more reductionist than others.

For example, OCD may be understood in different ways:

- Socio-cultural level – it involves behaviour most people would regard as odd (e.g. repetitive hand-washing).
- Psychological level – the individual's experience of having obsessive thoughts.
- Physical level – the sequence of movements involved in washing one's hands.
- Physiological level – hypersensitivity of the basal ganglia.
- Neurochemical level – underproduction of **serotonin**.

Which of these is the 'best' explanation of OCD is a matter of debate, but each level is more reductionist than the one before.

Psychology can be replaced by a *hierarchy* of reductionism.

Psychology can be placed in a hierarchy of science, with the more precise and 'micro' of these at the bottom (e.g. physics), and the more general and 'macro' at the top (e.g. sociology).

Researchers who favour reductionist accounts of behaviour see psychology as ultimately being replaced by explanations derived from those sciences lower down in the hierarchy.

Biological reductionism
Physiological and neurochemical level.

We are biological organisms made up of physiological structures and processes – all behaviour is at some level biological and can be explained through neurochemical, neurophysiological, **evolutionary** and genetic influences.

This assumption has been successfully applied to the explanation and treatment of mental illness.

Environmental reductionism
Physical level, behaviourist stimulus-response links.

The **behaviourist** approach is built on environmental reductionism – behaviourists study observable behaviour and break complex learning up into simple stimulus-response links.

So the key unit of analysis occurs at the physical level – the behaviourist approach is not concerned with **cognitive** processes at the psychological level. The mind is regarded as a 'black box' – irrelevant to our understanding of behaviour.

One strength of holism is it can explain key aspects of social behaviour.

There are some social behaviours that only emerge within a group context and cannot be understood at the level of individual group members.

For example, the effects of **de-individuation** of prisoners and guards in the Stanford prison **experiment** could not be understood by studying the participants as individuals – it was the interactions between the people that mattered.

This shows that holistic explanations are needed for a more complete understanding of behaviour than reductionist approaches.

Some behaviours only emerge within a group context. It would take a brave man to do this on his own...

One limitation of holism is that it is impractical.

Holistic explanations tend not to lend themselves to rigorous scientific testing and become vague and speculative as they become more complex.

For example, if we accept there are many factors contributing to depression, it is difficult to establish which is most influential and which to use as a basis for therapy.

This suggests that when it comes to finding solutions for real world problems lower level explanations may be more applicable.

One strength of reductionism is its scientific credibility.

A reductionist approach often forms the basis of scientific research. Target behaviours are reduced to constituent parts to create **operationalised** variables.

This makes it possible to conduct experiments or record observations (behavioural categories) in meaningful and reliable ways.

This gives psychology greater credibility, placing it on equal terms with the natural sciences lower down in the reductionist hierarchy.

One limitation of reductionist approaches is lack of validity.

Reductionist explanations at the level of genes or neurotransmitters oversimplify complex phenomena and so lose validity. They fail to analyse the social context of the behaviour – but this is where the behaviour derives its meaning.

Physiological processes in pointing one's finger are the same in any context. But an analysis of these processes does not tell us *why* the finger is pointed (e.g. to draw attention, as part of a raised hand to answer a question, or as an aggressive act).

This means that reductionist explanations can only ever form part of an explanation.

KNOWLEDGE CHECK

1. Using examples, explain what is meant by 'levels of explanation in psychology'.
   (4 marks)
2. Outline biological reductionism and environmental (stimulus-response) reductionism in psychology.
   (6 marks)
3. Evaluate reductionism in psychology.
   (6 marks)
4. Some psychologists believe that behaviour can only be fully understood by considering the whole person. Other psychologists believe behaviour has to be broken up into its constituent parts to be analysed.

   With reference to these two positions, discuss holism and reductionism in psychology.
   (16 marks)

A strength of both holism and reductionism is the interactionist approach.

Interactionism in the context of holism and reductionism considers how different levels of explanation combine and interact.

For example, the **diathesis-stress model** explains mental disorders such as schizophrenia as the outcome of predisposition (often genetic) which is triggered by some stressor (often psychological).

This model has led to a more multi-disciplinary and holistic approach to treatment (e.g. combining drugs and family therapy) and is associated with lower relapse rates.

Idiographic and nomothetic approaches

Spec spotlight

Idiographic and nomothetic approaches to psychological investigation.

There's always one isn't there – trying to make a point.

Point. Pencil. Geddit? Never mind.

Apply it

Sabiha, a teacher, decides to set up a classroom debate. She arranges it so half the class have to support the idiographic approach to psychological investigation and the other half have to support the nomothetic approach. Each side has to come up with: an example of their approach from an area of psychological research; an outline of their approach; two strengths of their approach; one limitation of their approach.

Outline each of the above for each side of the debate.

The idiographic approach

The study of *unique experience*.	The idiographic approach aims to describe the nature of the individual. People are studied as unique entities with their own subjective experiences, motivations and values. There is no attempt to compare these to a larger group standard or norm.
Associated with *qualitative* research methods.	The idiographic approach is associated with methods in psychology that produce qualitative data (e.g. **case studies**, unstructured interviews and other self-report measures). This reflects one of the central aims of idiographic research – to describe the richness of human experience and gain insight into the person's unique way of viewing the world.
Includes *humanistic* psychology and the *psychodynamic* approach.	**Humanistic psychology** is the best example of the idiographic approach. Rogers and Maslow were interested only in documenting the conscious experience of the individual or 'self', rather than producing general laws of behaviour. The **psychodynamic approach** is often thought of as idiographic because of Freud's use of the case study method. But Freud also assumed he had identified universal laws of behaviour and personality development (the language of the nomothetic approach).

The nomothetic approach

The production of *general laws*.	The main aim of the nomothetic approach is to produce general laws of behaviour. These provide a benchmark against which people can be compared, classified and measured. Future behaviour can then be predicted and controlled.
Associated with *questionnaires* and *psychological tests*.	The nomothetic approach is most closely associated with methods defined as reliable and scientific within psychology (e.g. questionnaires and psychological tests). These involve the study of larger numbers of people to establish how people are similar (which also tells us how people differ from one another).
Includes *behaviourist*, *cognitive* and *biological* research.	The nomothetic approach looks at findings from large numbers of people which are analysed for statistical significance. **Behaviourist**, **cognitive** and biological research would meet the criteria of the nomothetic approach. Questionnaires that test characteristics such as personality or IQ are used to diagnose abnormality and predict behaviours.

One strength is the idiographic approach provides rich data.

The idiographic approach provides a complete and global account of the individual, such as the study of HM.

A single case may generate hypotheses for further study (e.g. the case of HM in memory research helped our understanding that some procedural memories are more resistant to amnesia).

Such findings from unique cases may reveal important insights about normal functioning which may contribute to our overall understanding of behaviour.

One limitation of the idiographic approach may be its lack of scientific rigour.

Supporters of the idiographic approach may have to acknowledge the subjective and restrictive nature of their work.

One criticism of Freud is that many of his key concepts (e.g. the Oedipus complex) were largely developed from the detailed study of a single case (e.g. Little Hans).

Meaningful **generalisations** cannot be made without further examples, which means conclusions tend to rely on the subjective interpretation of the researcher and are therefore open to bias.

One strength of the nomothetic approach is the scientific value of the research.

The processes involved in nomothetic research tend to be more scientific, mirroring those employed within the natural sciences.

These processes include **standardised procedures**, assessing reliability and **validity**, and using statistical analyses to demonstrate significance.

This arguably gives the discipline of psychology greater scientific credibility.

One limitation of the nomothetic approach is the loss of the whole person.

The preoccupation within the nomothetic approach on general laws, prediction and control has been accused of 'losing the whole person' within psychology.

Knowing there is a 1% lifetime risk of developing schizophrenia tells us little about what life is like with it. In lab tests of memory participants are treated as a set of scores rather than as individual people.

This means, in its search for general laws, the nomothetic approach may sometimes overlook the importance of human experience.

A strength is the two approaches may be complementary not contradictory.

Rather than seeing idiographic and nomothetic approaches as either/or alternatives, we can consider the same issue or topic from both perspectives, depending on the nature of the research question.

Research on gender development attempts to establish general patterns of behaviour (e.g. Bem's androgyny scale) alongside case studies of atypical development (e.g. the case of David Reimer).

The goal of modern psychology is to provide rich, detailed descriptions of human behaviour as well as the explanation of such behaviour within the framework of general laws.

Teri knew she was different. Very few other people would have paired a brown jacket with a grey scarf.

REVISION BOOSTER

This is where a thorough understanding of research methods is so useful. The nomothetic–idiographic debate is closely linked to choice of methodology (much less so about theory). Your understanding of the debate can only be improved by looking again at research methods.

KNOWLEDGE CHECK

1. Using an example of each, outline idiographic and nomothetic approaches to psychological investigation.
   (3 marks + 3 marks)
2. Explain **two** differences between idiographic and nomothetic approaches to psychological investigation.
   (3 marks + 3 marks)
3. Discuss **one** criticism of nomothetic approaches to psychological investigation.
   (4 marks)
4. Describe and evaluate idiographic **and/or** nomothetic approaches to psychological investigation.
   (16 marks)

Ethical implications of research studies and theory

Spec spotlight

Ethical implications of research studies and theory, including reference to social sensitivity.

No one could accuse Janet of being 'socially sensitive'.

Apply it

A group of university researchers carried out a study of the academic abilities of primary school-aged children. Their participants came from several schools within a short distance of the university. They found that children from Afro-Caribbean backgrounds on average showed the lowest academic ability. Children from far-east Asian backgrounds had the highest ability.

Explain the ways in which this research could be considered socially sensitive.

Three essays

Note that for this topic there are three possible 16-mark essays that could be set:

Discuss ethical implications of research studies.

Discuss ethical implications of research.

Discuss social sensitivity in psychological research.

In all three cases the socially sensitive issues in research studies would be creditworthy. So focus your revision on that. If the essay is just on socially sensitive research, then general ethical implications would not be creditworthy.

Ethical implications

Ethical issues arise due to *conflict*.	Ethical issues arise when there is a conflict between: • Psychology's need for **valid** and valuable research. • Preserving the rights and dignity of participants.
Wider ethical implications of research are *hard to predict*.	Researchers can control the methods they use and how they treat participants. They have less influence on how findings are presented in the media, how their work impacts public policy and how it affects perception of some groups in society.

Socially sensitive research

Research with *social consequences* (e.g. criminality or race).	Socially sensitive research – there are potential social implications, either directly for the participants in research or the class of individuals represented by the research. For example: • Research investigating genetic basis of criminality might have far-reaching consequences for those who take part or for the broader social groups the participants represent. • Studies that tackle socially sensitive 'taboo' topics such as race or sexuality attract attention from the public.
Researchers should not avoid this type of research.	Some forms of research are socially sensitive but psychologists should not 'shy away' from them. Because of the importance of such research, psychologists may have a social responsibility to carry it out (Aronson 1999).
Concerns for socially sensitive research include *implications*, *public policy* and *validity*.	Sieber and Stanley (1988) have identified concerns: 1. *Implications*: some studies may give 'scientific status' to prejudice and discrimination (difficult to predict at outset). 2. *Uses/public policy*: what would happen if it was used for the wrong purpose? Findings may be adopted by the government for political ends or to shape public policy. 3. *Validity of the research*: some findings presented as objective in the past turned out to be fraudulent.
Burt's research on IQ had consequences for UK schoolchildren.	Burt was a leading psychologist influential in establishing the 11+ examination in the UK. This was used to decide whether children could go to grammar school based on their 'natural' intelligence (with a significant impact on life opportunities). Burt's view was that intelligence is genetic, based on his studies of twins showing a heritability coefficient of +.77 (Burt 1955). But discrepancies in the data showed he made much of the data up, and invented two research assistants. He was publically discredited but the 11+ (and the related public policy) remained for many years.

One strength is there are benefits of socially sensitive research.

Scarr (1988) argues that studies of under-represented groups and issues may promote greater understanding to help reduce prejudice and encourage acceptance.

Socially sensitive research has benefitted society (e.g. research into unreliability of eyewitness testimony has reduced the risk of miscarriages of justice within the legal system).

This suggests that socially sensitive research may play a valuable role in society.

As the only Accrington Stanley supporter, Brian (5th row, 3rd from the left) felt very much in the minority. Was he being too sensitive?

Another strength is understanding how to frame questions.

Sieber and Stanley (1988) warn that how research questions are phrased and investigated may influence the ways findings are interpreted.

Kitzinger and Coyle (1995) note how research into so-called 'alternative relationships' has been guilty of 'heterosexual bias' – homosexual relationships were judged against heterosexual norms.

This suggests that investigators must approach their research with an 'open mind' and be prepared to have their preconceptions challenged to avoid misrepresenting minority groups.

A strength is understanding potential damage from socially sensitive research.

Socially sensitive research has been used by governments and other institutions to shape social policy, despite the sometimes dubious nature of the findings (e.g. Burt's research into IQ).

Packard (1957) claimed sales of Coca-Cola and popcorn increased when images of the products were flashed on cinema screens too quickly for audiences to be aware of them (subliminal). It was later revealed Packard had made his findings up!

Research that seeks to manipulate the public has obvious ethical implications. It also raises the question of who benefits from such research – which may be particularly difficult to manage once the research is 'out there'.

One limitation of socially sensitive research is it may be used for social control.

In the 1920s and 30s, a large number of US states enacted legislation that led to the compulsory sterilisation of many of its citizens.

These people were judged to be 'feeble-minded' and a drain on society (e.g. those of 'low intelligence', drug/alcohol addicts and the mentally ill). Some psychologists argued they were 'unfit to breed'.

The fact that socially sensitive research has been used to 'prop up' discriminatory practices in the past is an argument against its widespread adoption.

KNOWLEDGE CHECK

1. With reference to **either** research studies **or** theories, explain what is mean by 'ethical implications'. *(3 marks)*

2. Outline **one or more** ethical implication(s) of research studies in psychology. *(4 marks)*

3. Outline **two** ethical implications of theories in psychology. *(2 marks + 2 marks)*

4. Discuss the ethical implications of research studies **and/or** theories in psychology. Refer in your answer to social sensitivity.
(16 marks)

Another limitation is that costs and benefits may be difficult to predict.

Research that carries ethical implications (or is socially sensitive) is scrutinised by an ethics committee – it is their job to weigh up the costs and benefits of the research.

However, some of the social consequences of research involving vulnerable groups may be difficult to anticipate.

Assessments of the 'worth' of such research are typically subjective, and the real impact of research can only ever be known once it has been made public.

Sexual selection and human reproductive behaviour

Spec spotlight

The evolutionary explanations for partner preferences, including the relationship between sexual selection and human reproductive behaviour.

Cute, but pretty dangerous. That's love for you.

Apply it

Michael is a 65-year-old businessman who owns a big yacht and a massive house. He has just married Catherine who is 22. She is Michael's fourth wife; as he gets older he seems to marry younger and younger women. Catherine wants four children, but Michael has a history of having affairs outside marriage. Catherine told him if she ever caught him doing that to her, she'd take 'appropriate physical action'.

How does evolutionary theory for partner preference explain both Michael's and Catherine's behaviour?

Sexual selection

Anisogamy – differences between male and female sex cells.	Male cells (sperm) are small, mobile and continuously produced from puberty to old age. Female cells (ova) are larger, static and produced at intervals for a limited number of years.
Anisogamy related to *mating strategies.*	Consequences of anisogamy are that there are plenty of fertile males but fewer females. This gives rise to different mating strategies – inter-sexual and intra-sexual.

Inter-sexual selection

Selection of mates between sexes (e.g. females selecting males or males selecting females).

Female strategy – quality over quantity.	Females make a greater investment of time, commitment and other resources before, during and after birth. Need to be choosier than males so seek a male who will provide healthy offspring and support them with resources.
Impact on mating behaviour.	Preferences of both sexes determine attributes that are passed on – e.g. if height is a genuine marker of fitness in males, the females who choose the tallest mates will have greater reproductive success and innate preferences are passed on. Over time this leads to taller and taller men being selected (runaway process).

Intra-sexual selection

Selection of mates within sexes (e.g. males competing with other males for mates).

Male strategy – quantity over quality.	Males do best if they reproduce as frequently as possible. Competition is necessary as females are a limited resource and are choosy. Males who compete successfully pass on their genes to the next generation and therefore those traits are perpetuated.
Impact on mating behaviour.	Intra-sexual selection pressures lead to certain patterns of human reproductive behaviour: • Male aggression – the most aggressive males are more likely to reproduce. • Male preference for youthful and fertile women because these are signs of fertility leading to reproductive success.

One strength is support for the relationship with intra-sexual selection.

Buss (1989) surveyed over 10,000 adults in 33 countries asking about partner preference.

He found that females valued resource-related characteristics more than males (e.g. good financial prospects). Males valued reproductive capacity (e.g. good looks and youth).

This supports sex differences due to anisogamy and partner preferences derived from sexual selection theory.

Another strength is support for the relationship with inter-sexual selection.

Clark and Hatfield (1989) sent students to approach other students and ask 'I have been noticing you around campus. I find you to be very attractive. Would you go to bed with me tonight?'

No female students agreed in response to requests from males. But 75% of males did agree to female requests.

This supports the suggestion of female choosiness and that males have evolved a different strategy to ensure their reproductive success.

One limitation is the relationship ignores social and cultural influences.

Partner preferences have impacted over time by changing social norms and cultural practices. These have occurred too rapidly to be explained in **evolutionary** terms.

Chang et al. (2011) report that some preferences have changed and others have remained the same over 25 years in China.

This suggests that both evolutionary and cultural influences must be taken into account when explaining human reproductive behaviour.

Another strength is support from waist–hip ratio research.

Singh (1993, 2002) measured waist–hip ratio (WHR) preferences of males for females.

Findings were that any hip and waist size can be attractive as long as the ratio of one to the other is 0.7 (thought to signify that the female is fertile but not currently pregnant).

This shows that evolutionary factors are reflected in patterns of human reproductive behaviour through partner preferences.

A final strength is support from lonely hearts research.

Waynforth and Dunbar (1995) studied lonely hearts advertisements in American newspapers to see how men and women describe the qualities they desired in and offered to a potential partner.

They found women tended to offer physical attractiveness and indicators of youth and sought resources. Men offered resources and sought youth and physical attractiveness.

These findings support the evolutionary suggestions that women will seek resources whilst men are more focused on signs of reproductive fitness.

REVISION BOOSTER

What are your evaluations like? Why not try and make them more like ours? Start with your initial point – a strength or a limitation in most cases. Then... elaborate! Develop your evaluation point in three more steps, just as we've done on all of these AO3 pages. Have a close look at each one to see what they have in common.

Which of the tiny two-dimensional men should Rebecca choose?

KNOWLEDGE CHECK

1. In relation to evolutionary explanations for partner preference, explain what is meant by 'sexual selection'. *(3 marks)*

2. Outline the evolutionary explanation for partner preference. *(6 marks)*

3. Evaluate the relationship between sexual selection and human reproductive behaviour. *(6 marks)*

4. 'To put it bluntly,' says Donald, 'women want to settle down with a man to provide for her and men just want to spread their seed around as much as possible.'

   With reference to evolutionary explanations for partner preferences, describe and evaluate the relationship between sexual selection and human reproductive behaviour. *(16 marks)*

Factors affecting attraction: self-disclosure

Spec spotlight

Factors affecting attraction in romantic relationships: self-disclosure.

They were at a fairly advanced stage in their relationship, but this was the first time Alice revealed she had five kids.

Apply it

Marina is talking about her marriage to Jacob. 'We make time to talk to each other every day. We take it in turns, no interruptions. We used to talk about how our days had been, what we had been doing, that sort of thing. But these days we talk about stuff that really matters, how we feel about things. And we talk about everything; there are no secrets between us.'

Explain how Marina's and Jacob's experience illustrates the role of self-disclosure in romantic relationships.

Know your onions

Altman and Taylor used a metaphor to explain deepening self-disclosures. It's like an onion – we 'peel away' layers of ourselves from the surface down to our inner core. A useful way of thinking about the process.

Self-disclosure

Important *early* in a relationship	Self-disclosure refers to revealing intimate information to another person.
	For example, revealing your likes and dislikes, hopes and fears, interests and attitudes. We share what really matters to us.
	Most people are careful about disclosing too much too soon.
	Ultimately self-disclosure plays an important role in the development of a relationship.

Social penetration theory (Altman and Taylor 1973)

Self-disclosure limited at start.	It is a gradual process of revealing your inner self to someone else.
	Revealing personal information is a sign of trust.
	Partner then has to reciprocate and reveal personal information.
Penetration leads to development.	As romantic partners increasingly disclose more information they 'penetrate' more deeply into each other's lives.
	Thus they gain a greater understanding of each other.
Breadth is narrow.	Both breadth and depth of self-disclosure are key according to the social penetration theory.
	Breadth is narrow at the start of a relationship because if too much information is revealed this may be off-putting and one partner may decide to quit the relationship.
Depth increases.	As a relationship develops more layers are gradually revealed.
	We are likely to reveal more intimate information including painful memories, secrets, etc.

Reciprocity of self-disclosure

Need for *reciprocity* for a relationship to develop	Reis and Shaver (1988) suggest that, in addition to a broadening and deepening of self-disclosure, there must be reciprocity.
	Successful relationships will involve disclosure from one partner which is received sensitively by the other partner.
	In turn this should then lead to further self-disclosure from the other partner.

One strength is support from research studies.

Sprecher and Hendrick (2004) found strong **correlations** between several measures of satisfaction and self-disclosure in heterosexual couples.

Men and women who used self-disclosure and those who believed their partners also disclosed were more satisfied with and committed to their romantic relationship.

This supports the concept of self-disclosure being a key component of committed romantic relationships.

After an ill-advised game of cat's cradle, Tim and Amanda had been entangled for nearly seven hours.

Another strength is real-life applications.

Hass and Stafford (1998) found that 57% of gay men and women reported that open and honest self-disclosure was a maintenance strategy.

Couples used to 'small talk' can be encouraged to increase self-disclosure in order to deepen their own relationships.

This highlights the importance of self-disclosure and suggests the theory can be used to support people having relationship problems.

One limitation is the theory does not apply to all cultures.

Tang et al. (2013) concluded that people in the US (**individualist** culture) self-disclose significantly more sexual thoughts and feelings than people in China (**collectivist** culture).

Both levels of self-disclosure are linked to relationship satisfaction in those cultures but nevertheless the pattern of self-disclosure is different.

Social penetration theory is therefore a limited explanation of romantic relationships and not necessarily **generalisable** to other cultures.

Another limitation is self-disclosure linked to relationship breakdown too.

Sometimes breakdown of relationships is characterised by a reduction in self-disclosure, however this is not always the case.

Duck's (2007) phase model of the breakdown of relationships recognises that couples often discuss their relationship with each other in intimate detail (i.e. self-disclose) yet this may not be sufficient to save the relationship.

This suggests that increased self-disclosure may not always lead to positive developments in a relationship.

A final limitation is that much of the research is correlational.

Studies such as Sprecher and Hendrick (2004) have found a positive correlation between self-disclosure and satisfaction.

However, we cannot assume that the relationship is a causal one.

This suggests that such research provides only limited support for the theory.

KNOWLEDGE CHECK

1. Explain what is meant by 'self-disclosure' in relation to factors affecting attraction in romantic relationships. *(3 marks)*

2. In relation to factors affecting attraction in romantic relationships, outline research into self-disclosure. *(6 marks)*

3. Identify and discuss **one** criticism of research into self-disclosure as a factor affecting attraction in romantic relationships. *(4 marks)*

4. Asad fancied Sabiha and asked her out on a date. Halfway into a lovely evening he said, 'I really want to get married and have lots of kids as soon as possible – it's really important to me.' Sabiha decided not to go on a second date.

   With reference to Asad and Sabiha's experience, describe and evaluate research into self-disclosure as a factor affecting attraction in romantic relationships.
   (16 marks)

Factors affecting attraction: Physical attractiveness

Spec spotlight

Factors affecting attraction in romantic relationships: physical attractiveness, including the matching hypothesis.

Sure he looks angelic now but imagine that face screaming at 4 in the morning.

Apply it

Most people agree that Gaby is very physically attractive. They think she comes across as a very nice and kind person too. When people wonder why she is single, Gaby replies it's because she hasn't found anyone in her league yet!

Explain how Gaby's experience illustrates the role of physical attractiveness in romantic relationships.

Longer-term attraction

It helps to remember that this topic is not a theory of how romantic relationships start. It is about factors affecting attraction in relationships of any duration. This means that research into the role of attraction in longer-term relationships is relevant (e.g. McNulty et al. 2008).

The importance of physical attraction

Symmetry.	Shackelford and Larsen (1997) found that people with symmetrical faces are rated as more attractive. It is thought that this is a signal of genetic fitness that cannot be faked (which makes it an 'honest' signal). The associated 'robust' genes are likely to be passed on and therefore symmetry is perpetuated. Explanations based on physical attractiveness are **evolutionary** ones – we have evolved a liking for attributes that signal high quality.
Baby face features seen as attractive.	Neotenous (baby face) features are thought to trigger protective and caring instincts, related to the formation of attachment in infancy. This is also an evolutionary explanation because features that strengthen attachment are **adaptive**.
Beyond the *formation stage.*	Attractiveness is important after the formation stage of a relationship. For example, McNulty et al. (2008) found that initial attractiveness continued to be an important feature of the relationship after marriage.
Halo effect describes how physical attractiveness is generalised.	We hold preconceived ideas about the attributes of attractive people. We believe that all their other attributes are overwhelmingly positive. For example, Dion et al. (1972) found that physically attractive people are consistently rated as kind, strong, sociable and successful compared with unattractive people.

Matching hypothesis (Walster *et al.* 1966)

We *choose a partner* whose attractiveness matches ours.	The hypothesis states that we choose partners that are of the same level of attractiveness to ourselves. To do this we need to assess our own value to a potential partner. For example, if we judge ourselves as 6/10 then we are likely to seek a mate of a similar level of attractiveness.
Choosing a partner is a compromise.	Evolutionary theories suggest we should seek the most attractive mates. However, we have to also balance the potential for being rejected because the partner we aim for is 'out of our league' in terms of attractiveness. So we compromise by 'matching' attractiveness.

One strength is research support for the halo effect.

Palmer and Peterson (2012) found that physically attractive people were rated more politically knowledgeable and competent than unattractive people.

This has implications and suggests politicians might be elected merely because they are considered physically attractive by enough voters.

This shows that the halo effect can be observed in real-life situations.

Touching to think that their shared love of repulsive yellow jackets had brought them together.

One limitation is not everyone considers physical attractiveness important.

Those who scored highly on the MACHO scale (sexist attitudes) were more influenced by physical attractiveness when judging likeability from a photograph and basic biographical data. (Towhey 1979).

As low scorers were less sensitive to this influence, it would seem that there are individual differences in the importance placed upon physical attractiveness.

This suggests that the effects of physical attractiveness can be moderated by other factors and may not be as significant a consideration in relationship formation for all partners.

Another limitation is mixed support for the matching hypothesis.

Walster et al.'s (1966) initial study failed to support the theory as they found students preferred partners who were more physically attractive rather than matching their level.

However, Feingold's (1988) **meta-analysis** of studies of 'actual' partners found a significant **correlation** in ratings of attractiveness between them.

These findings from more realistic studies support the hypothesis even though the original studies did not.

REVISION BOOSTER

Your own experience of relationships is useful here. Have you found yourself subject to the halo effect? How valid do you think it really is? Do you assume that attractive people are also kind, honest, helpful and so on? If you can apply a psychological theory to your own experience, that's a kind of revision. It could help you to understand the information and retain it. And you'll be thinking about psychology – always a good thing!

... *however*, don't include such anecdotal material in an exam answer. It is unlikely to gain marks.

One strength is there is cultural consistency in what is considered attractive.

Cunningham et al. (1995) found large eyes, small nose and prominent cheekbones in females were rated as highly attractive by white, Asian and Hispanic males.

Wheeler and Kim (1997) found that Korean and US students judged physically attractive people to be more trustworthy, mature, concerned for other people and friendly.

This consistency suggests physical attractiveness is culturally independent and may have evolutionary roots.

KNOWLEDGE CHECK

1. Outline research into physical attractiveness as a factor affecting attraction in romantic relationships. *(6 marks)*

2. In relation to factors affecting attraction in romantic relationships, outline the matching hypothesis. *(6 marks)*

3. Describe **one** study of physical attractiveness as an explanation of attraction in romantic relationships. *(6 marks)*

4. Discuss **two** factors affecting attraction in romantic relationships. *(16 marks)*

A limitation is that online dating research has not supported its assumptions.

Taylor et al. (2011) found online daters sought dates with partners who were more attractive than themselves and did not consider their own level of attractiveness.

This research involved actual dating choices (meeting people online is becoming increasingly popular) yet it does not support the matching hypothesis.

It may therefore be that the matching hypothesis no longer explains preferences regarding physical attractiveness in a useful way.

Factors affecting attraction: Filter theory

Spec spotlight

Factors affecting attraction in romantic relationships: filter theory, including social demography, similarity in attitudes and complementarity.

You've got two minutes my friend – impress me! Speed dating: the ultimate filtering opportunity.

Apply it

Martin and Claire first met at university where they were on the same corridor in halls of residence.

Yuan and Xia met on a demonstration against fox-hunting.

Gurmeet and Debina married 20 years ago. They enjoy telling each other about their different hobbies and interests.

Explain how the experiences of each of these couples illustrates elements of the filter theory of romantic relationships.

REVISION BOOSTER

Always think 'less is more' – writing about fewer things gives you the opportunity to demonstrate your detailed understanding.

Filter theory (Kerckhoff and Davis 1962)

Field of availables and *field of desirables*.	Explains attraction in terms of attitudes and personalities. 1. First we consider the *field of availables* (pool of potential partners who are accessible to us). 2. From this we select the *field of desirables* via three filters of varying importance at different stages of a relationship.

Social demography (1st level filter)

Such as *social class* and/or *education*.	Demographics are features that describe populations; social demographics include geographical location and social class. You are more likely to meet and have meaningful encounters with people who are physically close and share other features with yourself (e.g. same social class). Anyone who is too 'different' (too far away, too middle class) is not a potential partner and is 'filtered out' before the next stage.

Similarity in attitudes (2nd level filter)

Sharing beliefs and values.	Important to the development of romantic relationships only for couples who had been together less than 18 months. In early stages of a relationship agreeing on basic values promotes better communication and self-disclosure.
Law of attraction.	Byrne (1997) found that similarity in attitudes causes mutual attraction. Where such similarity does not exist it is found that often the relationship fades after only a few dates.

Complementarity (3rd level filter)

Partners meet *each other's needs.*	Partners complement each other when they have traits that the other lacks. For example, one partner may enjoy making the other laugh, and in turn this partner enjoys being made to laugh.
Important in *longer term/ later stages* of a relationship.	Complementarity is thought to give the romantic partners a feeling of togetherness and 'making a whole'. For example, partners will feel like they are meeting each other's needs if one likes nurturing (caring for and looking after another) and the other enjoys being looked after.

One strength of the theory is research support.

Winch (1958) found that similarities of personality, interests and attitudes between partners are typical of the early stages of a relationship but complementarity of needs increases in importance.

This supports at least two of the filters proposed in filter theory and also suggests that the filters may determine the development of the relationship.

This means that the **validity** of the theory has been supported in surveys of actual relationships.

One limitation is the lack of **replication** of the original findings.

Levinger (1974) has suggested that social change and difficulties in defining the depth of a relationship could be the reason for lack of replicability.

Kerckhoff and Davis (1962) assumed that partners together over 18 months were more committed. This may not be the case in all cultures or cases today.

The overall applicability of filter theory (e.g. to other cultures and types of relationship) is therefore questionable.

Another limitation is that there are questions about the direction of effect.

Anderson et al. (2003) found that cohabiting partners experienced emotional convergence, becoming more similar over time.

Furthermore, Davis and Rusbult (2001) suggest that attitude alignment also takes place (i.e. their attitudes change to become more similar to each other's).

This evidence suggests that similarities are the effect of having a relationship rather than the cause, as suggested by filter theory.

A further limitation is that the theory lacks **temporal validity**.

As the dating world has changed and moved increasingly online, social demography has taken on less importance.

For example, the likelihood of dating someone outside our culture has increased. This is not predicted by the initial level of filtering in the model.

These social changes in dating bring into question the temporal validity of filter theory as a factor in attraction.

A limitation is that complementarity may not be more important than similarity.

Anderson et al. (2003) found that similarity does increase over time but complementarity is not a feature in all relationships.

Davis and Rusbult (2001) discovered an attitude alignment effect in longer-term relationships, again suggesting that similarity is an effect of initial attraction and not the cause.

This suggests that the complementarity filter may not be reached in the case of all relationships and therefore the validity of filter theory is questioned.

Aw – how lovely, sharing everything. Who would have thought less than three years later they'd be arguing over who gets custody of the goldfish?

KNOWLEDGE CHECK

1. In relation to factors affecting attraction in romantic relationships, explain what is meant by 'social demography', 'similarity in attitudes' and 'complementarity'.
   (2 marks + 2 marks + 2 marks)

2. Outline **two or more** factors affecting attraction in romantic relationships. *(6 marks)*

3. Discuss strengths **and/or** limitations of filter theory as an explanation of factors affecting attraction in romantic relationships.
   (10 marks)

4. When it comes to relationships, some people believe 'opposites attract' and others think 'birds of a feather flock together'.

   With reference to both these points of view, describe and evaluate filter theory. *(16 marks)*

Theories of romantic relationships: SET

Spec spotlight

Theories of romantic relationships: social exchange theory.

Little did he know the box contained nothing but a post-it and written upon it was the single phrase, 'You're dumped'.

Apply it

Two counselling psychologists are writing a report on what makes a good relationship. They conclude that both partners know what they want from a relationship and have to get at least that out of it, otherwise they start wondering if they'd be happier elsewhere. A relationship is all about rewards and costs – if it is not profitable then it will not last.

How does the social exchange theory of relationships explain the psychologists' conclusions?

Social exchange theory (SET)

SET assumes relationships are guided by the *minimax principle*.	Thibault and Kelley (1959) proposed that relationships could be explained in terms of economics – it is an exchange of goods or less tangible things such as doing a favour. Satisfaction is judged in terms of profit (the perceived value of costs minus the value of rewards). Partners are motivated to minimise the costs to themselves whilst maximising rewards. Profitable relationships continue; unprofitable relationships fail.
Nature of *costs and rewards*.	Costs may include loss of time or stress. Rewards may include sex, praise or companionship. Opportunity cost also needs to be accounted for (i.e. the recognition that investment in a given relationship is at the 'cost' of expending those resources elsewhere).
CL is a measure of profit.	Comparison level (CL) is a judgment of the reward level we expect in a relationship, determined by relationship experiences and social norms. We will generally pursue a relationship where the CL is high but some people (e.g. with low self-esteem) may have low CLs.
CLalt is an additional measure of profit.	Comparison level for alternatives (CLalt) involves considering whether we might gain more rewards and endure fewer costs in a different relationship, assuming that (as in most cultures) we can only select one partner. We will remain in a relationship, despite available alternatives, when we consider it is more rewarding than the alternatives.
CLalt depends on our *current relationship*.	Duck (1994) suggests that there are always alternatives around. If the costs of our current relationship outweigh the rewards, then alternatives become more attractive. But if we are in a satisfying relationship we may not even notice them.
Four stages of relationships.	• *Sampling* stage involves exploring rewards and costs by experimenting in our relationships (not just romantic ones) and observing others. • *Bargaining* stage occurs at start of a relationship where romantic partners negotiate around costs and rewards. • *Commitment* stage is where relationships become more stable. Costs reduce and rewards increase. • *Institutionalisation* stage is when partners become settled because the norms of the relationship are established.

One limitation is SET assumes that all relationships are exchange based.

Clark and Mills (2011) argue that *exchange relationships* may involve profit (e.g. work colleagues) but *communal relationships* (e.g. romantic partners) involve giving and receiving of rewards without thinking of profit.

At the start of a romantic relationship tallying of exchanges might be viewed with some suspicion and even distaste.

This suggests that SET may not provide a suitable explanation for all types of relationships.

Rory tried to convince himself that he would rather watch football – but actually, he loved Bake Off.

Another limitation concerns the direction of effect.

It is assumed dissatisfaction occurs when costs outweigh rewards or alternatives seem more attractive, but Miller (1997) found people who said they were in a committed relationship spent less time looking at images of attractive people.

Furthermore 'less time spent looking' was a good predictor of the relationship continuing at a two-month follow up.

Therefore, SET may have the wrong direction of cause and effect. Rather than lack of profit leading to dissatisfaction it can be argued that we do not consider the profit until after we become dissatisfied.

REVISION BOOSTER

Are abbreviations acceptable? Students sometimes ask if these 'shortcuts' (e.g. 'SET', or indeed 'e.g.') are OK to use in exam answers. Would they annoy the examiner? The answer is that they are acceptable for recognised terms, and you won't annoy the examiner (examiners never get annoyed). If in doubt that the examiner will recognise the abbreviation, you should write out the term in full the first time you use it. Then, you can abbreviate to your heart's content.

A further limitation is that SET does not consider equity in relationships.

SET focuses on comparison levels but ignores the fact that many romantic partners desire fairness or equity.

Hatfield *et al.* (1984) found that couples in equitable relationships were more satisfied than those who saw themselves as over- or underbenefitting.

This evidence suggests SET is a limited explanation of relationships, supported by only a proportion of the research findings.

Another limitation is that it deals in concepts that are hard to quantify.

Research studies tend to **operationalise** rewards and costs superficially (e.g. money) but in reality rewards and costs are difficult to define and are subjectively judged.

Also it is unclear what the values of CL and CLalt must be before dissatisfaction threatens a relationship. This is a key issue in understanding relationship breakdown.

The inability to accurately quantify the key concepts of SET make it very difficult to produce **valid** research support.

KNOWLEDGE CHECK

1. Outline the social exchange theory of romantic relationships. *(6 marks)*

2. Outline any **one** theory of romantic relationships. *(6 marks)*

3. Explain **two** criticisms of the social exchange theory of romantic relationships. *(3 marks + 3 marks)*

4. Dom has been going out with Shelley for one month. He tells his friend, 'She keeps buying me presents and doing nice things – it's hard work keeping up with her!'

   Discuss the social exchange theory of romantic relationship, with reference to the above scenario. *(16 marks)*

One limitation is that research often involves artificial tasks and conditions.

Research often consists of game-playing and distribution of rewards and costs in a scenario where 'partners' are together just for the study.

More realistic studies which have used partners in actual relationships have been less supportive of SET.

The support for SET is weakened by the lack of validity of the studies and the fact that more realistic studies fail to support its assertions.

Theories of romantic relationships: Equity theory

Spec spotlight

Theories of romantic relationships: equity theory.

In the see-saw of life, the best relationships are all about balance.

Dan is explaining to Mike the secret of his long relationship with his girlfriend. 'You both have to feel you're getting something good out of it,' he says. 'Things don't have to be equal, but they do have to be fair. And you have to talk together about how to make things fair.'

Explain how Dan's wise advice supports the equity theory of romantic relationships.

Equity and exchange

It is easy to feel muddled about the difference between these two. In social exchange theory contentment is about what you get, even though there is an exchange of 'goods'. In equity theory it isn't about what you get, it's about a feeling of fairness. You might be getting the best deal but still feel unsatisfied.

The role of equity

Most people have a *need for equity* in relationships.	*Social exchange theory* suggests that partners seek equality or a balance between costs and benefits. In contrast Walster *et al.* (1978) propose that equity is more important where both partners' level of profit should be roughly the same.
Underbenefitting and *overbenefitting* can lead to dissatisfaction.	The underbenefitted partner is likely to be the least satisifed and their feelings may be evident in anger and resentment. The overbenefitted partner may feel less dissatisfied but is still likely to feel discomfort and shame.
Equity is about the *fairness* of the ratios.	It's not the size or amount of the rewards and costs that matters – it's the ratio of the two to each other. For example, if one partner puts a lot into the relationship but at the same time gets a lot out of it, then that will seem fair enough.

Consequences of inequity

Sense of inequity impacts *negatively* on relationships.	The greater the perceived inequity, the greater the dissatisfaction: equity theory predicts a strong positive **correlation** between the two. This applies to both the overbenefitted and underbenefitted partner.
Changes in equity occur during a relationship.	At the start of a relationship it may feel perfectly natural to contribute more than you receive. If that situation carries on as the relationship develops and one person continues to put more into the relationship and get less out of it, then satisfaction with the relationship may fail.
Inequity *has to be addressed* at times.	The underbenefitted partner will work hard to make the relationship more equitable if they believe it is possible to do so and that the relationship is salvageable. The greater the inequity the more work is required to restore equity. The change could be a **cognitive** rather than a behavioural one. For example the partner might revise their perceptions of rewards and costs so that the relationship feels more equitable to them, even if nothing actually changes. If the perception of rewards and costs are revised then actual abuse can become accepted as the norm for that relationship, for example reframing 'cruelty' as a form of rough treatment for your own good.

One strength is that equity theory has research support.

Utne *et al.* (1984) found that newly-weds who considered their relationship equitable were more satisfied than those who considered themselves as over- or underbenefitting.

So it would seem that profit is not the key issue in judging relationships, rather it is equity.

This research supports the central predictions of equity theory supporting its **validity** as an explanation of romantic relationships.

Newlyweds don't consider profit when judging their relationship – though it obviously helped that Lionel was the son of a millionaire.

One limitation is that equity theory may not be valid in all cultures.

Aumer-Ryan *et al.* (2007) found couples in an **individualist** culture linked satisfaction to equity but partners in a **collectivist** culture were most satisfied when they were overbenefitting.

This was true of both men and women, suggesting it is a consistent social rather than gender-based difference.

The assumption of the theory that equity is key to satisfying relationships in all cultures is not supported. The theory is limited in its ability to account for all romantic relationships.

Another limitation is that there are individual differences.

Huseman *et al.* (1987) suggest that some people are less sensitive to equity than others.

Some partners are happy to contribute more than they get (*benevolents*, underbenefitted). Others believe they deserve to be overbenefitted and accept it without feeling distressed or guilty (*entitleds*).

This shows that far from being a universal characteristic, a desire for equity is subject to individual differences.

REVISION BOOSTER

Ironically, there is an intimate relationship (see what I did there?) between equity theory and SET. That's no surprise because equity theory developed in response to perceived limitations of SET. But this means that it would be a great idea to revise these two theories together. You could even use equity theory (carefully) to evaluate SET in an essay.

On the other hand, don't get them mixed up. In short, make sure you know the similarities and differences between them.

A further limitation is that equity theory may not apply to all relationships.

Clark and Mills (2011) suggest a need to distinguish between types of relationship (e.g. romantic ones and business ones).

Studies show that equity does play a central role in some relationships (e.g. casual friendships) but there is limited support for its importance in others.

There is limited support for equity theory in terms of romantic relationships and it may be better at explaining other forms of relationship.

A final limitation is satisfying relationships don't become more equitable.

Berg and McQuinn (1986) found that equity did not increase in their **longitudinal** study of dating couples, as equity theory would predict.

The theory does not distinguish between those relationships which ended and those that continued. Variables such as self-disclosure appeared to be more important.

This is a strong criticism because it was based on real couples studied over time.

KNOWLEDGE CHECK

1. Outline the equity theory of romantic relationships. *(6 marks)*
2. Briefly outline **two** theories of romantic relationships. *(3 marks + 3 marks)*
3. Discuss **one** criticism of equity theory of romantic relationships. *(4 marks)*
4. Describe and evaluate the equity theory of romantic relationships. *(16 marks)*

Theories of romantic relationships: Rusbult's model

Spec spotlight

Theories of romantic relationships: Rusbult's investment model of commitment, satisfaction, comparison with alternatives and investment.

She'd hoped for Paris but, as Carl had insisted all that weekend, Blackpool is just as nice.

Apply it

Hana is in a relationship but her commitment is wavering. In the past, she did a lot to keep things going but now she wonders if she would get more out of a relationship with someone else, or be better on her own. But she thinks of all the good times she has had and everything she has put into her current relationship.

Explain how Hana's experience illustrates the elements of Rusbult's investment model of romantic relationships.

REVISION BOOSTER

Write very brief essay plans for each possible essay and then practise writing the essay out in full from these skeleton plans. Time yourself – 20 minutes for a 16-mark essay.

Rusbult's investment model

An *extension* of SET.	Rusbult's investment model (2011) further developed SET, suggesting that commitment depends on satisfaction level, comparison with alternatives and investment size.
	A satisfying relationship is one where the partners are getting more out of the relationship than they expect, given social norms and their previous experiences.
Satisfaction level and *CLalt* and *investment* determine commitment.	Investment – the resources associated with a romantic relationship which would be lost if the relationship ended.
	Satisfaction level – the extent to which partners feel the rewards of the romantic relationship exceed the costs.
	Comparison with alternatives (CLalt) – a judgement about whether a relationship with a different partner would reduce costs and increase rewards.
Two types of investment: *intrinsic* and *extrinsic*.	Intrinsic – any resources put directly into the relationship (e.g. money, energy and self-disclosures).
	Extrinsic – investments that previously did not feature in the relationship (i.e. were external to it) which are now closely associated with it (e.g. a jointly purchased house, children, shared memories).
	If investments are increasing and satisfaction is high, then the relationship is likely to continue.
Commitment determined by satisfaction + alternatives + investment.	High levels of satisfaction (more rewards with few costs) + the alternatives are less attractive + the sizes of their investment are increasing = partners will be committed to the relationship.
Satisfaction versus commitment.	Commitment matters more than satisfaction.
	This explains why, for example, a dissatisfied partner stays in a relationship when their level of investment is high. They will be willing to work hard to repair problems in the relationship so their investment is not wasted.
Relationship maintenance mechanisms.	Committed partners use maintenance behaviours to keep the relationship going, for example:

- Promoting the relationship (accommodation).
- Putting their partner's interests first (willingness to sacrifice).
- Forgiving them for any serious transgressions (forgiveness).
- A partner may be unrealistically positive about their partner (positive illusions).
- A partner may be negative about tempting alternatives/ other people's relationships (derogation of alternatives).

One strength is that there is research support for the investment model.

Le and Agnew's (2003) review found that satisfaction, comparison with alternatives and investment size all predicted relationship commitment. Where commitment was greatest, relationships were most stable and lasted longest.

The support is particularly strong given that the results were true for men and women in either heterosexual or homosexual relationships.

This suggests that the claim that these factors are universally important in relationships is **valid**.

Another strength is it can explain why people may stay in abusive relationships.

Rusbult and Martz (1995) found that women who reported making the greatest investment and who had the fewest attractive alternatives were the most likely to return to the partners who had abused them.

The concept of satisfaction as important to relationship duration cannot explain this tendency but the level of commitment can.

This is a strength because it explains the apparently inexplicable behaviour of staying in an abusive relationship.

One limitation of the model is that it oversimplifies investment.

Goodfriend and Agnew (2008) argue that there is more to investment than just the resources you have already put into a relationship.

Early in a relationship partners make very few actual investments but they do invest in future plans. It is future plans that motivate partners to commit so that the plans can become reality.

This means that the original model is a limited explanation as it fails to consider the true complexity of investment.

One strength is that its supporting evidence is based on self-report techniques.

Self-report techniques are an appropriate research method since the model is based on subjective judgements about size of investment and alternatives.

This is a good approach because what matters is the partners' subjective perceptions of their investments.

This is a strength because it is a more valid test of the model than, for example, experimental research.

One limitation of much of the research is the use of correlations.

Strong correlations have been established between the factors within the model.

But no matter how strong the correlation it does not follow that one variable causes the other.

As such we cannot conclude from this which factors, if any, might cause commitment.

Doting parents Rick and Tanya would make their kids run around for 11 hours a day. It was the only way they'd be guaranteed any sleep.

KNOWLEDGE CHECK

1. In relation to theories of romantic relationships, explain what is meant by the terms 'commitment', 'satisfaction' and 'investment'.
   (2 marks + 2 marks + 2 marks)

2. Briefly outline **two** theories of romantic relationships. *(6 marks)*

3. Briefly evaluate Rusbult's investment model of romantic relationships. *(6 marks)*

4. Cath and Katie are discussing what is important in a successful relationship. Cath says, 'The more satisfied you are in a relationship, the more committed you will be to it.' Katie disagrees: 'I think if you commit to a relationship and work at it, that makes it more satisfying.'

   Discuss Rusbult's investment model of romantic relationships. Refer to Cath's and Katie's comments in your answer. *(16 marks)*

Theories of romantic relationships: Duck's phase model

Spec spotlight

Theories of romantic relationships: Duck's phase model of relationship breakdown: intra-psychic, dyadic, social and grave-dressing phases.

It had seemed like hours since she last spoke. Aaron was beginning to regret asking if he could go on a fortnight's holiday to Ibiza with 'the lads'.

Apply it

Adam is brooding on his unhappiness in his relationship with his girlfriend.

Ramona and Giles are both unhappy and have started discussing what they are going to do next.

Kelvin and Briony have told their friends and family that they are getting relationship counselling.

a. Identify which stage of Duck's model each couple is experiencing. Briefly summarise the main features of these stages. Relate your summaries to the couples above.

b. There is another stage in Duck's model – identify it and write an example of your own. Also write a brief statement about the main feature(s) of the stage.

Duck's phase model

Breakdown is a *process*.	Duck (2007) proposed a phase model of relationship breakdown.
	He argued that the ending of a relationship is not a one-off event but a process that takes time and goes through four distinct phases.
Each phase has a *threshold*.	Each phase is characterised by a partner reaching a threshold where their perception of the relationship changes.
	The partner may reassess and decide the relationship isn't so bad, halting the process of breakdown.
	Or they cross the threshold and move on to the next stage of the model.
Intra-psychic phase.	Threshold – 'I can't stand this anymore', indicating a determination that something has to change.
	A partner becomes dissatisfied with the relationship in its current form. They then brood on the reasons for this and this will usually focus on their partner's shortcomings.
	The dissatisfied partner tends to keep this to themselves but may share their thoughts with a trusted friend, weighing up the pros and cons of continuing.
Dyadic phase.	Threshold – 'I would be justified in withdrawing'.
	Once a partner concludes that they are justified in ending the relationship they have to discuss this with their partner. Dissatisfactions about equity, commitment, etc. are aired.
	The phase may vary in length and in intensity of hostility and anxiety.
Social phase.	Threshold – the dissatisfied partner concludes, 'I mean it'.
	Once a partner wants to end the relationship they will seek support particularly from joint friends.
	These friends may be encouraged to choose a side but others may try and prevent the break-up by acting as a go-between.
	Once the news is public though this is usually the point of no return.
Grave-dressing phase.	Threshold – 'It's now inevitable'.
	Once the end becomes inevitable then a suitable story of the relationship and its end is prepared for wider consumption.
	This is likely to include an attempt to ensure that the storyteller will be judged most favourably.
	This creation of a personal story in addition to the public one is necessary so the partner can 'move on'.

One limitation of the model is that it is incomplete.

Rollie and Duck (2006) added a fifth *resurrection phase* in which ex-partners begin to use what they have learned from the last relationship to prepare for a future one.

The refined version also clarifies the point that movement through the stages is neither linear nor inevitable and partners may return to an earlier phase.

This suggests that the original phase model is therefore only a partial explanation of the process of relationship breakdown.

Another limitation is that supporting evidence is based on retrospective data.

Interviews about the process tend to take place after the breakdown, not during it. Such retrospective data may not be reliable.

It is almost impossible to study breakdown in the earlier stages without potentially interfering with the ongoing process.

This means that the model is based on limited information about the start of the breakdown process and so is incomplete as a description.

One strength is its application to helping people reverse the process.

The model suggests that some repair strategies might be more effective at one stage rather than another. For example, in the intra-psychic stage partners could brood more positively.

It would be less helpful to encourage brooding if a person had already reached the social phase.

This suggests that the model can lead to supportive suggestions that may help people through this difficult time in their lives.

A limitation is that it focuses on how rather than why breakdown occurs.

Flemlee (1995) suggests a 'fatal attraction' theory stating that the attributes that partners found attractive at the start of a relationship can often become too much.

For example, someone who was attracted to a 'so funny' partner may then decide to end the relationship because the other person 'fails to take life seriously'.

This highlights the fact that Duck's model only tells us what happens and not why.

One further limitation is that much research is based on **individualist** cultures.

Moghaddam *et al.* (1993) propose relationships in individualist cultures are mostly voluntary and end quite often, whilst in **collectivist** cultures relationships are more frequently 'obligatory' and less easy to end.

The whole concept of a relationship differs between cultures and therefore the process of relationship breakdown is likely to differ.

This is a limitation because it means that the model can only be applied to some cultures and types of relationship.

They weren't talking since Simon had refused to take back his comment that Jonathan's vest was 'garish'.

KNOWLEDGE CHECK

1. Briefly outline the intra-psychic and social phases of Duck's phase model of relationship breakdown.
   (3 marks + 3 marks)

2. Outline Duck's phase model of romantic breakdown.
   (6 marks)

3. Briefly evaluate Duck's phase model of relationship breakdown. *(6 marks)*

4. This item appeared on a news website: 'It's over! (Or is it?) Psychologists today claimed relationships do not end overnight. Breaking up is a process that takes time and goes through several phases. But the experts believe relationships can be saved at almost every stage.'

   With reference to the issues in this item, discuss Duck's phase model of relationship breakdown. *(16 marks)*

Virtual relationships in social media

Spec spotlight

Virtual relationships in social media: self-disclosure in virtual relationships; effects of absence of gating on the nature of virtual relationships.

The therapist had suggested that Jen was starting to become a bit obsessive about Minecraft – but she didn't care.

Apply it

Jimmy and Thomasina have never met, but they interact on social media all the time. They have both had self-esteem issues in the past, because they think themselves unattractive. So they were glad that they were able to get to know each other online before exchanging images of each other. Jimmy sometimes worries that typed words on Facebook aren't enough to express how he feels. Thomasina is anxious that she doesn't know the real Jimmy.

How can research into virtual relationships in social media explain Jimmy's and Thomasina's relationship?

Self-disclosure

Self-disclosure is different in *FtF* and *online* relationships.	Increasing use of social media has led to research on differences between the relationships formed and maintained online and those formed and maintained face-to-face (FtF).
	Self-disclosure is crucial in FtF relationships so psychologists have turned their attention to its role and nature in virtual relationships – also known as computer-mediated communication (CMC).
Reduced cues in CMC may lead to *less self-disclosure*.	*Reduced cues theory* (Sproull and Kiesler 1986) suggests that CMC relationships are less effective due to the lack of nonverbal cues (e.g. physical appearance, emotional responses) – in FtF relationships we rely on these cues.
	Lack of cues about emotional state (voice and facial expressions) leads to **de-individuation**.
	People then feel freer from the constraints of social norms (**disinhibition**) and this leads to blunt and even aggressive communication and a reluctance to self-disclose.
CMC relationships may involve *more self-disclosure*.	*Hyperpersonal model* (Walther 2011) suggests that early self-disclosure means that CMC relationships develop quickly. Such relationships can become more intense and intimate.
	However, CMC relationships can also end more quickly because of high excitement level but low levels of trust.
Self-disclosure differs in CMC because *online image can be manipulated*.	The sender of a message can be selective about what and how they present themselves when self-disclosing.
	This, along with the feeling of anonymity, means that people may feel *less* accountable for their behaviour and disclose more than they would to their nearest non-online partners.

Absence of gating

CMC *allows relationships to start* where they may not in FtF.	McKenna and Bargh (1999) argue that facial disfigurements or a stammer may be obstacles to a FtF relationship.
	However, starting a relationship online means that 'gates' are not there.
	A relationship can develop and once self-disclosure becomes deeper the gates become less of an issue.
Absence of gating has *benefits*.	Without the obstacles of FtF communication people are free to create different online identities and overcome various barriers.
	For example, a shy person can become more extravert online and their personality is no longer an obstacle.
	However, there is also scope for people to create an untrue persona (e.g. a man can become a woman).

One limitation is lack of research support for the reduced cues theory.

Walther and Tidwell (1995) assert that cues in CMCs are simply different from those in FtF ones. They found that there are plenty of cues in CMCs, just not the nonverbal ones that we recognise in FtF communication.

Emoticons and acrostics are considered effective substitutes in CMCs for the lack of usual nonverbal cues, so the proposal that there are reduced cues in CMCs appears unfounded.

This suggests that there may be no differences in self-disclosure between CMC and FtF relationships, which does not support reduced cues theory.

One strength of the hyperpersonal model is its supporting research.

Whitty and Joinson (2009) found supporting evidence for both hyperhonest and hyperdishonest online disclosures.

Questions asked in online discussions tend to be direct, probing and intimate and responses direct and to the point, quite different from FtF conversations.

This is consistent with the prediction of the model that these are distinctive types of disclosure in CMC.

One limitation of explanations is that they do not distinguish types of CMC.

From online e-commerce forms through to Facebook and to online dating, the level of self-disclosure varies considerably.

People disclose more in areas that they consider private (e.g. Facebook statuses that will only be seen by 'friends') and disclose less on webforms that involve the collection of data.

This means that the **validity** of theories that consider all CMC in the same way will be limited.

Another limitation of explanations is they do not recognise CMCs as multimodal.

Theories need to include the fact that relationships are usually conducted both online and offline.

The interaction between people online will influence the interaction in the FtF relationship, including the level and speed of self-disclosure. As such these two kinds of communication have to be considered together and not separately.

This suggests that current theories may underestimate the complexity of virtual relationships.

One strength is support for absence of gating.

McKenna and Bargh (2002) found that lonely and socially anxious people were able to express their 'true selves' more in CMC than in FtF situations.

Of the romantic relationships that initially formed online, 70% survived more than two years, higher than for relationships formed in the offline world.

This suggests that CMC can be helpful to support people who are socially anxious to build confidence in forming relationships.

Every time she drank a cup of water she was reminded of Grant – bland, tasteless and a bit of a drip.

REVISION BOOSTER

This topic should be right up your street. What an opportunity to use real-life examples to improve your revision. A carefully chosen example can be really useful in an essay. How do you decide which Facebook profile picture to use? Could it be anything to do with an image you want to present to others? Not even a little bit perhaps? But remember that anecdotal material is not creditworthy in an exam answer.

KNOWLEDGE CHECK

1. Outline research into virtual relationships in social media.
   (6 marks)
2. Outline research into self-disclosure in virtual relationships. *(6 marks)*
3. Briefly evaluate research into absence of gating on the nature of virtual relationships.
   (6 marks)
4. This article appeared in a magazine: 'Psychologists express concern over online anonymity. People are closing their Facebook accounts because they would rather not have to read abusive posts on their timelines.'

   Discuss virtual relationships in social media. Refer in your answer to the issues raised in the article. *(16 marks)*

Parasocial relationships

Spec spotlight

Parasocial relationships: levels of parasocial relationships, the absorption-addiction model and the attachment theory explanation.

It wasn't the first time Maxwell had been mistaken for a celebrity – but the fact they thought he was Justin Bieber came as a bit of a surprise.

Apply it

To begin with, Tim enjoyed watching Game of Thrones. *He followed each series and liked to discuss the episodes with his colleagues at work.*

Eventually, Tim spent more and more time telling his colleagues all about Game of Thrones. *He felt strongly that he and Cersei Lannister had a lot in common and fantasised about being her.*

Recently, Tim has described himself as Game of Thrones' *biggest fan. He thinks about Cersei all the time. He has spent a lot of money on merchandise and is in debt. He is planning to go to work dressed as Cersei.*

Identify the levels of parasocial relationship that Tim displays. Outline how **two** theories explain how Tim's parasocial relationship begins and progresses.

Levels of parasocial relationships

CAS assesses celebrity attraction.	The *Celebrity Attitude Scale* (CAS) was used by Maltby *et al.* (2006) to identify three levels of parasocial relationship.
Three levels: Entertainment-social, intense-personal and borderline pathological.	First level is 'entertainment-social level'. This is the least intense level where celebrities are viewed as sources of entertainment and fuel for social interaction.
	Second level is 'intense-personal level', an intermediate level where someone becomes more personally involved with a celebrity and this may include obsessive thoughts.
	Third level is 'borderline pathological level', the strongest level of celebrity worship where fantasies are uncontrollable and behaviour is more extreme.

The absorption-addiction model

Explains parasocial relationships in terms of people's *life deficiencies*.	McCutcheon (2002) suggests that parasocial relationships can make up for personal deficiencies (e.g. lack of fulfilment).
	Parasocial relationships also provide an escape from mundane lives.
	People may be triggered towards a higher level by stressful life events such as a bereavement.
Model has *two* components.	Absorption: Seeking fulfilment in celebrity worship motivates an individual to focus their attention on the celebrity, to become absorbed in the celebrity's existence and identify with them.
	Addiction: Like a physiological addiction, the individual needs to increase their 'dose' of involvement to gain satisfaction. This may lead to more extreme behaviours and delusional thinking.

The attachment theory explanation

Links *early attachment* problems to parasocial relationships.	Bowlby's attachment theory suggests that early difficulties in attachment may lead to difficulties in forming successful relationships later in life.
	Such difficulties may lead to a preference for parasocial relationships to replace those within one's own social circle as parasocial relationships do not require the same social skills.
Insecure attachment types are linked to parasocial relationships.	Ainsworth (1979) identified two attachment types associated with unhealthy emotional development: insecure–resistant and insecure–avoidant.
	Insecure–resistant types are most likely to form parasocial relationships because they want to have their unfulfilled needs met in a relationship where there is no real threat of rejection.
	Insecure–avoidant types prefer to avoid the pain and rejection of any type of relationship, either social or parasocial.

One strength is research support for the absorption-addiction model.

Maltby *et al.* (2005) studied female adolescents who reported an intense personal relationship with a female celebrity whose body shape they admired. These females tended to have a poor body image (often a precursor to an eating disorder).

Maltby *et al.* (2003) linked the entertainment-social level with extravert personality traits, the intense-personal category with neurotic traits, and the borderline pathological level with psychotic personality types.

Both studies support the model because they show a **correlation** between the level of celebrity worship and different or disordered psychological functioning.

One limitation of the absorption-addiction model is it lacks explanatory power.

The model describes the characteristics of people at different levels of intensity but does not explain why the different forms develop.

This does not help us to prevent the more dangerous and disturbing forms of parasocial relationships.

So the model is limited in its explanatory power and its application for supporting people whose celebrity worship has become problematic.

One limitation of the link to attachment theory is lack of support.

McCutcheon *et al.* (2006) found that participants with insecure attachments were no more likely to form parasocial relationships with celebrities than participants with secure attachment styles.

This is the key assumption of this explanation and failure to find support for it raises crucial questions about the explanation's **validity**.

This is a limitation of using attachment theory to explain parasocial relationships because it shows that it has little predictive strength.

One strength of attachment explanations is cross-cultural support.

Schmid and Klimmt (2011) found similar levels of parasocial attachment to Harry Potter in an **individualist** culture (Germany) and a **collectivist** culture (Mexico).

So it would seem that this tendency is not culturally specific.

This suggests that the need to form parasocial relationships may be universal and innate, and may be an **adaptive** behaviour.

One limitation is methodological issues limit the validity of the research.

Most of the research studies use self-report techniques to collect data. These can be affected by forms of bias, for example **social desirability bias**.

Most of the studies also use correlational analysis. Despite strong correlations between celebrity worship and body image causal links cannot be made.

This means that there is no evidence to show that parasocial relationships are caused by specific experiences.

Fans of Harry Styles are likely to run in only 'one direction' – towards him!

KNOWLEDGE CHECK

1. Using an example, explain what is meant by 'levels of parasocial relationships'.
   (4 marks)

2. Outline the attachment theory explanation of parasocial relationships.
   (6 marks)

3. Evaluate the absorption-addiction model of parasocial relationships. *(6 marks)*

4. Denise has just started at secondary school. Her parents are concerned because she watches Zoella's YouTube channel a lot more than she used to. Denise spends more time talking about Zoella than she does doing her homework.

   Using Denise's experience as an example, discuss research into parasocial relationships.
   (16 marks)

Sex and gender

Spec spotlight

Sex and gender. Sex-role stereotypes.

Of course people would make reference to their featureless faces and the fact that their heads were not in contact with the rest of their bodies – but Polly and Dilbert loved each other, and that was all that mattered.

A recent report by psychologists concluded that parents (and others) still tend to treat boys and girls differently. 'The 'pinkification' of girls has progressed to the point where almost all advertising aimed at girls is for something pink. Toys and activities aimed at boys usually involve aggression and competition. Girls' and boys' playground activities are just as gender-related as they were 50 years ago. Even some teachers have different expectations of boys and girls, especially in maths and sciences.'

Use your knowledge of sex, gender and sex-role stereotyping to discuss the issues raised in the report.

Sex and gender

Sex is a biological status (innate).

Someone's sex is biologically determined by their genetic make-up, namely their chromosomes.

Chromosomes influence hormonal and anatomical differences that distinguish males and females (e.g. reproductive organs, body shape and hair growth).

In reality sex and gender are terms often used interchangeably – which can cause some confusion.

Gender is a psychosocial status (nurture).

Gender, described as masculine or feminine, reflects all the attitudes, behaviours and roles we associate with being male or female.

Whilst biological sex cannot change despite sex change surgery, gender is more fluid and an individual can also become more masculine or feminine.

GID is where sex and gender do not correspond.

For most people their biological sex and gender identity correspond.

However, some people experience *gender identity disorder* (GID) when their biological sex does not reflect the way they feel inside and the gender they identify themselves as being.

Gender reassignment surgery allows people to bring their sexual identity in line with their gender identity.

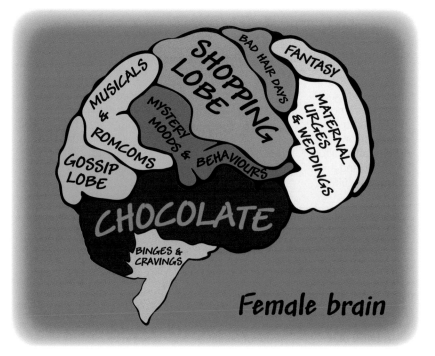

Female brain

Sex-role stereotypes

Sex-role stereotypes are *social expectations*.	Sex-role stereotypes are shared by a culture or group and consist of expectations regarding how males and females should behave.
	These expectations are transmitted through a society and reinforced by members of it (e.g. parents, peers, etc.).
Sex-role stereotypes *may or may not be* **valid**.	Some expectations have some basis in reality.
	For example, in many cases it might be the male in a heterosexual couple who is responsible for DIY whilst the female buys and sends the birthday cards from both of them.
	However, there is no biological reason for this to be the case.
	Many sex-role stereotypes are incorrect assumptions and can lead to sexist and damaging attitudes.
	For example, the stereotype that women are too emotional to cope with high-powered jobs.
Research confirms sex-role stereotypes in the media.	A study of TV adverts (Furnham and Farragher 2000) found that men were more likely to be shown in autonomous roles within professional contexts, whereas women were often seen occupying familial roles within domestic settings.
	This along with other studies demonstrates both the existence of sex-role stereotypes and the role the media has in reinforcing them.

Nurse or doctor? The irony was that Nathan was neither but since he'd passed the first aid course, he'd taken to wearing scrubs at the office.

REVISION BOOSTER

This topic is likely to have just short-answer questions and likely not to involve evaluation. If you were set a discuss question (such as question 4 below) then some of the counterpoints can be used to make a discussion, or use your knowledge of research methods.

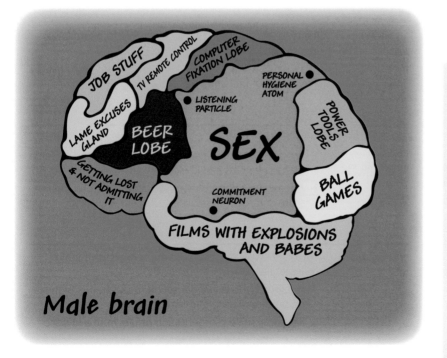

KNOWLEDGE CHECK

1. Briefly distinguish between sex and gender. *(3 marks)*
2. Outline research into sex and gender. *(6 marks)*
3. Describe **one** study into sex-role stereotypes. In your answer refer to what the researcher(s) did and what they found. *(6 marks)*
4. Brian makes sure the car is working properly, puts the bins out and is responsible for the TV remote control. Shirley does most of the housework, including the cooking, and is the one who remembers everybody's birthdays.

   With reference to Brian and Shirley's behaviour, discuss research into sex-role stereotypes. *(8 marks)*

Androgyny and the BSRI

Spec spotlight

Androgyny and measuring androgyny including the Bem Sex Role Inventory.

Androgyny – not so much a 'look' as a state of mind.

REVISION BOOSTER

Androgyny is a key term, named in the specification. Like other such key terms, you need to make sure you can write a brief description/ explanation of it for up to 3 marks.

Apply it

Two psychology students want to conduct a study into the link between androgyny and psychological well-being. They consider using the Bem Sex Role Inventory to assess androgyny, but are aware that it has been criticised. They don't know enough about the issues to make a decision, so they turn to you for advice.

Using your knowledge of how psychologists measure androgyny, how would you advise the students?

Defining androgyny

Androgyny is a *balance* of masculine and feminine characteristics.	Everyday understanding of the term androgyny relates to appearance as being neither female nor male. Psychologically it refers to the presence of a balance of masculine and feminine traits, behaviours and attitudes.
Androgyny is a *positive attribute*.	Bem (1974) suggested that high androgyny is associated with psychological wellbeing. Individuals who have a balance of masculine and feminine traits are better equipped to adapt to a range of situations. Androgyny needs to be distinguished from over-representation of opposite-sex characteristics. For example, a female who is very masculine or a male who is very feminine would not exhibit the necessary balance of male and female traits and may not be androgynous.

Measuring androgyny: The Bem Sex Role Inventory (BSRI)

Items on the BSRI are *masculine, feminine* or *neutral*.	Masculine items include dominant, competitive and athletic. Female items include gentle, affectionate and sympathetic. Neutral items are characteristics which do not apply more specifically to one sex than another, including sincere, friendly and unpredictable.
BSRI has *60 questions* and a *7-point scale*.	BSRI has 20 feminine, 20 masculine and 20 neutral trait items. Participants use a 7-point rating scale to rate each trait (1 is 'never true of me' and 7 is 'always true of me').
Masculine and feminine categorisation.	In total there are four categorisations that can be made: 1. A masculine categorisation results from a high score on masculine items and low score on feminine items. 2. A feminine categorisation results from a high feminine score and a low masculine score.
Androgynous and undifferentiated categorisation.	The other two categorisations are consistently high or consistently low: 3. An androgynous categorisation results from a high score on both masculine and feminine scales. 4. An unclassified categorisation results from a low score on both the masculine and feminine scales.

One strength is that the BSRI has been found to be both reliable and valid.

Development of the scale involved 50 males and 50 females judging 200 traits in terms of gender desirability. The top 20 in each case were used. Piloting it on over 1000 students confirmed that BSRI reflected their gender identity (**validity**).

Furthermore a follow-up study involving a smaller sample of the same students revealed similar scores when the students were tested a month later, suggesting high test-retest reliability.

Together this evidence suggests that the BSRI has a degree of both validity and test-retest reliability.

Expected behaviour for men and women has changed over time – as I was saying to my sister the other day when she walked off the rugby field.

One limitation is that links between well-being and androgyny are challenged.

Bem emphasised that androgynous individuals are more psychologically healthy because they are more able to deal with scenarios that demand a masculine, feminine or androgynous response.

Some researchers (e.g. Adams and Sherer 1985) have argued that people who display a greater proportion of masculine traits are better adjusted as these are more highly valued in Western society.

This suggests that Bem's assumption did not take adequate account of the social and cultural context in which it was developed.

Understanding yourself
The full version of the BSRI is available all over the internet. Your teacher might ask you to do this anyway, but why not fill it in for yourself? Become familiar with it and learn a few examples of masculine, feminine and neutral items for the exam.

Another limitation is gender identity cannot be reduced to a single score.

An alternative is the *Personal Attribute Questionnaire* (PAQ) which additionally measures instrumentality and expressionism, but the scale still suggests that gender identity can be quantified.

Golombok and Fivush (1994) suggest that gender identity is a more global concept and to understand it fully we must also consider the person's interests and perception of their own abilities.

This suggests that the BSRI is overly simple, but it also may just be difficult to measure gender identity.

REVISION BOOSTER
It really pays to practise writing 16-mark essays with your book shut and timing yourself – about 20 minutes for a 16-mark essay. Don't think it will magically come right on the day – test yourself.

A further limitation is the temporal and cultural validity of the BSRI.

Since the BSRI was developed over 40 years ago expectations have changed with regard to gender and behaviour.

There is also concern that the original judges who expressed their ideas about masculinity and femininity were all from the US.

This means that both the **temporal validity** and the cultural validity of the BSRI are questioned.

A final limitation is that questionnaires are subjective and biased.

A questionnaire assumes a degree of self-understanding that people may not have. Their answers may be determined by, for example, response bias (a pattern of responding).

Answers may also be influenced by **social desirability bias** where raters choose the answer which they think shows them in a favourable way.

The validity of the BSRI as a measure of androgyny is questioned because of the subjectivity and bias that arise from the use of such questionnaires.

KNOWLEDGE CHECK
1. Explain what is meant by the term 'androgyny'. *(3 marks)*
2. Outline research into androgyny. *(6 marks)*
3. Discuss **one** criticism of the Bem Sex Role Inventory. *(4 marks)*
4. Describe and evaluate how psychologists have measured androgyny. *(16 marks)*

The role of chromosomes and hormones

Spec spotlight

The role of chromosomes and hormones (testosterone, oestrogen and oxytocin) in sex and gender.

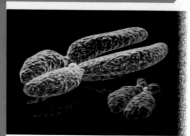

It's clear how the X chromosome got its name but why?

Apply it

Erika Schinegger won the women's world downhill skiing championship in 1966. She had a medical before the 1968 Winter Olympics that showed she was in fact chromosomally male. This news shocked Erika because she was raised as a girl. She discovered she had been born intersex. She underwent surgical and hormonal treatment to live as a man. Erik married and became a father.

What does Erik's experience tell us about the roles of chromosomes and hormones in sex and gender?

REVISION BOOSTER

No you have not slipped into a Biology revision book! The good news is these biological concepts are very factual. There is nothing to understand and students always do well on such topics. Be positive.

The role of chromosomes

Chromosome 23 determines biological sex.	Chromosomes are made from DNA – genes are short sections of DNA. Humans have 23 pairs of chromosomes – 23rd pair determines biological sex. Under a microscope these chromosomes are either X or Y shape. Female sex chromosome is XX and male is XY. A baby's sex is determined by whether the sperm that fertilises the egg is an X or a Y chromosome.
Y chromosome has *SRY gene.*	The Y chromosome carries a gene called the sex-determining region Y (SRY). This causes the testes to develop and androgens to be produced in a male embryo. Without androgens the embryo develops into a female.

The role of hormones

Gender *development* governed by hormones	Prenatally hormones act upon brain development and cause development of the reproductive organs. At puberty a burst of hormonal activity triggers the development of secondary sexual characteristics such as pubic hair. Males and females produce the same hormones but in different concentrations.
Testosterone Key role in male development and aggression.	**Testosterone** controls the development of male sex organs from the fifth month of foetal development. Testosterone linked to aggressive behaviour in both genders, in humans and animals. For example, Van de Poll *et al.* (1988) showed that female rats injected with testosterone became more physically and sexually aggressive.
Oestrogen Key role in female development and behaviour.	**Oestrogen** controls female sexual characteristics including menstruation. During the menstrual cycle some women experience heightened emotionality and irritability – pre-menstrual tension or pre-menstrual syndrome (a diagnosable disorder). In extreme cases PMS has been used (controversially) as a defence for violent behaviour in women.
Oxytocin Implicated in lactation and bonding.	Women typically produce **oxytocin** in larger amounts than men. • Stimulates lactation post birth. • Reduces the stress hormone cortisol. • Facilitates bonding. • May explain why females are more interested in intimacy in relationships than men – though amounts are the same in men and women when kissing and cuddling.

One strength is research support.

Dabbs et al. (1995) found, in a prison population, that offenders with the highest levels of testosterone were more likely to have committed violent or sexually-motivated crimes.

Van Goozen et al. (1995) found that male-to-female transsexuals (having oestrogen treatment) showed decreases in aggression and visuo-spatial skills; female-to-male transsexuals showed the opposite.

These studies support the role of sex hormones in gender-related behaviours such as aggression.

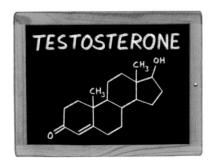

Aggression fuel.

REVISION BOOSTER

Have you checked out our revision advice on pages 4 to 9?

One limitation is that some evidence is contradictory.

Tricker et al. (1996) gave males either 10-weekly injections of testosterone or a **placebo** and found no significant differences in aggression.

Slabbekoorn et al. (1999) also demonstrated that sex hormones had no consistent effect on gender-related behaviour.

This research does not support the view that sex hormones determine behaviour.

Another limitation is the controversial nature of PMS as a medical category.

Rodin (1992) claims PMS is a social construction rather than a biological fact. Feminists claim this as an example of the medicalisation of the lives of women by explaining their emotions in purely biological terms.

Others have questioned the medical category pre-menstrual syndrome on the grounds that it stereotypes female experience and emotion.

This suggests that there may have been some over-exaggeration of the impact of hormones on behaviour.

A further limitation is that there is an overemphasis on nature.

Social learning theory points to social context in the learning of our gender identity and role, suggesting it is not considered when focusing on biology.

The biological explanation cannot easily explain cross-cultural differences. In Western society genders are becoming more androgynous but this is less so elsewhere.

This suggests that there is too much of an emphasis on nature in this approach to understanding sex and gender.

A final limitation is that biological accounts oversimplify a complex concept.

Biological approaches that reduce gender to the level of chromosomes and hormones have been accused of ignoring alternative explanations for gender development.

Other approaches stress thought processes (**cognitive** approach) or childhood experiences (**psychodynamic** approach).

Just focusing on a biological understanding ignores other possible influences which point to a more complex process in gender development.

KNOWLEDGE CHECK

1. Briefly explain the roles of testosterone, oestrogen and oxytocin in sex and gender.
   (2 marks + 2 marks + 2 marks)

2. Outline the role of chromosomes in sex and gender. *(6 marks)*

3. Evaluate research into the role of hormones in sex and gender. *(6 marks)*

4. This item appeared in a newspaper: Cheat! Caster Semenya is no woman. The South African 800m runner has no ovaries, and three times the normal level of testosterone for a woman. 'She' has internal testes and in our book that makes 'her' a man. This newspaper says, 'Don't let Caster compete as a woman.'

   With reference to the issues in the above item, discuss the role(s) of chromosomes **and/or** hormones in sex and gender. *(16 marks)*

Atypical sex chromosome patterns

Spec spotlight

Atypical sex chromosome patterns: Klinefelter's syndrome and Turner's syndrome.

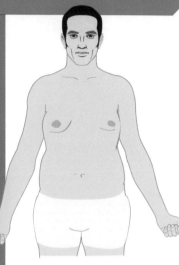

The additional breast tissue and soft body contours associated with a man who has Klinefelter's syndrome.

A woman with Turner's syndrome may have a wide 'webbed' neck, a broad 'shield' chest and low set ears.

Klinefelter's syndrome

XXY chromosomal structure	About 1 in 750 males have Klinefelter's syndrome. Individuals who have this condition are biological males with male anatomy but an additional X chromosome. 10% of cases are identified prenatally but up to 66% may not be aware of it. Diagnosis often comes about accidentally via a medical examination for some unrelated condition.
Physical characteristics – lack of body hair, health problems.	Some physical effects of XXY chromosome structure are: • Reduced body hair compared to a typical male. • Some breast development at puberty (gynaecomastia). • Underdeveloped genitals. • More susceptible to health problems that are usually associated with females, such as breast cancer.
Psychological characteristics – poor language skills, shy.	Klinefelter's syndrome is often linked to psychological characteristics such as: • Poorly developed language skills and reading ability. • Passive, shy and lacking interest in sexual activity. • Tend not to respond well to stressful situations. • Problems with what are called executive functions, such as problem-solving.

Turner's syndrome

X0 chromosomal structure.	1 in 5000 females have Turner's syndrome. Caused by an absence of one of the two X chromosomes leading to 45 rather than 46 chromosomes.
Physical characteristics – sterility and immature body shape.	Individuals with Turner's syndrome have the following physical characteristics: • No menstrual cycle as their ovaries fail to develop, leaving them sterile. • A broad 'shield' chest and no developing of breasts at puberty. • Characteristic low set ears and a 'webbed' neck. • Hips are not much bigger than the waist.
Psychological characteristics – high reading ability, social immaturity.	Psychological characteristics of Turner's Syndrome include: • Higher-than-average reading ability. • Lower-than-average performance on spatial, visual memory and mathematical tasks. • Tendency to be socially immature.

One strength of the research is its contribution to the nature–nurture debate.

Comparing chromosome-typical and atypical individuals highlights psychological and behavioural differences. For example, people with Turner's syndrome tend to have a higher verbal ability than 'typical' females.

From such results we might logically infer that these differences have a biological basis resulting from the abnormal chromosomal structure.

This adds to our understanding of the nature–nurture debate and suggests that innate influences have a powerful effect on psychology and behaviour.

One limitation is the lack of a causal relationship.

It is possible that the impacts of environmental and/or social influences are more important than the research suggests.

For instance, social immaturity in females with Turner's syndrome may be due to the way others respond to their physical immaturity rather than to a biological cause related to their chromosomes.

We cannot assume from this research alone that observed psychological and behavioural differences are due to nature.

Another strength is that the research has practical applications.

Herlihy et al. (2011) showed that individuals identified and treated from a very young age had significant benefits compared to those who had been diagnosed in adulthood.

Further research will increase the likelihood of earlier diagnosis and an increased understanding of the issues faced by those with the syndromes.

Such research has a direct benefit to people who have these atypical chromosomal patterns as well as potentially increasing our understanding of atypical development.

Another limitation is that the samples are unrepresentative and atypical.

Individuals with unusual conditions, particularly those with conditions that impact upon their physical appearance, are unlikely to be treated the same way as their peers.

This means that it is difficult to disentangle the relative contribution of nature and nurture to gender differences.

Overall this makes it difficult to generalise from the cases studied to all people who may have the conditions, especially as life experiences may have a significant impact.

A further limitation is that typical sex and gender may have been exaggerated.

If research into atypical chromosomal patterns is to contribute to the nature–nurture debate then we are assuming that we can compare atypical and typical gender behaviours.

However, studies such as Maccoby and Jacklin (1974) identified significantly more differences within the sexes than between them, questioning whether there are in fact typical behaviours.

This means that the research into atypical sex chromosome patterns may have only a limited role in helping our understanding of the usual development of sex and gender.

Apply it

Ryan is 16 and has very little body hair. He is very uncoordinated and clumsy. He is tall with long limbs and is also developing some breast tissue.

Tamara is 18 and has never had a period. She has recently been diagnosed as infertile. Her body shape suggests she has not been through puberty.

a. These are some of the physical characteristics of people with Klinefelter's and Turner's syndromes. Outline what Ryan's and Tamara's *psychological* characteristics are likely to be.

b. How can people like Ryan and Tamara help us understand gender?

REVISION BOOSTER

Here's a very common evaluative point: 'The study was correlational, so it did not establish cause and effect.' That's too easy. It's a useful way of remembering the issue for yourself. But in an exam answer, you should be doing more with it. Fully explain the point for maximum credit – what are the alternative factors involved, or the direction of causality?

KNOWLEDGE CHECK

1. Using an example, explain what is meant by the term 'atypical sex chromosome pattern'. (3 marks)

2. Outline **one** atypical sex chromosome pattern. (6 marks)

3. Evaluate research into **either** Klinefelter's syndrome **or** Turner's syndrome. (6 marks)

4. Describe and evaluate research into Klinefelter's syndrome **and/or** Turner's syndrome. (16 marks)

Cognitive explanations: Kohlberg's theory

Spec spotlight

Cognitive explanations of gender development, Kohlberg's theory, gender identity, gender stability and gender constancy.

Hopefully you've got my trousers in that briefcase, dear – I couldn't leave the house all day.

Apply it

Here are some comments made by children:

Claire: 'When I grow up I'm going to be a daddy.'

Ollie: 'Pop has long hair. He must be a lady.'

Justin: 'That man's wearing a dress; he looks funny.'

a. Approximately how old do you think Claire, Ollie and Justin are?

b. Identify the stages of gender development they are at.

c. Outline how Kohlberg's theory explains each of these examples of gender development.

Kohlberg's theory

A *cognitive developmental* approach.	**Cognitive** because a child's *thinking* about their gender is emphasised.
	Developmental because it is concerned with *changes* in thinking over time.
Gender development *parallels intellectual development*.	Piaget (see pages 110 to 113) proposed that the way a child thinks changes with age – they become capable of more logical and abstract thinking.
	This can be applied to gender development.
	Kohlberg identified three stages in gender development, related to Piaget's ideas.
	There are gradual rather than sudden transitions between stages and consequently the ages are approximate.
Stage 1 *Gender identity*, from about 2 years old.	Children are able to correctly identify themselves as a boy or a girl and are assumed to have developed gender identity.
	By 3 years, most children are able to identify other people as male or female, and can select the correct pictures when asked, 'Which one of these is like you?'
	Their understanding of gender appears limited to labelling and they have no sense of the permanence of gender.
	For instance, a boy at this stage may say 'when I grow up I will be a mummy'.
Stage 2 *Gender stability*, from about 4 years old.	Children realise that they will stay the same gender.
	However, they still find it challenging to apply this logic to:
	• Other people (e.g the idea that a man remains a man even if he grows his hair long).
	• Other situations (e.g. believing that people change sex if they engage in activities which are more often associated with the opposite gender – such as a female builder or a male nurse).
Stage 3 *Gender constancy*, from about 6 years old.	Children now recognise that gender remains constant and consistent across time and situations.
	And can apply this to other people as well as to themselves.
	They may be amused by someone with external appearance of the other sex (e.g. a man in a dress), but they understand he is still a man.
Gender constancy = the *start of a search* for gender-appropriate role models.	Gender constancy also marks the point when children begin to seek out gender-appropriate role models to identify with and imitate.
	Kohlberg suggests that once the child has a fully developed and internalised concept of gender at the constancy stage, they look for evidence which confirms it.

One strength is that there is supporting research evidence.

Slaby and Frey (1975) showed children images of males and females doing the same tasks. Young children spent equal time watching males and females.

Children in the gender constancy stage spent longer looking at the same sex because they identified with them.

This supports the idea that children change the way they process information about same- and opposite-sex people as they get older (i.e. they are thinking differently).

I want to tell my parents that I'm getting rather fed up with being forced to crawl through this flimsy polythene tube but, unfortunately, my age-appropriate but underdeveloped linguistic skills prohibit me from doing so. So, the tube it is then.

Another strength is support from the biological approach.

Kohlberg's stages are heavily influenced by changes in the developing child's brain and subsequent cognitive and intellectual maturation.

The biological basis of the theory is supported by Munroe *et al.*'s (1984) cross-cultural evidence of Kohlberg's stages in countries as far afield as Kenya, Samoa and Nepal.

This suggests that gender development has a considerable maturational element and universality, supporting a biological approach.

REVISION BOOSTER

Approximate ages for each stage in Kohlberg's theory are included here. It's worth learning them so you can use them in the exam to give that little bit more detail that could make your answer stand out from the rest.

One limitation is that gender-appropriate behaviour might begin earlier.

Bussey and Bandura (1992) found that children as young as 4 years old reported 'feeling good' about playing with gender-appropriate toys and 'bad' about doing the opposite.

This contradicts what Kohlberg would predict since he proposed that the final stage of gender constancy (when gender-appropriate models are sought) does not occur until around 6 years old.

This suggests that Kohlberg's theory is wrong because children have acquired gender-appropriate concepts earlier.

Another limitation is that the validity of the original interviews is questionable.

Kohlberg's original interviews were conducted with children as young as 2 or 3 years old. Questions were tailored to their age.

However, it is argued that Kohlberg may not have acknowledged that their ideas about gender may have been more complex than they could articulate.

This means that the support offered for the theory is limited and may not be valid.

KNOWLEDGE CHECK

1. In relation to cognitive explanations of gender development, explain what is meant by 'gender identity' and 'gender constancy'.
   (3 marks + 3 marks)

2. Outline Kohlberg's theory as a cognitive explanation of gender development. *(6 marks)*

3. Discuss **one or more** criticisms of Kohlberg's theory of gender development.
   (6 marks)

A further limitation is social learning theory challenges a focus on maturation.

Evidence suggests that boys have a less flexible concept of gender role and show greater resistance to opposite-sex activities than girls.

This cannot be explained by a maturational theory. The evidence suggests that social influences (social learning theory) may play a more significant role in gender development than Kohlberg suggested.

Therefore understanding gender development in terms of 'thinking' may be too simple and social learning theory's focus on the role of socialisation may be a more appropriate explanation of what occurs.

4. Ryan is 5 years old. When his mum tells him that daddy has a new job as a nurse, Ryan is shocked. 'Does that mean daddy is a lady now?' he asks.

   With reference to Ryan's comment, discuss **one** cognitive explanation of gender development. *(16 marks)*

Cognitive explanations: Gender schema theory (GST)

Spec spotlight

Cognitive explanations of gender development, gender schema theory.

Apply it

Jessica is 6 years old and is talking to her mum about what she wants to do when she grows up. 'I want to be a doctor because doctors are caring and kind,' says Jessica. 'That's nice,' says her mum, 'and will you get married?' 'Yes I will,' replies Jessica, 'and I'll wear a beautiful pink wedding dress with a bow in my hair and carry flowers.' 'Lovely,' says her mum, 'and what will your husband wear?' Jessica thinks for a minute and finally replies, 'I don't really know what boys wear at weddings.'

Use your knowledge of gender schema theory to explain the conversation between Jessica and her mum.

Are you in with the in-crowd? This bunch would be an ingroup for a boy but an outgroup for a girl.

Gender schema theory

GST suggests *understanding changes with age*.	Martin and Halverson's gender schema theory (GST), like Kohlberg's theory, is also **cognitive**-developmental, i.e. thinking changes with age.
	Like Kohlberg's theory, GST also suggests that children actively structure their own learning of gender.
	This contrasts with **social learning theory (SLT)** which suggests that children passively observe and imitate role models (SLT is discussed on page 104).
Gender schema contain and *organise our knowledge* of gender.	**Schema** are mental constructs that develop via experience (with some basic, limited ones present from birth).
	They are used by us to organise our knowledge.
	Gender schema contain what we know in relation to gender and gender-appropriate behaviour.
Gender schema *develop after gender identity*.	Martin and Halverson suggest that first a child establishes gender identity (around 2–3 years).
	The child then begins to look around for further information to develop their schema.
GST places *search for gender-appropriate information earlier*.	Martin and Halverson's idea is that the search for gender-appropriate information occurs much earlier than Kohlberg suggested.
	Kohlberg proposed that children needed to first achieve gender constancy (around the age of 7 years) but GST proposes a more gradual and earlier development process.
Gender schema develop and *determine behaviour*.	Gender-appropriate schema expand over time to include a range of behaviours and personality traits based on stereotypes (e.g. boys liking trucks and girls liking dolls).
	The schema direct the child's behaviour, (e.g. 'I am a boy so I play with trucks.'). This reinforces existing ideas about gender.
	By 6 years of age Martin and Halverson suggest children have acquired a rather fixed and stereotypical idea about what is appropriate for their gender.
	For example, having the belief that girls are calmer and more interested in dolls and prams than boys are.
Ingroup information is remembered better than outgroup.	Children pay more attention to, and have a better understanding of, the schema appropriate to their own gender (ingroup) than those of the opposite sex (outgroup).
	Ingroup identity bolsters the child's level of self-esteem as there is always a tendency to judge ingroups more positively.
	At around 8 years of age children develop elaborate schema for both genders.

One strength is that GST has research support.

Martin and Halverson (1983) found that children under 6 years of age remembered more photographs of gender-consistent behaviour than of gender-inconsistent behaviour a week later. They tended to change the sex of the person carrying out the inconsistent activity.

Additionally Martin and Little (1990) found that children under the age of 4 years, despite lack of gender stability and gender constancy, still demonstrated strongly sex-typed behaviours and attitudes.

This support for gender schema, along with evidence against Kohlberg's theory, suggests that GST might be a more **valid** explanation.

Another strength is that GST can explain young children's rigid gender beliefs.

The idea of ingroup schema explains why children discount information that conflicts with existing schema in favour of information that confirms ingroup schema.

Similarly, children display ingroup bias in paying more attention to information that is relevant to their own experience.

This suggests that gender schema theory can explain many aspects of young children's thinking about gender.

Cannot compute! Images of females occupying a stereotypical male role would be ignored or misremembered by children.

A further strength is that GST can complement Kohlberg's theory.

Stangor and Ruble (1989) suggest that gender schema and gender constancy are different processes. A schema relates to the organisation of memory – it enables children to store information.

In contrast gender constancy is about motivation – once children have a firm idea of what it means to be a boy or a girl (gender constancy) then they are motivated to engage in gender-appropriate activities.

So together the two theories can provide quite a detailed account of how gender development occurs.

One limitation is that the importance of schema has been exaggerated.

Focus on cognitive factors at the expense of social factors (parental influence and reinforcement) is not desirable.

Overlooking social factors means that the theory does not really explain why gender schema develop and take the form that they do.

This suggests that the theory oversimplifies the process of gender development.

Another limitation is there may be no link between schema and behaviour.

A prediction is that schema determine behaviour. As such gender behaviour can be changed by challenging schema or stereotypes.

But schema do not always determine behaviour (e.g. couples with strong views about sex equality may still organise chores on stereotypical lines).

This challenges GST because the basis of the theory is that attitudes do determine behaviour.

REVISION BOOSTER

One kind of question in the exam is the 'mini essay' (worth 8 or 10 marks, for example). Clearly, not as much material is required for one of these compared with a full-blown 16-marker. So consider this as you revise the five evaluative points on each AO3 page. Which are your 'favourites'? Which would you opt for if you only needed two or three? Go for the ones that you can explain and elaborate most fully. In a mini essay never try to squeeze in all five – less is more.

KNOWLEDGE CHECK

1. Outline **one** cognitive explanation of gender development. *(6 marks)*

2. Outline gender schema theory as a cognitive explanation of gender development. *(6 marks)*

3. Discuss gender schema theory as a cognitive explanation of gender development. *(8 marks)*

4. Outline and evaluate **two** cognitive explanations of gender development. *(16 marks)*

Spec spotlight

Psychodynamic explanation of gender development, Freud's psychoanalytic theory, Oedipus complex; Electra complex; identification and internalisation.

Nigel had decided it was never too early to teach his son the basic skills in life. Tomorrow – driving lessons.

Apply it

Tors is a 5-year-old boy who, up until now, wanted to spend most of his time with his mum. He resisted being with his dad and always sought out his mum when he was upset or distressed. However, recently Tors has preferred to spend time with his dad and is no longer interested in the cuddles he used to enjoy from mum. He is even copying some of his dad's behaviour.

a. How can Tors's behaviour be explained by Freud's psychoanalytic theory of gender development? Refer in your answer to the concepts of Oedipus complex, identification and internalisation.

b. Write a brief scenario like the one above, but illustrating a girl's experience at the same age, to reflect the concept of the Electra complex.

Freud's psychoanalytic theory

Phallic stage is the key time for gender development.	Freud's **psychodynamic** developmental theory explains five psycho-sexual stages: oral, anal, phallic, latent and genital.
	Pre-phallic stage: children have no concept of gender identity. They are bisexual in the sense that they are neither masculine nor feminine.
	Phallic stage: around 3–6 years, boys experience the Oedipus complex and girls experience the Electra complex.
Oedipus complex in boys. Desire for mother and hatred of father.	During the phallic stage boys develop incestuous feelings towards their mother. They want their mother for themselves.
	Thus they feel a jealous hatred for their father who has what the boy desires (the mother).
	Boys recognise that their father is more powerful. They fear that, on discovering their desire for their mother, their father will castrate them.
Electra complex in girls. Resentment of mother and in competition with her.	Jung used the term Electra complex to describe the conflict that girls experience. Freud called it penis envy.
	During the phallic stage girls feel competition with their mother for their father's love.
	Girls also resent their mother because they believe that she is responsible for their lack of a penis.
Resolution of conflict is through *identification* with the same-sex parent.	For a boy the conflict between his desires and his castration anxiety is resolved when the boy gives up his love for his mother and begins to identify with his father.
	Girls acknowledge that they will never have the penis that they desire. They substitute this with a desire to have their own children and through this they finally identify with their mother and her gender.
Identification with same-sex parent leads to *internalisation*.	Boys adopt the attitudes and values of their father, and girls adopt those of their mother.
	Freud referred to this process as internalisation of parents' identity. This happens all at once.
Little Hans **case study** illustrates the Oedipus complex.	Little Hans was a 5-year-old boy with a morbid fear of being bitten by a horse. His fear appeared to stem from an incident when he had seen a horse collapse and die in the street.
	Freud's interpretation was that Hans's fear of horses represented his actual fear of being castrated by his father because of Hans's love for his mother.
	Freud suggested that Hans had transferred his fear of his father onto horses via displacement (a defence mechanism).

One limitation is the lack of support for the Oedipus complex.

The theory predicts that the more punitive a father is the more robust his son's sense of gender identity.

However, Blakemore and Hill (2008) found that the reverse was true and that boys with more liberal fathers tend to be more secure in their masculine identity.

This suggests that Freud's explanation of the role of this complex in gender identity is not borne out in research and therefore it has limited **validity**.

Another limitation is Freud's theory does not fully explain female development.

Freud's idea of penis envy has been criticised as merely reflecting the era he lived and worked in, where males held so much of the power.

Horney (1967) argued that in fact men's womb envy was more prominent (a reaction to women's ability to nurture and sustain life).

This challenges the idea that female gender development was founded on a desire to want to be like men (an **androcentric bias**).

Lloyd was jealous of Maria for many reasons – she had a better job, a fancier computer and, of course, she had a womb.

A further limitation is the theory relies on a child having different-gender parents.

The theory assumes that boys and girls require both a male and female parent for normal gender development. It would follow that if they are not both present then we would expect an adverse effect on a child's gender development.

Golombok *et al.* (1983) found that children from single-parent families went on to develop normal gender identities and Green (1978) found only 1 out of 37 children who were raised by gay or transsexual parents had a non-typical gender identity.

This suggests that typical gender development does not require two parents of different genders and does not necessarily follow the process that Freud laid out.

REVISION BOOSTER
What are your evaluations like? Why not try and make them more like ours? Start with your initial point – a strength or a limitation in most cases. Then…elaborate! Develop your evaluation point in three more steps, just as we've done on all of these AO3 pages. Have a close look at each one to see what they have in common.

Another limitation is that Freud's methods of investigation lack scientific rigour.

Freud based his account on unconscious concepts which make the theory untestable, unlike other explanations which are testable and based on objective, verifiable evidence from controlled studies.

According to Popper, this makes Freud's theory *pseudoscientific* (not genuine science) as his key ideas cannot be falsified (i.e. proved wrong through scientific testing).

This means that Freud's theory of gender development is considered of less value than other theories which can be empirically tested.

KNOWLEDGE CHECK

1. With reference to Freud's psychoanalytic theory of gender development, explain what is meant by the 'Oedipus complex' and the 'Electra complex'.
   (3 marks + 3 marks)

2. Outline Freud's psychoanalytic theory of gender development. *(6 marks)*

3. Briefly evaluate Freud's psychoanalytic theory of gender development. *(5 marks)*

4. Some psychologists believe that boys and girls go through different processes of gender development. But both sexes experience identification and internalisation.

   Describe and evaluate **one** psychodynamic explanation of gender development. Refer in your answer to the concepts of identification and internalisation. *(16 marks)*

A final limitation is this theory disagrees with other theories on gender identity.

Freud claimed that before the age of 6 years the child is bisexual. At the end of the phallic stage the child identifies with the same-sex parent and no further development takes place.

In contrast, for example, Kohlberg described a complex process where children acquire gender identity at around 2 years, gender stability around 4 years and gender constancy at age 6.

This suggests that Freud underestimated the complexity and gradual process that occurs in gender development.

Social learning explanation of gender development

Spec spotlight

Social learning theory as applied to gender development.

Apply it

Louis, a 4-year-old boy, is very boisterous and active and sometimes quite aggressive when he plays. He enjoys the rough and tumble of wrestling with his dad and prefers toys such as soldiers, guns, etc.

Lionel is quite a feminine boy who enjoys playing with dolls and playing make-up games with his mum. He chose to dress as a 'zombie bride' at Halloween.

Explain how social learning theory would account for both Louis' and Lionel's gender development.

Modelling

Modelling can refer to when a fashion model models some clothing – or it can mean a form of learning where individuals learn a particular behaviour by observing another individual performing that behaviour.

Hang on – it's the same thing!

Yes, Gary was a male model, handsome and the envy of his friends – but it was some comfort to them that, at 22, he still couldn't put a coat on properly.

Social learning theory applied to gender development

Gender is learned *observation* and *reinforcement* in a social context.	**Social learning theory (SLT)** acknowledges the role of social context in gender development. Gender behaviour is learned from observing others and being reinforced for the imitation of the behaviour. SLT draws attention to the influence of the environment (nurture) in shaping gender development. Influences can include peers, parents, teachers, culture and the media.
Gender-appropriate behaviours are *differentially reinforced*.	Children are reinforced for gender-appropriate behaviour. For example, boys may be praised for being active and assertive and punished for being passive or gentle. Differential reinforcement explains why boys and girls learn distinctly different gender behaviours – they are reinforced for different behaviours, which they then reproduce.
Vicarious reinforcement and punishment.	Vicarious reinforcement: If the consequences of another person's behaviour are favourable, that behaviour is more likely to be imitated by a child (e.g. if a girl sees her mother being complimented when wearing a pretty dress and make-up). Vicarious punishment: If the consequences of behaviour are seen to be unfavourable (i.e. punished), behaviour is less likely to be imitated (e.g. if a little boy sees another boy teased for displaying feminine or 'sissy' behaviour they are unlikely to copy it).
Children will identify with *role models*.	A child will identify with people around them that they perceive to be 'like me' or like someone 'I want to be'. These role models tend to be: <ul><li>Part of the child's immediate environment (parents, teachers, siblings, etc.).</li><li>In the media (pop or sports stars).</li><li>Attractive, high status.</li><li>The same sex as the child.</li></ul>
Behaviour can be *modelled* by someone and then imitated.	**Modelling** in gender development occurs in two ways: <ol><li>A mother may *model* stereotypically feminine behaviour when tidying the house or preparing dinner.</li><li>When a girl copies her mother setting the table, or attempts to 'feed' her doll using a toy bottle, she is *modelling* the behaviour she has observed.</li></ol>
Mediational processes – the **cognitive** factors that determine the production of an observed behaviour.	Four mediational processes in learning gender behaviour: <ul><li>Attention: For instance, a little boy might follow closely what his favourite footballer does.</li><li>Retention: Remembering the skills of the footballer and trying to reproduce these when he plays.</li><li>Motivation: Desire to be like his hero.</li><li>Motor reproduction: Be physically capable of doing it.</li></ul>

One strength is supporting evidence for differential reinforcement.

Smith and Lloyd (1978) observed adults with 4–6-month-old babies who (irrespective of their actual sex) were dressed half the time in boys' clothes and half the time in girls' clothes.

Babies assumed to be boys were encouraged to be adventurous and active and given a hammer-shaped rattle. Babies assumed to be girls were reinforced for passivity, given a doll and praised for being pretty.

This suggests that gender-appropriate behaviour is stamped in at an early age through differential reinforcement and supports the SLT explanation of gender development.

Smith and Lloyd's study included a doll and a hammer-shaped rattle. Which this isn't. This is a doll with a hammer. And it's a little scary.

Another strength is that SLT can help explain changing gender roles.

Stereotypically masculine and feminine behaviour is less rigid than it was. SLT can explain it as a shift in social expectations/norms leading to changes in what is reinforced.

However, there has been no corresponding change in people's basic biology within the same period so the **biological approach** cannot explain changes over time.

This means SLT offers a more complete explanation of recent gender development than other alternatives.

One limitation is that SLT does not explain the developmental process.

SLT acknowledges that there are some physical and intellectual age limitations on gender-related behaviours but generally implies that modelling of gender-appropriate behaviour can occur at any age.

However, Dubin (1992) suggests that despite a child observing the behaviour of same-sex role models at an early age, the selection and imitation of such behaviour comes later.

Thus the influences of age and maturation on gender development are not properly considered by SLT and therefore the explanation is incomplete.

REVISION BOOSTER

If you were an athlete preparing for a big race you would do lots of timed practice runs. You should do the same with your exam answers. Shut your book and try to write answers to the questions below – you have just over a minute per mark. Afterwards, criticise your own answer.

Another limitation is that SLT does not fully consider biological factors.

The case of David Reimer (biological male, castrated at birth, raised as a female, male identity) suggests that it is not possible to override biological influence.

Now psychologists tend to accept that there are innate differences between boys and girls and these are reinforced through social interaction and cultural expectations.

So SLT only provides a partial explanation of the process of gender development. An interactionist account is a more complete explanation.

A further limitation is that SLT cannot explain unconscious influences.

Both SLT and Freud explain gender development through 'identification' with same-sex individuals.

The theories differ in the level of consciousness. SLT suggests that mediational processes are conscious whereas Freud talked in terms of unconscious processes.

This assumption that our gender behaviour is determined by factors within our control may be a limitation of SLT.

KNOWLEDGE CHECK

1. Outline social learning theory as applied to gender development. *(6 marks)*
2. Distinguish between the social learning explanation of gender development and the psychodynamic explanation. *(4 marks)*
3. Evaluate social learning theory as applied to gender development. *(6 marks)*
4. Discuss social learning theory as applied to gender development. Refer to another explanation of gender development in your answer. *(16 marks)*

The influence of culture and media on gender roles

Spec spotlight

The influence of culture and media on gender roles.

In some cultures owning a tractor is a good way to advertise your wealth and resources. Just saying...

Culture and gender roles

Nature versus nurture.	Nature: If a gender behaviour is consistent across cultures we consider it innate or biological.
	Nurture: If a gender behaviour is culturally specific we consider this is due to the influence of shared norms and socialisation.
The role of *nurture* – Mead's research.	Mead's (1935) research on tribal groups of New Guinea supported the cultural determination of gender roles. • Arapesh: gentle and responsive (similar to the Western stereotype of femininity). • Mundugumor: aggressive and hostile (similar to the Western stereotype of masculinity). • Tchambuli women were dominant and they organised village life; men were passive and considered to be decorative (reverse of Western gender behaviour).
The role of *nature* – Buss's research.	Buss (1994) found consistent mate preferences in 37 countries studied across all continents. In all cultures: • Women sought men offering wealth and resources. • Men looked for youth and physical attractiveness. Munroe and Munroe (1975) found that in most societies, division of labour is organised along gender lines.

The media and gender roles

Same-sex media role models preferred.	Children are most likely to imitate role models who are the same sex as they are and who are engaging in gender-appropriate behaviour. This maximises the chance of gender-appropriate behaviours being reinforced.
The *media* creates gender stereotypes.	Bussey and Bandura (1999) found that the media provides clear gender stereotypes, for example: • Men are independent, ambitious and advice-givers. • Women are dependent, unambitious and advice-seekers. Furnham and Farragher (2000) found that men were more likely to be shown in autonomous roles within professional contexts, whereas women were often seen occupying familial roles within domestic settings.
Correlation between media exposure and gender-stereotypical views.	McGhee and Frueh (1980) found that children who have more exposure to popular forms of media tend to display more gender-stereotypical views in their behaviour and attitudes. The research also suggested that people gain information through the media about the likely success or otherwise of adopting gender-typical behaviours, i.e. vicarious reinforcement.

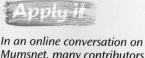

In an online conversation on Mumsnet, many contributors voiced concerns that what their children like to watch on TV reinforces gender role stereotypes. Others were optimistic that things are changing, arguing that films such as Frozen *and* Brave *challenge traditional stereotypes.*

With reference to these **two** positions, explain how the media can influence gender roles.

One limitation is that Mead's findings have been challenged.

In a follow-up study of Samoan people Freeman (1983) claimed that Mead misled participants and had been heavily influenced by her preconceptions.

However, Freeman's research was similarly criticised for lack of objectivity. He selected research to support his own viewpoint.

This raises questions over the quality of the research offered in relation to the influence of culture and media on gender roles.

Another limitation is that imposed etic may affect the validity of findings.

Cross-cultural research is typically undertaken by Western researchers, using theories and methods developed in the West. It is suggested that they impose their own understanding upon the people they are studying.

Berry et al. (2002) claimed that imposed etics can make methods and findings meaningless. This is the use of methods developed in one culture to assess behaviour in another culture.

This suggests that conclusions from cross-cultural research may not be valid. The inclusion of at least one member of the local population in the research team (as Buss did) is a way of guarding against this possibility.

A further limitation is that research does not resolve the nature–nurture debate.

Cross-cultural research can show what is biological and what is due to the impact of cultural practices on gender-role behaviour, but practically it is impossible to separate the two.

At birth children start learning from their society about gender-role norms. It is impossible to determine where nature (biology) stops and nurture (social influence) begins.

It is likely that the true explanation of gender development will be a constant interaction between both nature and nurture.

One limitation with research on the media is that it is correlational.

Media output might be reflecting social norms about males and females but it could also be that the media is the cause of such norms.

Children without regular media exposure are rarely available for the comparisons necessary to establish the direction of the media's effect.

This means we cannot assume that the media is responsible for causing gender roles.

A further limitation is that counter-stereotypes also exist in the media.

Such counter-stereotypes challenge notions of masculinity and femininity. Pingree (1978) found that gender stereotyping was reduced if children were shown adverts with women in non-stereotypical roles.

However, Pingree also found that pre-adolescent boys' stereotypes became stronger following exposure to the non-traditional models.

Therefore the prediction that counter-stereotypes will reduce gender stereotyping is not always supported.

As far as gender is concerned, neither route provides the best answer.

KNOWLEDGE CHECK

1. Outline research into the influence of culture on gender roles. (6 marks)
2. Describe one study into the influence of the media on gender roles. In your answer explain what the researcher(s) did and what they found. (6 marks)
3. Evaluate research into the influence of either culture or the media on gender roles. (6 marks)
4. Describe and evaluate research into the influence of culture and/or the media on gender roles. (16 marks)

Atypical gender development

Spec spotlight

Atypical gender development: gender identity disorder; biological and social explanations for gender identity disorder.

The High Court in October 2016 heard the case of a mother who was 'absolutely convinced that her 7-year-old son perceived himself as a girl'. The boy (referred to as 'X') wore girls' clothes to school, was registered as a girl with the local doctors' surgery and showed 'feminine mannerisms'. He played with girls' toys and was said to 'disdain his penis' and wanted to have it removed.

How would biological **and** social explanations of gender identity disorder explain X's experience?

Twin studies

MZ twins share 100% of genes but DZ twins only 50% (on average) – so we would expect a greater likelihood of both MZ twins developing GID if it is mostly genetic.

This is because both MZ and DZ twins are raised together in the same environment, but MZ twins have a greater degree of genetic similarity than DZs.

Separation anxiety can be avoided by symbiotic fusion. Er... come again?

Gender identity disorder (GID)

GID occurs where sex and gender *do not correspond*.	Gender identity disorder (GID): a mismatch between a person's biological sex and their gender identity.
	Some individuals identify themselves as transgender and may opt for gender reassignment surgery, becoming transsexual.
GID is a *psychological disorder* in DSM-5.	**DSM**-5 specifically excludes atypical gender conditions with a biological basis (e.g. Klinefelter's syndrome).
	It is still possible that GID may have a biological basis.
Brain sex research looks at the *BSTc*.	Brain sex theory suggests that GID is caused by brain areas that are incompatible with a person's biological sex.
	The focus of research is dimorphic areas of the brain (i.e. areas that take a different form in males and females).
	Zhou *et al.* (1995) studied the *bed nucleus of the stria terminalis central division* (BSTc) – this is 40% larger in males than in females.
	Post-mortem studies of six male-to-female transgender individuals had a BSTc of the typical female size.
	Kruijver *et al.* (2000) also found that these individuals had an average BSTc neuron number in the female range.
Genetic basis for GID indicated in twin studies.	Coolidge *et al.* (2002) found a GID prevalence of 2.3% in a sample of twins and suggested that 62% of these cases could be accounted for by genetic variance.
	Heylens *et al.* (2012) found that nine (39%) of their sample of **MZ twins** were concordant for GID; but none of the **DZs** were.
Psychoanalytic theory explains male GID in terms of separation anxiety.	Ovesey and Person (1973) suggest GID is caused by a child experiencing extreme separation anxiety before gender identity has been established.
	The boy fantasises about a symbiotic fusion with his mother to relieve his anxiety and remove his fear of separation.
	As a result the boy 'becomes' the mother and thus adopts a female gender identity.
	Stoller (1973) found that GID males did describe overly close mother–son relationships that would lead to greater female identification and confused gender identity in the long-term.
GST (**cognitive** theory) explains that counter-stereotypical activities create androgynous **schema**.	Liben and Bigler (2002) extended gender schema theory (GST):
	• First pathway: gender schema are learned and these direct gender-appropriate attitudes and behaviour as part of 'normal' development.
	• Second 'personal' pathway: personal interests may become more dominant and this in turn influences a child's gender schema. For example, a boy who plays with dolls may come to believe that playing with dolls is for boys as well as for girls. This leads to androgynous behaviour and in a small minority may lead to GID.

One limitation is that brain sex theory assumptions have been criticised.

Hulshoff Pol *et al.* (2006) found that transgender hormone therapy affected the size of the BSTc, which means that differences in transgender brains may be due to the therapy rather than a cause of GID.

In addition Chung *et al.* (2002) claim that prenatal hormonal influences (that affect the size of the BSTc) are not triggered until adulthood.

This evidence casts doubt on the idea that dimorphic brain differences are present in early childhood.

TRANS**GENDER**

Say it loud and proud.

One limitation of the biological explanation is twin study evidence is weak.

Twin studies actually show low **concordance rates** for GID. It is also difficult to separate the impact of **nature and nurture** as twins (especially MZ) may share similar environments.

GID is rare and therefore sample sizes in twin studies tend to be extremely small, limiting the extent to which effective **generalisations** can be made.

This means that we cannot rely on evidence from twin studies to support a genetic role in GID.

Another limitation of the biological explanation is it may oversimplify GID.

Biological explanations are criticised for reducing complex conditions to a genetic, neuro-anatomical and/or hormonal level, overlooking social or psychological factors.

It is likely that a full explanation would need to include an interaction between nature and nurture.

So biological theories of GID are unlikely to provide a complete explanation.

One limitation of the psychoanalytic explanation of GID is it lacks support.

Rekers (1986) actually suggests that gender disturbance in boys is more likely to be associated with the absence of the father than fear of separation from the mother.

The assumption that GID is caused by separation anxiety is difficult to test (e.g. fantasies about the mother occur at an unconscious level which means the individual may be unaware of them and so can't report them).

Overall there is a lack of research support for the psychoanalytical explanation of GID and the concept is basically not testable, a serious limitation of any theory.

One limitation of cognitive theory of GID is lack of explanatory power.

Liben and Bigler's (2002) theory describes GID rather than explaining how someone may become interested in activities that are not consistent with their own sex.

The theory also does not explain how such activities bring about the development of non sex-typed schema.

So other theories of GID (e.g. brain sex theory) may be more useful because they are explanatory.

KNOWLEDGE CHECK

1. In relation to atypical gender development, explain what is meant by 'gender identity disorder'. *(3 marks)*

2. Briefly outline **one** biological and **one** social explanation for gender identity disorder. *(3 marks + 3 marks)*

3. Evaluate research into atypical gender development. *(6 marks)*

4. Psychologists debate the causes of gender identity disorder. Some believe it is the outcome of biological influences, whereas others emphasise the role of social and psychological factors.

   With reference to the debate outlined above, discuss **two** explanations for gender identity disorder. *(16 marks)*

Piaget's theory of cognitive development

Spec spotlight

Piaget's theory of cognitive development: schemas, assimilation, accommodation, equilibration.

Confused? Yousef was experiencing what psychologists refer to as a state of disequilibrium.

Apply it

Adelaide is 8 years old and is going shopping for clothes with her mum. She has been shopping before so she knows what's involved in choosing something she likes. For the first time ever, Adelaide is allowed to go to the checkout and pay for her shopping herself. She is unclear about what to do and appears a bit anxious in case she gets it wrong. But she asks her mum to explain, and is much happier when she has. Adelaide said afterwards, 'That was easy – I know what to do now for next time.'

Use your knowledge of Piaget's theory of cognitive development to explain Adelaide's experience.

REVISION BOOSTER

It's crucial that you understand the differences between assimilation and accommodation – otherwise you won't really have a detailed understanding of Piaget's theory. Both terms are named on the specification, so be prepared to describe/explain them for up to 3 marks.

Piaget's theory of cognitive development

Maturation causes changes in the way children think.	Piaget asserted that children do not just know less than adults, they actually reason differently. Maturation is the key to how children's thinking changes – it is not just a matter of learning more. Piaget also looked at children's learning, in particular at two aspects: • The role of motivation in development. • The question of how knowledge develops.
Schema are units of knowledge.	Our knowledge of the world is represented in the mind and organised in **schema**. **Cognitive** development includes the construction of increasingly detailed schema. Children are born with a few schema but construct new ones during infancy, including the 'me-schema' in which all the child's knowledge about themselves is stored. As adults we build schema for people, objects, physical actions and also for more abstract ideas like justice or morality.
Disequilibrium creates motivation to learn.	When a child cannot make sense of their world because existing schema are insufficient, they feel a sense of disequilibrium which is uncomfortable. To escape this, and adapt to the new situation, the child explores and learns more. The result is a state of equilibration.
Equilibration is the preferred mental state.	Equilibration is a pleasant state of balance and occurs when experiences in the world match the state of our current schema.
Assimilation = new experiences understood within existing schema.	Any new experience creates disequilibrium because, as yet, it does not fit our existing schema. Assimilation takes place when the new experience does not radically change our understanding of the schema so we can incorporate the new experience into our existing schema. For example, when a child with dogs at home meets another dog of a different breed, the child will simply add the new dog to their dog-schema (assimilation).
Accommodation = new experiences require major schema change.	An experience that is very different from our current schema cannot be assimilated. Accommodation involves the creation of whole new schema or wholesale changes to existing ones. For example, a child with pet cats who has not come across dogs (has no dog-schema) on meeting a dog will initially try to incorporate the dog into their cat schema. When the dog acts rather differently (e.g. sitting when told to, barking, etc.), then the child needs to do something more dramatic than assimilation. The child will accommodate by forming a separate dog-schema. Both development and equilibration have taken place.

One strength of this theory is the supporting evidence.

Howe *et al.* (1992) put 9–12-year-olds in groups to discuss how objects move down a slope. They found that the level of children's knowledge and understanding increased after the discussion.

Crucially though, the children did not reach the same conclusions or pick up the same facts about movement down a slope.

This supports Piaget's idea that children learn through forming personal mental representations.

Piaget thought that children's cognitive development would be enhanced through contact with other children – though, as this picture shows, that perhaps depends on the child.

A further strength is that Piaget's ideas revolutionised teaching.

Activity-oriented classrooms allow children to learn in a more natural way. The children actively engage in tasks that allow them to construct their own understanding of the curriculum.

For example, in early years' classrooms learning is focused around play and discovering new aspects of the world.

This is a strength of Piaget's theory because it has had a positive impact directly on education and we continue to seek out active ways of allowing learning to occur.

One limitation is that Piaget underestimated the role of other people.

Piaget recognised teachers are important for setting up discovery situations for children but other theories suggest that the role of others in learning is more central.

For example, Vygotsky argued that learning is more of a social process and more advanced learning is possible only with the help of experts or peers.

This suggests that Piaget's theory is somewhat limited in its explanation of the cognitive development process.

A further limitation is that the role of equilibration may be overemphasised.

Piaget believed that disequilibrium and removal of its associated discomfort was the motivating factor in cognitive development.

However, not all children are equally motivated to remove disequilibrium. Piaget studied children from middle-class families who may well have been more motivated to learn than other children.

As the role of equilibration was a central part of his explanation this weakens the **validity** of his theory.

KNOWLEDGE CHECK

1. In the context of Piaget's theory of cognitive development, explain what is meant by the terms 'schema' and 'equilibration'.
   (2 marks + 2 marks)

2. In relation to Piaget's theory of cognitive development, distinguish between assimilation and accommodation. Use examples in your answer.
   (3 marks)

3. Outline Piaget's theory of cognitive development.
   (6 marks)

4. Discuss Piaget's theory of cognitive development.
   (16 marks)

A final limitation is that the full role of language is not acknowledged.

To Piaget language is just a cognitive ability that develops in line with other abilities.

Other researchers such as Vygotsky have placed a lot more importance on language development suggesting it is crucial to broader cognitive development.

If language is central to learning and it is not fully examined in the theory, then the theory is limited in its validity.

Piaget's stages of intellectual development

Spec spotlight

Piaget's theory of cognitive development: stages of intellectual development. Characteristics of these stages, including object permanence, conservation, egocentrism and class inclusion.

Until 7 years of age children are egocentric and assume that the view they have represents the view of others. Observe this kid. To the rest of us, he's stood in the middle of a field – to him, he's found the perfect hiding place.

Apply it

Calvin has two young children – Hazel aged 4 years and Hector aged 8 years. Whenever Calvin asks his children if they want some juice, Hazel insists on having it in her special cup which is tall and thin. She always refuses the alternative short and fat cup. Hector thinks this is funny – he is happy to have any cup because he can see when daddy pours the juice that they both get the same amount.

Identify which of Piaget's stages of intellectual development Hazel and Hector are at. Explain which cognitive skill is illustrated here.

Class inclusion

Class inclusion is the idea that classifications have subsets.

Piaget's stages of intellectual development

Four stages each with a different level of *reasoning ability*.	Piaget's theory explains how our knowledge of the world is acquired through **schema** and disequilibrium/equilibration.
	He also explained **cognitive** development as a set of stages, each characterised by a different level of reasoning ability.
	Exact ages vary from child to child but he proposed that all children develop through the same sequence of stages.
Sensorimotor stage (0–2 years approx.) includes *object permanence*.	A baby's focus is on physical sensations and basic coordination between what they see and their body movement.
	Babies also come to understand that other people are separate objects, and they acquire some basic language.
	They also develop object permanence (the understanding that objects still exist when they are out of sight):
	• Before 8 months, children immediately switch their attention away from an object once it is out of sight.
	• After 8 months children continue to look for it. This suggests that children then understand that objects continue to exist when removed from view.
Pre-operational stage (2–7 years) includes *egocentrism* and lack of *class-inclusion*.	Egocentrism was tested in the three mountains task (Piaget and Inhelder 1956).
	Children were shown three model mountains, each with a different feature: a cross, a house or snow.
	Pre-operational children tended to find it difficult to select a picture that showed a view other than their own.
	Class inclusion is tested, for example, using a picture of five dogs and two cats and asking, 'Are there more dogs or animals?'
	Children under 8 years tend to respond that there are more dogs (Piaget and Inhelder 1964).
	Younger children cannot simultaneously see a dog as a member of the dog class and the animal class.
Concrete operations stage (7–11 years) includes *logical reasoning*.	By the start of this stage, children have mastered conservation and are improving on egocentrism and class inclusion.
	However, they still have some reasoning problems – they are only able to reason or operate on physical objects in their presence (concrete operations).
Formal operations stage (11+ years) includes *syllogisms*.	Abstract reasoning develops – being able to think beyond the here and now. Children can now focus on the form of an argument and not be distracted by its content.
	For example, they can process syllogisms: 'All yellow cats have two heads. I have a yellow cat called Charlie. How many heads does Charlie have?' The answer is two but younger children are distracted by the fact that cats do not have two heads.

One limitation is that the theory was based on tests that may lack validity.

McGarrigle and Donaldson (1974) found that in a conservation of number task, if the counters were moved accidentally by a 'naughty teddy', 72% of children under 7 correctly said the number was the same as before.

This suggests that Piaget underestimated the conservation ability of children aged 4–6 years. Piaget's method may have led the children to think something must have changed (or why would the researcher ask the question?).

This is a limitation because it calls into question the nature of the pre-operational stage of intellectual development.

Another limitation is that lack of class inclusion ability is questioned.

Siegler and Svetina (2006) found that, when 5-year-olds received feedback that pointed out subsets, they did develop an understanding of class inclusion.

This was contrary to Piaget's belief that class inclusion was not possible until a child had reached the necessary intellectual development at 7 years of age.

This again calls into question the validity of Piaget's stages.

A further limitation is that the assertions about egocentrism are not supported.

Hughes (1975) found that even at 3½ years a child could position a boy doll in a model building with two intersecting walls so that the doll could not be seen by a policeman doll.

This suggests that children are able to decentre and imagine other perspectives much earlier than Piaget proposed.

This again suggests the manner of Piaget's studies and tasks led him to underestimate children's intellectual abilities and that the resultant stages were incorrect.

A limitation is that children's abilities were both under- and overestimated.

As well as underestimating what young children can do, Piaget may have overestimated other abilities such as achieving formal operations.

In addition there is evidence that, with practice, children can achieve logical thinking earlier than Piaget suggested.

This challenges some of the basic principles of his theory if some stages are not universal and progression is not just due to maturation.

A final limitation is his view that intellectual development is a single process.

Studies of children with autistic spectrum disorder (ASD) suggest that intellectual abilities may develop independently as such children are typically very egocentric but develop normal reasoning and language.

This evidence supports a domain-specific rather than a domain-general view of intellectual development.

This suggests that a basic assumption of Piaget's theory (that cognitive development is domain-general) may not be valid for all examples of development.

This really is a naughty teddy; he's having a wee behind the door.

KNOWLEDGE CHECK

1. In relation to Piaget's stages of intellectual development, explain what is meant by 'object permanence' and 'conservation'. Use examples in your answer.
   (3 marks + 3 marks)

2. Identify **one** stage of Piaget's theory of intellectual development and outline the features of this stage. *(4 marks)*

3. Describe **one** study into Piaget's stages of intellectual development. *(4 marks)*

4. Describe and evaluate Piaget's stages of intellectual development. *(16 marks)*

Vygotsky's theory of cognitive development

Spec spotlight

Vygotsky's theory of cognitive development, including the zone of proximal development and scaffolding.

Scaffolding. Helping learners negotiate the intellectual challenges of life. I'm wasted in this job, I should have been a poet.

An expert

An expert is any person with more knowledge. This can be an adult or could be a peer.

Jamela trains primary teachers and spends a lot of time in the classroom observing trainees. She has noticed that the best teachers spend time with individual children. They can quickly identify where the child is in their understanding and what they need to know to progress further. These teachers use various strategies to capture and keep the child's interest. They get them started on a task and encourage them to keep going with it. Good teachers also get children to do lots of work in pairs.

Use your knowledge of Vygotsky's theory of cognitive development to explain Jamela's observations.

Vygotsky's theory of cognitive development

The theory stresses the role of *social processes*.	Vygotsky agreed with Piaget that children develop reasoning skills sequentially but believed that this process was mainly dependent on social processes.
	Vygotsky claimed knowledge is:
	• First *intermental* (between someone more expert and someone less expert).
	• Then *intramental* (within the individual).
Cultural differences in learning are explained through differing experiences.	Reasoning abilities are acquired via contact with those around us and as a result there will be cultural differences in **cognitive** development because we all grow up and learn about the world surrounded by cultural values and beliefs.
	Children pick up the mental 'tools' that are most important for life from the world they live in.
ZPD is the gap between current and potential capabilities.	The zone of proximal development (ZPD) is the gap between:
	• What a child knows or can do alone, and
	• What the child is capable of, following interaction with someone more expert.
	Vygotsky claimed that the role of a teacher was to guide the child through this gap to as full a level of understanding as the child's developmental ability would allow.
Increased skills and reasoning ability from experts.	For Vygotsky cognitive development was not just about acquiring more facts but about becoming more skilled at reasoning.
	The most advanced (formal) reasoning can only be achieved with the help of experts, not simply through exploration.
Experts use *scaffolding* to help learner cross the ZPD.	Wood *et al.* (1976) suggest a number of features of scaffolding including:
	• Recruitment – engaging learner's interest.
	• Reduction in degrees of freedom – focusing learner and getting started.
	• Direction maintenance – motivating learner to persevere.
Progressive scaffolding strategies.	Wood *et al.* also identified progressive strategies that can be used to scaffold learning. For example, prompts might be (from most to least help):
	• Demonstration (e.g. mother draws an object with crayons).
	• Preparation for child (e.g. mother helps child hold crayon).
	• Indication of materials (e.g. mother points to crayons).
	• Specific verbal instruction (e.g. mother says, 'How about using the green crayon?').
	• General prompt (e.g. mother says, 'Now draw something else.').

One strength is evidence for the ZPD.

Roazzi and Bryant (1998) found that 4–5-year-olds performed better on a 'number of sweets' challenge when working with peers (who offered support on estimating) rather than alone.

This demonstrated that children can develop more advanced reasoning skills when working with more expert people.

This therefore supports the **validity** of ZPD as a developmental concept.

How many sweets? Er... certainly fewer than there were before he turned up.

Another strength is support for the idea of scaffolding.

Conner and Cross (2003) observed 45 children at intervals between the ages of 16 and 54 months, finding that mothers used less direct intervention as children developed.

This shows how the level of help given by an expert partner declines over time as suggested by the process of scaffolding.

This supports Vygotsky's claim that scaffolding is a good description of the process by which children move through their ZPD.

REVISION BOOSTER

In question 4 below you are required to refer to the scenario. If you don't then the maximum mark you could get is 12 because 4 of the 16 marks are for application (and 6 for AO1 and 6 for AO3). Applying your knowledge is a tricky skill and well worth practising – there are a lot of marks at stake.

A further strength is the practical applications of Vygotsky's ideas.

Van Keer and Verhaeghe (2005) found that 7-year-olds tutored by 10-year-olds, in addition to their whole-class teaching, progressed further in reading than a **control group** who only had class teaching.

This evidence suggests that Vygotsky was correct in assuming that more able people, even if they are essentially peers, can enhance development and learning.

This supports both the validity and usefulness of the theory.

KNOWLEDGE CHECK

1. In the context of Vygotsky's theory of cognitive development, what is meant by the terms 'zone of proximal development' and 'scaffolding'? *(2 marks + 2 marks)*

A limitation is that not all children respond identically to learning opportunities.

Howe et al. (1992) found 9–12-year-olds who had group discussions about the movement of objects down a slope showed better understanding after the discussion but did not all pick up the same facts.

So even when children experience the same interaction or experience they do not necessarily have the same level or nature of cognitive development.

Vygotsky's theory can be criticised for not fully explaining the differential rate of development of different children whereas Piaget's concept of maturation can.

2. Outline Vygotsky's theory of cognitive development. *(6 marks)*

3. Describe research into scaffolding in the context of Vygotsky's theory of cognitive development. *(6 marks)*

Another limitation is that not all individual differences are acknowledged.

Both Piaget and Vygotsky assume that processes of learning are essentially universal. However, not all children may learn effectively in a social situation.

The personality of the learner and style of processing may differ and need to be taken into account in explaining their cognitive development.

Practically, Vygotsky's theory may not be helpful in understanding the learning processes of every child and the idea may not be applicable to all.

4. Uriah is an Ofsted inspector. Over the years he has noticed that excellent learning happens when children who can do a task help children who cannot do it yet.

   Discuss Vygotsky's theory of cognitive development. Refer to Uriah's experience in your answer. *(16 marks)*

Baillargeon's explanation of infant abilities

Spec spotlight

Baillargeon's explanation of early infant abilities, including knowledge of the physical world; violation of expectation research.

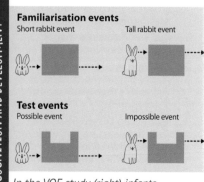

An impossible event?

Apply it

Some babies are watching the 'mouse man'. The mouse man is magic – he can make a mouse appear out of a handkerchief and then disappear, just like that. He forms a 'mouse' from his handkerchief, which peeks out from his hand. Then it turns back into a handkerchief. The babies watch this very carefully – some of them even seem to smile at what the mouse man is doing.

Explain why the babies might be so fascinated by the mouse man. Refer to violation of expectations and Baillargeon's explanation of infant abilities in your answer.

Familiarisation events

Short rabbit event   Tall rabbit event

Test events

Possible event   Impossible event

In the VOE study (right) infants were first 'familiarised' with the task (top row). They were then shown the test events to see how they would react.

Baillargeon's explanation of infant abilities

Object permanence is due to poor motor skills.	Baillargeon suggested that infants in the sensorimotor stage may have a better-developed understanding of the physical world than proposed by Piaget.
	Piaget suggested that infants did not reach for a hidden object because they lacked an understanding of object permanence. Baillargeon suggested it might be because they didn't have the necessary motor skills.
VOE research used to investigate infant abilities.	Baillargeon considered that the methods used by Piaget led him to underestimate children's abilities.
	She developed the violation of expectation (VOE) technique to compare infant reactions to an expected and an unexpected event and thus was able to make inferences about the infant's **cognitive** abilities (see Key study below).
Innate *PRS* gives infant a basic world understanding.	Baillargeon *et al.* (2012) proposed that we are born with a physical reasoning system (PRS) to enable us to learn details of the physical world more easily. This primitive awareness becomes more sophisticated as we learn from experience.
	Baillargeon referred to *object persistence* (similar to Piaget's object permanence) and claimed that this was one such ability.
PRS means infants are *predisposed to attend* and learn from impossible events.	Infants identify *event categories*. Each event category corresponds to one way in which objects interact and children learn about these from birth.
	An innate PRS means that, when an infant is shown an impossible occurrence (tall rabbit event where tall rabbit does not appear), it draws their attention. This will help them to develop their understanding of the physical world.

Key study: Baillargeon and Graber (1987) VOE research

Procedure	24 infants, aged 5–6 months, were shown a tall or a short rabbit passing behind a screen with a window:
	• Possible condition – the tall rabbit can be seen passing the window but the short one cannot.
	• Impossible condition – neither rabbit appeared at the window.
Findings	The infants looked for an average of 33.07 seconds (impossible condition) compared to 25.11 seconds (possible condition).
	This was interpreted as meaning that the infants were surprised at the impossible condition.
	This was presumably because they knew that the tall rabbit should have reappeared at the window.
	This demonstrates an understanding of object permanence at less than 6 months of age.

One strength is the VOE technique provides a better understanding of infants.

Piaget assumed that when an infant failed to search for a hidden object, the infant thought it no longer existed.

Another interpretation would be that they were simply losing interest, but use of the VOE technique enables us to control this possibility.

This means that Baillargeon's explanation provides a more **valid** account of infant abilities than Piagetian theories.

One limitation is that it is hard to judge what an infant understands.

Using the VOE technique we are predicting how a baby might behave if a violation of expectations occurred. However, they might not actually look longer at impossible events than possible events.

Additionally, infants might look for different lengths of time at different events just because they see them as different not necessarily because they have recognised them as impossible.

This raises questions about the validity of the VOE for investigating infant understanding.

A further strength is PRS can explain why physical understanding is universal.

Hespos and van Marle (2012) point out that basic physical properties are understood by almost everyone (e.g. if you drop something it will land on the floor).

The fact that this understanding is universal suggests that it is innate. If it were not innate we would expect cultural differences which have not been found.

Baillargeon argued that the PRS was innate and this is well supported.

A limitation is VOE assumes behavioural responses indicate understanding.

Piaget distinguished between understanding and acting in accordance with a principle. Looking longer, even if it is because the scene is impossible, is not the same as reasoning about the physical world.

This suggests that Piaget and Baillargeon are considering two different processes.

This means that Baillargeon's research is not actually a criticism of Piaget's conclusions.

A strength is the findings are consistent with research on other abilities.

Pei et al. (2007) found that infants can use crude patterns to judge distance from an early age but that more subtle texture differences require more experience.

Distance perception therefore appears to be another innate system that becomes more sophisticated with age like the PRS.

Therefore, it is likely many cognitive systems develop at least partially in tandem and the fact that other abilities develop in the same way as VOE is supportive of Baillargeon's PRS theory.

Ey up, here he comes again – that psychologist just won't leave me alone.

REVISION BOOSTER

In an exam answer, be careful how you express the criticisms made of Piaget by Baillargeon (and Vygotsky). Neither of them disagree with Piaget's theory in its entirety – they suggest how it can be developed and refined. Be clear about what these refinements are – Baillargeon's focus was on how Piaget's methodology led him to underestimate young children's abilities.

KNOWLEDGE CHECK

1. Using examples, explain what is meant by 'knowledge of the physical world' in relation to Baillargeon's explanation of early infant abilities. *(3 marks)*

2. Describe **one** study into violation of expectation in the context of Baillargeon's explanation of early infant abilities. In your answer, explain what the researcher(s) did and what was found. *(6 marks)*

3. Evaluate research into Baillargeon's explanation of early infant abilities. *(6 marks)*

4. Describe and evaluate Baillargeon's explanation of early infant abilities. Refer to evidence in your answer. *(16 marks)*

Social cognition: Selman's levels of perspective-taking

Spec spotlight

The development of social cognition: Selman's levels of perspective-taking.

Oh yeah, all Selman thinks about is how other people would feel if I was rescued – how would Holly feel, how would her Dad feel, how would her friend feel? Well, no one ever asks how I would feel. Maybe I like being stuck up here. Maybe I don't want to be rescued... has anyone considered that?

Guys? Guys – come back, I was only joking! Help!

Apply it

Peggy is 11 and her brother Pavel is 7. They both have a tablet, but their parents try to keep their use to a minimum. So Peggy and Pavel are not allowed to use them in bed, for instance. Pavel says, 'I want to use it in bed because I like it and it's mine.' But his sister explains to him, 'Mummy and daddy don't want us to stay up all night playing games on our tablet. They want us to go to sleep – it's for our own good.'

Use your knowledge of Selman's theory of the development of social cognition to explain Pavel's and Peggy's comments.

CHAPTER 7: COGNITION AND DEVELOPMENT

Selman's levels of perspective-taking

Domain-general versus *domain-specific*.	Selman (1971, 1976) disagreed with Piaget's domain-general approach to development and proposed that social perspective-taking develops separately from other aspects of **cognitive** development (domain-specific).
Perspective-taking assessed with *scenarios*.	Selman's assessment procedure involved asking children to take the role of different people in a social situation and consider how each person felt.
	One scenario featured a child called Holly who has promised her father she will no longer climb trees, but who then comes across her friend whose kitten is stuck up a tree.
	The child participant was asked to explain how each person (Holly, her friend and her father) would feel if Holly did or did not climb the tree to rescue the kitten.
Selman's stage theory begins with *egocentrism*.	Selman (1976) found that children of different ages responded in different ways. He used these differences to build a stage theory of how thinking about social situations changes. • Stage 0 (3–6 years) *Socially egocentric* – a child cannot distinguish between their own emotions and those of others nor explain the emotional states of others.
Children *progressively* see another person's perspective.	• Stage 1 (6–8 years) *Social information role-taking* – a child can now distinguish between their own point of view and that of others, but can only focus on one perspective at a time. • Stage 2 (8–10 years) *Self-reflective role-taking* – a child can explain the position of another person and appreciate their perspective but can still only consider one point of view at a time. • Stage 3 (10–12 years) *Mutual role-taking* – a child is now able to consider their own point of view and that of another at the same time.
The final stage focuses on *social conventions*.	• Stage 4 (12 years +) *Social and conventional system role-taking* – a child recognises that understanding others' viewpoints is not enough to allow people to reach agreement. Social conventions are needed to keep order.
Selman added *three further elements* to fully explain social development.	(1) *Interpersonal understanding:* this is what Selman measured in his earlier research. Being able to take different roles is evidence that we understand social situations. (2) *Interpersonal negotiation strategies:* we also have to develop skills in how to respond to the social situations. This could include learning to negotiate and manage conflict. (3) *Awareness of personal meaning of relationships:* in addition to understanding and managing social situations we also need to be able to reflect on social behaviour in the context of life history and the full range of relationships.

One strength is that there is strong research evidence.

Selman (1971) found positive **correlations** between age and the ability to take different perspectives.

This is supported by **longitudinal** follow-up studies (e.g. Gurucharri and Selman 1982) which confirm that perspective-taking develops with age.

This is a strength of the levels idea generally, particularly as it is supported by a range of evidence.

Bullies were actually found not to have perspective-taking deficits. They were just mean. Plain and simple.

One limitation is mixed evidence as to how important perspective-taking is.

Buijzen and Valkenburg (2008) found a negative correlation between age, perspective-taking and coercive behaviour. This suggests that perspective-taking is important in developing prosocial behaviour.

However, Gasser and Keller (2009) found that bullies displayed no difficulties in perspective-taking.

We cannot therefore conclude from such mixed evidence that perspective-taking enables socially desirable behaviour.

REVISION BOOSTER

Disagree with one of our conclusions? Great! We don't claim to be perfect but we are getting better.

Try to write your own, improved version.

Another strength is the theory helps understand some atypical development.

Marton *et al.* (2009) compared 8–12-year-old children diagnosed with ADHD with a **control group**, looking at performance on perspective-taking tasks. They found those with ADHD did worse on scenario understanding.

The ADHD group also did worse on identifying the feelings of each person involved and evaluating the consequences of different actions.

This means that research has identified a key social cognitive deficit in this group of people, supporting the usefulness of the theory in helping us to ultimately intervene and support people with atypical development.

*ADHD (sometimes referred to as 'ADD') stands for **attention deficit hyperactivity disorder**, a condition characterised by inappropriate inattention, impulsiveness and motor hyperactivity which is inappropriate for a child's age.*

KNOWLEDGE CHECK

1. Explain what is meant by the term 'social cognition'. *(4 marks)*

2. In the context of the development of social cognition, outline Selman's levels of perspective-taking. *(6 marks)*

Another limitation is only one aspect of social development is considered.

Selman's theory looks only at cognitive factors whereas children's social development involves more than their developing cognitive abilities.

For example, internal factors (e.g. empathy) and external factors (e.g. family atmosphere) are important and it is likely social development is due to a combination of these.

Therefore, it can be argued that to consider the one element of perspective-taking in isolation gives an oversimplified account of social development.

3. In relation to the development of social cognition, describe **one** study of Selman's levels of perspective-taking. *(6 marks)*

4. Parents post on a website about their children's ability to understand other people's points of view. Parents with more than one child agree that it all depends on how old they are.

A strength is support for learning perspective-taking through experience.

Wu and Keysar (2007) found that young adult Chinese participants did significantly better in perspective-taking than matched Americans.

This indicates that the development of perspective-taking is influenced by socio-cultural inputs and not just maturity.

This supports Selman's assumption that both maturity level and the social environment contribute to perspective-taking development.

Describe and evaluate Selman's levels of perspective-taking as an explanation of the development of social cognition. *(16 marks)*

Social cognition: Theory of mind (ToM)

Spec spotlight

The development of social cognition: theory of mind, including theory of mind as an explanation for autism; the Sally–Anne study.

Mum, where's my chocolate? I don't want to be in the psychological study anymore, I just want my chocolate!!

False belief

A false belief is a belief in something that is incorrect. For example, Maxi holds a false belief that the chocolate is in the blue cupboard. ToM enables a person to understand that what is in your mind is not the same as what is in someone else's mind, i.e. you or the other person may have a false belief.

The Sally–Anne task

Sally puts the marble in her basket

While Sally is away Anne moves the marble to her box

When Sally returns, where will she look for her marble?

Theory of mind (ToM)

ToM is the ability to *mind-read*.	ToM is not a theory like 'Piaget's theory' but a personal theory or belief about what other people know, are feeling or thinking. It is tested via different methods depending on age.
Testing ToM in toddlers – *beads in a jar*.	Meltzoff (1988) allowed children to observe adults placing beads into a jar. • **Experimental condition**: adults appeared to struggle with this and dropped the beads. • **Control condition**: adults successfully placed the beads in the jar. In both conditions toddlers successfully placed the beads in the jar, suggesting that they were imitating what the adult intended to do rather than what they actually did, demonstrating ToM.
Testing ToM using a *false belief task*.	Wimmer and Perner (1983) told 3–4-year-olds a story in which: • Maxi left his chocolate in a blue cupboard in the kitchen. • After Maxi's mother had used some of the chocolate in her cooking she placed the remainder in a green cupboard. The children had to say where Maxi would look for his chocolate – most 3-year-olds incorrectly said that Maxi would look in the green cupboard whilst most 4-year-olds correctly identified the blue cupboard, demonstrating ToM.
Testing ToM using the *Sally–Anne task*.	Children were told a story involving two dolls, Sally and Anne. • Sally places a marble in her basket. • Sally leaves the room. • Anne moves the marble to her box. • Sally returns. • Where does Sally look for her marble? In order to understand that Sally does not know that Anne has moved the marble, you need an understanding of Sally's false belief about where it is.
Lack of ToM demonstrated in children with *ASD*.	Baron-Cohen *et al.* (1985) used the Sally–Anne task to test 20 high-functioning children diagnosed with autistic spectrum disorder (ASD), a **control group** of 14 children with Down's Syndrome and 27 children without a diagnosis. 85% of children in the control group correctly identified where Sally would look for her marble but only 20% of the ASD group did, suggesting that ASD involves a ToM deficit.
Testing ToM using the *Eyes Task*.	Older children with ASD can succeed on false belief tasks, despite problems with empathy, social communication, etc. This questions whether ASD can be explained by ToM deficits. Baron-Cohen *et al.* (1997) developed the Eyes Task as a more challenging test of ToM and found that adults with high functioning ASD struggled. This supports the idea that ToM deficits might be the cause of ASD.

One limitation is the low **validity** of false belief tasks.

Bloom and German (2000) suggest that false belief tasks require other **cognitive** abilities (e.g. memory) as well as ToM. Studies that provide visual aids to help with memory of false belief stories have found that younger children may succeed.

Furthermore, a child can have a well-developed ToM and still struggle with false belief tasks. And children who cannot perform well on false belief tasks still enjoy pretend-play, which requires a ToM.

These two arguments suggest that false-belief tasks do not measure ToM, which challenges the validity of ToM research.

Woman: 'I wonder what he's thinking. I wonder if he's wondering what I'm thinking. Maybe we're thinking the same thing.'

Man: 'I wonder if United are winning.'

Another limitation is it's difficult to distinguish ToM from perspective-taking.

It is suggested that many of the methods used to study ToM (including the Sally–Anne task) could actually be measures of perspective-taking.

In addition, Rehfeldt *et al.* (2007) suggest perspective-taking tasks are also able to distinguish between ASD children and others.

If ToM is basically the same as perspective-taking then the concept lacks any usefulness.

Paul is 2½ years old and has left his favourite teddy carefully on his bookshelf. While he was at nursery, his mum tidied his room and placed his teddy in a box by his bed.

Using your knowledge of theory of mind, suggest where Paul would look for his teddy and explain why.

One strength is the application to understanding ASD.

ToM research has been useful in helping us understand the differing experiences of people with ASD. Baron-Cohen even suggests that ASD is a direct result of ToM.

Tager-Flusberg (2007) reports that recent research does not support the idea that ToM problems are specific to ASD and that all people with ASD have ToM deficits.

This means that ASD and ToM may not be as closely linked as was once believed and ToM is only a partial explanation for ASD.

A limitation is that there is no clear understanding of how ToM develops.

Perner *et al.* (2002) adopted a Piagetian approach and suggested that ToM develops in line with other cognitive abilities (domain-general). This view suggests ToM is based on an innate ability which develops with age.

However, Astington (1998) takes a more Vygotskian approach, focusing on the social influences that affect ToM and suggesting we internalise our ToM during early interactions with adults.

A lack of understanding of the origins of ToM should not stop us using the idea, though it would be preferable to understand where the difficulties come from as that may inform treatments for ASD.

KNOWLEDGE CHECK

1. In relation to the development of social cognition, outline the Sally–Anne study. **(6 marks)**
2. In the context of the development of social cognition, outline theory of mind as an explanation for autism. **(6 marks)**
3. Describe **one** study of the theory of mind explanation of the development of social cognition. In your answer, explain what the researcher(s) did and what was found. **(6 marks)**
4. Discuss theory of mind as an explanation of the development of social cognition. **(16 marks)**

Another limitation is that the validity of the Eyes Task is questioned.

The Eyes Task is criticised because looking at a static pair of eyes is different from real-life experiences of seeing a face as part of a dynamic interaction.

As such, conclusions about ToM that result from the use of the task lack validity.

This suggests that the Eyes Task is not a valid and realistic measure of ToM and questions the conclusions about ASD.

Social cognition: The mirror neuron system

Spec spotlight

The role of the mirror neuron system in social cognition.

Makes you feel like yawning? That'll be your mirror neurons.

Apply it

Two brothers are sitting opposite each other colouring in drawings. Their mum is watching them. Slowly, Lachlan lifts his right hand, points his finger and picks his nose with it. Without any fuss at all, Lancelot does exactly the same thing. Mum has noticed this before in other ways too and she wonders what the explanation could be.

With reference to psychological research, explain how mirror neurons could be responsible for Lachlan's and Lancelot's contagious nose-picking.

The role of mirror neurons

Mirror neurons respond to *motor activity* of others.	Rizzolatti *et al.* (2002) noted that the same area of the monkey's motor cortex became activated when: • Monkeys observed a researcher reaching for his lunch. • The monkey itself reached for food. The researchers later confirmed that it was the same brain cells firing.
Mirror neurons help us experience the *intentions* of others.	Gallese and Goldman (1998) suggested that mirror neurons respond not just to observed actions but to intentions behind behaviour. We need to understand the intentions of others in order to interact socially. Research on mirror neurons suggests we actually simulate the action of others in our own brains and thus experience their intentions through our mirror neurons.
Mirror neurons implicated in development of *ToM*.	It has also been suggested that mirror neurons play an important role in perspective-taking and theory of mind (ToM). Mirror neurons can fire in response to others' actions and intentions and this underlies ToM.
Mirror neurons may be key to *human social evolution*.	Ramachandran (2011) suggested that mirror neurons have shaped human **evolution**, in particular how we have evolved as a social species. Mirror neurons enable us to understand intention, emotion and perspective. These are fundamental requirements for living in large groups with the complex social roles and rules that characterise human culture.

Mirror neurons and autistic spectrum disorder (ASD)

Mirror neurons may underlie understanding of *ASD*.	ASD is associated with problems related to social-**cognitive** abilities, such as difficulty with perspective-taking, understanding intention, emotion and ToM. It follows that people with ASD might have a poor mirror neuron system.
The *'broken mirror' theory* of ASD is based on mirror neurons.	Ramachandran and Oberman (2006) have proposed the 'broken mirror' theory of ASD. According to this theory ASD develops due to neurological deficits, including dysfunction in the mirror neuron system. Such dysfunction prevents a child imitating and understanding social behaviour in others. Researchers have observed that, in infancy, children who are later diagnosed with ASD typically mimic adult behaviour less than children with no diagnosis. This may demonstrate innate problems with the mirror neuron system.

One strength is research support for the role of mirror neurons.

Haker et al. (2012) demonstrated via **fMRI** scans that Brodmann's area (part of the brain rich in mirror neurons) is involved in contagious yawning (a simple example of human empathy).

Mouras et al. (2008) found when men watched heterosexual pornography, activity in the *pars opercularis* (rich in mirror neurons) was seen immediately before sexual arousal. This suggests that mirror neurons produced perspective-taking, making the pornography arousing.

Both studies support the importance of mirror neurons in social cognition showing that regions of the brain believed to be rich in mirror neurons activate when empathy or perspective-taking take place.

'Look pal, quit staring or there's gonna be trouble.' Dermot was not quite old enough to understand how mirrors work.

One limitation is the difficulties involved in studying the system in humans.

Evidence for mirror neuron activity usually comes from brain scanning. This technique identifies activity levels in regions of the brain but cannot measure activity in individual brain cells.

Inserting electrodes is the only way of measuring activity at a cellular level and is not ethically possible in humans.

Mirror neuron research is therefore based on inferences from measuring general activity in areas of the brain and as such cannot provide direct evidence of mirror neuron activity.

REVISION BOOSTER

You could get this question in the exam: 'Explain what a mirror neuron is' for 3 marks. Nice! But let's face it, you're more likely to get, 'Explain the role of the mirror neuron system in social cognition' for 6 marks. So consider very carefully what that word 'role' means (in understanding intentions, enabling perspective-taking, allowing social evolution).

Another limitation is mixed evidence for the link with ASD.

Hadjikhani (2007) supports the link between ASD and mirror neuron deficits by finding a smaller thickness of the *pars opercularis* in ASD participants.

Other studies using fMRI have shown lower activity in brain areas associated with mirror neurons in participants with ASD.

However, not all such findings have been **replicated** so the reliability of the results remains questionable and consequently the evidence linking ASD to mirror neurons is mixed.

A further limitation is an inability to isolate specialist cells.

Hickok (2009) questions whether mirror neurons exist. This is controversial as other researchers (e.g. Mukamel et al. 2010) do believe there are isolated mirror neurons.

Hickok argues that we only know mirror neurons by their function and have failed thus far to be able to identify individual cells and point to their differences from other neurons.

This challenges the existence of specialist neurons carrying out the mirroring – but it does not deny that the function described is carried out in the brain.

KNOWLEDGE CHECK

1. In the context of social cognition, explain what is meant by the 'mirror neuron system'. *(3 marks)*
2. Outline research into the mirror neuron system in social cognition. *(6 marks)*
3. Briefly evaluate the role of the mirror neuron system in social cognition. *(4 marks)*
4. Discuss the role of the mirror neuron system in social cognition. *(16 marks)*

A final limitation is how mirror neurons function to support social cognition.

Hickok also questions the role of mirror neurons in social cognition even if they do exist.

Hickok suggests that their role may have more to do with using others' behaviour to plan our own.

This suggests that there is still work to do in this area before firm explanations can be made about the role of mirror neurons in social cognition.

Diagnosis and classification of schizophrenia

Spec spotlight

Classification of schizophrenia. Positive symptoms of schizophrenia, including hallucinations and delusions. Negative symptoms of schizophrenia, including speech poverty and avolition.

Reliability and validity in diagnosis and classification of schizophrenia, including reference to co-morbidity, culture and gender bias and symptom overlap.

Auditory hallucinations.

REVISION BOOSTER

You have just over a minute to spend writing for each mark – but make sure you give that time to the short-answer questions. It's probably easier to boost your mark on these rather than on essay questions.

Aiden is an 18-year-old student. He has said to his friends that a voice has told him he has been singled out for great things. Aiden's conversations have changed – he rarely gets to the end of a sentence, he seems distracted all the time and often repeats himself.

Explain why Aiden might be diagnosed with schizophrenia. Refer to positive and negative symptoms.

Classification of schizophrenia

No single defining characteristic.	Schizophrenia is a collection of seemingly unrelated symptoms. There are many misconceptions and exaggerations surrounding the nature of schizophrenia.
DSM-5 and ICD-10 differ.	**DSM**-5: one positive symptom must be present (delusions, hallucinations or speech disorganisation). **ICD**-10: two or more negative symptoms are sufficient for diagnosis (e.g. avolition and speech poverty).

Symptoms of schizophrenia

Positive symptoms = additional experiences beyond those of ordinary existence.

1: *Hallucinations.*	Sensory experiences that have no basis in reality or distorted perceptions of real things. Experienced in relation to any sense. For example, hearing voices or seeing people who aren't there.
2: *Delusions.*	Beliefs that have no basis in reality – make a person with schizophrenia behave in ways that make sense to them but are bizarre to others. For example, beliefs about being a very important person or the victim of a conspiracy.

Negative symptoms = loss of usual abilities and experiences.

1: *Avolition.*	Severe loss of motivation to carry out everyday tasks (e.g. work, hobbies, personal care). Results in lowered activity levels and unwillingness to carry out goal-directed behaviours.
2: *Speech poverty.*	A reduction in the amount and quality of speech. May include a delay in verbal responses during conversation. DSM emphasises speech disorganisation and incoherence.

Issues in diagnosis

Key issues.	1. Reliability: the extent to which the diagnosis of schizophrenia is consistent. 2. **Validity**: the extent to which the diagnosis and classification techniques measure what they are designed to measure, in this case to measure schizophrenia. 3. Co-morbidity: occurrence of two illnesses together which confuses diagnosis and treatment. 4. Symptom overlap: when two or more conditions share symptoms, questioning the validity of the classification.

One limitation of a diagnosis of schizophrenia is low reliability.

Cheniaux *et al.* (2009) had two psychiatrists independently diagnose 100 patients using both DSM and ICD criteria.

Inter-rater reliability was poor. One psychiatrist diagnosed 26 with schizophrenia using DSM and 44 using ICD. Second psychiatrist diagnosed 13 with DSM and 24 with ICD.

This inconsistency between mental health professionals and the different classification systems is a limitation of the diagnosis.

Schizophrenia is often 'co-morbid' with depression.

An additional limitation in the diagnosis of schizophrenia is validity.

A standard way to assess validity of a diagnosis is **criterion validity** – do different assessment systems arrive at the same diagnosis for the same patient?

Cheniaux *et al.*'s study shows that schizophrenia is much more likely to be diagnosed using ICD than DSM.

This suggests that schizophrenia is either over-diagnosed in ICD or under-diagnosed in DSM. This is poor validity and a weakness of the diagnosis.

A further limitation in the diagnosis of schizophrenia is co-morbidity.

Co-morbidity is when two or more conditions occur together. If conditions occur together a lot of the time it might call into question whether they are actually a single condition.

Buckley *et al.* (2009) concluded that around half of patients with a diagnosis of schizophrenia also have a diagnosis of depression (50%) or substance abuse (47%).

In terms of classification, if very severe depression looks like schizophrenia and vice versa, it may be they are a single condition. This confusing picture is a limitation.

Another limitation is gender bias in the diagnosis of schizophrenia.

Longenecker *et al.* (2010) reviewed studies of the prevalence of schizophrenia and concluded that since the 1980s men have been diagnosed more often than women.

Cotton *et al.* (2009) found female patients typically function better than men. This may explain why some women escape diagnosis because their better interpersonal functioning may bias practitioners to under-diagnose schizophrenia.

This is a problem because men and women with similar symptoms may experience differing diagnoses.

A final limitation is cultural bias in the diagnosis of schizophrenia.

African-Americans and English people of African origin are much more likely to be diagnosed with schizophrenia in the UK. Rates in the West Indies and Africa are not high, so this is not due to genetic vulnerability.

Higher diagnosis rates in the UK may be because some behaviours classed as positive symptoms of schizophrenia are 'normal' in African cultures (e.g. hearing voices as part of ancestor communication).

This highlights an issue in the validity of diagnosis because it suggests that individuals from some cultural backgrounds are more likely to be diagnosed than others due to bias.

REVISION BOOSTER

These issues – validity, reliability, co-morbidity – may be quite familiar to you by now. It would be straightforward to write a general description of these concepts in an exam answer, but try to avoid this even in a short-answer question. You must THINK LINK – explain clearly how the concepts relate to schizophrenia, use examples and evidence to make the link and keep your answer relevant.

Also, in an essay, you must use the concepts of validity, reliability, etc., as evaluation – therefore you must shape them as we have tried to do here.

KNOWLEDGE CHECK

1. Briefly describe **two** symptoms of schizophrenia.
   (2 marks + 2 marks)
2. Distinguish between positive and negative symptoms of schizophrenia. *(4 marks)*
3. In relation to diagnosis and classification of schizophrenia, explain what is meant by 'co-morbidity' and 'symptom overlap'. Use examples in your answer.
   (3 marks + 3 marks)
4. Discuss reliability and validity in the diagnosis and classification of schizophrenia. *(16 marks)*

Biological explanations for schizophrenia

Spec spotlight

Biological explanations for schizophrenia: genetics, the dopamine hypothesis and neural correlates.

Twin studies

MZ twins share 100% of genes but DZ twins only 50% (on average) – so we would expect a greater likelihood of both MZ twins developing schizophrenia if it is mostly genetic.

This is because both MZ and DZ twins are raised together in the same environment, but MZ twins have a greater degree of genetic similarity than DZs.

Genetic basis

Schizophrenia *runs in families*.	Strong relationship between genetic similarity of family members and likelihood of both developing schizophrenia.
	Gottesman's (1991) family study found **MZ twins** have a 48% shared risk of schizophrenia. **DZ twins** have a 17% shared risk and siblings (about 50% genes shared) have a 9% shared risk (see graph on left).
Schizophrenia is *polygenetic* and *aetiologically heterogeneous*.	Existence of different candidate genes indicates the following: • Each individual gene confers a small increased risk of schizophrenia (i.e. schizophrenia is polygenetic). • Different combinations can lead to schizophrenia (i.e. schizophrenia is aetiologically heterogeneous). Ripke *et al.* (2014) studied 37,000 patients and found 108 separate genetic variations associated with increased risk; many coded for the **dopamine** neurotransmitter.

As genetic similarity increases so does the probability of sharing schizophrenia. Source: Gottesman (1991)

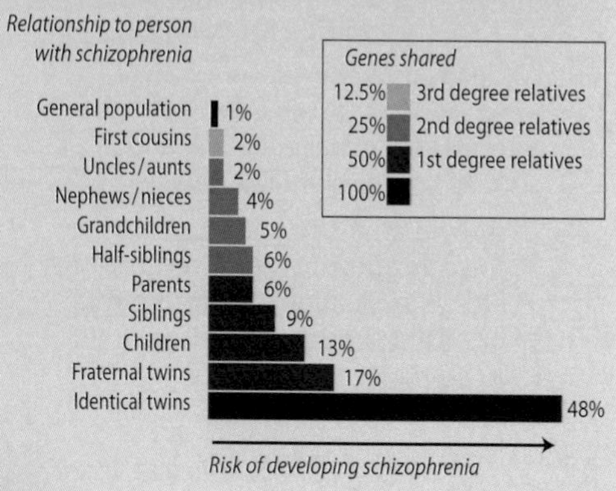

Relationship to person with schizophrenia

Genes shared
12.5% 3rd degree relatives
25% 2nd degree relatives
50% 1st degree relatives
100%

General population 1%
First cousins 2%
Uncles/aunts 2%
Nephews/nieces 4%
Grandchildren 5%
Half-siblings 6%
Parents 6%
Siblings 9%
Children 13%
Fraternal twins 17%
Identical twins 48%

Risk of developing schizophrenia

Findings from Gottesman's study.

Dopamine hypothesis

Role of *dopamine*.	Dopamine (DA) is widely believed to be involved in schizophrenia because it is featured in the functioning of brain systems related to the symptoms of schizophrenia.
Hyperdopaminergia linked to subcortex.	High dopamine activity in subcortex (central areas of the brain) associated with hallucinations and poverty of speech (e.g. excess of dopamine receptors in Broca's area).
Hypodopaminergia: linked to prefrontal cortex.	More recent versions of the hypothesis have focused on low levels of dopamine in the prefrontal cortex (responsible for thinking and decision-making).

REVISION BOOSTER

Many students oversimplify the dopamine hypothesis: 'High dopamine levels cause schizophrenia.' But it's not as simple as that, as hopefully you can see from this spread.

Neural correlates

Brain activity linked with *symptoms*.	Neural correlates are measurements of the structure or function of the brain that correlate with the positive or negative symptoms of schizophrenia.
Avolition + ventral striatum.	Ventral striatum is involved in anticipation of reward (related to motivation). Loss of motivation (avolition) in schizophrenia may be explained by low activity levels here. Juckel *et al.* (2006) found a negative **correlation** between ventral striatum activity and overall negative symptoms.
Hallucinations + superior temporal gyrus.	Allen *et al.* (2007) found that patients experiencing auditory hallucinations recorded lower activation levels in the superior temporal gyrus and anterior cingulate gyrus.

One strength is the strong evidence for genetic vulnerability to schizophrenia.

The Gottesman (1991) family study clearly shows how genetic similarity and shared risk of schizophrenia are closely related.

Adoption studies (Tienari et al. 2004) show children of people with schizophrenia are still at heightened risk of schizophrenia if adopted into families without a history of schizophrenia.

So schizophrenia may not be entirely genetic, but there is overwhelming evidence that genetic factors make some people more vulnerable.

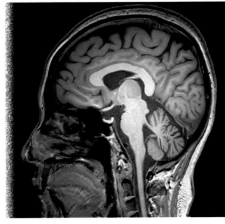

Is schizophrenia a problem in the brain?

One limitation is that there is mixed support for the dopamine hypothesis.

Dopamine agonists (e.g. amphetamines) that increase dopamine can induce schizophrenic-like symptoms in people without schizophrenia. Antipsychotic drugs that lower dopamine can be effective in reducing symptoms.

However, some of the candidate genes identified code for the production of other neurotransmitters such as glutamate.

This suggests that dopamine cannot provide a complete explanation for schizophrenia and that it is just one important factor.

Scarlett does not know that the man she has called 'dad' all her life is not her biological father. Her mum is now concerned because Scarlett is planning to start a family, and they never got round to telling her the truth. Scarlett's biological father had schizophrenia and her mum thinks the 'family curse' might be passed on to her grandchildren.

Use your knowledge of schizophrenia to explain why Scarlett's mum is both right and wrong to be concerned.

Another limitation is the correlation–causation problem.

The question that remains is whether unusual activity in the brain causes the symptoms or whether there are other possible explanations for the correlation.

A negative correlation may suggest that low activity in the ventral striatum *causes* avolition. But it could be that avolition means that less information passes through the striatum *resulting* in the low activity.

Therefore, although neural correlates exist, they tell us relatively little about the causes of schizophrenia.

One strength is that the role of mutation supports the genetic explanation.

Schizophrenia can take place in the absence of family history of the disorder (e.g. through mutation of paternal DNA in sperm cells caused by radiation, poison or viral infection).

Brown et al. (2002) found a link between paternal age (associated with increased risks of mutation) and risk of schizophrenia, increasing from 0.7% in fathers under 25 to 2% in fathers over 50.

This evidence supports the importance of genetic factors in the development of schizophrenia.

KNOWLEDGE CHECK

1. In relation to biological explanations for schizophrenia, explain what is meant by 'neural correlates'. *(3 marks)*

2. Outline the dopamine hypothesis as a biological explanation for schizophrenia. *(6 marks)*

3. Evaluate genetics **or** neural correlates as a biological explanation for schizophrenia. *(6 marks)*

4. Describe and evaluate **two or more** biological explanations for schizophrenia. *(16 marks)*

One limitation is that it is clear that the environment is also involved.

After all, the probability of developing schizophrenia even if your identical twin has it is less than 50%.

There is evidence that environmental factors (e.g. family functioning during childhood) can also play a role in the development of schizophrenia.

This suggests that schizophrenia may be the result of a combination of **biological** and psychological approaches (as acknowledged by the interactionist approach).

Psychological explanations for schizophrenia

Spec spotlight

Psychological explanations for schizophrenia: family dysfunction and cognitive explanations, including dysfunctional thought processing.

Schizophrenia may be caused by communication problems.

Apply it

Connor is being interviewed by a psychiatrist because he is experiencing disturbing symptoms. He believes that aliens from Mars are beaming ideas into his head. The interview is difficult because Connor finds it hard to concentrate and his conversation is very disorganised. He mixes up words so his speech doesn't make sense.

How could the psychiatrist explain Connor's behaviour in terms of cognitive factors?

Delicious dates

'Do we have to remember all these dates?' Every teacher is asked this about 83 times a year. The answer is, 'No. Although the examiner will be impressed if you can remember the main ones...' We provide the dates in this guide just to give you a sense of psychology's timeline.

Family dysfunction

Schizophrenogenic mothers Rejecting and controlling.	Fromm-Reichmann's (1948) **psychodynamic** explanation based on patients' early experiences of 'schizophrenogenic mothers' (mothers who cause schizophrenia). These mothers are cold, rejecting and controlling, and create a family climate of tension and secrecy. This leads to distrust and paranoid delusions and schizophrenia.
Double-bind theory Conflicting family communication.	Bateson *et al.* (1972) described how a child may be regularly trapped in situations where they fear doing the wrong thing, but receive conflicting messages about what counts as wrong. They cannot express their feelings about the unfairness of the situation. When they 'get it wrong' (often) the child is punished by withdrawal of love – they learn the world is confusing and dangerous, leading to disorganised thinking and delusions.
Expressed emotion Criticism and hostility lead to relapse in patients.	Expressed emotion (EE) is the level of emotion (mainly negative) expressed towards the schizophrenic patient and includes: • Verbal criticism of the patient. • Hostility towards them. • Emotional over-involvement in their life. High levels of EE cause stress in the patient, a primary explanation for relapse in patients with schizophrenia.

Cognitive explanations

Dysfunctional thought processing.	Lower levels of information processing in some areas of the brain suggest cognition is impaired. For example, reduced processing in the ventral striatum is associated with negative symptoms.
Metarepresentation leads to hallucinations.	Metarepresentation is the **cognitive** ability to reflect on thoughts and behaviour (Frith *et al.*1992). This dysfunction disrupts our ability to recognise our thoughts as our own – could lead to the sensation of hearing voices (hallucination) and having thoughts placed in the mind by others (delusions).
Dysfunction of central control leads to speech poverty.	Frith *et al.* (1992) also identified dysfunction of central control as a way to explain speech poverty – central control being the cognitive ability to suppress automatic responses while performing deliberate actions. People with schizophrenia experience derailment of thoughts and spoken sentences because each word triggers automatic associations that they cannot suppress.

One limitation is that evidence for family relationships is often retrospective.

Read *et al.* (2005) reviewed 46 studies and concluded that 69% of all adult female inpatients with schizophrenia (59% of men) had a history of physical and/or sexual abuse in childhood.

But most of this evidence is based on information about childhood experiences gathered after the diagnosis. The symptoms may have distorted the patients' recall of their childhood experiences.

This creates a problem with the **validity** of the evidence.

Another limitation is that the evidence for family-based explanations is weak.

Poor childhood experiences may be associated with schizophrenia, but there is little evidence to support the importance of schizophrenogenic mothers, expressed emotion or double-bind.

These theories are mainly based on clinical observation of patients (open to interpretation). They have also historically led to blaming of parents already suffering over their child's symptoms.

These issues undermine the appropriateness and credibility of the family-based explanation.

Family evidence for schizophrenia may be flawed.

One strength is support for different information processing.

Stirling *et al.* (2006) compared 30 patients with schizophrenia with 18 non-patients (**control group**) on cognitive tasks (e.g. in the Stroop Test participants had to name the ink colour of colour words).

Patients took over twice as long as the control group to suppress the impulse to read the word and to name the ink colour instead. This supports Frith's theory of central control dysfunction. Other evidence also shows that processing differs in schizophrenic patients.

However, it is not clear whether these faulty cognitions are merely the proximal cause (i.e. cause of the symptoms) or the underlying distal cause (i.e. the origins of the disorder).

REVISION BOOSTER

Only family dysfunction and dysfunctional thought processing are named on the specification as psychological explanations for schizophrenia. There are plenty of others, but don't feel you have to learn additional material. LESS IS MORE! It is much better to have a really clear understanding of two explanations than to know a little bit about lots of them.

Another limitation is biological factors are sometimes overlooked.

Psychological explanations can be hard to reconcile with biological ones (e.g. genetics). If the biological explanations are valid, how do they fit with psychological ones?

Perhaps both biological and psychological factors can separately produce the same symptoms – this raises the question of whether both outcomes are really schizophrenia.

Alternatively, we can view this in terms of the **diathesis-stress model** where the diathesis may be biological or psychological.

KNOWLEDGE CHECK

1. In relation to psychological explanations for schizophrenia, explain what is meant by 'dysfunctional thought processing'. *(3 marks)*
2. Briefly outline **two** psychological explanations for schizophrenia.
   (3 marks + 3 marks)
3. Explain **one** criticism of cognitive explanations for schizophrenia. *(4 marks)*
4. Outline and evaluate family dysfunction as a psychological explanation for schizophrenia. In your answer refer to another explanation for schizophrenia. *(16 marks)*

A final limitation of the cognitive explanation is direction of causality.

It remains unclear whether cognitive factors are a cause or a result of the neural correlates and abnormal neurotransmitter levels in schizophrenia.

For example, does dysfunctional metarepresentation reduce levels of **dopamine** in the superior temporal gyrus? Or is the direction of causality the reverse?

This questions the validity of the cognitive approach in explaining the underlying origins of the condition.

Biological therapies for schizophrenia: Drug therapy

Spec spotlight

Drug therapy: typical and atypical antipsychotics.

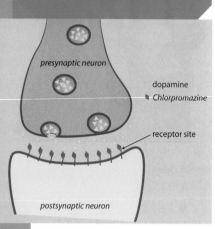

presynaptic neuron

dopamine
■ *Chlorpromazine*

receptor site

postsynaptic neuron

Chlorpromazine *acts as a dopamine antagonist, i.e. it acts against dopamine, in this case by blocking dopamine receptors at the postsynaptic neuron.*

REVISION BOOSTER

Typical and atypical antipsychotics are named on the specification. This means you could be asked to outline one or the other or both. For the full 6 AO1 marks, it's very unlikely you would have to describe just one of them. So your best strategy is to revise 3 marks' worth of AO1 material for both.

REVISION BOOSTER

Don't feel you have to memorise the exact content of the critical points given here. The explanations are meant to show you how to fully elaborate your point – provide evidence, examples, elaboration and finally link back/draw a conclusion. Trying to memorise all the details may just mean you have too much in your head. But do try to remember some of the detailed information to give your point critical power.

Typical antipsychotics

Dopamine antagonists.	Typical antipsychotic drugs (e.g. *chlorpromazine*) have been around since the 1950s.
	They work by acting as antagonists in the dopamine system and aim to reduce the action of dopamine – they are strongly associated with the dopamine hypothesis.
Block dopamine receptors in the synapses.	Dopamine antagonists work by blocking dopamine receptors in the synapses in the brain, reducing the action of dopamine.
	Initially, dopamine levels build up after taking *chlorpromazine*, but then production is reduced.
	This normalises neurotransmission in key areas of the brain, which in turn reduces symptoms like hallucinations.
Chlorpromazine also has sedation effect.	*Chlorpromazine* also has an effect on histamine receptors which appears to lead to a sedation effect.
	Therefore it is also used to calm anxious patients when they are first admitted to hospital.

Atypical antipsychotics

Target *dopamine* and **serotonin**.	Atypical antipsychotics such as *Clozapine* have been used since the 1970s.
	The aim of these drugs was to improve effectiveness of drugs in suppressing psychoses such as schizophrenia and also minimise the side effects.
	They typically target a range of neurotransmitters including dopamine and serotonin.
Clozapine acts on dopamine, glutamate and serotonin to improve mood.	*Clozapine* binds to dopamine receptors as *chlorpromazine* does but also acts on serotonin and glutamate receptors.
	This drug was more effective than typical antipsychotics – clozapine reduces depression and anxiety in patients as well as improving **cognitive** functioning.
	It also improves mood, which is important as up to 50% of people suffering from schizophrenia attempt suicide.
Risperidone is as effective as *clozapine* but safer.	*Risperidone* was developed because *clozapine* was involved in the deaths of some patients from a blood condition called agranulocytosis.
	Risperidone like *clozapine* binds to dopamine and serotonin receptors.
	But *risperidone* binds more strongly to dopamine receptors and is therefore more effective in smaller doses than most antipsychotics and has fewer side effects.

One strength is the evidence shows antipsychotics are moderately effective.

Thornley *et al.* (2003) reviewed data from 13 trials (1121 participants) and found that *chlorpromazine* was associated with better functioning and reduced symptom severity compared with **placebo**.

There is also support for the benefits of atypical antipsychotics. Meltzer *et al.* (2012) concluded that *clozapine* is more effective than typical antipsychotics, and that it is 30–50% more effective in treatment-resistant cases.

Therefore the evidence suggests that antipsychotics are reasonably effective.

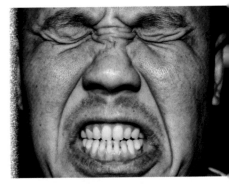

Antipsychotics may have serious side effects.

One limitation of antipsychotic drugs is side effects (mild, serious and fatal).

Typical antipsychotics are associated with dizziness, agitation, sleepiness, weight gain, etc. Long-term use can lead to lip-smacking and grimacing due to dopamine super-sensitivity.

The most serious side effect is *neuroleptic malignant syndrome* (NMS) caused by blocking dopamine action in the hypothalamus (can be fatal due to disrupted regulation of several body systems).

Atypical antipsychotics were developed to reduce side effects but some still exist and this is a serious limitation of antipsychotic drug therapies.

Coral is a 19-year-old university student recently diagnosed with schizophrenia. Her parents are concerned because Coral's psychiatrist has prescribed antipsychotic drugs. The psychiatrist explains that the drugs are atypical antipsychotics. They want to know the difference between these and other antipsychotics. They also want reassurance that the drugs Coral is getting are effective without many side effects.

Use your knowledge of drug therapy to outline what the psychiatrist could tell Coral's parents.

Another limitation is the theoretical objection to the use of antipsychotic drugs.

The use of these drugs is strongly tied up with the dopamine hypothesis and the idea that there are higher than usual levels of dopamine in the subcortex in the brain.

But there is evidence that this may not be correct and that dopamine levels in other parts of the brain are too low rather than too high. If so, antipsychotics shouldn't work.

This has undermined the faith of some people that any positive effects are actually due to the pharmacological effects of antipsychotics.

A further limitation is doubts about the true effectiveness of antipsychotics.

Healy (2012) suggests that data from some successful trials have been published multiple times, exaggerating the positive effects. Also, most studies only review short-term effects.

Healy also suggests that as antipsychotics have powerful calming effects, it is easy to demonstrate that they have a positive effect on patients despite the fact they may not be effective in reducing psychosis.

This suggests that the effectiveness of antipsychotics may be overestimated by much of the empirical research.

A final limitation is that antipsychotic drugs may simply be a 'chemical cosh'.

Antipsychotics may have been used in hospital situations to calm patients and make them easier for staff to work with, rather than to benefit the patients themselves.

Short-term use of antipsychotics to calm patients is recommended by the National Institute for Health and Care Excellence (NICE).

However, this practice is seen by some as a human rights' abuse This raises ethical issues in the use of antipsychotic drugs with schizophrenia patients.

Psychological therapies for schizophrenia

Spec spotlight

Cognitive behaviour therapy and family therapy as used in the treatment of schizophrenia. Token economies as used in the management of schizophrenia.

CBT is a form of talking therapy.

Zara has returned home after a spell on a hospital psychiatric ward. She has schizophrenia and now lives with her mother, two brothers and sister. The family has always been very close and emotions often run high. Although Zara's symptoms are now under control, her community psychiatric nurse is concerned that she might suffer a relapse. The nurse discusses with Zara's family the possibility of family therapy.

Explain how family therapy could help Zara. Use research evidence to support your explanation.

REVISION BOOSTER

Because CBT, family therapy and token economies are all named on the specification, you need to revise all three of these psychological therapies – you could be asked questions specifically on any one of them.

If a 16-mark essay was asked on just one of these there is about 120 words for each explanation on this page, which is enough for the 6 AO1 marks in an essay.

Cognitive behaviour therapy (CBT)

Identify and change *irrational thoughts*.	The aims of **CBT** in general are to help patients identify irrational thoughts and try to change them.
	This may involve discussion of how likely a patient's beliefs are to be true, and consideration of less threatening possibilities.
CBT helps patients to *understand* their symptoms.	Patients are helped to make sense of how their delusions and hallucinations impact on their feelings and behaviour.
	For example, a patient may hear voices and believe they are demons so they will be very afraid.
	Offering explanations for these symptoms reduces anxiety and helps the patient realise their beliefs are not based on reality.

Family therapy

Reduce *expressed emotion* (EE) in the family.	Family therapy is with families rather than individual patients, aiming to improve communication and interaction in the family.
	Family therapists try to reduce stress within the family that may contribute to patient's risk of relapse (reduce levels of EE).
Improve family function by e.g. reduction of guilt and improve understanding.	Pharaoh *et al.* (2010) identified a range of strategies family therapists use to reduce the likelihood of relapse and readmission to hospital. For example:
	1. Reduce stress of caring for a relative with schizophrenia.
	2. Improve ability of family to anticipate and solve problems.
	3. Reduce guilt and anger in family members.
	4. Improve beliefs about and behaviour toward schizophrenia.

Token economies

Tokens used to reinforce desirable behaviours (*operant conditioning*).	Token economies are reward systems (**operant conditioning**) used to manage the behaviour of patients with schizophrenia who spend long periods in psychiatric hospitals.
	Tokens (e.g. coloured discs) are given to patients who carry out desirable behaviours (e.g getting dressed, making a bed, etc.).
	This reward reinforces the desirable behaviour and because it is given immediately prevents 'delay discounting' (reduced effect of a delayed reward).
Tokens are *secondary reinforcers*.	Tokens have no value in themselves but can be swapped later for tangible reward (e.g. sweets, a walk outside, etc.).
	They are secondary reinforcers because they only have value due to the learned association (**classical conditioning**) with innate primary reinforcers.

One limitation of psychological therapies is research shows limited benefits.

Jauhar *et al.* (2014) found CBT had a significant but small effect on positive and negative symptoms. McMonagle and Sultana (2009) found only one of three studies of token economies that used **random allocation** showed improvement.

Pharaoh *et al.* reviewed effectiveness of family therapy and found moderate evidence for the reduction of hospital readmissions over one year and some improvement to quality of life – but the evidence was inconsistent.

Overall there is only modest support for the effectiveness of psychological therapies.

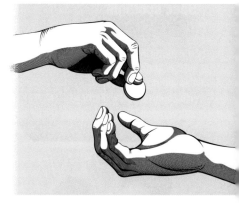

Token economy systems to treat schizophrenia may be effective but ethically questionable.

Another limitation is that psychological therapies may help but not cure.

CBT helps patients make sense of their symptoms. Family therapy reduces the stress of living with schizophrenia. Token economies help to make patients' behaviour more socially acceptable.

These things are all worth doing, but should not be confused with curing schizophrenia.

Biological therapies do not cure schizophrenia either but they do reduce the severity of the symptoms and thus may be more desirable.

A further limitation relates to ethical issues.

Token economy systems are controversial because severely ill patients cannot get privileges because they are less able to comply with desirable behaviours than moderately ill patients – so severely ill patients suffer discrimination.

Also, CBT may challenge a person's paranoia – but might that interfere with their freedom of thought? If, for example, CBT challenges a patient's beliefs in a controlling government, that could stray into modifying their politics.

Ethical issues like these make psychological therapies for schizophrenia controversial.

REVISION BOOSTER

Question 2 below includes the word 'how'. This means you must focus on what a therapist would actually do when delivering treatment.

Another limitation is the quality of some evidence.

Small-scale studies that compare patients before and after psychological therapies have found positive results.

But these studies often lack a **control group** or lack random allocation to conditions – but they are included in reviews.

This may mean that the effectiveness of psychological therapies is overestimated by the evidence.

A final limitation is alternative psychological therapies are under-researched.

For example, NICE recommends art therapy, if a qualified art therapist is available who has experience working with schizophrenia patients.

However, these therapies are not well researched so it is unclear how effective they are.

This questions whether under-researched therapies should be made available to patients.

KNOWLEDGE CHECK

1. In relation to the management of schizophrenia, explain what is meant by the term 'token economy'. Use an example in your answer. *(4 marks)*

2. Explain how cognitive behaviour therapy is used as a treatment of schizophrenia. *(6 marks)*

3. Evaluate family therapy as a treatment of schizophrenia. *(6 marks)*

4. Cognitive behaviour therapy, family therapy and token economies are all used in the treatment and management of schizophrenia.

    Describe and evaluate **two or more** of these treatments of schizophrenia. *(16 marks)*

The interactionist approach to schizophrenia

Spec spotlight

The importance of an interactionist approach in explaining and treating schizophrenia; the diathesis-stress model.

Can a genetic vulnerability be 'triggered' by cannabis use to lead to schizophrenia?

Apply it

Lorenzo was sexually abused as a child. At 14 years old, he started smoking very powerful cannabis.

Amaya and Cecilia are identical twins. Their father is schizophrenic. Amaya is at university facing very important final exams.

Explain how an interactionist approach can help us understand the risk of Lorenzo, Amaya and Cecilia developing schizophrenia.

REVISION BOOSTER

In a 16-mark essay you don't have to write everything on this spread. What is here is actually more than 1000 words!! For a 16-mark essay you probably only have time to write 500 words – but don't cut down the elaboration of the AO3 points. Better to do four elaborated points rather than five briefer ones.

The interactionist approach

***Diathesis-stress model**: vulnerability + trigger = schizophrenia.*	*Diathesis* means vulnerability; *stress* in this context refers to negative psychological experiences. The diathesis-stress model says both a vulnerability and a stress trigger are needed to develop schizophrenia.
Meehl's model: gene + stress = schizophrenia.	In the original diathesis-stress model, diathesis was entirely the result of a single 'schizogene'. Meehl (1962) argued that someone without this gene should never develop schizophrenia, no matter how much stress they were exposed to. But a person who does have the gene is vulnerable to the effects of chronic stress (e.g. a *schizophrenogenic mother*). The schizogene is necessary but not sufficient for the development of schizophrenia.
Modern understanding of *diathesis*.	It is now believed that diathesis is not due to a single 'schizogene'. Instead it is thought that many genes increase vulnerability. Also, diathesis doesn't have to be genetic. It could be early psychological trauma affecting brain development. For example, child abuse affects the hypothalamic-pituitary-adrenal (HPA) system, making a child vulnerable to stress.
Modern understanding of *stress*.	A modern definition of stress (in relation to diathesis-stress) includes anything that risks triggering schizophrenia (including psychological stress). For example, cannabis use can increase the risk of schizophrenia up to seven times depending on dose – probably because it interferes with the **dopamine** system.

Treatment according to the interactionist approach

Antipsychotic medication and *CBT*.	Turkington *et al.* (2006) suggest it is possible to believe in biological causes of schizophrenia and still practise **CBT** to relieve psychological symptoms. But this requires adopting an interactionist model – it is not possible to adopt a purely **biological approach**, tell patients that their condition is purely biological (no psychological significance to their symptoms) and then treat them with CBT.
UK adopts *more interactionist* approach compared to US.	In Britain it is increasingly standard practice to treat patients with a combination of drugs and CBT. In the US there is more of a conflict between psychological and biological models of schizophrenia and this may have led to slower adoption of the interactionist approach.

One strength is support for the dual role of vulnerability and stress.

Tienari et al. (2004) studied children adopted away from schizophrenic mothers. The adoptive parents' parenting styles were assessed and compared with a **control group** of adoptees with no genetic risk.

A child-rearing style with high levels of criticism and conflict and low levels of empathy was implicated in the development of schizophrenia but only for children with a high genetic risk.

This is very strong direct support for the interactionist approach – genetic vulnerability and family-related stress combine in the development of schizophrenia.

Parenting style could contribute to the onset of schizophrenia.

One limitation is that the original diathesis-stress model is too simplistic.

Multiple genes increase vulnerability, each with a small effect on its own – there is no schizogene. Stress comes in many forms, including dysfunctional parenting.

Researchers now believe stress can also include biological factors. For example, Houston et al. (2008) found childhood sexual trauma was a diathesis and cannabis use a trigger.

This shows that the old idea of diathesis as biological and stress as psychological has turned out to be overly simple.

REVISION BOOSTER

Always start an evaluation paragraph with the lead-in line (such as 'One strength is support for the dual role of vulnerability and stress') to alert the examiner that you are about to evaluate. It makes marking so much easier.

Another strength is the usefulness of the interactionist approach in treatment.

Tarrier et al. (2004) **randomly allocated** 315 patients to (1) medication + CBT group, or (2) a medication + supportive counselling group, or (3) a control group.

Patients in the two combination groups showed lower symptom levels than those in the control group (medication only) – but no difference in hospital readmission.

Studies like this show that there is a clear practical advantage to adopting an interactionist approach in the form of superior treatment outcomes.

KNOWLEDGE CHECK

1. Outline the interactionist approach in explaining and treating schizophrenia. *(6 marks)*

2. Describe the importance of the diathesis-stress model in explaining and treating schizophrenia. *(6 marks)*

3. Discuss **one** criticism of the interactionist approach in explaining and treating schizophrenia. *(4 marks)*

One limitation is we don't know exactly how diathesis and stress work.

There is strong evidence to suggest that some sort of underlying vulnerability coupled with stress can lead to schizophrenia.

But we do not understand the mechanisms by which symptoms of schizophrenia appear and how both vulnerability and stress produce them.

This does not undermine support for the approach, but it does mean we have an incomplete understanding of the actual mechanism.

4. Thea has been diagnosed with schizophrenia. Her father was also schizophrenic and she had a traumatic and unpredictable childhood. She is now taking antipsychotics each day and attending CBT sessions.

   Referring to Thea's experience, discuss the diathesis-stress model in the context of explaining **and** treating schizophrenia. *(16 marks)*

A further limitation is the treatment-causation fallacy.

Turkington et al. (2006) argue the fact that combined biological and psychological therapies are more effective than either on their own does not necessarily mean the interactionist approach to schizophrenia is correct.

Similarly the fact that drugs help does not mean that schizophrenia is biological in origin. This error of logic is called the *treatment-causation fallacy*.

It means that the superior outcomes of combined therapies should not be over-interpreted in terms of evidence in support of the interactionist approach.

Explanations for food preferences: Evolutionary

Spec spotlight

Explanations for food preferences: the evolutionary explanation, including reference to neophobia and taste aversion.

It had been a long day.

REVISION BOOSTER

You will never need more than 6 marks' worth of material to describe the evolutionary explanation (or any explanation). So let's do the maths. This is about 150–200 words. If you know six basic points and can write 25 words (on average) for each, then you'll be fine. That's why the AO1 pages of this guide are divided into six points.

Apply it

Kassidy is just a year old and seems to have some firm food preferences. He likes crisps and definitely does not like vegetables. He pulls a 'yuk' face whenever his parents try to get him to eat broccoli. His older sister Gianna went through a similar phase but soon started eating different things. But now she is at primary school she is refusing to try anything new.

How would evolutionary explanations for food preference explain Kassidy's and Gianna's behaviour?

Evolutionary explanations for food preferences

Preference for *sweetness* because reliable signal of high-energy food.	Steiner (1977) found sugar on tongues of newborn babies produced positive facial expressions (upturned mouth corners).
	Fructose is especially sweet and babies consume large amounts if allowed – this makes **evolutionary** sense because fructose is a 'fast-acting' sugar in fruit, providing energy quickly.
Preference for *salt* because used in many cell functions.	Salt taste preference appears in humans at about 4 months.
	Harris *et al.* (1990) found breastfed infants at 16–25 weeks preferred salted cereal – breast milk is low in salt, so this suggests salt preference is innate and not learned.
Preference for *fat* because high in calories and makes foods palatable.	High-calorie foods were usually unavailable to ancestors so learning a preference for fat was an advantage for survival.
	Fat has twice the calories of equivalent carbohydrate/protein – a preference for fat is an efficient route to energy consumption.
	Fat also makes food taste pleasant (palatability) and appeals to other senses (e.g. smell).

Neophobia

Innate unwillingness to try unfamiliar foods that could cause harm.	Food neophobia most pronounced from 2 to 6 years of age.
	Birch (1999) claims neophobia appears when children start to explore and encounter foods independently of parents. Untried foods are potentially dangerous; neophobia is **adaptive** because the child is less likely to eat something causing illness or death.
	Neophobia reduces when we learn specific foods won't poison us – then it is replaced by a different evolutionary mechanism encouraging a varied diet of important nutrients.

Taste aversion

Innate ability to *quickly learn to dislike foods* that may cause harm.	Seligman's (1971) *biological preparedness* concept says we acquire some aversions quicker than others – generally to objects/situations of greatest threat to our ancestors' survival.
	Garcia and Koelling (1966) found rats acquired taste aversion to sweetened water when paired with poison (**classical conditioning**) but not when paired with electric shocks.
	This is an adaptive response aiding survival.
Bitterness: example of an adaptive taste aversion.	Bitter compounds are usually a reliable warning sign of toxins in food – it benefits survival to detect these quickly.
	Steiner (1977) found negative facial expressions in babies in response to bitter taste before any learning of preference – strongly suggests innate mechanism.

One strength of the evolutionary explanation is some research supports it.

Torres *et al.*'s (2008) review of studies concluded humans have a tendency to prefer high-fat foods in periods of stress.

This suggests preference for fat-provided energy to fuel more effective fight or flight response in stressful times.

This supports the explanation because it shows preference is adaptive, giving ancestors survival advantage over those without it.

What? Seriously, what? Do I have something on my face?

One strength is the explanation involves a plausible evolutionary mechanism.

Alcock *et al.* (2014) argue that food preferences evolved as an adaptive response to gut microbes – these influence the host's behaviour to increase its own survival.

De Weerth *et al.* (2013) found a link between infant colic and gut microbes. Pain of colic causes baby to cry so parents increase feeding, delivering more nutrients to the baby's gut, benefitting the microbes.

This suggests ancestors' food preferences were not for their benefit but enhanced survival chances of gut microbes – showing the evolutionary mechanism at work.

Delicious dates

'Do we have to remember all these dates?' Every teacher is asked this about 83 times a year. The answer is, 'No. Although the examiner will be impressed if you can remember the main ones...' We provide the dates in this guide just to give you a sense of psychology's timeline.

One limitation of the explanation is individual differences in taste aversion.

Drewnowski *et al.* (2001) found some people cannot taste the bitter chemical PROP (6-n-propylthiouracil) but others are very sensitive to it and avoid foods containing it.

But bitter compounds (flavonoids, polyphenols) in some foods (soy products, green tea, red wine) may protect against cancer. People who could not detect bitterness could eat foods with anti-cancer properties – an adaptive preference.

PROP insensitivity may be inherited – difficult for evolutionary theory to explain when taste aversion is so important for ancestors' survival (although insensitivity may be linked to something that offered ancestors different survival benefit, i.e. protection against cancer).

Another limitation of the explanation is that neophobia is maladaptive.

Neophobia is a good example of adaptation beneficial to ancestors' survival chances.

But now it is maladaptive because most food is bought from retailers, so safer and more plentiful than ever.

In the modern environment, neophobia restricts variety of children's diet by limiting what they eat.

KNOWLEDGE CHECK

1. In relation to the evolutionary explanation for food preferences, explain what is meant by 'neophobia' and 'taste aversion'.
   (3 marks + 3 marks)

2. Outline the evolutionary explanation for food preferences. Refer in your answer to neophobia **and** taste aversion. *(6 marks)*

3. Briefly evaluate the evolutionary explanation for food preferences. *(4 marks)*

4. Discuss the evolutionary explanation for food preferences. *(16 marks)*

A final limitation is that there are cultural influences on food preferences.

Cashdan (1998) argues that culture plays a major role in determining which foods are accepted and rejected, and also a role in ethnic identity.

Someone brought up in a Jewish Kosher household would probably be repulsed by the idea of eating prawn cocktail with a non-Jewish neighbour.

Food preferences are more difficult to change than other elements of culture (e.g. dress style). Culture influential in preferences, but ignored by evolutionary explanations.

Explanations for food preferences: The role of learning

Spec spotlight

The role of learning in food preference, including social and cultural influences.

Classical conditioning

UCS unconditioned stimulus
UCR unconditioned response
NS   neutral stimulus
CS   conditioned stimulus
CR   conditioned response

Before conditioning:
UCS produces UCR

During conditioning:
NS associated with UCS and becomes CS

After conditioning:
CS produces CR

They loved watching the telly. Imagine how much more they'd enjoy it if they actually turned it on.

Madison has just started at primary school and at lunchtime carefully watches what her friends have to eat. Two friends always have vegetables and love eating them but Madison has never liked them. In class the children all enjoy playing a game on their tablets where they get points for collecting healthy food. Within a few months Madison starts eating all her vegetables, whereas she never did before.

What role does learning play in food preferences? Explain Madison's behaviour in terms of this theory.

The role of learning in food preference

Classical conditioning through *flavour-flavour learning*.	We develop preference for new food by associating it with flavours we already like.
	We innately prefer sweetness so we learn to prefer new foods by sweetening them.
	This association eventually leads to liking new food on its own.
Operant conditioning – children's preferences *reinforced* by parents.	Parents provide rewards (e.g. praise) or punishments for eating certain foods – but it is still hard to establish preference (e.g. to green vegetables) in children using rewards.
	Therefore classical conditioning is probably a more powerful form of food preference learning than operant conditioning.

Social influences

Social learning theory explains social influences such as *family*.	**Social learning theory (SLT):** children acquire food preferences of role models they observe eating certain foods, especially if the model is rewarded and the child identifies with them.
	Family influences: these are the most obvious social influence on preference learning because parents are 'gatekeepers' of children's eating.
Other social influences include *peers* and *media*.	Peer influences: Birch (1980) found children changed vegetable preferences in response to observing other children.
	Media influences: non-family models become important as children get older and more independent of parents' food choices, e.g. TV adverts for 'unhealthy' foods (containing salt, sugar, fat), promoted by characters children identify with.

Cultural influences

Cultural influences on food preferences exerted through *cultural norms*.	Cultural influences are the most reliable indicator of food preferences.
	Cultural norms establish preferences (e.g. attitudes towards what constitutes a 'proper meal'). For example:
	• 'Meat and two veg' – Sunday roast dinner is a common cultural ideal in British households.
	• In Britain and France the cultural tradition is to eat every part of an animal (offal – kidneys, liver, etc.); less so in the US where the preference is steaks/burgers.
Cultural influences involve *classical conditioning* and *vicarious reinforcement*.	Classical conditioning: we associate many foods we eat as adults with happiness growing up (enjoyable times with friends and family, culturally-specific feasts).
	Vicarious reinforcement: culture influences which foods parents present to children, children see parents enjoying these foods (rewarding).

One limitation is classical conditioning alone is not enough.

Flavour-flavour learning explains food preferences and aversions – but evidence is much stronger for aversion learning than preference learning.

For example, Baeyens *et al.* (1996) found pairing new food with a soapy-flavoured chemical (Tween) created a lasting aversion to the food.

This suggests that flavour-flavour learning is less crucial than other learning processes (e.g. repeatedly feeding child a new food without sweetening it).

Christmas. A time for family, culturally-determined food values and horrific jumpers apparently.

Another limitation is that social learning influences are mostly short-term.

Family influences on preferences can last a lifetime, but social learning effects of TV are less persistent.

Hare-Bruun *et al.* (2011) found children who watched most TV also had most unhealthy food preferences. This link was much weaker in a six-year follow-up, and disappeared altogether for girls.

This suggests that the effects of TV are mostly short-term. As children get older, close friends are more powerful social influences on long-term preferences.

A strength of the learning explanation is it can account for multiple influences.

Chilli is one of the most widespread spices in the world. It causes a characteristic 'burn' which is aversive in all cultures. People innately dislike chilli yet still eat it.

In cultures where chilli is traditionally used, children are carefully, gradually and repeatedly exposed to it until 'almost everyone... is converted from a chilli hater to a chilli liker by the age of six years...' (Rozin 2006).

This is a strength of the learning explanation because it shows family and cultural influences can switch innate food aversion into preference via learning and experience.

A strength of the learning explanation is research support for SLT.

Jansen and Tenney (2001) found children's most preferred taste was an energy-dense drink taken at the same time as a teacher who clearly enjoyed it.

Watching someone else enjoy a drink is vicariously reinforcing, especially if you identify with the person (their teacher).

This is a strength because it supports the roles of vicarious reinforcement and identification in social learning of preferences.

Another strength is research support for cultural influences.

A big cultural change in Western societies is the increasing availability of food outside the home, plus a decline in family mealtimes and cooking.

46% of spending on food in the US is food eaten outside the home. American adolescents eat 30% of their meals outside the home, half in fast-food restaurants.

This shows that wider cultural changes do influence the foods people prefer.

KNOWLEDGE CHECK

1. Explain **one** social influence on the learning of food preference. *(3 marks)*
2. Outline social **and/or** cultural influences on the learning of food preference. *(6 marks)*
3. Evaluate the role of learning in food preference. *(6 marks)*
4. Maricel is explaining to Jade what he and his family from the Philippines eat. They like sapin-sapin, a rice and coconut dessert. Jade explains that she and her family love fish and chips.

   Outline and evaluate the roles of social **and** cultural influences on food preferences. Refer to Maricel's and Jade's conversation in your answer. *(16 marks)*

Neural and hormonal mechanisms in eating behaviour

Spec spotlight

Neural and hormonal mechanisms involved in the control of eating behaviour, including the role of the hypothalamus, ghrelin and leptin.

The hypothalamus. A little structure with a big appetite.

hypothalamus

Abbreviate!

VMH. LH. NPY. CCK. There are many common abbreviations that are acceptable – so don't feel you have to memorise all those big words. You can just use the abbreviations.

Apply it

Olga is already obese and is continuing to gain weight. She feels hungry most of the time even though she eats a lot of snacks between meals. But it's never long before she wants to eat again. She eats more than everyone else when she goes out for a meal with her friends. Olga finds her eating behaviour difficult to explain, and wonders if there is something physically wrong with her.

Using your knowledge of neural **and** hormonal mechanisms involved in the control of eating behaviour, explain why Olga has gained weight.

Neural mechanisms

Hypothalamus controls neural and hormonal mechanisms (and maintains homeostasis).	Hypothalamus regulates level of glucose (energy source) in blood. Glucose strongly influences eating behaviour. Neural: glucose-sensing neurons in hypothalamus detect fluctuations in blood glucose concentration. Hormonal: hypothalamus regulates glucose by directing insulin and anti-insulin hormones (e.g. glucagon) in the pancreas. Homeostasis: hypothalamus plays key role in maintaining blood glucose homeostasis within narrow range of values.
Dual-centre model of eating.	Two structures of hypothalamus provide homeostatic control: • 'On switch', lateral hypothalamus (LH). • 'Off switch', ventro-medial hypothalamus (VMH).
Lateral hypothalamus (LH) – on switch.	LH contains cells to detect glucose levels in liver. LH is activated when glucose falls below a certain level ('set point') so the person becomes hungry, triggering a motivation to eat. *Neuropeptide Y* (NPY) also secreted. NPY injected into rats' hypothalamus cause them to eat excessively, becoming obese.
Ventro-medial hypothalamus (VMH) – off switch.	Eating leads to a rise in levels of glucose in the bloodstream and liver (glycogen) – detected by cells in VMH. VMH is triggered once levels increase past a set point – LH activity is inhibited at the same time, so the person becomes satiated (feels full and stops eating). Damage to VMH – Reeves and Plum (1969) studied a woman whose weight doubled in two years. She had a tumour on her VMH causing the normal 'stop eating' function to fail.

Hormonal mechanisms

Ghrelin – appetite stimulant (secreted by stomach).	The longer we go without food (more empty stomach) the more ghrelin is released – the level is detected by receptors in the *arcuate nucleus* of the hypothalamus. When levels rise above a set point the arcuate nucleus signals LH to secrete NPY. Wren *et al.* (2001) found intravenous ghrelin caused a short-term increase in amount of food eaten. Ghrelin level doubles just before a meal and decreases very quickly afterwards.
Leptin – appetite suppressant (secreted by adipose cells).	Leptin blood level increases with fat level and is detected by VMH – part of VMH satiety mechanism. Level of leptin increases beyond a set point – person feels full and stops eating. Licinio *et al.* (2004) studied a rare genetic condition – inability to produce leptin associated with severe obesity. Individuals treated with leptin replacement therapy saw 40% average weight loss and 49% reduction in food intake over 18 months.

AO3
Evaluation

Neural and hormonal mechanisms in eating behaviour

One strength of the dual-centre model is research support.

Hetherington and Ranson (1942) found lesioning VMH of rats made them hyperphagic (overeating) and severely obese. But lesions often damage other parts of the brain.

Gold (1973) found lesions limited to VMH do not produce hyperphagia. This only happened when the paraventricular nucleus (PVN) of hypothalamus was also damaged.

However, this finding is disputed because it has not been **replicated** – overwhelming consensus is that VMH lesions do cause overeating, as predicted by the model.

One limitation of the model is that it is oversimplified.

Valassi *et al.* (2008) argue that even putting social, psychological, and cultural factors to one side, biological contributions to eating behaviour are numerous.

CCK (cholecystokinin) is a hormone – activates the nerve, sending signals to hypothalamus to 'stop eating' – this may be a more powerful appetite suppressant than leptin.

This is a limitation of the model because it presents a relatively straightforward homeostatic account not accurately reflecting the true complexity of eating control.

Another limitation is that the model ignores social and cultural influences.

Woods (2004) claims that the glucostatic view of the dual-centre model is outdated. LH detects falls in glucose levels and stimulates hunger only in 'emergency' of severe energy deprivation.

Normal meal onset is not so much under neurochemical control and is usually initiated by social/cultural lifestyle factors (e.g. traditional times of day for eating).

This is a limitation because it shows a purely **biological approach** to understanding eating behaviour and ignores potentially more influential non-biological factors.

A further limitation is that the model is mostly based on animal research.

We should be cautious about extrapolating findings to humans without considering differences between species that may make **generalisations** invalid.

This is because eating behaviour is more complex in humans than in rats. There are more influences affecting human eating behaviour (e.g. social, psychological, cultural factors).

But studying rats may be a **valid** way of understanding neural and hormonal mechanisms – likely to be similar because most structures found in a human brain are in a rat brain (e.g. hypothalamus).

A strength is that the model gives rise to potentially useful applications.

There is an obesity epidemic in Western nations, so the benefits of finding successful treatments are huge – financial savings for NHS/economy and quality of life for individuals.

Our understanding of eating behaviours must be as complete as possible. Increasing knowledge of neural and hormonal mechanisms can contribute but we must not assume any single explanation has all the answers.

This is a strength because understanding complex interactions between nervous system and hormones makes treatments for obesity and anorexia realistic (e.g. Licinio *et al.*'s research into leptin deficiency).

I'm not overweight, just big-boned.

REVISION BOOSTER

'Neural' refers to how the nervous system/brain controls eating behaviour. 'Hormonal' is about how the endocrine system controls eating behaviour. As is often the case, the wording of the specification means you might have to write about one or the other or both. So getting them mixed up would be bad news for your marks.

KNOWLEDGE CHECK

1. Briefly outline the roles of the hypothalamus, ghrelin and leptin in the control of eating behaviour.
   (2 marks + 2 marks + 2 marks)

2. Describe the neural **and** hormonal mechanisms involved in the control of eating behaviour. *(6 marks)*

3. Briefly evaluate the roles of ghrelin **and** leptin in the control of eating behaviour. *(4 marks)*

4. Discuss neural **and/or** hormonal mechanisms involved in the control of eating behaviour. Refer to research evidence in your answer. *(16 marks)*

Biological explanations for anorexia nervosa

Spec spotlight

Biological explanations for anorexia nervosa, including genetic and neural explanations.

Is there a genetic basis to eating disorders such as anorexia?

Twin studies

MZ twins share 100% of genes but DZ twins only 50% (on average) – so we would expect a greater likelihood of both MZ twins developing anorexia nervosa if it is mostly genetic.

This is because both MZ and DZ twins are raised together in the same environment, but MZ twins have a greater degree of genetic similarity than DZs.

A counselling psychologist runs a therapy group for young women with anorexia nervosa. As she has been doing this for several years, she has noticed that many of her clients are not the only ones in their families to have this disorder. Most of them have a female relative, often a mother or grandmother, who also had anorexia. Some have relatives with other disorders, especially depression.

Use your knowledge of neural **and** genetic explanations for anorexia to explain the psychologist's experience.

Genetic explanations

Studies of MZ and DZ twins show anorexia nervosa (AN) *runs in families*.	Holland *et al.* (1988) found **MZ concordance rate** of 56% but only 5% for **DZs**. Treasure and Holland (1995) found MZ concordance of 65%, with 32% for DZs – still strong evidence for the role of genes.
Researchers have found many *candidate genes* (e.g. Ephx2).	Candidate-gene association study (CGAS) by Scott-Van Zeeland *et al.* (2014) sequenced 152 candidate genes possibly linked with features of AN and found only one gene significantly associated with AN: Ephx2 (epoxide hydrolase 2). This codes for an enzyme involved in cholesterol metabolism – many people in acute phase of AN (when symptoms are severe) have abnormally high levels of cholesterol.
Genome-wide association studies (GWAS) look at the whole collection of human genes.	In contrast with CGAS, GWAS make no assumptions about which genes might be involved in anorexia. Boraska *et al.* (2014) identified 72 separate genetic variations but none were significantly related to AN – possibly because the study was not sensitive enough to detect genetic influences.

Neural explanations

Effects of **serotonin** and **dopamine** studied through *metabolites*.	Neurotransmitter levels in nervous system not studied directly – researchers measure levels of metabolites (chemical byproducts) instead. Main metabolite of serotonin is 5-HIAA (5-hydroxyindoleacetic acid). Main metabolite of dopamine is HVA (homovanillic acid).
Serotonin involved in many AN-related behaviours (e.g. obsessiveness).	Bailer and Kaye (2011) found low levels of 5-HIAA in people with AN return to normal after short-term weight recovery – levels actually increase beyond normal in long-term. Attia *et al.* (2014) found AN patients who did not return to pre-illness weight responded less well to serotonin agonists (drugs) than AN patients restored to a healthy weight. The pattern of results clearly indicates underactivity of the serotonin system in AN.
Decreased *dopamine* levels associated with AN.	Kaye *et al.* (1991) found HVA lower in recovered AN patients compared with controls. Bailer *et al.* (2012) gave amphetamine to participants to increase dopamine release – healthy participants experienced pleasure but AN patients experienced anxiety. Eating increases dopamine release so perhaps AN patients restrict food intake to reduce their anxiety levels.

One limitation of twin studies is 'equal environments' may be incorrect.

MZ and DZ concordance rates are only comparable if MZ and DZ twins are treated with equal degrees of similarity (equal 'environments'). Studies assume this is true.

But MZ twins are treated more similarly than DZs by parents, other family members, friends, teachers. They spend more time together and may even have a closer bond than DZs.

Greater environmental similarity for MZs suggests heritability estimates are artificially inflated and genetic influences on AN are not as great as twin studies suggest.

Studies of MZ (and DZ) twins may be complicated by their very similar environments.

A limitation of gene studies is that AN is polygenic.

Many studies (e.g. Pineiro et al. 2010) show that the search for a single gene is futile. Several candidate genes have been put forward only to 'fall by the wayside' in later research.

No one gene can be responsible for a wide variety of physical and psychological symptoms in AN (e.g. appetite loss, body image distortions, fear of weight gain).

Single-gene studies divert attention and resources from understanding true polygenic nature of AN – many genes make important but modest contributions.

A strength of the dopamine explanation is it is supported by research evidence.

Kaye et al. (1999) found levels of dopamine metabolite HVA lower in recovered AN patients compared with controls. Recovered participants were normal in weight and not restricting their diets.

Most studies measure HVA in people currently experiencing symptoms – so weight loss/ malnutrition could account for lower dopamine levels. But Kaye et al.'s study avoids these **confounding variables**.

Because lower HVA levels persisted after recovery, it suggests that disturbance of dopamine metabolism may be a cause of AN and not an effect – this confirms the **validity** of the explanation.

A limitation of the serotonin explanation is other neurotransmitters are involved.

Nunn et al. (2012) argue serotonin alone does not distinguish between people with and without AN. Serotonin accounts for some features of AN but not others.

AN is better explained by considering interaction between serotonin and noradrenaline. Other neurotransmitters (e.g. **GABA**) are also involved.

This is a reminder that neurotransmitter systems do not operate in isolation; instead there are complex interactions. But the explanation is recent and remains to be fully tested.

A limitation is AN cannot be understood in terms of genes alone.

Abraham (2008) argues AN is best understood in terms of genes that create a vulnerability to AN (diathesis) that only expresses itself when the individual tries to lose weight (a stressor) – the **diathesis-stress model**.

People lose weight for many social, cultural or psychological reasons. This means non-biological risk factors play a triggering role, as do many perpetuating factors that maintain disordered eating behaviours.

This suggests that biological explanations are still valid, but not entirely valid on their own. They must be seen in a wider context of other contributory non-genetic factors which may limit biological effects.

REVISION BOOSTER

You should understand the background behind twin studies (i.e. what MZ and DZ concordance rates mean). But don't spend exam time explaining it, otherwise what you write will be too generic. Focus instead on what the difference between MZ and DZ twins tells us about the genetics of anorexia.

KNOWLEDGE CHECK

1. In relation to anorexia nervosa, explain what is meant by the term 'neural explanations'. *(3 marks)*

2. Distinguish between genetic and neural explanations for anorexia nervosa. *(4 marks)*

3. Evaluate the neural explanation for anorexia nervosa. *(6 marks)*

4. Many psychologists believe that anorexia nervosa runs in families. Others argue that most cases are due to chemical imbalances in the brain.

   Describe and evaluate **one or more** biological explanations for anorexia nervosa. Use research evidence in your answer. *(16 marks)*

Psychological explanations for anorexia nervosa: FST

Spec spotlight

Psychological explanations for anorexia nervosa: family systems theory, including enmeshment, autonomy and control.

Some researchers think anorexia may be an expression of a need for independence.

Apply it

Prudence is a teenager who is eating less and less and losing weight. She is fed up because her mum is always getting at her about everything. She feels very strongly that she is not a child anymore, but is always treated like one. No one ever lets her do anything. Prudence's mum is very irritated with Prudence because she seems ungrateful for all the nice things her parents give her. Prudence wants to talk about this with her parents, but they always change the subject.

Use family systems theory to explain why Prudence is losing weight and is vulnerable to developing anorexia nervosa.

REVISION BOOSTER

In a 16-mark essay you don't have to write everything on this spread. What is here is actually more than 1000 words!! For a 16-mark essay you probably only have time to write 500 words – but don't cut down the elaboration of the AO3 points. Better to do four elaborated points rather than five briefer ones.

Family systems theory (FST)

Family systems theory (FST) is a **psychodynamic** theory of anorexia nervosa (AN) by Minuchin *et al.*	The family is a complex social system – interactions between family members become tightly structured around the AN sufferer's symptoms distracting attention away from the family's many interpersonal conflicts.
	Minuchin *et al.* (1978) identified four main features of a typical anorexic family, as listed below.
(1) *Enmeshment*: members of anorexic families are too involved with each other.	In anorexic families the boundaries are 'fuzzy' – poorly defined roles and lack of leadership. Family members spend lots of time together, impinge on each other's privacy, speak for each other assuming they know their views. Self-identities of each member are tied up with one another.
	Adolescent daughter in an anorexic family tries to differentiate her identify and assert her independence by refusing to eat.
(2) *Overprotective*: family members constantly defend each other from external threats.	Obsessive nurturing reinforces family loyalty leaving no room for independence.
	Palazzoli (1974) described an enmeshed family in which the mother of a daughter with AN saw her role as a personal sacrifice. The mother felt that all her decisions were for her daughter's benefit and not her own. It is then much easier to blame the anorexic daughter when things go wrong.
(3) *Rigidity*: interactions within anorexic family are extremely inflexible.	Family members deny the need for change and try to keep things as they are. Problems arise when situations change due to pressure – the family is too rigid to adapt so is thrown into crisis.
	For example, an adolescent daughter seeks independence but the rest of the family quash her attempt at self-differentiation. Predictable outcome is dysfunctional behaviour, often AN.
(4) *Conflict avoidance*: family prevents or suppresses conflict.	Family members take whatever steps necessary to prevent or suppress conflict (e.g. no discussion of issues where difference of opinion might arise). So problems are not resolved and continue to fester until crisis develops.
	Anorexic daughter continues to refuse to eat, starves herself, and her family refuses to accept there is anything to discuss.
Bruch added *need for autonomy* and control as a family issue.	Bruch (1978) suggested AN is caused by an adolescent daughter's struggle to achieve autonomy and control. The mother, domineering and intrusive, does not accept the daughter's need for independence.
	The confused daughter expresses this in major symptoms of AN – distorted body image, inability to identify hunger and overwhelming feeling of loss of control. She controls her destiny by controlling her body – the thinner she gets, the greater the degree of control.
	She gains autonomy by disrupting her dependent relationship with her mother.

One strength of FST is evidence to support the role of autonomy.

Brockmeyer et al. (2013) found 112 female AN patients showed significantly greater desire to be autonomous than healthy controls.

This matches Strauss and Ryan (1987) who found female AN patients showed greater disturbances of autonomy – more controlling style of regulating own behaviour; less differentiation between selves and other family members.

These findings support FST because they show the desire for autonomy (especially when prevented) is a risk factor for AN in daughters.

The obvious implication of FST is that therapy should be family-focused as is the case with BFST.

One limitation of FST is much of the evidence is inconsistent.

Aragona et al. (2011) found families of female AN patients no more enmeshed/rigid than non-AN families. Study used self-reports; others use observer/interviewer ratings.

Studies have different outcomes depending on how variables are measured – it is difficult to test predictions about vague concepts like enmeshment and autonomy.

This inconsistency is a major limitation of FST, because it means that research has failed to reliably identify a 'typical anorexic family'.

FST was originally developed to explain the effects of family dysfunction on many psychological disorders in terms of different family relationships. But because AN overwhelmingly affects adolescent females, FST has focused on the mother–daughter relationship almost to the exclusion of all others. You might want to consider this from the point of view of gender bias.

Another strength of FST is therapies based on it have success in treating AN.

Behavioural family systems therapy (BFST) aims to disentangle family relationships and reduce parental control over AN patient's eating.

Robin et al. (1995) found six out of 11 AN patients recovered after 16 months of BFST, and three more recovered after another year. FST-based therapy appears successful.

However, the study was not blinded because 'recovery' was assessed by psychologists who knew which patients underwent BFST. Risk of bias is too great to draw firm conclusions.

A limitation is research does not show family dysfunction is a cause of anorexia.

Enmeshment, rigidity, overprotectiveness and conflict avoidance may be consequences of having a daughter with AN.

However, perhaps it doesn't matter whether the family is the cause of AN or not – symptoms become intimately linked to family dynamics anyway.

But scientific psychology seeks causes to explain behaviour so AN can be predicted/treated – FST research cannot do this.

A strength of FST is it can explain features of AN that other theories cannot.

FST can explain tendency for AN to first appear in adolescence and explain significantly greater incidence in females.

FST reflects the reality that the overwhelming majority of people with AN are adolescent females (outnumbering males 9 to 1).

However, it's also true that FST has trouble accounting for AN in males and AN that does not appear in adolescence.

KNOWLEDGE CHECK

1. In relation to the family systems theory of anorexia nervosa, explain what is meant by the terms 'enmeshment' and 'autonomy'. *(2 marks + 2 marks)*

2. Explain the difference between autonomy and control in the context of family systems theory of anorexia nervosa. *(3 marks)*

3. Describe **one** psychological explanation for anorexia nervosa. *(6 marks)*

4. Using evidence, outline and evaluate family systems theory as a psychological explanation for anorexia nervosa. *(16 marks)*

Psychological explanations for anorexia nervosa: SLT

Spec spotlight

Psychological explanations for anorexia nervosa: social learning theory, including modelling, reinforcement and media.

The term 'model' does not refer to a model such as Cara Delevingne – it is a generic term referring to someone on whom we model our behaviour. It might of course be the case that you model yourself on someone who is a model.

Apply it

A researcher has interviewed several young women who have anorexia nervosa. They give many reasons for why they have lost weight, but one is very common. Most say they would love to be like the very thin models and celebrities they see on TV and read about in magazines. They are apparently attracted by the glamorous lifestyles, wealth and attention.

Explain the researcher's finding using your knowledge of social learning theory.

Social learning theory (SLT)

Social learning theory (SLT) explains *direct and indirect* learning.	Direct learning of anorexia nervosa (AN) involves **classical** and **operant conditioning** of an individual's behaviour.
	Indirect learning involves observation of other people – behaviour is modelled/imitated if it is vicariously reinforced.
AN acquired indirectly through *modelling* an *observed model.*	Four main features of a model in AN:
	1. Provides 'template' to imitate (modelling).
	2. Can exist in real life (e.g. family member) or be symbolic (e.g. cartoon character).
	3. Modifies social norms by establishing acceptable or usual behaviour (e.g. child observes older sibling restricting food intake and learns this is 'normal').
	4. Especially influential if child identifies with model (e.g. respects model or perceives them as glamorous and associates their thinness with desirable characteristics).
Vicarious reinforcement increases chance that eating behaviour will be imitated.	Observer sees model rewarded (praised) and learns behaviour (losing weight) has positive consequences – observer is then more likely to imitate behaviour.
	Family members are major sources of vicarious reinforcement because their behaviour can be repeatedly observed over time.
	If older child's food restriction behaviour is regularly rewarded, younger sibling experiences many instances of vicarious reinforcement that make imitation more likely and frequent.
The *media* is a powerful transmitter of cultural ideals of body shape/size.	Western cultural ideal body shape for women has become thinner over time (e.g. Size Zero).
	Women may identify with glamour of celebrities and media figures who conform to 'thin ideal' – they are then motivated to lose weight and achieve thinness (dieting, exercise, laxatives).
	Behaviour vicariously reinforced by fame and success observed in female role models.

Key study: Dittmar *et al.* (2006) SLT and AN

Procedure	162 British girls aged 5–8 years were shown images of either Barbie dolls, Emme dolls or control objects (flowers, etc.).
	If Barbie was scaled up to adult human size, her waist would be 39% smaller than most AN patients. Emme dolls have a bigger more realistic body shape.
Findings	Girls who saw Barbie images significantly more dissatisfied with own body shape and had significantly lower body esteem.
	Young girls identify with Barbie because of glamour associated with body shape – makes them vulnerable to developing AN.

One strength of the SLT explanation is research supports it.

Becker *et al.* (2011) found the most significant predictor of eating disorders in adolescent females on the island of Fiji was how many of their friends and schoolmates had access to the media.

SLT predicts that individual girls are more likely to acquire AN when friends in their social network watch TV (even if she does not) and discuss what they have seen.

This suggests favourable discussion of thin celebrities encourages reinforcement of behaviour seeking thinness – direct (praise from friends for losing weight) and vicarious (thin celebrities praised by friends).

Another strength is SLT explains cultural changes linked to AN.

AN is still less common in non-Western cultures but incidence rates are increasing rapidly – SLT explains this in terms of changing cultural norms.

Chisuwa and O'Dea (2010) found increased rates of AN in Japan in the last 40 years, as traditional values favouring plumpness are displaced by the Western cultural thinness ideal.

SLT shows this change is driven in part by media representations of female body shape aimed especially at adolescents.

Is the Western preoccupation with thinness a result of media and cultural icons (like Barbie)?

One limitation of SLT is that it fails to explain why AN is not more common.

Most young women are exposed to role models of thinness in media but only some develop AN – another factor must be involved.

Could be a **diathesis**, i.e. underlying vulnerability to develop AN which may be genetic or environmental (e.g. significant childhood trauma).

So explanation of AN that accommodates biological and non-biological factors is more **valid** than one based on social learning processes alone.

Another strength of SLT is that it explains gender differences in AN.

The eating disorder 'bigorexia' is increasingly common in Western men who wish to develop a muscular body shape without gaining fat.

SLT explains this with the same processes as anorexia: identification (with male celebrities), modelling (observing behaviours in the media and imitating them) and vicarious reinforcement (seeing that some behaviours are rewarded).

Evidence (e.g. Jones and Morgan 2010) supports SLT prediction that bigorexia is an eating disorder prevalent in men who respond to cultural ideals about masculinity transmitted through media.

A further strength of SLT is that it gives rise to treatment applications.

Social learning methods are incorporated into many treatment approaches to AN, especially where immediate weight gain is an urgent priority.

For example, modelling as a treatment provides a pattern of healthy eating behaviour for AN patients to imitate (celebrities who offer alternative to 'thin ideal').

This is a strength because the validity of SLT is increased if practical applications derived from it are effective.

KNOWLEDGE CHECK

1. In relation to the social learning theory of anorexia nervosa, explain what is meant by the terms 'modelling' and 'reinforcement'.
   (3 marks + 3 marks)

2. Outline the social learning theory of anorexia nervosa.
   (6 marks)

3. Describe **one** study of the social learning theory of anorexia nervosa. In your answer refer to what the researcher(s) did and what was found. *(6 marks)*

4. Lillia is 14 and her mum has had depression and eating disorders since Lillia was small. Lillia and her mum often shop together for food and eat together, although her mum rarely finishes a meal. Her dad often talks about how beautiful Lillia's mum is and comments on how similar Lillia and her mum are.

   Discuss **one** biological and **one** psychological explanation for anorexia nervosa. Refer to Lillia and her mum in your answer.
   (16 marks)

Psychological explanations for anorexia nervosa: Cognitive

Spec spotlight

Psychological explanations for anorexia nervosa: cognitive theory, including distortions and irrational beliefs.

A distorted perception of body image may be at the root of anorexia.

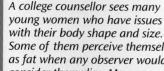

A college counsellor sees many young women who have issues with their body shape and size. Some of them perceive themselves as fat when any observer would consider them slim. Many are very high-achieving students, but they all report spending hours and hours on their work, often stressing over the smallest things. They tend to make very harsh judgements of their own abilities, including their ability to lose weight.

Using your knowledge of psychological theories of anorexia, explain the cognitive processes that these young women are experiencing.

Cognitive theory

Cognitive distortions are a cause of anorexia nervosa (AN).	Distorted perception of body image is central to the diagnosis of AN in **DSM**-5 (2012) – so it makes sense that **cognitive** distortions may be a cause of AN.
	People with AN filter experiences of life through the three factors identified below.
Factor 1 *Disturbed* perceptions about body shape and weight.	Murphy *et al.* (2010) argue that the main clinical features of AN stem from disturbed perceptions.
	These cause preoccupations with thoughts of food, eating, body shape.
	Leads to behaviours such as food restriction and checking (e.g. constantly looking in mirror). People with AN misinterpret emotional states as 'feeling fat', even as they get thinner.
Overestimation of body size and weight.	Williamson *et al.* (1993) asked AN patients and a healthy **control group** to estimate current and ideal body sizes.
	Found that AN participants' estimates were significantly less accurate, with a marked tendency to overestimate size.
	Their ideal body size was significantly thinner than for controls.
Factor 2 *Irrational beliefs* defy logic.	Irrational beliefs are views and attitudes about AN that do not make sense.
	Such thoughts give rise to automatic negative thoughts (Beck), for example:
	• 'If I don't control my weight, I'm worthless' (all-or-nothing thinking).
	• 'I ate half a biscuit, I've got no willpower' (catastrophising).
Perfectionism is a key irrational belief in AN.	A person who exhibits perfectionism:
	• Feels they must meet demanding standards in all areas of life but especially eating, body shape, weight loss.
	• Uses intensive record-keeping to ensure they are achieving their goals.
	• Raises standards even higher once targets are reached – forever pursuing unrealistic goals in a vicious cycle of irrational perfectionism and starvation.
Factor 3 *Cognitive inflexibility* (e.g. difficulty in set-shifting).	AN patients have problems switching fluently between tasks requiring a different set of cognitive skills (set-shifting). They apply the same skills in a changed situation where they are no longer useful.
	Treasure and Schmidt (2013) proposed the *cognitive interpersonal maintenance model* of AN: when vulnerable person begins weight loss process, they rigidly persist and continue to perceive themselves as needing to lose weight. They cannot switch to a more **adaptive** way of thinking about body size. Weight loss is a solution to a problem that no longer exists, but they can't perceive this accurately.

One strength of the explanation is research support for cognitive distortions.

Sachdev et al. (2008) scanned AN patients' brains and found less activation (compared with healthy controls) in areas involved in attention when participants viewed images of *own* bodies.

But there was no difference in activation between AN patients and controls when shown images of *other people's* bodies.

This suggests cognitive distortions exist in AN, but may be limited to the individual's own body image and not extend to bodies in general.

Cognitive distortions may be limited to an individual's own body image.

Another strength is that there is support for perfectionism.

Halmi et al. (2012) found childhood perfectionism was a significant predictor of later development of AN in 728 women aged over 16.

Perfectionism preceded onset of AN, so is a potential causal risk factor for developing the disorder.

However, participants had to think back to childhood to recall perfectionism so recall probably distorted, artificially increasing the link with the development of AN.

One limitation is that there is some contradictory research.

Cornelissen et al. (2013) found no significant differences between AN patients and healthy women in terms of accuracy in estimating own body size.

We cannot distinguish between body size estimates of non-AN and AN women – this challenges the role of body image distortion in cognitive theories.

However, other studies do support the role of cognitive distortions in AN. Gardner and Brown (2014) argue that conflicting findings are due to different techniques used to estimate body size.

A further strength is treatment applications from the cognitive explanation.

Grave et al. (2014) used enhanced **CBT** and found substantial weight increase in 26 hospitalised AN patients. This was maintained one year after discharge.

CBT is based on the view that AN patients will not recover unless cognitive distortions and irrational beliefs about food, eating, body shape and size are corrected.

Findings of the study fulfil predictions derived from cognitive theory of AN, strengthening its **validity** as an explanation of AN.

A limitation is cognitive distortions and irrational beliefs may not cause AN.

Shott et al. (2012) found younger AN patients no worse at set-shifting than healthy controls, but older patients were.

So, cognitive inflexibility does not make individuals vulnerable to developing AN – it is instead a consequence of the disorder. Very little research shows cognitive distortions exist before the onset of AN.

If cognitive distortions are merely symptoms of AN and not a cause, this undermines the validity of the cognitive explanation and severely limits its usefulness.

REVISION BOOSTER

Students are often disappointed to find they haven't got as many marks for evaluation as they thought. This is usually because they aren't evaluating – they're describing. For example, you could evaluate the cognitive theory of AN by addressing the evidence for cognitive distortions. But if all you do is say what the evidence is ('Sachdev did some brain scans and what he found was…'), then that's not evaluation.

KNOWLEDGE CHECK

1. In relation to the cognitive theory of anorexia nervosa, explain what is meant by the terms 'distortions' and 'irrational beliefs'. Use examples in your answer.
   (3 marks + 3 marks)

2. Briefly outline research into distortions **and** irrational beliefs in relation to the cognitive theory of anorexia nervosa. *(6 marks)*

3. Briefly evaluate **two** psychological explanations for anorexia nervosa. *(6 marks)*

4. Describe and evaluate the cognitive theory of anorexia nervosa. Refer to distortions **and** irrational beliefs in your answer. *(16 marks)*

Biological explanations for obesity

Spec spotlight

Biological explanations for obesity, including genetic and neural explanations.

Obesity rates run in the family.

Apply it

Ptolemy is a 12-year-old boy who is clinically obese. His dad is also seriously overweight and has Type 2 diabetes. But his mum is within the normal weight range.

Tate and Lyle are teenage twins who are both very overweight. There are several obese people in their family.

Nazir has been under a lot of stress for several months, in her work and at home. She copes with this by eating and therefore is now obese. She gets no pleasure from eating anymore but it distracts her from the stress.

Use these cases to describe how genetic **and** neural factors explain obesity.

REVISION BOOSTER

Write a very brief essay plan for each possible essay and then practise writing the essay in full from the plan. Time yourself – 20 minutes for a 16-mark essay.

Genetic explanations

Obesity runs in *families*.	Family-related patterns in terms of body mass index (BMI) – a characteristic transmitted from parents to offspring.
Examples of family-related patterns come from *family and twin studies*.	Family studies: BMI **concordance rates** for obesity in first-degree relatives are 20–50% (Chaput *et al.* 2014). Twin studies: **MZ** concordance rates for obesity are 61–80% – very substantial genetic component (Nan *et al.* 2012).
Genetic inheritance of obesity is *polygenic*.	No single genetic cause of obesity – many genes involved with small effects interacting to produce overall outcome. Locke *et al.* (2015) found 97 genes associated with variations in BMI but accounted for only 2.7% of BMI variation – up to 400 genes may be involved in heritability of obesity. Plus there are other ways of measuring obesity (e.g. waist–hip ratio) so different genes may influence different aspects of obesity.

Neural explanations

Neurotransmitters such as **serotonin** and **dopamine**.	Serotonin: regulates eating behaviour by influencing activity of hypothalamus. Dopamine: crucial role in brain's reward and motivation system involving hypothalamus, hippocampus and amygdala.
Low serotonin levels.	Serotonin signals to hypothalamus we have eaten to satiety. Dysfunctions of serotonin system from stress or co-morbid disorders (e.g. depression) – may be genetically inherited. Results in abnormally low levels of serotonin and therefore inaccurate satiety signals sent to hypothalamus. The result is that eating behaviour is **disinhibited** (i.e. not controlled), leading to carbohydrate cravings (i.e. desire for energy-dense foods including sugars) causing weight gain through excess calories.
Low dopamine levels.	Dopamine activity associated with pleasure from eating and associated cues (e.g. smell of food). Wang *et al.* (2001) found obese people have fewer dopamine D2 receptors in the *striatum* than normal-weight controls. Low dopamine means this neurotransmitter cannot perform usual pleasurable reward function in response to eating. Overeating is an attempt to increase dopamine and activate reward centres in the brain, providing pleasure. Obesity is the outcome of food addiction operating neurochemically like other addictions.

One limitation of the genetic explanation is that twin studies are not conclusive.

Twin studies try to control for environmental influences by comparing concordance rates of MZ and **DZ twins** – since in both cases each pair of twins is raised together.

However, the approach is only **valid** if MZ and DZ twins are treated with equal degrees of similarity – but some researchers argue MZ twins are treated more similarly than DZs.

This suggests that twin studies may overestimate extent of genetic influences, indicating obesity is not an inevitable outcome of genetic risk because environmental factors play an essential role.

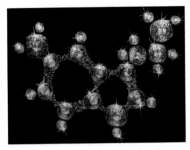

A serotonin molecule – low levels are implicated in obesity.

Another limitation is that there is evidence contradicting the role of genes.

Paracchini *et al.* (2005) conducted **meta-analysis** of 25 studies investigating genes possibly involved in regulating leptin (LEP gene) and leptin receptors (LEPR gene).

But the study found no evidence of a link between these genes and obesity. Whatever the role of leptin in obesity, it does not have a solely genetic basis.

This suggests that obesity is a complex phenomenon and other non-genetic factors are important in its causation and development.

One strength of the neural explanation is evidence for the role of serotonin.

Ohia *et al.* (2013) highlight the importance in obesity of one serotonin receptor in particular – the 2C receptor.

Studies of 'knockout' mice (specific genes are removed) with no functioning 2C receptors show they develop late-onset obesity.

This is a strength because it is evidence of a link between obesity and a dysfunctional serotonin system, at least in mice.

Another strength is that there is also evidence for the role of dopamine.

There may be a genetic basis to dysfunctions of the dopamine reward system – DRD2 gene codes for the D2 receptor implicated in obesity.

Ritchie and Noble (2003) found that people who inherited one version of the DRD2 gene had 30–40% fewer D2 receptors compared to people with other versions.

This supports the view that people with low dopamine levels (fewer D2 receptors) experience less dopamine-activated pleasurable reward from eating – so more likely to overeat.

A strength of **biological approaches** is they give rise to treatment applications.

Biological research is revealing physiological mechanisms as plausible causes of obesity – and each is a candidate for new treatments.

Realistic future treatments include drugs to correct dopamine or serotonin deficiencies and personalised medicine tailored to an individual's genetic profile.

The ability to produce better treatments supports the validity of biological explanations (genes and neurotransmitter dysfunction) because predictions derived from these explanations would be fulfilled.

KNOWLEDGE CHECK

1. Briefly distinguish between genetic and neural explanations of obesity.
   (3 marks)

2. Briefly outline **one or more** genetic explanation(s) for obesity. *(4 marks)*

3. Identify and briefly discuss **one** biological explanation for obesity. *(5 marks)*

4. This item appeared on a news website: 'Obesity crisis is all in the genes. Psychologists said yesterday that obesity runs in families. But others have pointed out that this does not mean that obesity is definitely genetic.'

   With reference to the issues raised in this item, outline and evaluate **two** biological explanations for obesity.
   (16 marks)

Psychological explanations for obesity

Spec spotlight

Psychological explanations for obesity, including restraint theory, disinhibition and the boundary model.

The restrained eater has to think about food much of the time.

REVISION BOOSTER

An exam question may require you to write about just one of these explanations – or it may require psychological explanations. In the case of the latter don't make the mistake of describing all three as you will have far too much AO1.

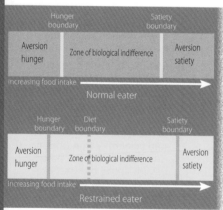

Herman and Polivy's boundary model: restrained eaters do not eat according to their biological needs, as normal eaters do.

Restraint theory (Herman and Polivy 1975)

Restricting food intake.	Dieters restrain eating (deliberately restrict food/calorie intake) which is self-defeating.
Restrained eaters exert **cognitive control**.	Restrained eater has to *think* about eating much of the time. They categorise foods into 'good' and 'bad' and create rules about which foods are allowed and which are forbidden.
The outcome of restrained eating is *paradoxical*.	Restrained eater becomes more preoccupied with food not less. No longer eats when hungry and stops when full. Eating behaviour becomes **disinhibited** (not controlled) and they eat more and gain weight – opposite outcome to goal.

Disinhibition

Restraints loosened.	Period of restrained eating often followed by disinhibited eating in which individual eats as much as they want.
Disinhibitors lead to loss of control.	A disinhibitor is a food-related cue, either internal (e.g. mood, feeling depressed) or external (e.g. media images). Restrained eaters are sensitive to these cues and vulnerable to loss of control leading to unrestrained eating (a binge).
Disinhibition controlled by cognitive factors.	For example, distorted thinking maintains disinhibited eating for remainder of binge. For example, all-or-nothing thinking – no point stopping: 'I blew it, I might as well eat all of this.'

The boundary model (Herman and Polivy 1984)

Biological process: Both hunger and satiety are aversive.	Hunger: when energy levels dip below 'set point' we feel aversive state of hunger and are motivated to eat. Satiety: eating to fullness creates aversive state of discomfort so we are motivated to stop eating.
Psychological process: ZBI.	Zone of biological indifference (ZBI): when we feel neither hungry nor full (i.e. the area between hunger and satiety boundaries). In this zone psychological factors (cognitive and social) have more influence than biological ones on food intake.
ZBI wider for restrained eaters.	People who restrict food intake have lower hunger boundary and higher satiety boundary. So more of their eating behaviour is under cognitive rather than biological control – making them vulnerable to disinhibition.

One strength of these explanations is supporting evidence.

Wardle and Beales (1988) **randomly allocated** 27 obese women to a diet, exercise or **control group**.

Restrained eaters (diet group) ate significantly more (consumed most calories) because they experienced occasional disinhibition and binged beyond feeling full.

Findings support the view that restraint is a causal factor in overeating which inevitably leads to weight gain and obesity.

Another strength of these explanations is evidence confirms role of media.

Boyce and Kuijer (2014) showed dieters and non-dieters slideshows with images of thinness. Food intake measured in ten-minute 'taste test' when they were allowed to eat as much as they liked from four bowls.

Restrained eaters ate significantly more after seeing media images of thinness but no difference in responses to neutral images.

Suggests images common in our culture are disinhibitors triggering eating in restrained eaters – a pathway to weight gain and obesity predicted by restraint theory.

Disinhibition is a causal explanation of binge eating.

One limitation of these explanations is contradictory evidence.

Savage *et al.* (2009) measured dietary restraint, disinhibition and weight in 163 women at the start of the study and every two years after a six-year period.

They found that restrained eating while dieting leads to weight loss rather than gain in the short to medium term (significant negative **correlation**).

This is a limitation because the finding is the opposite outcome to that predicted by restraint theory, challenging its **validity**.

Another limitation of these explanations is that restraint is multifaceted.

Two forms of restraint are *rigid restraint* (all-or-nothing approach to limiting food intake) and *flexible restraint* (allows limited amounts of 'forbidden' foods without triggering disinhibition).

Only rigid restraint is likely to lead to obesity – this could explain why Savage *et al.* (2009) found that restrained eating can produce weight loss.

Boundary model presents restraint as a single behaviour so does not reflect its true nature as uncovered by research – makes this a limited approach to understanding obesity.

One strength of the boundary model is it gives rise to practical applications.

The boundary model predicts that the paradoxical outcome of restricting food intake is disinhibition, overeating, weight gain and obesity. Restricting food intake triggers psychological mechanisms that make weight loss difficult.

This defies common sense and the 'quick fix' culture of the dieting industry, which promises weight loss by restricting certain foods and blames the individual if it doesn't work.

This suggests that the boundary model is potentially effective because it opens up alternative routes to successful weight loss (e.g. training dieters to eat at a slower rate, Zandian *et al.* 2009)

Apply it

Charity is on a diet but her weight is going in the wrong direction. She thinks about food more than she used to and notices the smells of food all the time. Her friends mean well but are always asking her how the diet is going. When Charity has a bad day at work, she thinks about how she is going to treat herself to a piece of chocolate – but ends up eating the lot.

Explain Charity's behaviour in terms of restraint, disinhibition and the boundary model. Use some research evidence in your answer.

KNOWLEDGE CHECK

1. Distinguish between restraint theory and disinhibition as psychological explanations for obesity. *(3 marks)*
2. Briefly outline the boundary model as an explanation for obesity. *(4 marks)*
3. Briefly evaluate disinhibition as an explanation for obesity *(4 marks)*
4. Describe and evaluate psychological explanations for obesity. *(16 marks)*

Explanations for the success and failure of dieting

Spec spotlight

Explanations for the success and failure of dieting.

REVISION BOOSTER

Exam questions will always use the wording of the specification. So, in this case, you will only be asked about 'the success and failure of dieting'. Use one or more of these explanations to discuss this. One may be enough. Less is always more.

Bear in mind. Just stop thinking about me. Can't do it, can you?

Apply it

A friend of yours is a dietician. He advises obese people about how to lose weight. He helps them to devise diets that will lead to weight loss and reduce the risk of Type 2 diabetes. However, he has noticed that the more he helps some people, the more likely they are to put weight on rather than lose it. He works out that there must be quite a lot of psychology involved – weight loss is not just a physical thing. He asks you for some advice that he can pass on to his clients.

What advice would you give your friend? Outline some reasons why diets fail and how they can be successful. Base your advice on psychological evidence.

The spiral model (Heatherton and Polivy 1992)

Diet failure leads to *sense of personal deficiency*.	Food-restricted dieting often begins in adolescence when body shape leads to low self-esteem and desire to lose weight.
	Initial success but weight is often regained leading to a sense of personal deficiency (e.g. 'I didn't try hard enough').
Downward spiral created.	Dieters do not radically rethink their approach. They make a bigger effort and experience more frustration and emotional distress making them vulnerable to **disinhibited** eating.
	Metabolic changes in body make weight loss physically more difficult (e.g. ghrelin levels increase, leptin levels decrease).
	Result is more failure followed by more attempts to 'diet harder', lowering of self-esteem, increase in depression.

Ironic processes theory (Wegner *et al.* 1987)

Being on a diet increases *preoccupation* with food.	Asking people not to think about a white bear almost guarantees they do. Paradoxical outcome of trying to suppress a thought is to make it more likely.
	Dieters label certain foods as 'forbidden' so they become more salient (i.e. they stand out). Leads to increased thinking about food and disinhibition of eating, loss of control, excessive food intake, dieting failure.
Trying to *distract yourself* doesn't work.	Distraction (e.g. reading a book) requires mental activity – so dieter has less **cognitive** capacity to suppress thoughts of food.
	Central irony of restrained-eating diet – to be successful at preventing thoughts of food, dieter has to spend their time, energy and undivided attention trying not to think about food.

Restraint, disinhibition and the boundary model

Restraint leads to disinhibition and failure in dieting.	Dieters make conscious effort to restrain eating, therefore behaviour is under cognitive control.
	Dieters tend to experience cognitive distortions and are vulnerable to internal and external food-related cues tempting them to break their diet.
	Eating may become disinhibited and many calories are consumed very quickly – resulting in the dieter losing no more weight than someone not dieting.
Boundary model suggests when you pass *preset limit* you give up control.	Dieters do not regulate eating in response to feelings of hunger or satiety – instead they set themselves a limit on how much food they think they should eat.
	If they eat past this point they continue to eat until they are full on basis of 'What the hell, I might as well'.

One strength of the spiral model is it has practical uses.

Heatherton and Polivy (1992) argue that a key lesson of the model is to prevent lowering of self-esteem and thus avoid worst consequences of diet failure.

For example, people who think about *avoiding* putting on weight rather than trying to lose it are less likely to experience disinhibited eating because their self-esteem is higher (Lowe and Kleifield 1988).

This is a strength of the model because it proposes several ways that dieting can become successful, involving 'breaking out' of the spiral at various points to promote self-esteem.

People who think about avoiding putting on weight are more likely to make a success of dieting.

One strength of ironic processes theory is it has research support.

Adriaanse *et al.* (2011) found exposure to statements like 'When I am sad, I will not eat chocolate' reinforced association between 'being sad' and 'eating chocolate'. Made link accessible in memory and recall more likely.

This so-called *ironic rebound effect* is behavioural as well as cognitive because snack diaries showed participants ate more unhealthy snacks and calories than the **control group** in the following week.

This confirms the difficulty in suppressing thoughts of eating once they become accessible in memory. Shows how thinking of self as dieting leads to failure. This supports **validity** of ironic processes theory as explanation of dieting.

One limitation of ironic processes is that they have minimal effects.

Evidence shows ironic processes operate in eating behaviour but it is unclear how far they account for success and failure of dieting.

Effects of ironic processes exaggerated in 'snapshot' laboratory **experiments** and less relevant to real-life attempts to lose weight over longer period of time.

This suggests other factors are likely to be more important in determining a diet's success (e.g. self-esteem as proposed by the spiral model).

Another strength of ironic processes theory is it has practical applications.

The theory suggests overeating is more likely when the dieter has to draw on cognitive resources for doing another activity.

So Boon *et al.* (2002) suggest dieting is more successful when dieter pays full attention to eating – no eating in front of TV, reading at mealtimes, conversations over dinner.

This is a strength because theory offers practical ways ironic processes can be overcome or avoided and therefore helps increase chances of dieting success.

A limitation is all explanations struggle to account for individual differences.

Ogden (2010) suggests theories claiming dieting is counterproductive have trouble explaining why some people lose weight even when preoccupied with food.

These people are a minority but include anorexics who lose weight through restricted eating and people with an internal locus of control (believe in their own control).

So theories lack validity because they don't apply to all cases of people dieting to lose weight – not full explanations to predict who is likely to fail or succeed in losing weight.

KNOWLEDGE CHECK

1. Outline **one** explanation for the success and failure of dieting. *(6 marks)*
2. Describe **one** study of the success and failure of dieting. *(6 marks)*
3. Briefly evaluate **one** explanation for the success and failure of dieting. *(4 marks)*
4. Leander and Uday are arguing about diets. Leander reckons just being on one means it won't work. Uday believes they do work, and is about to start on his most recent one which involves cutting down drastically on carbohydrates.

   Discuss **one or more** explanation(s) for the success and failure of dieting. Refer to Leander's and Uday's positions in your answer. *(16 marks)*

The physiology of stress

The physiology of stress, including general adaptation syndrome, the hypothalamic-pituitary-adrenal system, the sympathomedullary pathway, and the role of cortisol.

Stressors come in many forms.

Apply it

When Luther thinks about his upcoming exams, he sweats and shakes, his heart beats faster and he feels sick. The same thing happened when his girlfriend told him they were splitting up. And when he sang and played guitar in the college concert. He responded to these very different situations in basically the same way.

a. Use your knowledge of the physiology of stress to explain what is happening to Luther when he experiences these symptoms.

b. Apply what you know about the general adaptation syndrome to explain why his responses in different situations are so similar.

General adaptation syndrome (GAS) (Selye 1936)

First stage: *Alarm reaction.*	**Sympathetic branch** of the **autonomic nervous system (ANS)** activated by hypothalamus.
	Stimulates adrenal medulla to release adrenaline and noradrenaline to prepare body for fight or flight.
Second stage: *Resistance.*	Body tries to adapt by combating stressor.
	Body's resources consumed at harmful rate (e.g. stress hormones eventually damage heart).
	Parasympathetic branch activated to conserve energy.
Third stage: *Exhaustion.*	Adaptation to chronic stressor fails because resources needed to resist are drained.
	Symptoms of sympathetic arousal (e.g. raised heart rate). Adrenal glands damaged, immune system suppressed.
	Stress-related illnesses now likely (e.g. hypertension, coronary heart disease and depression).

The physiological stress response

Acute (short-term) stress response.	Immediate response to stressor: Hypothalamus activates sympathetic branch of ANS.
Sympathomedullary pathway (SAM), also called fight or flight response.	Stimulates adrenal medulla to release adrenaline and noradrenaline into bloodstream (heart beats faster, muscles tense, liver converts stored glycogen into glucose to provide energy to fuel fight or flight response).
	Once stressor stops: **parasympathetic nervous system** activated and physiological arousal decreases – priority now is energy conservation, rest and digest response.
Chronic (long-term) stress response.	If stressor continues: HPA now activated.
Hypothalamic-pituitary-adrenal system (HPA).	Hypothalamus produces corticotropin releasing factor (CRF).
	Detected by anterior lobe of pituitary gland and causes release of adrenocorticotropic hormone (ACTH).
	ACTH detected by adrenal cortex which secretes cortisol.
Cortisol is the major stress hormone.	Cortisol affects glucose metabolism and restores energy.
	Has other effects (e.g. suppresses immune system).
	HPA is self-regulating via negative feedback loop – cortisol in bloodstream monitored at pituitary and hypothalamus.
	High levels of cortisol trigger reduction in both CRF and ACTH, resulting in corresponding reduction in cortisol.

One strength of the GAS is that there is evidence to support it.

Selye (1936) subjected rats to stressors (e.g. extreme cold, surgical injury). Found the same collection of responses ('syndrome') regardless of stressor.

Stress was a general body response appearing after 6–48 hours that was not unique to specific stressor. He tracked response to stressor through resistance and exhaustion stages.

This suggests the body's general response to a stressor is a physiological reality as Selye argued, at least in rats.

One limitation of the GAS is that it may not be a general response to stressors.

Key to the GAS is that the stress response is non-specific (i.e. it is always the same, regardless of stressor).

Mason (1971) **replicated** Selye's procedures with monkeys. Effects varied depending on stressor (extreme cold increased urinary cortisol; extreme heat reduced it).

This challenges the central concept of Selye's theory by showing specific stressors can produce specific patterns of responses, undermining the **validity** of the GAS.

Another limitation of research on the physiological stress response is male bias.

If an ancestral female responded with fight or flight this created a risk for her children because it left them vulnerable (they are defenceless if mother runs away).

Taylor (2006) argues that the 'traditional' stress response applies mostly to males. More **adaptive** in females is 'tend and befriend' (threat is met with tending offspring and befriending females for social support).

The assumption that fight or flight is a valid explanation of the stress response in all humans is a reflection of an **androcentric bias** towards male physiology.

Another limitation is that psychological factors are ignored.

Much research is on animals so physiological accounts of stress ignore psychological factors. Lazarus (1999) argues we **cognitively** appraise a stressor by deciding if it's a threat (primary appraisal) and if we have the resources to cope (secondary appraisal).

In Speisman et al.'s (1964) study students watched a gruesome medical procedure on film while their heart rates were measured. If traumatic nature of operation emphasised, heart rates increased; if described as a voluntary rite of passage, heart rates decreased.

It is difficult for a purely physiological explanation to account for this finding. It shows that humans are not as passive in the face of stressors as physiological theories assume.

A strength of research is that it offers real-life benefits.

Addison's disease is rare disorder of adrenal glands (cannot produce cortisol). Stress can trigger life-threatening Addisonian crisis (confusion, abnormal heart rhythm, drop in blood pressure).

Can be treated with self-administered cortisol replacement therapy and patients lead relatively normal lives. But need to be aware of stressful situations when medication should be increased.

Further understanding of physiological stress response could lead to improved treatments matched to precise stressor (e.g. acute or chronic).

De-stressors come in many forms.

REVISION BOOSTER

The maximum you will have to write to describe the general adaptation syndrome is about 150–200 words. This is the amount appropriate for a 6-mark answer. That's about 40 words for each of the three stages of the GAS plus some general background.

KNOWLEDGE CHECK

1. In relation to the physiology of stress, describe the general adaptation syndrome. *(6 marks)*

2. Outline the role of cortisol in the physiology of stress. *(6 marks)*

3. In relation to the physiology of stress, outline the hypothalamic-pituitary-adrenal system **and** the sympathomedullary pathway. *(6 marks)*

4. Describe and evaluate research into the physiology of stress. *(16 marks)*

The role of stress in illness

Spec spotlight

The role of stress in illness, including reference to immunosuppression and cardiovascular disorders.

The immune system

The immune system protects bodies from invading germs and other foreign bodies (antigens) by deploying several defensive cells, for example T cells and natural killer (NK) cells.

Scientific proof that stress can affect your mascara.

Apply it

Ursula recently became a fully-trained firefighter who frequently faces situations of great danger. She has to make life-or-death decisions which have consequences for herself, her colleagues and others. She has sleep problems and more arguments with her partner than she used to. She also has more colds than she did, and has had a few chest pains.

Referring to psychological research, explain why Ursula might be ill more than she used to be.

Immunosuppression

Immune system suppressed.	Directly: Cortisol produced by the hypothalamic-pituitary-adrenal system (HPA) inhibits production of immune cells.
	Indirectly: Stress influences lifestyle behaviours (smoking, drinking) that have a negative effect on immune functioning.
Chronic stress of *exams* → decrease in NK and killer T cells.	Kiecolt-Glaser *et al.* (1984) obtained blood samples from 75 medical students, tested before the exam period (low-stress) and on the day of the first exam (high-stress). They also completed questionnaires measuring sources of stress and self-reported psychological symptoms.
	The activity of natural killer (NK) and killer T cells decreased between first and second samples – evidence of an immune response suppressed by a common stressor.
	Decline was greatest in students who reported feeling lonely and experiencing other sources of stress (e.g. life events).
Chronic stress of *caring for ill relative* → increase in immune antibodies.	Kiecolt-Glaser *et al.* (1991) compared health and immune functioning of caregivers (looking after a relative with Alzheimer's) with a matched group of non-caregivers.
	Over 13 months caregivers showed an increase in antibodies to Epstein-Barr Virus but no increase in control participants.
	Caregivers also had infectious illnesses on significantly more days and higher levels of depression (32% of caregivers met criteria for clinical depression; 6% of **control group**).

Cardiovascular disorders (CVDs)

Stress associated with *CVDs* (CHDs and stroke).	CVDs are disorders of heart and blood vessels – including coronary heart disease (CHD) and stroke (blocked blood vessels in the brain).
	Some evidence shows stress has immediate effects on CVDs (acute) as well as longer-term effects (chronic).
Acute stress caused by *watching football match* → CVDs.	Wilbert-Lampen *et al.* (2008) looked at incidences of heart attacks during football matches (sudden emotional arousal – an acute stressor) played in Germany during the 1996 World Cup.
	On days Germany played, cardiac emergencies increased by 2.66 times compared with a control period – acute emotional stress of watching favourite football team more than doubled participants' risk of suffering a cardiovascular event.
Chronic stressors e.g. *workplace stressors* → heart attack.	Yusuf *et al.*'s (2004) INTERHEART study compared 15,000 people who'd had a heart attack (myocardial infarction, MI) with a similar number of people who had not.
	Several chronic stressors had a strong link to MI including workplace stress and stressful life events – role of stress greater than obesity and third behind smoking and cholesterol.

One limitation is that some research shows stress can benefit immunity.

An assumption underlying stress and illness research is that stress suppresses the immune system. But some studies show stress can have immunoenhancing effects.

Dharbhar (2008) subjected rats to mild stressors which stimulated a major immune response. Immune cells (e.g. lymphocytes) flooded into bloodstream and body tissues in preparation for physical damage.

This suggests acute and chronic stressors do not affect immune system in the same way. This shows the relationship between stress, the immune system and illnesses is complex and not fully understood.

Graham brought a new meaning to the phrase 'getting stuck into a book'.

One strength is research shows a link between immunosuppression and cancer.

There is support for the immunosuppressive effects of stress from studies of illnesses other than CVDs (e.g. development of cervical cancers are affected by immune functioning).

Pereira *et al.* (2003) studied HIV-positive women. After one year, women who experienced many stressful life events were more likely to develop pre-cancerous lesions of the cervix than those who had fewer stressful events.

This study demonstrates that effects of stress on the immune system may have wider and more direct consequences on health and illness than research into CVDs has indicated.

REVISION BOOSTER

There are three topics from these pages mentioned on the specification – the role of stress in illness, immunosuppression and CVDs. You could get a question on any of these. 'The role of stress in illness' means you can write about either or both of the other two (remember: less is more). But a question specifically on immunosuppression or CVDs is a different matter.

Another limitation is the link between stress and illness is mostly indirect.

Stress can have both direct and indirect effects on CVDs. But the evidence for stress as an indirect precipitating factor in CVDs is much stronger than evidence that it directly causes CVDs.

Stress can increase risk of heart attack in people who already have CVDs. Orth Gomer et al. (2000) found that marital conflict for women with CVDs created stress that tripled the risk of heart attack.

This is different from showing stress causes CVDs to develop in the first place, especially when most people who experience stressors do not develop illnesses at all.

Another strength is research into stress and illness may have real-life benefits.

Dharbhar's research (2008) may eventually lead to patients being given low doses of stress hormones before surgery to improve their chances of making a full recovery afterwards.

Kiecolt-Glaser and Glaser (1992) found students who took a relaxation training programme seriously had better immune functioning during their exam period than those who didn't bother with it.

This is a strength because real-life applications increase research's **validity** by confirming relevance of concepts underlying them (e.g. effects of stress on the immune system).

A further limitation is that research focuses on short-term, artificial stressors.

Researchers conduct studies using certain stressors (short-term acute ones, e.g. mild shocks or unfair money distribution) that are easily manipulated in the laboratory.

Controlled research tells us about one type of stressor but not the other. Even chronic stressors in controlled studies are highly artificial (e.g. noise, electric shocks).

Therefore controlled research on acute and chronic stress often lacks **external validity**.

KNOWLEDGE CHECK

1. In relation to the role of stress in illness, explain what is meant by 'immunosuppression' and 'cardiovascular disorders'. *(3 marks + 3 marks)*

2. Describe **one** study into the role of stress in illness. In your answer refer to what the researcher(s) did and what was found. *(6 marks)*

3. Briefly evaluate the role of stress in illness. *(4 marks)*

4. Fabrizio is experiencing increasingly ill health, from niggly sniffles to aches and pains and an irregular heartbeat. His girlfriend thinks it is because of stress, as Fabrizio lost his job recently.

   Discuss the role of stress in illness. Refer to immunosuppression, cardiovascular disorders and Fabrizio's experience in your answer. *(16 marks)*

Sources of stress: Life changes

Spec spotlight

Sources of stress: life changes.

They'd found the perfect dress – now all they needed were the shoes...

Apply it

Two psychology students conduct a survey of their fellow sixth-formers. They want to identify the experiences that are most stressful for students. Some have sadly lost family members; for others, their parents have divorced. Some have moved to the college from a different part of the country; others have celebrated the arrival of a baby in their family. All of them have been through important exams. The psychology students find that the people who have experienced most events are the ones who report being depressed, anxious and physically ill.

Use your knowledge of life changes to explain the psychology students' findings. Support your explanation with some evidence.

Life changes as a source of stress

Sources of stress are often the *big events* in our lives.	Major sources of stress are the really important things that happen to us from time to time. For example, getting married/divorced, close relative dies, financial state changes (better or worse), new child is born.
Life changes require *significant adjustment*, so are stressful.	Life changes are stressful because you make major psychological adjustment to adapt to changed circumstances – the bigger the change, the greater the adjustment and associated stress. Life changes are cumulative – they add together to create more stress because they require even more change to adapt. Applies as much to positive life changes as to negative ones.
Life changes measured using *SRRS*, calculating LCUs.	Holmes and Rahe's (1967) *Social Readjustment Rating Scale* (SRRS) gives number of life change units (LCUs). The higher the LCU value, the more adjustment the life change needs, making it more stressful (e.g. divorce is 73 LCUs; marriage is 50). Participants tick all the life changes they recall over previous months (usually 12).
Life changes linked to illness if *LCUs more than 300*.	Rahe (1972) suggested scoring under 150 LCUs means you are likely to experience reasonable health in following year. Between 150 and 300 LCUs means you have 50% chance of experiencing illness the next year. Over 300 LCUs means an 80% chance.

Key study: Rahe *et al.* (1970) Life changes and illness

Procedure	US Navy personnel assigned to three ships completed a version of the SRRS called *Schedule of Recent Experiences* (forerunner to SRRS). Total LCU score was calculated for each participant for a six-month period before tour of duty – every illness on board ship was reported to the medical unit. At the end of the tour, an independent researcher reviewed the medical records and calculated an illness score for each participant. Neither participants nor on-board medical staff aware of the purpose of study or what data were being used for.
Findings	Researchers found significant positive **correlation** (of +.118) between LCU scores for six months before departure and illness scores aboard ship. Those who experienced most stressful life changes in the final six months before leaving had most (severe) illnesses on ship. Researchers concluded life changes were a reasonably robust predictor of later illness.

One strength of the life changes concept is supportive research evidence.

Lietzén *et al.* (2011) found a high level of life change was a reliable predictor of asthma onset. Link not explained by known risk factors (e.g. pet at home or smoking).

Study after study has found a moderate but significant positive correlation between stress of life changes and illnesses.

Some research is especially supportive because it is prospective – methodologically powerful because it predicts illness in the future based on past life changes.

One limitation of life changes research is it ignores individual differences.

Life changes do not affect everyone in the same ways. For example, the stress a woman feels if she becomes pregnant depends on various things, such as whether it was planned or unexpected.

Byrne and Whyte (1980) tried to predict who would experience myocardial infarction (heart attack) based on life change scores. This only worked when they took into account the subjective interpretations participants gave to their life changes.

This suggests that the classic life changes approach fails to consider the impact of individual differences in how life changes are perceived, reducing the **validity** of this approach as an explanation of stress.

'Yellow and green should never be seen.' Sid had heard it all before – but it was Christmas and he was determined to make a point.

Another limitation of life changes research is it assumes all change is stressful.

The SRRS mixes together different types of life changes (e.g. positive and negative). But positive and negative changes may have different effects.

Turner and Wheaton (1995) found negative life changes caused most stress measured by the SRRS. Could be due to frustration associated with negative life changes.

This challenges the validity of the life changes approach, suggesting that a global measure should be abandoned in favour of looking at effects of specific life changes.

REVISION BOOSTER

It really pays to practise writing 16-mark essays with your book shut and timing yourself – about 20 minutes for a 16-mark essay.

A further limitation is life changes may be rather unimportant sources of stress.

Lazarus argues that daily hassles are more important sources of stress than life changes because the accumulative effect of many minor stressors is greater than that of a few, relatively rare major events.

DeLongis *et al.* (1988) studied married couples, finding that more hassles meant more health problems (e.g. headaches), but there was no such relationship between life changes and illnesses.

Failure to find a correlation between life changes and illnesses in this study casts doubt on validity of life changes as a predictor of stress and suggests daily hassles may be the more useful concept.

KNOWLEDGE CHECK

1. In relation to sources of stress, explain what is meant by 'life changes'. Use examples in your answer.
(4 marks)

2. Describe **one** study into life changes as a source of stress. In your answer refer to what the researcher(s) did and what they found. *(6 marks)*

3. Evaluate research into **one** source of stress. *(6 marks)*

A final limitation of life changes research is that most of it is correlational.

Many studies measure life changes (using SRRS) and illness (frequency and/or severity) and find a positive correlation between them – higher LCU score, higher 'illness score'.

Because we are not justified in drawing conclusions about cause and effect based on correlational analysis, we cannot claim that stress of life changes causes illness.

This is a limitation because it is possible that another causal factor (e.g. having less money) could explain relationship. This means effects of life changes on illness are most likely to be indirect.

4. Tad and Tadita have both had a stressful year. Tad split up with his wife and had to move house and start a new job. Tadita got married and had a baby.

   Outline and evaluate life changes as a source of stress. Refer to Tad's and Tadita's experiences in your answer.
(16 marks)

Sources of stress: Daily hassles

Spec spotlight

Sources of stress: daily hassles.

Mental note: buy more post-its!

Apply it

Hadrian has noticed the following about daily life. The laptop always takes longer to boot up when you need it most. The weather can be beautiful until you go on holiday, when it pours down. What you are looking for is always in the last place you look. A pound coin dropped on the floor always rolls miles away. Hadrian believes that these experiences are frustrating and irritating and gang up on us to cause us harm.

a. Use research on daily hassles to explain Hadrian's experiences.

b. What is the evidence that he is right?

c. Is there another explanation?

REVISION BOOSTER

In a 16-mark essay you don't have to write everything on this spread. What is here is actually more than 1000 words!! For a 16-mark essay you probably only have time to write 500 words – but don't cut down the evaluation. That's worth 10 marks so it is always better to do more evaluation.

Daily hassles as a source of stress

Daily hassles are frequent and *everyday irritations* and frustrations.	According to Lazarus *et al.* (1980) daily hassles range from: • Minor inconveniences (e.g. can't find keys). • Greater pressures and difficulties (e.g. not enough time). Each hassle on its own does not have the impact of a significant life change – but their added effects leave us feeling stressed.
Stressfulness of daily hassles depends on *psychological appraisal.*	Primary appraisal: Lazarus argued that when we experience a hassle we engage in primary appraisal – we work out subjectively how threatening it is to psychological health. Secondary appraisal: if we deem that the hassle is threatening we engage in secondary appraisal – we subjectively consider how well equipped we are to cope with the hassle.
Daily hassles measured with *HSUP.*	*Hassles and Uplifts Scale* (HSUP) is a self-report measure of: • Hassles: how many experienced and how severe they are (e.g. losing things, not having enough time). • Uplifts: small, daily pleasant and enjoyable things that offset stress of hassles (e.g. getting on well with friends).
Effects of *life changes and daily hassles* are different.	Life changes have indirect effects – they are *distal* sources of stress. Daily hassles have direct and immediate effects on our everyday lives – they are *proximal* sources of stress.

Key study: Kanner *et al.* (1981) Hassles and psychological symptoms

Procedure	100 participants completed several scales: • *Hassles Scale* every month for nine consecutive months. • *Life changes scale* 2½ years before study started, again one month before and again at end of the study. • *Hopkins Symptom Checklist* to measure psychological symptoms of anxiety and depression.
Findings	Researchers found significant positive **correlations** between hassle frequency and psychological symptoms at start and end of study. The more hassles the participants experienced the more severe were the psychological symptoms of depression and anxiety. Hassles were a stronger predictor of psychological symptoms than life changes both during the ten months of the study and from 2½ years earlier.

One strength is the daily hassles concept has research evidence to support it.

Research by Ivancevich (1986) suggests daily hassles and life events both have effects on health, but daily hassles are more influential.

Daily hassles were better predictors of poor health, poor job performance and absenteeism from work compared with life changes.

This is a strength because a substantial body of research exists to suggest daily hassles are a more **valid** explanation of stress than life changes.

One limitation of daily hassles research is that it is mostly retrospective.

Participants complete checklists by recalling hassles experienced over a particular time period (e.g. past month).

The usefulness of any data that relies on retrospective recall depends on how accurate participants' memories are.

This suggests validity of hassles research may be doubtful because people may not accurately recall the number and strength of daily hassles.

Another limitation is that daily hassles may have less effect than life changes.

The *amplification hypothesis* suggests daily hassles contribute to illness only when we experience major life changes. Chronic stress of life change makes minor daily stressors seem worse than usual.

For example, for someone moving house (life change), losing an everyday item such as a key (hassle) might take on much greater significance than normal.

But it is the life change that is the real culprit and the daily hassle is just the immediate precipitating factor, suggesting that life changes have a greater impact.

Bad hair day? We've all had one.

A further limitation of the hassles concept is it can't explain gender differences.

Males and females differ in their interpretation of what hassles are.

Helms *et al.* (2010) argue that because men and women have different roles within most families, they experience the same everyday events differently (e.g. domestic chore becomes a hassle for whoever has to carry it out regularly).

This suggests the explanation of stress in terms of daily hassles is limited because it cannot account for why men and women differ in what they consider to be hassles.

A final limitation of hassles research is that it is mostly correlational.

Hassles research suffers from the same problems of drawing cause and effect conclusions as we saw in the case of life changes.

Despite consistent and significant correlations between hassles and illness, we cannot claim hassles cause illness. An intervening variable (e.g. being depressed) may cause both a tendency to report daily hassles and to report illnesses.

This means that most research cannot give us answers about the direct effects of hassles on physical and psychological symptoms of illness.

REVISION BOOSTER

A lot of research has addressed the issue of which is the best predictor of illness, life changes or daily hassles? You could tackle evaluation bearing this in mind. You could compare and contrast the two sources of stress. But keep your focus on the topic of the exam question.

KNOWLEDGE CHECK

1. Using examples, explain the difference between life changes and daily hassles.
   (4 marks)
2. Describe **one** study into daily hassles as a source of stress.
   (6 marks)
3. Briefly evaluate research into daily hassles as a source of stress. *(4 marks)*
4. Discuss daily hassles as a source of stress. Refer to **at least one** other source of stress in your answer. *(16 marks)*

Sources of stress: Workplace stress

Spec spotlight

Sources of stress: workplace stress, including the effects of workload and control.

No one can be that happy to do housework. Their secret? The bottles are filled with vodka.

REVISION BOOSTER

In an exam everyone feels some measure of anxiety – use your understanding of stress to help cope with exam anxiety.

Harmony is an A level student who is struggling under a big workload. She has six essays to do in ten days. She feels she is working harder than she did at GCSE. But because there is so much to do, she feels she has no control over her work. There's no time for planning and now she has another piece of work – she is part of a group preparing a presentation on workplace stress.

Using your knowledge of sources of stress, identify the features of Harmony's situation that make it particularly stressful. Explain how she might feel and why. Refer to some research in your explanation.

Research into workplace stress

Workload and control	Workload = the amount of work someone has to do. Can refer to underload as well as overload, but is usually the latter.
	Control = extent worker feels able to make own decisions, work independently, have more flexibility to set own pace (e.g. scheduling tasks themselves).
	Having job control acts as a buffer against the negative effects of workload because it reduces the amount of stress experienced.
Job demands – control model combines workload and control.	Karasek's (1979) job demands-control model states stressful demands of a job (e.g. workload) can lead to poor health, dissatisfaction and absenteeism – but this relationship is modified by amount of control the employee has over work.
	When two people have equally demanding workloads, only the one who lacks control over work becomes ill.

Key study 1: Bosma *et al.* (1997) Control and workplace stress

Procedure	Whitehall Studies were prospective studies of over 10,000 civil servants in a wide range of job grades.
	Devised a questionnaire to measure workload and job control.
	Participants also examined for symptoms of coronary heart disease (CHD) and followed up after five years.
Findings	Researchers found no **correlation** between workload and illness – so job demands were not a significant workplace stressor.
	But employees who reported low job control at the start of the study more likely to have CHD five years later – even when other risk factors (e.g. lifestyle, diet) statistically accounted for.
	Finding also existed across all job grades – status and support given to higher grade civil servants did not offset risk of developing CHD if job lacked control.

Key study 2: Johansson *et al.* (1978) Workload, control and stress

Procedure	**Natural experiment** in Swedish sawmill compared group of wood 'finishers' and group of cleaners.
	Measured employee illness, absenteeism, and levels of the stress hormones adrenaline and noradrenaline.
	Finishers had little control over work because it was dictated by the machine – but job demands were high because it was complex, skilled and carried a lot of responsibility.
Findings	Researchers found higher level of stress hormones in finishers overall – higher even before they got to work and increased over the day (but cleaners' levels decreased).
	More stress-related illness and absenteeism among finishers.

One limitation of the job demands-control model is that it is simplistic.

Lack of control and workload are significant stressors for many workers (at least in some cultures) but are not the only ones.

How much stress a worker experiences is the outcome of a complex interaction between the kind of work they do and how well they use coping mechanisms.

Job demands-control model ignores other factors and lacks **validity** because of simplistic focus on just two major job-related sources of stress.

Another limitation is the model may not explain cultural differences.

Györkös *et al.* (2012) reviewed cross-cultural studies and found a lack of job control was seen as stressful in **individualist** cultures (e.g. UK and US).

However, in **collectivist** cultures (e.g. China and other Asian countries) control was considered less desirable.

Concept of job control may be a Western notion reflecting individualist ideals of equity and personal rights. May not **generalise** to non-Western cultures which prioritise the good of wider society.

If I look stressed enough maybe I can sneak in a little kip and no one will notice...

A further limitation is evidence that having job control is more stressful.

Some research shows too much control can be a source of work stress. This depends on **self-efficacy**: the extent to which you believe you are capable of performing tasks successfully.

Meier *et al.* (2008) found employees with low self-efficacy felt more strain in jobs that gave more control. Reverse is true for employees with high self-efficacy – low control is more stressful.

People with low self-efficacy do not benefit from having greater control (e.g. in choices they have, greater flexibility to make decisions, etc.). They find it more stressful, which is not predicted by the model.

A limitation of the Whitehall Studies is that there are methodological problems.

Focus of Whitehall Studies was on control and job demands (workload) to test the demands-control model. Other potentially vital sources of stress were ignored (e.g. pay, conditions, job security).

These 'ignored' factors are confounded with employment grade. Civil servants in lower grades have less job security and poorer pay and conditions, in contrast with those in senior grades.

These are **confounding variables** reducing the validity of findings. This means it is difficult to know if the reason for illness was lack of job control or one of these other confounding variables.

A limitation of the sawmill study was it also had some methodological flaws.

This was a natural experiment because researchers were unable to **randomly allocate** workers to the two groups for obvious practical reasons.

So finishers and cleaners could have differed systematically in ways that might affect the outcome (e.g. finishers did a more skilled job than cleaners, so finishers may have been better trained and educated than cleaners).

This means the validity of the study is low because findings can be explained by factors other than the variable under investigation.

KNOWLEDGE CHECK

1. Outline research into the effects of workload **and/or** control on workplace stress.
   (6 marks)

2. Describe **one** study into the effects of workload on workplace stress. In your answer refer to what the researcher(s) did and what they found. *(6 marks)*

3. Evaluate research into the effects of control on workplace stress. *(6 marks)*

4. The following item appeared in a newspaper: 'Work kills, say psychologists. Experts yesterday told us what we all know already. If you have too much work to do, and you can't control it, then you will get ill.'

   Referring to the issues raised in this item, outline and evaluate research into the workplace as a source of stress. *(16 marks)*

Self-report measures of stress

Spec spotlight

Measuring stress: self-report scales (Social Readjustment Rating Scale and Hassles and Uplifts Scale) and physiological measures, including skin conductance response.

Apply it

An organisational psychologist has been asked by an NHS trust to measure levels of stress amongst its staff. Because he feels that just one measure is not enough to understand stress fully, he chooses two methods – one to measure people's feelings about the stress they experience, and the other to measure the physical effects of stress. He expects he will find a correlation between the two measures. His report will have to include a brief assessment of the advantages and disadvantages of both measures.

a. Describe **two** specific measures that would meet the psychologist's needs.

b. Briefly outline his assessment of them – what strengths and limitations could he include in his report?

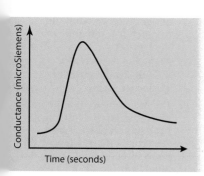

A typical skin conductance response (SCR): a slope at the start indicating the onset of the response, which then takes time to rise, reaches a peak and then decays in a long 'tail' on the trace, all within a few seconds.

Self-report measures of stress

SRRS 43 life events linked to change.	*Social Readjustment Rating Scale* (SRRS) created by Holmes and Rahe (1967) using medical records to identify events in patients' lives that happened not long before they became ill. 43 life events, involving major positive or negative life change.
LCU scores provide measure of stress.	Life change unit (LCU) calculated for each life event by asking a group of people to estimate readjustment required for each event, using marriage (500 units) as a baseline. SRRS is used by asking participants to indicate which life events they have experienced in the past 12 months – LCUs for these are added to give an overall (global) stress score.
Hassles scale 117 items.	Kanner *et al.* (1981) created *Hassles and Uplifts Scale* (HSUP) to measure daily hassles and uplifts as indicators of stress. Hassles Scale has 117 items selected from categories such as 'work', 'health' and 'environment' (e.g. 'troublesome neighbours', 'too much responsibility'). Measures severity of each hassle on a three-point scale: 'somewhat', 'moderately' or 'extremely severe'.
Uplifts scale 135 items.	135 Uplifts Scale items were produced from the same categories as the Hassles Scale – uplifts include 'getting enough sleep', 'liking fellow workers'. Individual identifies all the uplifts that apply and indicates their frequency over a specific time period (e.g. that day).

Physiological measures of stress

Stress arouses the ANS *producing sweat* which conducts electricity.	Stress creates arousal in **autonomic nervous system** (ANS). One consequence is that we sweat more – human skin is a good conductor of electricity and sweat enhances that – the more we sweat, the more conductance there is. To measure conductance: <ul><li>Electrodes are attached to index and middle fingers of one hand to detect sweating.</li><li>A tiny current (cannot be felt) is applied to electrodes to measure how much electricity is conducted.</li><li>Conductance can be measured (in microSiemens) – the signal is amplified and displayed on a screen.</li></ul>
SCR is a measure of stress.	*Tonic conductance* is skin conductance when we are not experiencing a stimulus (used as baseline). *Phasic conductance* occurs when something happens (e.g. shown an image or asked a question) – produces skin conductance response (SCR).

One limitation of SRRS and HSUP is the items are ambiguous.

Many items on stress measures are general categories rather than individual events so are open to interpretation by different participants in research studies.

Dohrenwend et al. (1990) found their participants interpreted items such as 'serious illness and injury' in a variety of ways from 'sprained arm' to 'a life-threatening heart attack'.

Intra-category variability reduces **validity** of self-report measures so it is difficult to assess the true relationship between stress, life events, hassles and illness.

Another limitation of the SRRS and HSUP is the contamination effect.

The SRRS and Hassles Scale are intended to be used as predictors of stress-related illness. But many items on both scales overlap with symptoms of physical and psychological disorders.

So, rather than predicting illness, these scales reflect it. Stress and illness are confounded (acting as **confounding variables**) with hassles and life changes, when they should be separate.

Some researchers believe self-report measures of stress are so compromised by methodological problems they should be replaced by direct observation of behaviour.

Another limitation is the SRRS and HSUP assess 'global' stress.

SRRS and HSUP provide one score combining many different aspects of the stressors they measure. The assumption is a single measure of stress can be used to predict any kind of illness.

It makes more sense to assume that there are specific types of life changes (or hassles) within these scales that may predict particular illnesses (e.g. several items on the SRRS which relate to loss).

Validity of these scales may be reduced because the overall score tells us very little. If the global score does not predict illness, then the scale has little practical value.

Well I fixed that leaky tap. That gushing sound? Yeah, sorry about that. I think you might need a plumber... and perhaps the fire service.

A limitation of the SRRS is muddling controllable and uncontrollable events.

Stern et al. (1982) found that uncontrollable life changes measured by the SRRS were reasonably reliable predictors of later physical illness whereas controllable changes were not.

This finding highlights the importance of taking into account the interpretations individuals place on items on a self-report scale.

A scale lacks validity if it cannot predict who becomes ill. Scales that cannot distinguish between controllable and uncontrollable life changes (and hassles) clearly fall into this category.

Validity revisited

Validity can be a confusing topic, but here it's happily straightforward. It's all about these questions: 'Does the method really measure stress? Or something else? How do we know it really measures stress?'

One limitation of the SCR is there are individual differences.

SCR measurement recognises people have different patterns of skin conductance, so baseline measure (tonic conductance) is taken before stimulus is presented.

However, some people are *stabiles* (SCRs vary little when they are at rest, and not much influenced by internal thoughts or external events). Others are *labiles* (produce a lot of SCRs even when resting).

This suggests the SCR measurement is not a straightforward matter of comparing baseline SCRs (tonic) against stimulated SCRs (phasic).

KNOWLEDGE CHECK

1. Distinguish between self-report scales and physiological measures in measuring stress. *(3 marks)*
2. Briefly outline skin conductance response as a way of measuring stress. *(4 marks)*
3. Evaluate self-report scales as ways of measuring stress. *(6 marks)*
4. Discuss **two** ways of measuring stress. *(16 marks)*

Individual differences in stress: Personality type

Individual differences in stress: personality types A, B and C and associated behaviours.

Ah this is the life... Eh? What water? And where did my front room go??

CVD? CHD?

What's the difference? CVD stands for cardiovascular disorder and refers to disorders of the heart (coronary) and blood vessels (vascular). So this includes heart attacks and strokes (lack of blood supply to the brain).

CVD also includes CHD, i.e. coronary heart disease. So CHD is a specific type of CVD.

It doesn't really matter if you get them mixed up but we thought we would make the difference clear!

For the twenty-seventh time today... I have never taken out payment protection insurance!

Type A and B

Type A Competitive, time urgent and hostile.	Friedman and Rosenman (1959) observed that patients with coronary heart disease (CHD) shared a pattern of behaviour, which they called Type A personality: • Competitive – driven, achievement-motivated, ambitious, aware of status. • Time urgent – fast-talking, impatient, proactive, multitaskers. • Hostile – aggressive, intolerant and quick to anger.
Type B Laid back.	Friedman and Rosenman also identified the characteristics of Type B personality – relaxed, tolerant, reflective, 'laid back' and less competitive than Type As.
Western Collaborative Group Study (WCGS)	3000 males in California medically assessed as free of CHD at the start of the study. Assessed for personality type by answering 25 questions in a structured interview. Interviews were conducted to incite Type A-related behaviour (e.g. interviewer would be aggressive and frequently interrupt).
Link to *CHD*.	Eight-and-a-half years later, 257 men had developed CHD. 70% of these assessed at the start of the study as Type A – considerably more than the Type Bs who developed CHD. Type As had higher levels of adrenaline and noradrenaline and higher blood pressure/cholesterol. Suggests Type A personality makes people vulnerable to stressors because impatience and hostility cause raised physiological stress response.

Type C

Type C Pathological niceness, repress emotions.	Type C people demonstrate pathological niceness, are 'people pleasers', compliant, passive and self-sacrificing. They avoid conflict by repressing emotions, especially anger (particularly relevant to cancer-proneness).
Link to *cancer*.	Temoshok (1987) proposed Type C is linked with cancer. Dattore *et al.* (1980) studied 200 veterans of the Vietnam War – 75 cancer patients and others with non-cancer diagnoses. Cancer patients reported significantly greater emotional repression and fewer depression symptoms (unlikely to acknowledge depression because repressing emotions). This is evidence of a link between Type C and cancer-proneness.

One strength of the Type A concept is there is research support.

Edigo et al. (2012) studied 150 Spanish men and women under 65 years of age who had had a stroke, and compared them with a matched control group.

Stroke sufferers were more likely to be Type A. This was true for both men and women and not explained by traditional lifestyle risk factors (e.g. smoking and diet).

The fact that recent research continues to support the view that Type A plays a role in CVD suggests that the concept has some validity.

One limitation of the role of personality in stress is contradictory evidence.

Some research shows Type B personality is associated with a greater risk of CHD than Type A.

Ragland and Brand (1988) followed up men from Friedman and Rosenman's original study who survived a heart attack. Type B survivors were more likely to die than Type As.

This finding demonstrates that the relationship between Type A/B personalities and illness is a complex one and not yet fully understood.

One limitation of the Type A concept is that it is too broad.

Type A personality includes too many different traits. Research focus moved to the hostility component of Type A (hostile people are selfish, manipulative, mistrusting and contemptuous).

Dembroski et al. (1989) reanalysed data from Friedman and Rosenman's study and found that ratings of hostility significantly predicted later incidence of CHD.

This certainly casts doubt on validity of the Type A personality (but also supports the view that some aspect of Type A personality is involved in CHD).

A further limitation of original Type A/B distinction is complex link with CHD.

Type A/B classification was modified by Friedman et al. (1985) because research produced many inconsistent and contradictory findings – 'Type A' may not be same as 'coronary-proneness'.

Some Type As are confident and active, and unlikely to develop CHD.

Some Type Bs are quiet and unaggressive because they suppress Type A characteristics (e.g. ambition and hostility), and may develop CHD.

This alteration has a significant effect on the validity of Type A and B concepts because it blurs the boundary between the two and makes it more difficult to use the concept of Type A to predict who is likely to develop CHD.

One limitation of the Type C concept is some contradictory evidence.

Greer and Morris (1975) found a link between emotional suppression typical of Type C and breast cancer, but only in women under 50.

Research into links between Type C and cancer is plagued by inconsistent findings and failures to replicate apparently significant results.

Type C may be very 'fragmented' rather than a single personality type. So, it is currently impossible to use Type C concept to predict who is likely to get cancer.

Apply it

Harold has a very responsible job with a major charity. He wants to lead the charity one day so he is always trying to do three things at once, impatiently rushing around. Harold is very demanding of everyone around him so he often snaps at them.

Henrika is a volunteer with a support group for children with autism. She is very laid back and relaxed with the children and their parents. She has an unhurried and calm approach to her work and life.

Hester's aim in life is to make sure everyone around her is happy. Because she wants to please everyone, she often 'bites her lip' and keeps her thoughts to herself. She often finds herself agreeing with the last person she spoke to.

Identify the three personality types described here. Use your knowledge of individual differences in stress to explain your choices.

KNOWLEDGE CHECK

1. In relation to individual differences in stress, explain what is meant by Type B and Type C personality. (3 marks + 3 marks)
2. Outline research into personality types in relation to individual differences in stress. (6 marks)
3. Describe one study of personality Type A in relation to individual differences in stress. In your answer refer to what the researcher(s) did and what they found. (6 marks)
4. Discuss one or more individual differences in stress. Refer to research evidence in your answer. (16 marks)

Individual differences in stress: Hardiness

Spec spotlight

Individual differences in stress: hardiness, including commitment, challenge and control.

Still trying, son (see our Year 1 Revision Guide).

Apply it

Kalil works for an organisation that helps young people cope with life's problems. He runs courses and activity weekends where teenagers learn the value of being able to stand up to stress and beat it. Kalil himself used to be addicted to heroin, but now he is determined to overcome all the setbacks that life throws at him. He tells the young people they can do the same by developing their 'Three Cs'.

a. Use your knowledge of individual differences in stress to explain what Kalil means by the 'Three Cs'.

b. How could the 'Three Cs' help the young people to overcome stress? Refer to **one** piece of research in your answer.

REVISION BOOSTER

Write a very brief essay plan for each possible essay and then practise writing the essay in full from this. Time yourself – 20 minutes for a 16-mark essay.

Hardiness

Hardiness *protects against stress*; 'existential courage'.	Kobasa (1979) proposed hardiness is a set of personality characteristics that protect us against stress. Maddi (1986) argues hardiness gives us 'existential courage' – the will or determination to keep going despite setbacks life throws at us and uncertainties about the future.
Three dimensions to hardiness: *commitment, challenge, control.*	Commitment: hardy people deeply involved in relationships, activities and selves. They throw themselves wholeheartedly into life, optimistic they will learn something valuable. Challenge: hardy people are resilient and welcome change as an opportunity or a challenge rather than a threat. They recognise life is unpredictable, but this is exciting and stimulating. Control: hardy people have a strong belief that they are in charge of events. They actively strive to influence environments rather than being powerless and passive observers of life passing by.

Key study 1: Kobasa (1979) Hardiness and stress

Procedure	Kobasa measured life changes of 670 male American middle and senior managers aged 40–49 years. Used *Schedule of Recent Experiences* (forerunner of SRRS) to identify who experienced high stress over previous three years. Also analysed absenteeism records and levels of illness.
Findings	Managers responded to same degree of stress very differently. Some were more resilient – they could tolerate high levels of stress without becoming ill or taking time off work. Kobasa interpreted this finding as confirming role of hardiness because resilient managers scored highly on the Three Cs.

Key study 2: Maddi (1987) Hardiness at work

Procedure	Maddi studied 400 managers and supervisors at the Bell Telephone company in the US over several years. The Bell Telephone company underwent one of the biggest reorganisations in American corporate history when thousands of people lost their jobs – also extremely stressful experience for those who stayed.
Findings	Significant declines in performance and health in about two-thirds of participants (e.g. heart attacks, strokes, depression and drug abuse). The managers who scored highly on measures of the Three Cs flourished – their health did not deteriorate, they felt happier and more fulfilled at work and were rejuvenated by the whole stressful experience.

One limitation of hardiness is the difficulty in measuring the concept.

Funk (1992) pointed out that most popular scales measure hardiness by asking questions about negative traits (e.g. powerlessness and alienation).

A hardy person gets low scores on these items, so scales may measure lack of neuroticism rather than hardiness as such because neuroticism is characterised by anxiety, fear, worry.

So, a substantial amount of research into the relationship between hardiness, stress and illness is based on measures of hardiness that lack **validity**.

Another limitation of hardiness is the Three Cs may not be equally important.

There seems to be an element of control at the heart of both commitment and challenge.

Also much research shows how important personal control is to well-being. So it's likely that control is a key factor determining hardy response to stressors.

Hull et al. (1987) recommend that research focuses on control and commitment only and abandons the challenge component altogether.

Another limitation is effects of hardiness on health are mostly indirect.

Contrada (1989) found hardy people had lower blood pressure, but was unable to choose between two explanations of this finding.

Being hardy could reduce physiological effects of stressors on the body. Alternatively hardy people might engage in healthy behaviours (e.g. taking regular exercise) so hardiness indirectly reduces risk of illness.

This makes it difficult to pinpoint the reasons why hardiness might be beneficial, which reduces the usefulness of the concept and raises doubts about its validity.

One strength of hardiness is that there is research evidence to support it.

The role of hardiness in relation to illness has been confirmed in a variety of research studies.

Contrada (1989) found students who scored highest on a measure of hardiness had lower levels of blood pressure in a stressful lab task. Lowest blood pressure was in students who were hardy and also had Type B personality.

This finding shows hardiness has a biological basis in the stress response (hardy participants had lower blood pressure). Suggests hardiness is a genuine characteristic of people who can resist stress.

Another strength of hardiness is that it has useful real-life applications.

Bartone et al. (2008) found that candidates who passed a four-week assessment course for the US Army Special Forces were significantly hardier than those who did not pass.

This and other research shows hardiness is linked to resilience against combat stress – so elite units of US military routinely assess candidates for hardiness. Training programmes aim to increase hardiness further.

This increases the validity of the hardiness concept because real-life application confirms relevance of concept to understanding stress (e.g. used to predict who will be able to resist stress).

Cut out that negativity!

REVISION BOOSTER

Personality type (previous topic) and hardiness are named on the specification so you could get questions specifically on these. Or the question could be on 'individual differences'. This is good news, because you can choose – one or the other or both. But be careful not to spend too long on AO1.

KNOWLEDGE CHECK

1. Define the terms 'commitment', 'challenge' and 'control' in relation to hardiness.
   (2 marks + 2 marks + 2 marks)
2. Outline research into hardiness. Refer in your answer to commitment, challenge and control. *(6 marks)*
3. Evaluate research into hardiness in relation to individual differences in stress. *(6 marks)*
4. Padraig works in a big college which is undergoing major changes. Some of his colleagues are showing signs of stress, but he does not feel stressed at all. He explains that this is a chance for him to develop, learn new things, and work hard to come through hard times.

   Describe and evaluate research into hardiness in relation to individual differences in stress. Refer to Padraig's experience in your answer. *(16 marks)*

Managing and coping with stress: drug therapy (benzodiazepines, beta blockers).

Er, I think I might need a glass of water.

Olympia is a teacher of children with learning support needs. After a few years in this very stressful job she found the demands overwhelming because her workload increased and she had less say in how she did things. One day she felt very light-headed and dizzy. She went to her doctor who measured her blood pressure and found it was very high. He immediately gave Olympia a tablet to take and a prescription for more of the drug. But Olympia would like to consider her options.

a. Explain how drug therapy could benefit Olympia.

b. Why is she right to consider alternatives?

Benzodiazepines (BZs)

BZs act on *CNS*.	BZs (e.g. diazepam) reduce the anxiety associated with stress by reducing central nervous system (CNS) arousal.
	They tap into one way the body naturally combats anxiety.
Mode of action of BZs involves **GABA**.	Gamma-aminobutyric acid (GABA) is a neurotransmitter that inhibits activity of most neurons in the brain.
	During synaptic transmission, GABA combines with GABA-A receptors on the postsynaptic neuron.
	This inhibits activity in the postsynaptic neuron making it less likely signals will be passed from one neuron to the next.
BZ drug molecules *combine with GABA receptors*.	BZs enhance this natural inhibition, so there is even less neuronal activity in the brain.
	BZ drug molecules combine with GABA receptors so channels in the receptors open more often (without being blocked) for chloride ions to enter the neuron.
	This makes the neuron more responsive to inhibitory effects of GABA and less responsive to other neurotransmitters – reducing activity throughout the CNS and anxiety.

Beta blockers (BBs)

BBs act on **sympathetic nervous system**.	Beta-adrenergic blockers (beta blockers) act on the sympathetic nervous system to reduce sympathetic arousal, a key part of stress-related anxiety.
	BBs (e.g. *atenolol*) are prescribed to reduce blood pressure and treat heart problems.
Mode of action of BBs involves *adrenaline and noradrenaline*.	Stress hormones adrenaline and noradrenaline are produced as part of the sympathomedullary (SAM) pathway.
	These hormones combine with beta-adrenergic receptors located throughout cardiovascular system (mainly in heart and blood vessels).
	This explains increased heart rate and blood pressure associated with stress.
BBs work by blocking *beta-adrenergic receptors*.	BBs stop beta-adrenergic receptors being stimulated by adrenaline and noradrenaline. This slows heart rate, reduces blood pressure, etc., reducing need for oxygen.
	BBs reduce stress-related anxiety without altering alertness because they don't operate directly on the brain. So they are ideal for people who want to eliminate physical symptoms of stress but remain alert (e.g. stage performers, surgeons).

One strength of BZs is high-quality research evidence shows they are effective.

In a **randomised controlled trial** (RCT), half the participants take a **placebo** (identical to drug but no effects) – knowing you are taking a drug has positive effects (placebo effect).

A recent review of high-quality RCT studies by Baldwin *et al.* (2013) concluded there is good evidence that BZs are significantly more effective than placebo in treating acute anxiety.

This suggests that BZs are effective in treating the main psychological component of stress (although the review did also find some BZs were less effective than others).

One strength of BBs is that research evidence shows they are effective.

Kelly (1980) concluded that BBs are effective for treating everyday anxieties associated with public speaking, exam nerves and even civil disturbances of living in Northern Ireland in 1970s.

BBs are also useful for people with social anxiety disorder in which fear of speaking in public is a major stressor. Because BBs reduce arousal they prevent further anxiety developing.

Studies consistently demonstrate BBs are an effective treatment for physical symptoms of stress but may be even more useful combined with other drugs such as BZs (Hayes and Schulz 1987).

One limitation of drug therapy is side effects.

Side effects of anti-stress drugs include drowsiness, respiration problems and paradoxical reactions (opposite outcomes to ones you expect from treatment, e.g. impulsive behaviours, uncontrollable emotional responses).

BBs also reduce heart rate and blood pressure too much in some patients and are not suitable for people with diabetes or severe depression. Patient might stop taking the drug because of side effects so anxiety symptoms return.

This means side effects need to be carefully weighed up against the benefits of the drug, and also against alternatives including psychological therapies (e.g. stress inoculation therapy).

Another limitation of drug therapy is that it only treats symptoms.

Drug therapy focuses on reducing symptoms of stress (mainly anxiety) and gives patient short-term relief.

Drug therapy does not attempt to treat root causes of stress so inappropriate treatment for chronic (long-term) stressors.

Long-term drug therapy for chronic stress may do more harm than good so psychological therapy might be more suitable.

A further limitation of BZs is that they are associated with dependence.

People become dependent on BZs when they need more of the drug over time to get the original effects and experience withdrawal when they stop taking it. Main symptoms are anxiety, depressed mood and sleep disturbances.

Ashton (2005) argues it is possible to manage withdrawal syndrome if done carefully with psychological support. Also points out this can be avoided by prescribing BZs for two to four weeks – but some doctors prescribe for months or even years.

Dependence can create greater problems for users of drug therapy than the stress it is intended to manage. So BZs should be used solely for intended purpose – to treat short-term anxiety.

Feeling better? Great. Now any chance I could have the glass back? It's my favourite.

REVISION BOOSTER

Note the phrase 'mode of action'. It's not on the specification, but it's crucial to your description of drug therapies. Explain *how* BZs and BBs work in the nervous system – be familiar with the physiological details.

KNOWLEDGE CHECK

1. In relation to managing and coping with stress, explain what is meant by 'drug therapy'. **(4 marks)**
2. Outline drug therapy as a way of managing and coping with stress. Refer to benzodiazepines **and** beta blockers in your answer. **(6 marks)**
3. Evaluate drug therapy as a way of managing and coping with stress. **(10 marks)**
4. In relation to managing and coping with stress, discuss drug therapy. **(16 marks)**

Of course I'm not stressed anymore, I'm euphoric!

Apply it

Our learning support teacher Olympia is now taking beta blockers to reduce her blood pressure. But she is investigating her other options for coping with stress. She speaks to a friend who tried stress inoculation therapy (SIT) and found it helped her a lot. So Olympia gets a referral to a clinical psychologist, who starts by telling her that there will be three stages to the therapy...

a. Outline the **three** stages of SIT. For each, give **one** practical way in which Olympia can be helped by SIT in her specific situation.

b. Use your knowledge of SIT to explain how effective the therapy could be for her.

Stress inoculation therapy (SIT)

SIT is a **cognitive behaviour therapy** focusing on how we think about stress.	Meichenbaum and Cameron (1973) identified phases of SIT – each focuses on practical steps needed to help the client.
	Phases are not completely distinct or in order – they overlap and there may be some going backwards before moving on.
Focus is on *cognitive appraisal*.	**Cognitive** appraisal: client learns to think differently – to see stressors as challenges that can be overcome.
	Client also educated to tell the difference between aspects of a stressful situation that can be changed and those that can't.
Phase 1 *Conceptualisation.* To understand stressors.	Client and therapist work together to identify and understand stressors the client faces.
	Client is educated about the nature of stress and its effects.
	There should be a warm and collaborative rapport between therapist and client.
	Client retains responsibility for their progress – client is the expert on his or her own stress experiences.
Phase 2 *Skills acquisition and rehearsal.* Coping self-statements	Client learns skills to cope with stress (e.g. relaxation, social skills, communication, cognitive restructuring).
	Major element of skills acquisition is learning to monitor and use self-talk – client uses coping self-statements ('You can do this!', 'Stick to the plan!') to replace anxious internal dialogue.
	Client plans in advance how to cope when stress occurs – how they can overcome it through skills they learn.
Phase 3 *Real-life application and follow-through.* Role play, homework tasks.	Therapist creates opportunities for client to try out skills in a safe environment. Various techniques are used to increase realism of stressful situations (e.g. role playing, visualisation, virtual reality, mobile apps).
	Learned skills are gradually transferred to the real world through homework tasks for client to deliberately seek out moderately stressful situations and use their coping skills in everyday life ('personal **experiments**').
	Client later feeds back to therapist for discussion and further work if necessary.
Inoculation gained through *relapse prevention.*	Therapist helps prepare the client to cope with setbacks – client learns to cognitively restructure setbacks as temporary learning opportunities and not permanent catastrophic failures.
	Part of inoculation is to identify potential problems in advance and plan how to deal with them.
	Involves therapist preparing the client to attribute success to their own skills and not to luck or chance or some other external agent (internal versus external locus of control).

One strength of SIT is its flexibility.

SIT incorporates a wide variety of stress management techniques in the skills acquisition phase. Can be used with individuals, couples, groups and in a variety of settings.

This means techniques can be tailored to specific needs – some skills are more suitable for elderly people or people with learning difficulties. Can even be adapted for use online.

This suggests that SIT is so flexible it has the potential to be an effective method of managing any form of stress, including in situations where people face racism and homophobia.

One limitation of SIT is that it is a very demanding therapy.

Clients must make big commitments of time and effort and be highly motivated. Training can be lengthy and involve self-reflection and learning new skills.

Applying SIT techniques to real life is especially challenging – some people find it difficult to use coping self-statements when experiencing the anxiety of a stressful situation.

These demands and sense of failure mean some people don't continue treatment, making it unsuccessful in many cases.

Tommy wasn't sure but he reckoned he might look the same even if his head was upside-down.

Another limitation of SIT is that success depends on control.

SIT is multidimensional – it uses many techniques to target a variety of stressors and symptoms. Unlikely that every aspect of this wide-ranging approach is equally effective.

Control may be the key factor explaining the effectiveness of SIT. As coping skills develop, client gains growing feeling of control over stressful situations.

This suggests that transfer of skills to everyday life does not work when client feels they cannot gain control over the situation.

A strength of SIT is research supporting its effectiveness.

Saunders *et al.*'s (1996) **meta-analysis** found SIT effective for reducing anxiety in performance situations (e.g. public speaking) and for enhancing performance under stress (e.g. doing better in exams).

They also found that SIT was as effective for people experiencing extreme anxiety as for those with moderate or normal levels of anxiety.

These findings are especially useful because they show that SIT reduces stress-related anxiety and also leads to improvements in actual performance.

Another strength is that SIT emphasises the importance of prevention.

SIT is 'future oriented' because it centres on inoculation and encourages clients to plan for what could happen, to be psychologically prepared not just for success but failure too.

This means that SIT is very far from being a 'quick fix', a criticism often levelled against physiological methods of stress management, such as drug therapy.

Therefore SIT identifies root causes of why a person is stressed. It gives clients skills and motivation to make real changes so the same situations do not arise again.

REVISION BOOSTER

When you describe SIT, focus on the practical details of how the therapy proceeds. What actually happens? What does the therapist do? And the client? There's a lot of material to choose from, and only 6 marks – not too difficult to give a detailed description of SIT, but dangerous if you do too much in an essay because you reduce the time for the AO3 writing.

KNOWLEDGE CHECK

1. Distinguish between stress inoculation therapy and **one other** way of managing and coping with stress. *(2 marks)*
2. Outline stress inoculation therapy as a way of managing and coping with stress. *(6 marks)*
3. Briefly evaluate stress inoculation therapy in relation to managing and coping with stress. *(4 marks)*
4. Describe and evaluate **two** ways of managing and coping with stress. *(16 marks)*

Managing and coping with stress: Biofeedback

Spec spotlight

Managing and coping with stress: biofeedback.

Of course Helen knew it was important to relax, but she still had to check her emails!

Apply it

Dr. Mair is preparing a presentation to a group of health workers about ways of coping with stress. Unfortunately, she knows little about biofeedback so she does some research. She speaks to several people who have experienced biofeedback. Some found it helped them, others didn't. But they were all able to help Dr. Mair understand how the procedure works.

Pretend you are Dr. Mair and prepare a short talk on biofeedback to explain its underlying concepts, the procedure involved and its effectiveness. Use some research evidence in your explanation.

Biofeedback

Biofeedback aims to control *involuntary* physiological processes.	Biofeedback trains people to control involuntary physiological processes (e.g. heart rate, muscle tension). Budzynski (1973) identified three phases, outlined below.
Phase 1 *Awareness* of own physiological response.	Client is connected to a machine which converts physiological activity into visual and/or auditory signal. • Muscular tension measured using electromyogram (EMG) – activity of muscles converted into tone of varying pitch. • Electroencephalogram (**EEG**) measures brain activity – shown on a screen. • Skin conductance responses (SCRs) indicate sweating activity and can similarly be displayed. Machines give visual or auditory feedback (i.e. a meaningful representation of physiological process being monitored).
Phase 2 *Learn to control* the physiological response.	Client applies learned stress management techniques. Client monitors the effect of changes – for example, can see that changed breathing causes change on visual display in the desired direction (e.g. altering the line of the graph). Biofeedback with children uses game-based interface – client adjusts physiological response to complete on-screen maze. Biofeedback from the machine is rewarding and reinforces client's behaviour, making further success more likely (i.e. **operant conditioning**).
Phase 3 *Transfer* what is learned to everyday life.	Once client becomes aware of their physiological response and how to control it (e.g. reducing heart rate), they transfer control to everyday life. They practise stress management techniques in stressful situations rather than in the therapy room.

Key study: Davis (1986) Biofeedback and cancer

Procedure	Biofeedback training involved 13 sessions lasting 45 minutes, over an eight-week period. Clients learned deep-breathing and relaxation techniques.
Findings	At an eight-month follow-up, levels of urinary cortisol and self-reported anxiety were significantly lower than at the start of the study. Cortisol levels increased in control participants who had no form of therapy. Researchers concluded this was evidence of significant stabilisation of the hypothalamic-pituitary-adrenal (HPA) system by biofeedback.

One strength of biofeedback is research evidence.

Lemaire et al. (2011) trained medical doctors to use a biofeedback device three times a day over a 28 day period. The doctors also completed a questionnaire measuring perception of how stressed they were.

Mean stress score for biofeedback users fell significantly over the course of the study. Corresponding score for a **control group** also fell but by a much smaller amount.

This suggests biofeedback has benefits in helping to improve the psychological state of someone experiencing stress.

One limitation of biofeedback is its effectiveness depends on what is measured.

Lemaire et al. (2011) found that biofeedback had very little effect on objective, physiological indicators of the stress response (e.g. cortisol levels).

Greenhalgh et al. (2009) found biofeedback was no more effective than other therapies in treating high blood pressure (a CVD). Also no more effective than **placebo** or no treatment.

Effectiveness of biofeedback depends on what you aim to 'treat'. It may help make individual 'feel better' but effects on stress-related risk factors for CVD much less clear.

A strength of biofeedback is it can improve other stress management methods.

Bussone et al. (1998) treated children suffering from tension headaches with either relaxation on its own or with BART (biofeedback-assisted relaxation therapy) i.e. relaxation + biofeedback.

Headache frequency reduced in both groups by 55% three months after treatment. However, improvements greater in BART group after one year and three years.

This suggests relaxation techniques are effective, but improved with biofeedback. So benefits of biofeedback may be as an aid to relaxation rather than a stress management technique in itself.

Another strength is biofeedback is a convenient stress management method.

Recent devices are about the size of a mobile phone. The client tries to change the colour of the device by controlling their breathing to reduce heart rate.

Further developments in 'wearable technology' (e.g. smartwatches) should make it even cheaper and easier to use biofeedback in stressful everyday situations.

Client aims to alter physiological responses without relying on the device, (i.e. encouraged to 'withdraw' over time as with drug therapy – although dependence on a device is less damaging to client's health than drugs).

A limitation is individual differences in effectiveness of biofeedback.

Biofeedback as a stress management method does not suit everyone.

Client has to understand relationship between physiological functioning and signals they receive and must be motivated to apply learned skills to alter signals in the real world.

Demands of biofeedback limit it as a method that everyone can use. But this is true of all methods, so no more a limitation of biofeedback than it is of SIT and drug therapy.

'So look,' said Lee excitedly, 'I can have exactly the same thing on my phone and my watch – at the same time!'

Who said technology is pointless?

REVISION BOOSTER

What are your evaluations like? Why not try and make them more like ours? Start with your initial point – a strength or a limitation in most cases. Then…elaborate! Develop your evaluation point in three more steps, just as we've done on all of these AO3 pages. Have a close look at each one to see what they have in common.

KNOWLEDGE CHECK

1. Explain the difference between biofeedback and stress inoculation therapy as ways of managing and coping with stress. *(4 marks)*
2. Outline biofeedback as a way of managing and coping with stress. *(6 marks)*
3. Evaluate biofeedback as a way of managing and coping with stress. *(6 marks)*
4. Two psychology teachers are discussing ways of coping with stress. Parveneh argues that drugs are the best option for most people. But Percy reckons that biofeedback is best because it worked for him.

   Discuss **two or more** ways of managing and coping with stress. Refer to the two psychology teachers in your answer. *(16 marks)*

Gender differences in coping with stress

Gender differences in coping with stress.

Clive reflected that perhaps his new bedroom wallpaper was, well... a bit random.

REVISION BOOSTER

Always think 'less is more' – writing about fewer things gives you the opportunity to demonstrate your detailed understanding. But, in a 16-mark essay, try to include something on each of the 6 points identified here.

Apply it

In times of stress, Rodrigo tries to tough it out with a 'stiff upper lip', tackling the issue just like he would any other problem. He was brought up to rely on himself and not to bother other people with his feelings. Gabriella has a different approach. She has lots of friends, so she gets help from as many of them as she can, especially her closest female friends. This helps to calm her and make her feel better about the situation.

Use your knowledge of gender differences in coping with stress to explain Rodrigo's and Gabriella's experiences.

Gender differences in coping with stress

Men tend to use *problem-focused* methods.	Lazarus and Folkman (1984) suggest problem-focused methods reduce stress by tackling root causes in a direct, practical and rational way.
	For example, taking control to remove or escape from stress, learning new skills such as time management or relaxation techniques.
Women tend to use *emotion-focused* methods.	Lazarus and Folkman suggest emotion-focused methods reduce stress indirectly by tackling the anxiety associated with a stressor.
	For example, various forms of avoidance such as keeping busy and using **cognitive** appraisal to think about the stressor more positively.
Men and women showed these differences in *coping with infertility*.	Peterson *et al.* (2006) assessed coping strategies of men and women diagnosed as infertile – using several measures, including the *Ways of Coping* questionnaire.
	Men are more likely to use planful problem-solving – feature of problem-focused approach.
	Women are more likely to accept blame and use various avoidance tactics – characteristics of emotion-focused approach.
Tend and befriend response in women.	Taylor *et al.* (2000) argue from an **evolutionary** perspective that fight or flight is disadvantageous for females because confronting or fleeing from a predator makes it hard to protect one's offspring.
	Different response has evolved in females – tend and befriend.
	• Tending is protecting, calming and nurturing offspring, blending in with environment.
	• Befriending involves seeking support from social networks at times of stress in order to cope.
Oxytocin drives tend and befriend response.	**Oxytocin** is mainly a female hormone. It promotes feelings of goodwill and affiliation with others, and helps the body recover more quickly from physiological effects of stressors.
	Taylor *et al.* (2002) found higher levels of oxytocin linked with lower cortisol levels only in female participants.
	Female sex hormone **oestrogen** increases effects of oxytocin, but male hormones (e.g. **testosterone**) reduce them – so oxytocin effects are stronger in women, creating reduced stress response.
Befriending tends to happen only with other women.	Women very strongly favour befriending in stressful situations – but selectively because generally only with other women.
	Lewis and Linder (2000) found most female participants preferred to wait for female support during a stressful experience rather than seek it from a man – might have evolved as a mechanism for protecting females and offspring against threatening males.

One limitation is role constraint theory misrepresents gender differences.

Role constraint theory argues that coping strategies are highly situation-specific, (e.g. work stressors lend themselves to problem-focused coping but emotion-focused strategies more suitable in relationships).

Matud (2004) found women and men experienced different types of stressful life changes (women more family-related and men more work-related). Women also used more emotion-focused coping than men.

This shows gender differences are due to men and women experiencing different stressors (predicted by role constraint theory) not reflecting something fundamental about being a man or a woman.

Another limitation is further evidence against gender differences in coping.

Porter and Stone (1995) found women reported more relationship-related stressors and men more work-related ones, as other research has shown.

But when this variation was accounted for, there were no important gender differences. Choice of coping style does not depend on gender but on nature of situation.

So, gender differences not because one coping method is 'female-preferred' and another 'male-preferred' but due to one working in a situation where the other doesn't.

We're laughing maniacally because we've had too much coffee!

REVISION BOOSTER

There are a few research studies here – you don't have to include all of them in your answer. But it is important to provide some specific evidence. If you just say that 'lots of studies support gender differences', then that's quite a weak evaluation point. You need to make it clear that you have knowledge and understanding of specific studies which support your arguments.

If studies are used as AO3 then focus on the conclusions not the procedures.

One limitation is some evidence shows there is no link with gender differences.

Peterson et al. (2006) discovered men and women used coping methods that did not fit the classic distinction between emotion-focused and problem-focused.

Seeking social support can be both emotion-focused and problem-focused. Women used it to seek information (problem-focused) and for emotional support (emotion-focused).

This suggests men and women use both methods depending on the nature of the stressor rather than gender differences as such.

A further limitation of gender difference research is that much is retrospective.

Participants think back to stressful occasions and recall methods they used to cope – this has an impact on the findings of research studies.

De Ridder (2000) found women reported using emotion-focused coping more than men only when recalling retrospectively. Difference disappeared when participants used method of reporting coping strategies at regular intervals in the day.

The gender difference is not robust if it only exists when a certain measurement method is used.

A strength of the 'tend and befriend' concept is evidence to support it.

Tamres et al. (2002) found women significantly more likely than men to seek social support – a central part of befriending response to stress.

Feldman et al. (2007) measured oxytocin in women during pregnancy and after birth. Women with highest levels formed stronger bond with baby.

These findings illustrate a growing body of research evidence suggesting several predictions derived from tend and befriend theory are **valid**.

KNOWLEDGE CHECK

1. Identify and explain **one** gender difference in coping with stress. *(4 marks)*
2. Outline research into gender differences in coping with stress. *(6 marks)*
3. Briefly evaluate research into gender differences in coping with stress. *(6 marks)*
4. Discuss gender differences in coping with stress. Refer to research evidence in your answer. *(16 marks)*

The role of social support in coping with stress

Awkward high-five alert!

The role of social support

Instrumental support is practical and tangible.	Schaefer *et al.* (1981) suggest instrumental support could be: • Physically doing something (e.g. giving someone a lift to the hospital). • Providing information (e.g. telling someone what you know about stress).
Emotional support expresses concern and affection.	Emotional support is what we provide when we say 'I really feel for you', or 'I'm sorry you're going through such a tough time' – it expresses warmth, concern, affection, empathy and love. Emotional support isn't intended to offer practical help, but to make the stressed person feel better, to lift their mood.
Esteem support increases a person's faith in themselves.	'Esteem' refers to how we regard someone else; high esteem means having respect and admiration. Esteem support is when we reinforce someone's faith in themselves and their belief in their ability to tackle a stressful situation. Increasing their confidence in themselves reduces feelings of stress.
All three are *interrelated* and can be provided without physical presence.	There is overlap between these types of support, e.g. being a 'shoulder to cry on' could conceivably involve all three types. Even practical instrumental support can help emotionally because of what it means to the individual who receives it, a sign of caring. What they have in common is they can be provided without physical presence – emotional and esteem support are given every day over online social networks (e.g. Facebook).

Key study: Cohen et al. (2015) Hugs as social support

Procedure	404 healthy adult participants telephoned every evening for 14 consecutive days to report how many hugs they'd received that day. Also completed questionnaire on perceived social support. Researchers placed participants in quarantine, exposed them to a common cold virus and monitored them for illness (stress acts as immunosuppressant so we expect people who are more stressed to become ill).
Findings	Participants who experienced most stress (interpersonal conflicts such as arguments) were most likely to become ill. Those who perceived they had greater social support had a significantly reduced risk of illness – hugs accounted for up to one-third of the protective effect of social support. Participants who had the most frequent hugs were less likely to become infected (or symptoms were less severe). This shows that perceived social support is a buffer against stress.

Apply it

Nadim helped Naomi with the shopping, cooking and cleaning after Naomi came out of hospital.

Raisa has had a very difficult year. But she is encouraged by the posts she reads on Facebook and Twitter from her friends and even people she doesn't know.

Wilmot got a letter through the post the other day. It was from a friend who knew he was depressed. The friend told Wilmot that she believed in him and was sure he'd pull through.

a. Identify the types of social support described here.

b. Do any of the cases describe more than one type of support?

c. Use your knowledge of coping with stress to explain what benefits social support brings.

One strength is research evidence to confirm beneficial effects.

A wealth of research links various forms of social support with well-being, and absence of support with illness.

Fawzy et al. (1993) found melanoma patients who were part of an emotional support group had better NK (immune) cell functioning six years later, and more likely to be alive and cancer-free than patients in **control group**.

Beneficial effects of social support can be substantial and long-lasting. **Validity** of findings is greater because study was well-controlled and prospective (social support predicted outcome several years on).

Another strength is that there are beneficial effects specifically for women.

Men have larger social networks than women, but in times of stress women are more likely to seek out and use social support as well as provide it.

Luckow et al. (1998) found in 25 out of 26 studies of gender differences in social support, women used support to cope with stress more than men (especially emotional support).

A consistent finding is that men and women use social support differently. Women live longer than men so this might suggest that the social support they have is benefitting them.

'Don't worry Chip, it'll soon be varnish day again.'

One limitation is that social support is not universally beneficial.

Instrumental support (e.g. information) is more valued from medical staff or teachers than from friends. Emotional support from a relative might not be helpful (e.g. feeling anxious if they insist on coming to doctor's appointment).

This might explain why online support from people we have never met face-to-face can sometimes help us cope better.

This shows that support is more beneficial when it is sought by the person needing it. They are in control and can decide who will provide the appropriate type of support.

Another limitation is that there are cultural differences.

Taylor et al. (2004) found Asian-Americans were much less likely to seek and use social support networks in times of stress compared with European-Americans.

Asian-Americans were concerned not to disrupt harmony of communities by raising their own problems. European-Americans viewed relationships as resources to cope with stressful situations.

This suggests that the benefits of social support are not universal but depend on culture. We should avoid assuming social support will improve well-being and health of everyone in all cultures.

KNOWLEDGE CHECK

1. Briefly explain **three** types of social support in coping with stress.
   (2 marks + 2 marks + 2 marks)
2. Outline research into the role of social support in coping with stress. *(6 marks)*
3. Evaluate the role of social support in coping with stress. *(8 marks)*
4. Outline and evaluate research into the role of social support in coping with stress. Refer to **at least two** types of social support in your answer.
   (16 marks)

A limitation of social support is its benefits depend on the presence of stress.

Buffering hypothesis (Cohen and Wills 1985) argues social support protects us against effects of stressors by creating psychological distance.

Support acts as a reserve that dampens the impact of stressors and allows us to cope better. When stress is absent social support provides no benefits.

So social support offered when people feel they are coping is actually unwelcome and may be offered for the benefit of the supporter.

Neural and hormonal mechanisms in aggression

Spec spotlight

Neural and hormonal mechanisms in aggression, including the roles of the limbic system, serotonin and testosterone.

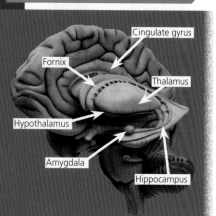

The limbic system is made up of several subcortical structures, of which the amygdala is most closely associated with aggression.

Apply it

Boris has frequently bullied other children at his primary school. His bullying is often physical and this time one of the teachers caught him slapping another child. But although he has been warned many times before, Boris continues to behave in this way – it's almost as if he can't help himself and behaves like this on the spur of the moment.

Use psychological evidence relating to both neural **and** hormonal mechanisms in aggression to explain Boris's behaviour.

REVISION BOOSTER

It really pays to practise writing 16-mark essays with your book shut and timing yourself – about 20 minutes for a 16-mark essay. Don't think it will magically come right on the day – test yourself.

Neural mechanisms in aggression

Reactivity of *limbic system* predicts aggressive behaviour.	Papez (1937) and Maclean (1952) identified the limbic system as including the cingulate gyrus, hypothalamus, fornix, amygdala. Speed and sensitivity of limbic system responses to stimuli are important predictors of aggressive behaviour in humans.
Amygdala is strongly associated with aggression.	The amygdala plays a key role in how we assess and respond to environmental threats. Gospic *et al.* (2011) carried out brain scans (**fMRI**) on participants in a lab-based game that provoked aggression. Scans showed aggressive reactions were associated with a fast and heightened response by the amygdala. Benzodiazepine (reduces arousal of the **autonomic nervous system**) taken before the game halved the number of aggressive reactions and also decreased amygdala activity.
Low level of *serotonin* results in reduced self-control and increased aggression.	Normal levels of serotonin in the *orbitofrontal cortex* are inhibitory and linked with reduced firing of neurons and associated with greater behavioural self-control. Decreased serotonin disturbs this mechanism, reduces self-control and increases impulsive behaviours, including aggression (Denson *et al.* 2012). Virkkunen *et al.* (1994) compared levels of a serotonin metabolite (breakdown byproduct, 5-HIAA) in cerebrospinal fluid of violent impulsive and non-impulsive offenders. Levels significantly lower in impulsive offenders – disturbance of this pattern implies disruption of serotonin functioning.

Hormonal mechanisms in aggression

Testosterone higher in men and linked to aggression.	**Testosterone** is a hormone responsible for the development of masculine features. It helps regulate social behaviour via influence on areas of the brain involved in aggression.
Studies of prison populations show role of testosterone in aggression.	Dolan *et al* (2001) found a positive **correlation** between testosterone levels and aggressive behaviours in male offenders in UK maximum security hospitals. Most suffered from personality disorders (e.g. psychopathy) and had histories of impulsively violent behaviour.
Animal studies show aggression linked to testosterone.	Animal studies (Giammanco *et al.* 2005) show **experimental** increases in testosterone are related to aggressive behaviour. Converse is also true – testosterone decrease leads to reduction in aggression in castration studies.

One limitation is the limbic system explanation excludes other possibilities.

The amygdala functions in tandem with the orbitofrontal cortex (OFC) to maintain self-control and inhibit aggression.

Coccaro *et al.* (2007) showed OFC activity is reduced in patients with psychiatric disorders that feature aggression.

This shows the regulation of aggression cannot be explained by the limbic system alone – it is highly complex.

One strength is that there is supporting evidence for the role of serotonin.

Research shows drugs that increase serotonin activity also reduce levels of aggressive behaviour.

Berman *et al.* (2009) found that participants given a serotonin-enhancing drug called *paroxetine* gave fewer and less intense electric shocks to a **confederate** than people in a **placebo** group.

This was only true of participants who had a prior history of aggressive behaviour, but is evidence of a link between serotonin function and aggression that goes beyond correlational findings.

Another strength is a plausible mechanism to explain testosterone's effects.

Mazur's (1985) *biosocial model of status* (BMoS) suggests changes in testosterone levels following a loss of status in a competition should affect aggressive behaviour afterwards.

In a lab-based competition, Mehta and Josephs (2006) found that 73% of the losers (whose testosterone levels rose afterwards) decided to rechallenge their opponent. But only 22% of the losers (whose testosterone levels fell) decided to do so.

These findings confirm the prediction from Mazur's BMoS and support the **validity** of testosterone as a plausible explanation of how aggressive behaviour is caused.

A limitation of the role of testosterone is that evidence in humans is mixed.

This is because some research shows hormones other than testosterone are also significantly involved in aggression.

Carre and Mehta's (2011) *dual-hormone hypothesis* claims high testosterone leads to aggression only when cortisol is low – high cortisol blocks its influence on aggressive behaviour.

The combined activity of testosterone and cortisol may be a better predictor of human aggression than testosterone alone.

A limitation of neural/hormonal explanations is that research is correlational.

This is because the alternatives are limited – studies with humans are impossible for ethical reasons and animal studies raise issues of **generalisability** to human aggression.

Research showing a correlation between serotonin and aggression risks oversimplifying the true mechanisms involved as other factors which influence or even cause aggression are overlooked.

This means that the neural and hormonal regulation of aggression is almost certainly more complex than our current understanding suggests.

Mr Angry lets off some steam.

REVISION BOOSTER

Evaluation points about methodology are criticisms of studies. But for this topic you have to evaluate the explanation rather than the study. If you criticise the methodology of a study you need to link this to the explanation/theory – how does this limitation affect our understanding of the neural/hormonal mechanisms involved in aggression?

KNOWLEDGE CHECK

1. Outline neural mechanisms in aggression. Refer to the roles of the limbic system **and** serotonin in your answer.
   (6 marks)

2. Outline the role of testosterone as a hormonal mechanism in aggression.
   (6 marks)

3. Briefly evaluate **either** neural **or** hormonal mechanisms in aggression. *(4 marks)*

4. Petra already has a criminal record for violence at the age of 20. She feels angry most of the time and then just lashes out when she 'boils over'. She feels she has no control over her behaviour. Petra also frequently feels depressed and may even have a sleep disorder.

   Describe and evaluate the role of neural **and** hormonal mechanisms in aggression. Refer to Petra's experience in your answer. *(16 marks)*

Genetic factors in aggression

Spec spotlight

Genetic factors in aggression, including the MAOA gene.

Twin studies

MZ twins share 100% of genes but DZ twins only 50% (on average) – so we expect greater similarities in aggressive behaviour between MZ twins if aggression is mostly genetic.

This is because both MZ and DZ twins are raised together in the same environment, but MZ twins have a greater degree of genetic similarity than DZs.

Lily and Millie tended not to settle their disputes over a cup of tea and a tête-à-tête.

Apply it

Pete has four older brothers who have all been in trouble with the law for violent offending. His mother and father were also very aggressive towards them all when they were growing up. Social services and the police were involved with the family several times. All of the boys were known as bullies at school, and now Pete appears to be bullying other children at his primary school.

Use your knowledge of genetic factors in aggression to explain why Pete is behaving like this.

Genetic factors in aggression

Twin studies show genetic factors account for about 50% of variance in aggressive behaviour.	Coccaro *et al.* (1997) studied adult male monozygotic (**MZ**) and dizygotic (**DZ**) twins. For direct physical aggression, the researchers found **concordance rates** of 50% for MZ twins and 19% for DZs. For verbal aggression the figures were 28% for MZ twins and 7% for DZ twins.
Adoption studies show genetic factors account for about 41% of variance in aggressive behaviour.	Similarities in aggressive behaviour between an adopted child and biological parents suggest genetic influences are operating; but similarities with adopted parents suggest environmental factors. Rhee and Waldman's (2002) **meta-analysis** of adoption studies found genetic influences accounted for 41% of the variance in aggression.
MAOA is linked to low **serotonin**.	Monoamine oxidase A (MAOA) is an enzyme – it 'mops up' neurotransmitters after a nerve impulse has been transmitted between neurons. It breaks down the neurotransmitter (e.g. serotonin) into constituent chemicals to be recycled or excreted (*catabolism*). Production of this enzyme is determined by the MAOA gene – a dysfunction in the operation of this gene may lead to abnormal activity of the MAOA enzyme, which affects levels of serotonin (low levels are linked to aggression).
One variant of the MAOA gene is nicknamed the *'warrior gene'*.	The 'warrior gene' is a variant of the MAOA gene that leads to low MAOA activity in the brain and is associated with aggressive behaviour. Brunner *et al.* (1993) studied 28 male members of a Dutch family repeatedly involved in impulsively aggressive violent criminal behaviours (e.g. rape, attempted murder, assault). These men had both abnormally low levels of MAOA in their brains and the low-activity version of the MAOA gene.
The most *violent domestic abusers* had the low-activity MAOA gene.	Stuart *et al.* (2014) studied 97 men from a treatment programme for domestic abusers, who had inflicted a form of aggression called *intimate partner violence* (IPV). Men with the low-activity MAOA gene were the most violent perpetrators of IPV – engaged in greatest psychological and physical aggression and inflicted worst injuries on partners.
Low MAOA gene activity linked to aggression *only when combined with early traumas*.	Frazzetto *et al.* (2007) found an association between antisocial aggression and the low-activity MAOA gene variant in adult males but only in those who experienced significant trauma (e.g. sexual or physical abuse) during the first 15 years of life. Those who had not experienced trauma were not especially aggressive as adults even if they possessed the low-activity MAOA gene variant. These findings together are strong evidence of a gene–environment interaction (sometimes called **diathesis-stress**).

One limitation of genetic factors is that they have been difficult to isolate.

It is difficult to separate genetic and environmental factors. Someone with an aggression-associated gene may only behave aggressively if the environmental conditions are suitable.

McDermott *et al.* (2009) showed that participants with the low-activity MAOA gene behaved aggressively in a lab-based task, but only when they were provoked.

This means that it has proven remarkably challenging to establish exactly how influential genes are in aggressive behaviour.

One limitation of the MAOA explanation is there are multiple genetic influences.

The sizes of genetic effects are statistically significant but actually quite small – so there are probably other genes involved in aggression.

Stuart *et al.* (2014) found that *intimate partner violence* (IPV) in men was associated with the serotonin transporter gene (5-HTT) – the combination of this and the MAOA gene was most closely linked with IPV.

Hundreds or thousands of genes interact in complex ways, casting doubt over any search for single candidate genes.

Gus tended to take paintballing a little too seriously...

Another limitation is that findings depend on how aggression is measured.

Methods of measuring aggression differ significantly between studies, and include self-reports, parent and teacher reports and direct observations.

In Rhee and Waldman's (2002) meta-analysis of 51 twin and adoption studies, genetic factors had a greater influence on aggression in studies using self-reports rather than parent or teacher reports.

Findings vary depending on how aggression is measured so it is difficult to 'pin down' the real causes of this behaviour and draw **valid** conclusions about the role of genetic (or other) factors.

A strength of MAOA explanation is support from prosocial behaviour research.

The low-activity variant of the MAOA gene is associated with greater aggression so presumably the converse is true – people with the high-activity variant should be more prosocial.

Mertins *et al.* (2011) found males with the high-activity MAOA variant were more co-operative in a lab-based task – they made fewer aggressive moves than participants with the low-activity variant.

This finding confirms the importance of the MAOA gene in aggressive behaviour. The two predictions of the MAOA explanation (i.e. antisocial and prosocial behaviour) are opposite sides of the same coin.

Another strength of the MAOA explanation is support from animal studies.

Genetic deletion techniques allow researchers to 'knockout' single genes in mice; an **experimental** manipulation that lets them observe the effects on aggression.

Godar *et al.* (2014) showed MAOA 'knockout' mice have increased brain serotonin and are hyper-aggressive. When serotonin is blocked by the drug *fluoxetine*, the mice revert to non-aggression.

These findings show MAOA must normally have some function in relation to serotonin, presumably keeping it at a 'normal' level by removing it from synapses.

KNOWLEDGE CHECK

1. Outline research into genetic factors in aggression. *(6 marks)*
2. Describe research into the MAOA gene in relation to genetic factors in aggression. *(6 marks)*
3. Evaluate research into genetic factors in aggression. Refer to the MAOA gene in your answer. *(6 marks)*
4. Estelle has been in trouble many times for fighting at school. She says the other kids provoke her, but she is aggressive towards just about everyone. Because Estelle's dad is in prison for serious assault, her mum says it's not surprising that Estelle is following in his footsteps.

   Describe and evaluate the role of genetic factors in aggression. Refer to Estelle and her family in your answer. *(16 marks)*

The ethological explanation of aggression

Spec spotlight

The ethological explanation of aggression, including reference to innate releasing mechanisms and fixed action patterns.

Apply it

Burak has just bought a new cat, Walker, and is worried that it might fight with the neighbour's cat. One day he sees Walker rearing up on his hind legs, meowing loudly, with his fur standing on end. He then noticed his neighbour's cat reacting in a similar way, whilst inching closer to Walker. Later he saw that Walker had no scratches or other injuries.

Using your knowledge of the ethological explanation of aggression, explain Walker's behaviour.

Aggression within a species (intra-species aggression) may end with an appeasement display. Doesn't look that playful does it?

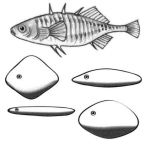

Tinbergen's stickleback models. A realistically shaped model (top) did not provoke aggressive behaviour because it lacked a red underbelly. All the other models did, despite their unstickleback-like shapes.

The ethological explanation of aggression

Aggression is *adaptive* to to (1) reduce competition and (2) establish dominance.	Aggression is beneficial to survival because it: 1. Reduces competition because a defeated animal is rarely killed but instead forced into territory elsewhere, reducing competition pressure. 2. Establishes dominance hierarchies. For example, a male chimpanzee's dominance gives him special status, including mating rights over females. Pettit *et al.* (1988) observed how aggression in playgroups played an important role in how some children became dominant over others – this is **adaptive** (therefore naturally selected) because dominance over others brings benefits.
Much aggression is *ritualistic* – a series of behaviours carried out in a set order.	Lorenz (1966) observed most intra-species aggression consisted mainly of ritualistic signalling (e.g. displaying teeth) and rarely became physical. Intra-species aggression usually ends with an appeasement display – indicates acceptance of defeat and inhibits aggression in the winner, preventing damage to the loser. This is adaptive because every aggressive encounter ending with the death of an individual could threaten existence of species.
IRM is triggered by an environmental stimulus.	An innate releasing mechanism (IRM) is a built-in physiological process or structure (e.g. a network of neurons in the brain). It acts as a 'filter' to identify threatening stimuli in the environment. An environmental stimulus (e.g. facial expression) activates the IRM. It triggers or 'releases' a fixed action pattern (FAP).
FAP is ritualistic, universal and ballistic.	A fixed action pattern (FAP) is a pattern of behaviours triggered by an IRM. Lea (1984) argues that a FAP is a relatively unchanging behavioural sequence (ritualistic) found in every individual of a species (universal) and follows an inevitable course which cannot be altered before it is completed (ballistic).

Key study: Tinbergen (1951) Male stickleback and aggression

Procedure	Another male entering a stickleback's territory in the mating season initiates a sequence of aggressive behaviours (a FAP) – red on the competing male's underbelly is the stimulus that triggers the IRM that in turn leads to the aggressive FAP. Tinbergen (1951) presented male sticklebacks with a series of wooden models of different shapes.
Findings	If the model had a red underside the stickleback would aggressively display and attack it – but no red meant no aggression. Tinbergen also found the aggressive FAP did not change from one encounter to another – once triggered it always ran its course to completion without any further stimulus.

One strength is that there is some supporting research evidence.

Research by Brunner et al. (1993) shows the low-activity variant of the MAOA gene is closely associated with aggressive behaviour in humans, suggesting an innate biological basis.

There is also evidence for IRMs for aggression in the brain – activity in the limbic system (especially the amygdala) triggers aggressive behaviour in humans and other animals.

As the ethological explanation argues that aggression is genetically determined, its validity is supported by evidence that demonstrates the genetic and physiological basis of aggression.

Keith was beginning to regret uttering the immortal words, 'What's a half-nelson?'

One limitation is that there are cultural differences in aggressive behaviour.

Nisbett et al. (1996) found that when white males from the southern United States were insulted in a research situation, they were more likely than northern white males to become aggressive.

This was only true for reactive aggression triggered by arguments, so Nisbett concluded the difference was caused by a culture of honour – impulsive aggression was a learned social norm.

It is difficult for ethological theory, with its view of aggression as instinctive, to explain how culture can override innate influences.

Another limitation is that there is some evidence against ritualistic aggression.

Goodall (2010) observed male chimps from one community systematically slaughter the members of another group in a coordinated and premeditated fashion.

This happened despite the victims offering signals of appeasement and defencelessness – these did not inhibit the aggression of the attacking chimps as predicted by the ethological explanation.

Goodall's observations challenge the view of the ethological explanation that aggression has evolved into a self-limiting and relatively physically harmless ritual.

Proactive and reactive aggression

There are huge problems in defining aggressive behaviour, but many psychologists accept the distinction between proactive and reactive aggression. Proactive aggression is cold, planned and unprovoked. Reactive aggression is angry and impulsive retaliation in the heat of the moment. Some of the research only applies to reactive aggression rather than all aggressive behaviour.

A further limitation is evidence that fixed action patterns are not that 'fixed'.

Hunt (1973) points out that sequences of behaviours that appear to be fixed and unchanging are greatly influenced by environmental factors and learning experiences.

This means that FAPs are more flexible than implied by the term 'fixed' (many ethologists now prefer the term *modal action pattern* to reflect this).

The flexibility of FAPs suggests aggressive behaviours are affected by environmental influences, challenging the validity of the ethological (biological) explanation.

A final limitation is unjustified generalisations to human aggression.

Lorenz did not study higher mammals such as primates, and Tinbergen chose not to study the extreme destructive violence that is a feature of human aggression.

But they both made generalisations from animal aggression to humans, including warfare. Lorenz extrapolated from the behaviour of individual animals to the behaviour of entire countries.

We should be cautious about making such generalisations, especially to a complex behaviour (e.g. warfare) which is the outcome of many interacting influences.

KNOWLEDGE CHECK

1. In relation to the ethological explanation of aggression, distinguish between innate releasing mechanisms and fixed action patterns. *(3 marks)*

2. Describe **one** study into the ethological explanation of aggression. *(6 marks)*

3. Evaluate the ethological explanation of aggression. *(6 marks)*

4. Discuss the ethological explanation of aggression. In your answer refer to innate releasing mechanisms **and** fixed action patterns. *(16 marks)*

Evolutionary explanations of human aggression

Spec spotlight

Evolutionary explanations of human aggression.

Barry wasn't the first man to lose his girlfriend to Pinterest – and he wouldn't be the last.

Mayra is a counselling psychologist who runs a therapy group for survivors of domestic abuse. Over the years, she has noticed that her clients have had similar experiences of abusive partners. For example, most abusers keep a close eye on what their partners are doing. Abusers ask a lot of questions about where their partners have been and who they've been with. Abusers also make threats of violence and, of course, often eventually become physically aggressive.

Using your knowledge of evolutionary explanations of human aggression, explain Mayra's clients' experiences.

Evolutionary explanations of human aggression

Men use aggressive *mate retention strategies* to avoid cuckoldry.	Men face the threat of cuckoldry (having to raise offspring that are not their own) – it is a waste of his resources because it contributes to survival of a rival's genes and leaves the 'father' with fewer resources to invest in his own future offspring. Men in our **evolutionary** past who could avoid cuckoldry were more reproductively successful – so psychological mechanisms have evolved to increase anti-cuckoldry behaviours in men (e.g. sexual jealousy felt more strongly by men than women). This drives the often aggressive mate retention strategies men use to keep their partners and prevent them from 'straying' – these were **adaptive** in our evolutionary history.
Mate retention strategies include *direct guarding and negative inducements*.	Wilson and Daly (1996) identify two major mate retention strategies involving aggression: • Direct guarding: a man's vigilance over a partner's behaviour (e.g. checking who they've been seeing). • Negative inducements: (e.g. threats of consequences for infidelity – 'I'll kill myself if you leave me.').
Mate retention strategies linked to *physical violence*.	Wilson et al. (1995) found women who reported mate retention strategies in partners were twice as likely to suffer physical violence at their hands – 73% of these women required medical attention and 53% said they feared for their lives. Men who used guarding (e.g. monitoring partner's movements) or negative inducements (e.g. threats to kill) were more likely to use physical violence against their partners – these retention behaviours reliably predicted husbands' use of aggression against their wives.
Bullying may be an adaptive form of aggression.	Bullying is a power imbalance in which a stronger individual uses aggression repeatedly against a weaker person. Researchers have traditionally viewed bullying as a maladaptive behaviour (e.g. due to poor social skills or childhood abuse) – but evolutionary ancestors may have used it as an adaptive strategy to increase chances of survival by promoting their own health and creating reproduction opportunities.
In men, bullying *ensures access to females* and reduces threats from males.	In men bullying suggests dominance, acquisition of resources, strength – and also wards off potential rivals (Volk et al. 2012). Characteristics associated with bullying deliver the ideal combination of access to more females and minimal threat from competing males – so aggressive bullying was naturally selected because these males would have reproductive success.
In women, bullying helps *secure partner's fidelity*.	Female bullying more often takes place within rather than outside a relationship, and is a method of controlling a partner. Women use bullying behaviour to secure a partner's fidelity, which means the partner continues to provide resources for future offspring – again, such behaviour would be naturally selected because it enhanced the woman's reproductive success.

One strength is research support for central evolutionary concepts.

Many research studies demonstrate that mate retention strategies are associated with sexual jealousy and aggression.

Shackelford et al.'s (2005) study is a dramatic example – direct guarding and negative inducements are overwhelmingly used by males, against both females and other males.

This suggests risk of infidelity, cuckoldry and aggression are linked and supports predictions from the explanation about the adaptive value of aggression.

The Lynx effect.

Another strength is the evolutionary explanation explains gender differences.

Males engage more often than females in aggressive acts, especially physical aggression (i.e. there are gender differences).

Campbell (1999) argues that aggression in females risks the survival of their offspring so a more adaptive strategy is to use verbal aggression to retain a partner who provides resources.

The fact that the evolutionary explanation can explain such gender differences in aggression (and predict them in research) increases the **validity** of this kind of approach.

A further strength is real-life applications.

Rigby (2010) reviewed several established anti-bullying interventions. Despite the availability of such interventions, bullying remains prevalent.

Most interventions fail to recognise that bullies bully because they gain advantages – it would make no sense for them to voluntarily give up the power they have over others without some form of compensation.

An evolutionary understanding of bullying as an adaptive behaviour can help us to devise effective anti-bullying interventions, to increase the costs of bullying and the rewards of prosocial alternatives.

One limitation is cultural differences in aggression.

The evolutionary explanation predicts aggression is present in all cultures because it is used everywhere to increase survival chances through greater reproductive success.

The !Kung San people of the Kalahari discourage aggression and those who use it lose status and reputation. The Yanomamo of Venezuela use aggression to gain status in their structured society.

The fact the !Kung San and the Yanomamo have such different experiences of, and attitudes towards, aggression suggests that this behaviour is not universal, contrary to evolutionary theory.

Another limitation is methodological issues with the research evidence.

It is extremely difficult to test hypotheses about the evolution of behaviours to solve problems of adaptation in our past, so research is correlational.

But even a very strong **correlation** does not allow us to conclude that evolutionary-related factors (e.g. sexual jealousy) cause aggression.

This makes it very difficult to establish precisely how valid an evolutionary explanation of aggression is.

KNOWLEDGE CHECK

1. In terms of human aggression, explain what is meant by the term 'evolutionary explanation'. *(3 marks)*
2. Describe **one** study of the evolutionary explanation of human aggression. In your answer refer to what the researcher(s) did and what was found. *(6 marks)*
3. Briefly evaluate the evolutionary explanation of human aggression. *(4 marks)*
4. This item appeared on a news website: 'Men are more jealous than women, say psychologists. Men abuse their partners to prevent them straying because they are jealous. Bullying could also be a way of attracting and keeping a partner. "You get this sort of behaviour in lots of different parts of the world," added the experts.'

    With reference to the issues raised in this item, outline and evaluate evolutionary explanations of human aggression. *(16 marks)*

Social psychological explanations: Frustration-aggression

Spec spotlight

Social psychological explanations of human aggression, including the frustration-aggression hypothesis.

A frustrating morning for Malcolm; he just couldn't get his wig to 'sit right'.

Frustration-aggression hypothesis

Frustration *always leads* to aggression, and aggression is always the result of frustration.	Dollard *et al.*'s (1939) hypothesis is based on the **psychodynamic** approach – aggression is a psychological drive similar to biological drives (e.g. hunger) and we experience frustration if our attempt to achieve a goal is blocked by an external factor.
	Frustration creates an aggressive drive leading to aggressive behaviour (violent fantasy, verbal outburst, physical violence).
Aggressive behaviour is *cathartic*.	Expression of the aggressive drive in behaviour is cathartic because the aggression created by the frustration is satisfied.
	This reduces the drive making further aggression less likely – we feel better for getting it 'off our chest'.
Aggression may be expressed *indirectly*.	Aggression may be expressed indirectly because the cause of frustration is:
	• Abstract (e.g. the government).
	• Too powerful and we risk punishment (e.g. a teacher who gave you a low grade).
	• Unavailable (e.g. the teacher left before you saw the grade).
	So our aggression is displaced (deflected) onto an alternative – one that is not abstract, is weaker and is available (an object, a pet, younger sibling, etc.).
The *weapons effect* shows that cues make aggression more likely.	Berkowitz and LePage (1967) found once students became frustrated in a lab task, they were more likely to give (fake) electric shocks when they could see a weapon next to them.
	Weapons effect shows that frustration only creates a readiness for aggression – and then aggressive cues in the environment make it more likely that aggression will happen ('The finger pulls the trigger, but the trigger may also be pulling the finger.')

Edith went to see her favourite rugby league club play in both the play-off final and the Challenge Cup final. They lost both. Each time, she was convinced her team would win, and was really excited and happy to be watching them. But after long journeys back home with late trains and missed buses, Edith arrived home angry and depressed. She immediately started an argument with her brother, and there is now a small dent in the wall where she kicked it.

Use your knowledge of the frustration-aggression hypothesis to explain Edith's behaviour.

Key study: Geen (1968) Frustration and aggression

Procedure	Male university students completed a jigsaw puzzle, during which level of frustration was manipulated in one of three ways.
	• For some participants the puzzle was impossible to solve.
	• Others ran out of time because another student (a **confederate**) kept interfering.
	• Others were insulted by the confederate.
	Then the participants gave (fake) electric shocks to the confederate whenever he made a mistake on another task.
Findings	Insulted participants gave the strongest shocks on average, then the interfered group, then the impossible-task participants.
	All three groups selected more intense shocks than a (non-frustrated) **control group**.

One strength is that there is research evidence.

Marcus-Newhall *et al.* (2000) conducted a **meta-analysis** of 49 studies of displaced aggression (aggressive behaviour directed against a target other than the one that caused frustration).

Participants who were provoked but unable to retaliate directly against the source of their frustration were significantly more likely to aggress against an innocent party than people who were not provoked.

The researchers concluded that displaced aggression is a reliable phenomenon, supporting a central concept of the hypothesis and increasing its **validity** as an explanation of aggression.

One limitation is that there is evidence that aggression is not cathartic.

Bushman (2002) found participants who vented their anger by hitting a punchbag became more angry and aggressive, rather than less.

Venting to reduce anger is like using petrol to put out a fire – but this is the advice many therapists give to clients.

This casts doubt on the validity of a central assumption of the hypothesis.

The most frustrating thing as far as Tommy was concerned was that he'd just ripped his nice new shorts.

Another strength is the original hypothesis was reformulated to fit the evidence.

Frustration does not always lead to aggression and aggression can occur without frustration. So Berkowitz (1989) argued frustration is just one of many aversive stimuli that create negative feelings.

Aggression is triggered by negative feelings generally rather than by frustration specifically. The outcome of frustration can be a range of responses; only one is aggression.

This is a strength because it highlights the flexibility of the hypothesis and is how science operates – a theory is adapted when evidence comes along that it cannot explain.

A further limitation is the effects of justified and unjustified frustration.

Dill and Anderson (1995) showed participants a paper-folding task but frustrated them by making it difficult to follow, either because the experimenter was in a hurry to meet his girlfriend (unjustified) or because his boss told him to be quick (justified).

Participants who experienced unjustified frustration produced most aggression (negative judgements of the experimenter). Justified frustration produced less aggression but more than the **control condition** (absence of frustration).

This finding shows that some forms of frustration can create more aggression than others – a serious challenge to the validity of the original hypothesis.

A strength is useful real-life applications.

Berkowitz's argument that 'the trigger can pull the finger' has featured in the gun control debate in the US.

Some states allow 'open carry', where a gun does not have to be concealed. But presence of a weapon acts as a cue to aggression making its use more likely.

Research into the weapons effect may reduce gun-related violence by showing that aggressive cues should be removed from the environment, saving lives.

REVISION BOOSTER

You might need to outline a study related to the frustration-aggression hypothesis for up to 6-marks of AO1. Geen's study is covered on the facing page but we haven't always provided such detail. Nevertheless, in the AO3 section, there is usually detail of procedures and conclusions of one study.

KNOWLEDGE CHECK

1. Outline the frustration-aggression hypothesis. *(6 marks)*
2. Describe **one** study that has investigated the frustration-aggression hypothesis. *(6 marks)*
3. Evaluate **one** social psychological explanation of aggression. *(6 marks)*
4. Two students worked very hard on their essays. Sadly, they both got a grade E. Camilla became very angry and head-butted a wall. Ricardo went very quiet and decided to have another go at the essay.

   Outline and evaluate **one** social psychological explanation of aggression. Refer to Camilla and Ricardo in your answer. *(16 marks)*

AO1
Description

Spec spotlight

Social psychological explanations of aggression, including social learning theory as applied to human aggression.

Social learning theory

A theory that explains behaviour in terms of direct reinforcement but also indirect reinforcement – learning from observing others and imitating their behaviour.

Gabriel watches a DVD of his favourite film (not Frozen, sadly). The film features lots of shooting and fighting and a bit of swearing as well. It's clear that the main character is a hero, despite behaving very aggressively. The next day in school, Gabriel swears at a teacher, runs around firing imaginary weapons and attacks some other boys.

How can social learning theory help us to explain Gabriel's behaviour?

Perhaps Gabriel should have watched Frozen *instead?*

REVISION BOOSTER

On these AO1 pages, there are nearly always six key points for each topic. This easily covers the descriptive content you would need for any essay – because description is worth 6 marks. Don't be tempted to over-describe.

Social learning theory (SLT) applied to aggression

Aggression learned directly through *positive* and *negative* reinforcement.	Bandura's **social learning theory (SLT)** acknowledged that aggression can be learned directly through **operant conditioning** (positive and negative reinforcement and punishment). For example, a child who angrily snatches a toy learns aggression brings rewards – direct positive reinforcement.
Most aggression learned indirectly, through *observation* and vicarious *reinforcement*.	Observational learning explains most aggressive behaviour. • A child observes models (e.g. parents) being aggressive and works out how aggressive behaviour is performed. • Children also observe the consequences of a model's aggressive behaviour – if it is rewarded the child learns aggression can be effective in getting what they want. This is vicarious reinforcement – it makes it more likely that the child will imitate the model's aggressive behaviour.
Social learning requires *attention, retention, reproduction* and *motivation*.	Four **cognitive** conditions are needed for observational learning to take place: • Attention: observer notices model's aggressive actions. • Retention: observer remembers model's aggressive behaviour and forms symbolic mental representation of it. • Reproduction: observer repeats behaviour. • Motivation: observer imitates behaviours if they have an expectation that behaving aggressively will be rewarding.
Self-efficacy increases each time aggression brings rewards.	Self-efficacy is the extent to which we believe our actions will achieve a desired goal. A child's confidence in their ability to be aggressive grows as they learn that aggression can bring rewards (e.g. child who regularly hits others to get a toy learns they have the motor skills to do so and this ability comes easily to them).

Key study: Bandura et al. (1961) Social learning of aggression

Procedure	Young children individually observed an adult model playing with toys, including an inflatable plastic toy called a 'Bobo doll'. Some children observed the model behaving aggressively towards the doll (e.g. throwing, kicking, plus verbal outbursts). Children were then taken to another room where there was a Bobo doll and other toys including ones the model had used.
Findings	Children in the 'aggressive model' condition imitated the behaviour they observed – the closeness of imitation was often remarkable, a direct copy including using specific objects and verbal phrases. Children in the 'non-aggressive model' condition showed almost no aggression later.

One strength is that there is supportive research evidence.

Poulin and Boivin (2000) found most aggressive boys (9–12 years old) formed friendships with other aggressive boys – 'training grounds' for antisocial behaviour.

This means they were exposed frequently to models of physical aggression (each other) and to its reinforcing consequences (including rewarding approval).

This shows that aggression increases in precisely the conditions predicted by SLT.

Parents should take care that their own aggressive behaviour doesn't 'rub off' on their children.

One limitation is that SLT cannot explain all forms of aggression.

Children who use proactive (cold, calculating) aggression have high self-efficacy – they are confident so they use aggression to achieve goals. This behaviour is well-explained by SLT.

But children who show reactive aggression (angry, impulsive) are hostile, suspicious of others, and do not use aggression to achieve anything except retribution in the heat of the moment.

This behaviour is less explicable from a social learning perspective, and may be better explained by an alternative such as Berkowitz's negative affect theory.

REVISION BOOSTER

Don't write in general terms about SLT (e.g. a non-specific outline of modelling or vicarious reinforcement). You have to *shape* what you know to explain aggression. The general rule is this: if you don't mention aggression throughout your answer, then it's unlikely to gain much credit.

Another strength is that SLT highlights the benefits of non-aggressive models.

People are not passive recipients of reinforcement – they shape their own aggressive behaviour by choosing situations which reward aggression.

A way to reduce aggression is to break this cycle by encouraging aggressive children to form friendships with children who do not habitually behave aggressively.

Providing children with models of non-aggressive behaviour is a practical benefit of understanding aggression as a social learning process, leading to a reduction in violence.

A further strength is useful real-life applications.

Huesmann and Eron (2013) argue that media portrayals of aggressive behaviour can be powerful influences on a child's acquisition of aggression.

This is especially true if a media character is rewarded for being aggressive (vicarious reinforcement).

Such effects support the predictions of SLT and can be applied to reducing aggressive behaviour by providing non-aggressive models in the media.

A limitation is SLT has difficulty explaining cultural differences in aggression.

Different cultures have different norms about which behaviours should be reinforced.

In some cultures (e.g. the !Kung San), social norms do not encourage aggression so aggressive models are unavailable for children to observe and vicarious reinforcement is rare. But !Kung San people still behave aggressively.

This suggests there is more to aggressive behaviour than social learning. Perhaps it is instinctive and therefore a **biological approach** is a more **valid** explanation of this cultural finding.

KNOWLEDGE CHECK

1. Briefly outline **two** social psychological explanations of aggression.   *(3 marks + 3 marks)*
2. Outline social learning theory as applied to human aggression.   *(6 marks)*
3. Evaluate social learning theory as applied to human aggression.   *(6 marks)*
4. Tabitha hangs out with a group of girls who have a reputation for bullying. She finds them interesting and exciting and she watches what they do very carefully. Tabitha is beginning to develop the confidence to bully other kids herself.

   With reference to Tabitha, describe and evaluate social learning theory as applied to human aggression.   *(16 marks)*

Social psychological explanations: De-individuation

Spec spotlight

Social psychological explanations of human aggression, including de-individuation.

Hugh's ill-judged disguise didn't really conceal his identity. And robbing the bank where he worked was probably not the brightest idea either.

Apply it

Toby is recounting his days back in the 1970s of travelling around Britain and Europe being a football hooligan. He and his mates would cover their faces and cause trouble, provoking the opposition. There would always be a big crowd of them, and sometimes they would rip up the terraces and start hurling concrete at rival supporters. And there would usually be a good old-fashioned shirtless pitch invasion.

Using your knowledge of de-individuation, explain Toby's behaviour.

REVISION BOOSTER

Exam questions may ask you to describe a study – it is always best to include some details of both procedures and findings.

De-individuation applied to aggression

De-individuation refers to reduced sense of personal responsibility.	Zimbardo (1969) argued behaviour is usually constrained by social norms – aggressive behaviour is usually discouraged. But when we become part of a crowd we lose restraint and may behave in emotional, impulsive and irrational ways – we become de-individuated and lose individual self-identity and responsibility for our own behaviour. Responsibility is shared throughout the crowd – we ignore social norms and experience less personal guilt at harmful aggression directed at others.
Anonymity is a major condition of de-individuation.	Several conditions of de-individuation promote aggression (e.g. darkness, uniforms) – a major one is anonymity. We have less fear of retribution because we are unidentifiable in a crowd – the bigger the crowd, the greater the anonymity. Anonymity provides fewer opportunities for others to judge us negatively.
Anonymity reduces *private self-awareness*.	Prentice-Dunn and Rogers (1982) argue that anonymity reduces private self-awareness because our attention is focused outwardly to the events around us. This means we think less about our own beliefs and feelings – we are less self-critical and evaluative.
Anonymity reduces *public self-awareness*.	Anonymity also reduces public self-awareness because we realise we are anonymous and our behaviour is less likely to be judged by others. We no longer care how others see us – we become less accountable for our aggressive and destructive actions.

Key study: Dodd (1985) Student de-individuation

Procedure	Dodd asked psychology students: 'If you could do anything humanly possible with complete assurance that you would not be detected or held responsible, what would you do?' Students knew their answers were anonymous. Three independent raters who did not know the hypothesis decided which categories of prosocial or antisocial behaviour the responses belonged to.
Findings	36% of responses involved a form of antisocial behaviour and 26% actual criminal acts (most common was 'rob a bank'). Only 9% of responses were prosocial behaviours (e.g. helping people). In terms of how people *imagine* they would behave, this study demonstrates a link between anonymity, de-individuation and aggressive behaviour.

One strength is there is supportive research evidence.

Douglas and McGarty (2001) looked at aggressive online behaviour in chatrooms and uses of instant messaging.

They found a strong **correlation** between anonymity and 'flaming', (posting hostile messages). The most aggressive messages were sent by those who hid their identities.

This suggests a link between anonymity, de-individuation and aggressive behaviour in a context that has even greater relevance today.

'Anonymity shapes crowd behaviour' (Dixon and Mahendran 2012).

One limitation is that there is some contradictory evidence.

Gergen et al. (1973) put strangers in a darkened room and told them to do what they wanted – they soon started kissing and touching each other.

This 'deviance in the dark' study was repeated with participants told they would be face-to-face with each other afterwards – touching and kissing was reduced.

Despite a guarantee of anonymity creating the conditions for de-individuation, aggressive behaviour was not an outcome of this study.

Original footage from the Gergen et al. (1973) study. Pretty racy stuff, eh?

Another limitation is de-individuation does not inevitably lead to aggression.

Johnson and Downing's (1979) female participants gave (fake) shocks to a **confederate**, either wearing masks, dressed as nurses or wearing their own clothes (**control condition**).

Masked participants gave more (intense) shocks and 'nurses' gave fewer at lower levels. 'Nurses' were more compassionate towards victims, in line with the prosocial role associated with a nurse's uniform.

Both aggression and prosocial behaviour are potential outcomes of de-individuation (not just aggression). Normative cues in the situation determine which is most likely to occur.

A strength is useful real-life applications.

De-individuation theory can help us to understand aggressive behaviour in online gaming services such as Xbox Live.

These services have features promoting de-individuation: reduction of personal identity (e.g. players using 'handles' to identify themselves) and an arousing immersive environment.

This real-life application confirms the relevance of de-individuation concepts to aggression (anonymity creates conditions of de-individuation and reductions in self-awareness).

KNOWLEDGE CHECK

1. Explain the difference between de-individuation and **one other** social psychological explanation of aggression. *(3 marks)*

2. Describe **one** study into de-individuation as a social psychological explanation of aggression. In your answer refer to what the researcher(s) did and what they found. *(6 marks)*

3. Evaluate de-individuation as a social psychological explanation of aggression. *(6 marks)*

4. Outline and evaluate **two or more** social psychological explanations of aggression. *(16 marks)*

A limitation is alternative explanations may account better for aggression.

Spears and Lea (1992) applied social identity theory (SIT) to de-individuation in their *Social Identity model of De-individuation Effects* (the SIDE model).

De-individuation leads to behaviour that conforms to local group norms (could be antisocial *or* prosocial) because anonymity shifts individual's attention from personal identity to social identity as group member.

Anonymity and reduced self-awareness do not have the wider effects predicted by the de-individuation explanation – aggression is not the inevitable outcome of a de-individuated state.

Institutional aggression in the context of prisons

Spec spotlight

Institutional aggression in the context of prisons: dispositional and situational explanations.

The Premier Lodge's 'panoramic sea view' wasn't quite what was described on the website.

REVISION BOOSTER

You might be asked about dispositional or situational explanations separately. There is plenty here for each of them – about 150 words of each which is enough for 6 marks of description. For evaluation include comparisons with the alternative model.

Apply it

A psychologist has been asked to prepare a report on a prison which has experienced an outbreak of violence amongst the inmates. She has visited the prison several times and her report notes that many inmates were involved in violent criminal gangs before they came to the prison. The prison itself has a harsh regime, where the rules do not seem to be applied consistently. Several of the prisoners are in solitary confinement and there is a high proportion of female staff. The budget for food has been cut several times.

Referring to issues raised in the psychologist's report, explain aggressive behaviour in prison.

Dispositional explanation – importation model

Institutional aggression results from *characteristics* of prisoners.	Irwin and Cressey (1962) argued that inmates bring with them (import) into prisons a subculture typical of criminality – including beliefs, values, norms, attitudes, learning experiences and personal characteristics (e.g. gender, race and class).
	Inmates import these to negotiate their way through the unfamiliar prison environment in which existing inmates use aggression to establish power, status and access to resources.
	Aggression is the result of individual characteristics of inmates and not of the prison environment.
Prisoner characteristics include *anger* and *traumatic experiences*.	DeLisi *et al.* (2011) studied juvenile delinquents in California institutions who imported several negative dispositional features.
	For example, childhood trauma, anger, histories of substance abuse and violent behaviour.
Outcomes include self-harm and prisoner violence.	Inmates in the DeLisi *et al.* study were more likely to engage in suicidal activity and sexual misconduct, and committed more acts of physical violence brought to the attention of the parole board (compared with a **control group** of inmates with fewer negative dispositional features).

Situational explanation – deprivation model

Institutional aggression due to stress created by *prison environment* itself.	Clemmer (1958) argued that harsh prison conditions cause stress for inmates who cope by behaving aggressively.
	Aggression is also influenced by another situational factor – an unpredictable prison regime that regularly uses 'lock ups' to control behaviour. This creates frustration and reduces access to 'goods' (e.g. television) even further.
	This is a recipe for aggression, which becomes an **adaptive** solution to the problem of deprivation.
Harsh conditions include psychological and physical factors.	Psychological factors (e.g. deprived of freedom, independence and heterosexual intimacy).
	Physical factors (e.g. deprivation of material goods increases aggressive competition amongst inmates to acquire them).
Prison-level factors are independent of prisoner's personality.	Steiner (2009) investigated factors predicting inmate aggression in 512 US prisons – inmate-on-inmate violence was more common in prisons where there were higher proportions of female staff, African-American inmates, Hispanic inmates, and inmates in protective custody for their own safety.
	These are prison-level factors because they are independent of individual characteristics of prisoners – they reliably predicted aggressive behaviour in line with the deprivation model.

One strength of the importation model is research support.

Camp and Gaes (2005) placed half of their male inmate participants in low-security Californian prisons and the other half in the second-highest category of prisons.

There was no significant difference in aggressive misconduct between the two groups – features of the prison environment are less important predictors of aggressive behaviour than characteristics of inmates.

This is strong evidence in favour of the dispositional explanation especially because there was **random allocation** of inmates to prisons of different security levels.

One limitation of importation model is an alternative may be better.

Dilulio (1991) claims the importation model is inadequate to explain institutional aggression because it ignores roles of prison officials and factors linked to running prisons.

He proposes an *administrative control model* (ACM) which states that poorly managed prisons are more likely to experience most serious forms of inmate violence (e.g. homicides, rioting).

According to the ACM, these factors are more influential in determining aggression than inmate characteristics, casting doubt over the **validity** of the dispositional explanation.

'That's the last time I agree to tidy up the loft,' thought Waneta.

One strength of the deprivation model is research support.

Individual-level factors can be predictors of aggression independent of the prison environment, but research shows that some situational variables are also highly influential.

Cunningham *et al.* (2010) analysed inmate homicides in Texas prisons and found motivations for the behaviours were linked to some of the deprivations identified by Clemmer.

As these are factors predicted by the deprivation model to make aggression more likely, these findings support the validity of a situational explanation.

One limitation of the deprivation model is contradictory research evidence.

The deprivation model predicts that a lack of freedom and heterosexual contact leads to high levels of aggression in prisons – but the available evidence does not support this.

Hensley *et al.* (2002) studied inmates of prisons allowing conjugal visits (i.e. to have sex). There was no link between involvement in these visits and reduced aggressive behaviour.

This shows situational factors do not necessarily affect prison violence, and casts some doubt on the validity of the deprivation model.

One limitation of both explanations is the interactionist model may be better.

Dobbs and Waid (2004) argue deprivation does not lead to violence unless it combines with the individual characteristics imported into the prison by inmates.

This is a more valid explanation because it explains the evidence and inmates' experiences of institutional aggression. It offers a fuller account because it explains a greater variety of aggressive behaviours.

It is also more realistic because it reflects the complex nature of institutional aggression, which is unlikely to have just one cause (or set of causes) as assumed by the importation and deprivation models.

KNOWLEDGE CHECK

1. With reference to institutional aggression, explain what is meant by 'dispositional' and 'situational' explanations.
   (3 marks)

2. Outline dispositional explanations of institutional aggression. *(6 marks)*

3. Evaluate situational explanations of institutional aggression. *(6 marks)*

4. Two psychology students are discussing aggression in prisons. One says, 'It's not surprising there's aggression in prisons when you look at the people in them.' The other disagrees, 'Well, I think it's more to do with the way prisons are run.'

   With reference to these arguments, discuss **two** explanations of institutional aggression in the context of prisons. *(16 marks)*

Media influences: Effects of computer games

Spec spotlight

Media influences on aggression, including the effects of computer games.

'Who called me a muppet?'

Two psychology students would like to investigate the effects of computer game violence on aggressive behaviour. But their teacher tells them they cannot show their participants any violent or aggressive material for ethical reasons. The students are concerned that this will have serious implications for their conclusions. They have to think very carefully about how they can carry out their study. So, knowing you are a top psychologist, they ask you for your help.

Outline to the students the types of study they could conduct. Explain the pros and cons of each one.

Always think 'less is more' – writing about fewer things gives you the opportunity to demonstrate your detailed understanding. For 6 marks AO1 you may not want to include all six of the points here so you have time for detail.

The effect of computer games on aggression

Studies are experimental, correlational and/or longitudinal.	**Experimental** studies – lab studies of short-term effects of computer games can demonstrate cause-and-effect.
	Correlational studies – can investigate real-life variables and are usually short-term.
	Longitudinal studies – correlational studies conducted over a period of time looking at long-term effects.
	Meta-analyses – bring together a variety of studies to give a judgement of size of the effect of violent media on aggression.
Experiment Violent computer games caused greater aggression.	Bartholow and Anderson's (2002) participants played a violent or non-violent computer game for ten minutes – then carried out the *Taylor Competitive Reaction Time Task*, a standard lab measure of aggression (choosing volume of noise blasts).
	Those who played the violent game selected significantly higher noise levels compared with non-violent players.
Correlation Positive correlation between aggression and violent computer-game-playing.	DeLisi *et al.* (2013) studied 227 juvenile offenders with histories of serious aggressive behaviour. Structured interviews used to gather data on aggression and violent computer-game-playing.
	Aggressive behaviour was positively correlated with how often they played violent computer games and how much they enjoyed them.
	Researchers claim the link is so well-established that computer game violence should be considered a significant risk factor.
Longitudinal Can predict aggression in adulthood.	Robertson *et al.* (2013) studied 1037 people born in New Zealand, measuring their TV viewing hours (all types of programme) at regular intervals up to the age of 26 years.
	Time spent watching TV was a reliable predictor of aggressive behaviour in adulthood (convictions for aggressive and violent crimes) and diagnosis of **antisocial personality disorder**.
	The most important media-related factor in influencing aggressive behaviour may be the amount of TV watched rather than whether it has violent content or not.
Meta-analysis Increased aggression across genders and cultures.	Anderson *et al.*'s (2010) meta-analysis of 136 studies included experimental, correlational and longitudinal research.
	Exposure to violent computer games was associated with increases in aggressive behaviours, thoughts and feelings.
	This applied to both males and females and across **collectivist** and **individualist** cultures.
Effects of violent game-playing on aggression greater than effect of smoke on cancer.	Anderson *et al.* (2010) claim the effect of violent game-playing on aggressive behaviour is greater than the effect of second-hand smoke on cancer.
	The analysis also showed no indication that **publication bias** influenced the results.

One limitation of experiments is that measures of aggression are artificial.

The *Taylor Competitive Reaction Time Task* measures aggression as the volume of noise selected by participants as punishment – an unrealistic measure.

Aggression measures in lab situations are also unrealistic because they do not involve retaliation – the experimenter gives the participant permission to be 'safely' aggressive.

This casts doubt on the **validity** of experimental studies and on the link between media violence and aggression.

Another limitation of experimental studies is the non-equivalence problem.

Experimental studies compare participants who play a violent computer game with those who play a non-violent one – but it is difficult to be sure that the two games are equivalent apart from the presence or absence of violence.

Przybylski *et al.* (2014) looked at two often-used games – Marathon 2 (a violent game using 20 keys) is much more complex than Glider Pro 4 (a non-violent game using just two keys). The difference in complexity is a **confounding variable**.

Participants may behave more aggressively after playing the violent game – but this could be due to frustration caused by the greater complexity of the game rather than the violence the players are exposed to.

Boy in blue: 'Yes, Mum's come home with a couple of encyclopedias from the bookshop!'

Boy in orange: 'Oh thank goodness. At last we can expand our minds rather than playing endless hours of FIFA.'

(True story)

One limitation of correlations is we cannot draw cause-and-effect conclusions.

No variables are manipulated or controlled, and there is no **random allocation** of participants to violent or non-violent media conditions.

A positive correlation between violent computer games and aggression can be explained by socialisation (violent games cause people to be aggressive) or selection (people who are already aggressive choose violent games).

The direction of causality cannot be settled by correlational studies so the finding does not help us choose between two hypotheses, leaving open the question of exactly how computer games influence aggression.

One limitation of longitudinal studies is confounding variables.

Longitudinal studies are conducted over quite lengthy periods of time (from several months to several years).

Many sources of aggression interact with media influences over this period (e.g. role models). It is difficult to separate them and assess contributions to aggressive behaviour.

Therefore it is impossible to conclude that it is violent media such as computer games (rather than confounding variables) that have affected aggression.

One limitation of all methodologies is publication bias.

There is a tendency for only statistically significant findings to be published.

This is a particular problem for meta-analyses because they generally only include published studies, which mostly show a significant effect.

So publication bias creates the false impression that the effects of violent media on aggression are greater than they actually are.

Media influences

Spec spotlight

Media influences on aggression. The roles of desensitisation, disinhibition and cognitive priming.

This is awful – there's no plot, no characterisation; the central protagonist is terribly one-dimensional.

Three friends all regularly watch violent films. Paige has been doing this for so long she no longer finds them exciting or interesting. Ichabod's friends have noticed that he seems more argumentative these days. Lacey used to be quite calm, but now it's like she's on a 'hair trigger' all the time. Things other people find funny she thinks are annoying.

Use your knowledge of media influences on aggression to explain these behaviours.

Roles of desensitisation, disinhibition and cognitive priming

Desensitisation = reduced *physiological* response (SNS arousal).	Normally when we witness aggression we experience arousal associated with the **sympathetic nervous system** (increased heart rate, blood pressure, sweat activity, etc.). But when children repeatedly view aggression on TV or play violent computer games they become habituated and the physiological effects are reduced (desensitisation) – i.e. a stimulus that is usually aversive has a lesser impact.
Desensitisation = reduced *psychological* response (e.g. less empathy for victim).	Repeated exposure to violent media promotes a belief that aggression as a method of resolving conflict is socially acceptable. Therefore negative attitudes towards violence weaken, less empathy is felt for victims, etc. (Funk *et al.* 2004). Weisz and Earls (1995) showed participants the film *Straw Dogs* (contains graphic rape scene). Male viewers showed greater acceptance of rape myths after watching a mock rape trial (compared with male viewers of a non-violent film). They also showed less sympathy to the victim and were less likely to find the defendant guilty (no similar effect for female participants).
Disinhibition = exposure to violent media *changes usual restraints*.	Most people believe violence and aggression are antisocial – so there are powerful social and psychological restraints against using aggression to resolve interpersonal conflicts. Violent media gives aggressive behaviour social approval, especially where effects on victims are minimised and appear justified. The effect is that the usual restraints on individuals are loosened (**disinhibited**) after exposure to violent media.
Disinhibition *enhanced* if aggression is rewarded.	It is not unusual for computer games to show violence being rewarded at the same time as its consequences are minimised or ignored. Such rewards strengthen the new social norms in the viewer.
Cognitive priming = a 'script' learned about how to behave to aggressive cues.	Repeated experience of aggressive media can provide us with a 'script' about how violent situations may 'play out'. Huesmann (1998) argues that this script is stored in memory so we become 'ready' (primed) to be aggressive. This is an automatic process because a script can direct our behaviour without us being aware of it. The script is triggered when we encounter cues in a situation that we perceive as aggressive.
Songs with *aggressive lyrics* may trigger violent behaviour.	Fischer and Greitemeyer (2006) investigated song lyrics as a form of media violence. Male participants listened to songs featuring aggressively derogatory lyrics about women. Compared with when they listened to neutral lyrics, participants later recalled more negative qualities about women and behaved more aggressively towards a female **confederate**. Similar results with female participants and 'men-hating' lyrics.

Apply it

One strength of desensitisation is research support.

Krahé et al. (2011) showed participants violent (and non-violent) film clips while measuring physiological arousal using skin conductance (see page 166).

Viewers of violent media showed lower arousal when watching violent film clips. Arousal was negatively correlated with unprovoked aggression in a 'noise blast' task.

This demonstrates lower arousal in violent media users reflecting desensitisation to the effects of violence leading to a greater willingness to be aggressive.

One limitation of desensitisation is catharsis may be a better explanation.

Krahé et al. (2011) failed to find a link between media viewing, lower arousal and reactive aggression.

This may be because catharsis occurred – viewing violent media acts as a safety valve, allowing participants to release aggressive impulses without behaving violently.

Desensitisation cannot explain this, which suggests aggression is not the outcome of desensitisation. Therefore catharsis may be the more **valid** explanation.

One strength of disinhibition is research support.

Berkowitz and Alioto (1973) showed a film depicting aggression as vengeance. Participants gave more (fake) electric shocks of longer duration to a confederate.

Media violence may disinhibit aggressiveness when it is justified – vengeance is a powerful justification for violence which is then seen as more socially acceptable.

This adds validity to the disinhibition concept because it demonstrates the link between removal of social constraints and subsequent aggressive behaviour.

Another strength of disinhibition is it can explain the effect of cartoon violence.

Kirsh (2006) argues that children do not learn specific behaviours from cartoon models (e.g. it is not possible to punch someone so their head spins round 360 degrees).

Children learn social norms instead – the aggression carried out by cartoon models is socially normative, especially when it goes unpunished.

This supports the disinhibition hypothesis because children learn from cartoons that aggression is rewarding and achieves goals in a socially acceptable way.

One strength of cognitive priming is useful practical applications.

Understanding how cognitive priming influences aggression can potentially save lives – whether situations break into violence depends on how individuals interpret cues which depends on scripts stored in memory.

Bushman and Anderson (2002) claim someone who habitually watches violent media accesses stored aggressive scripts more readily – so they are more likely to interpret cues as aggressive and resort to a violent solution.

This raises the possibility that effective interventions could reduce aggressive behaviour by challenging hostile cognitive scripts and encouraging habitual violent media users to consider alternatives (e.g. humour or negotiation).

The three faces of Steve.*

*Psychology in-joke – ask your teacher.

REVISION BOOSTER

Evaluation points like these aren't just for long essay-style questions. You might be asked for a single strength or limitation as part of a short-answer question. Also, some questions ask for a 'brief discussion' for 6 marks. For such questions, two or three of these points would do the job nicely.

KNOWLEDGE CHECK

1. Explain what is meant by the terms 'desensitisation' and 'disinhibition' in relation to media influences on aggression. *(2 marks + 2 marks)*

2. Outline the role of cognitive priming in media influences on aggression. *(4 marks)*

3. Briefly evaluate the role of disinhibition in media influences on aggression. *(4 marks)*

4. Discuss media influences on aggression. Refer in your answer to the roles of desensitisation, disinhibition and cognitive priming. *(16 marks)*

Defining and measuring crime

Spec spotlight

Problems in defining crime. Ways of measuring crime, including official statistics, victim surveys and offender surveys.

The 'living statues' in Oldham town centre were becoming really elaborate.

Wendy's house was burgled for the third time in a year. The first and second time, she reported the crimes to the police. They came and had a look round and gave her a crime number for her insurance company. She also had a visit from a nice woman from Victim Support. But then she heard nothing more. Wendy tells her friend that she didn't bother to report the latest burglary. Her friend replied, 'But if you don't report it then no one will know what the true level of crime is.'

Is Wendy's friend right? Use your knowledge of ways of measuring crime to explain your answer.

Problems in defining crime

Crimes are acts *against the law*.	Crime might be defined as any act that breaks the law and therefore warrants some form of punishment.
	However, this legalistic definition is complicated by the fact that what counts as a crime changes – both across time and across cultures.
Definitions of crime differ across *cultures*.	What is considered a crime in one culture may not be judged a crime in another.
	For example, in 2014 forced marriage was made illegal in the UK, yet this is still practised in some cultures.
Definitions of crime change *over time*.	At different historical times people define crime differently.
	For example, a parent's right to smack their child was outlawed in 2004.
	Homosexuality was considered a crime in this country until 1967, but attitudes and the law have changed so it is no longer a crime.

Ways of measuring crime

Official statistics: Government records of reported crime.	Official statistics are government records of the total number of crimes reported to police and recorded in the official figures.
	These are published on an annual basis and provide a 'snapshot' of the number of crimes occurring in the country and different regions.
	This allows the government to develop crime-prevention strategies and policing initiatives in response to the figures.
Victim surveys: People's experience of crime.	Victim surveys record people's experience of crime over a specific period.
	The *Crime Survey for England and Wales* (CSEW) asks people to document crimes they have been a victim of in the past year.
	50,000 households are randomly selected to take part. The results are published annually.
	In 2009, a separate survey was introduced to record the experiences of younger people aged 10–15.
Offender surveys: People self-report crimes they've committed.	Offender surveys involve individuals volunteering details of the number and types of crimes they have committed.
	These surveys tend to target groups of likely offenders based on 'risk' factors, such as previous convictions, age, social background, etc.
	The survey looks at indicators of repeat offending, trends in drug and alcohol use, etc.

One limitation is official statistics may underestimate crime.

Some commentators suggest that so many crimes go unreported to the police that only around 25% of offences are included in the official statistics. The other 75% of offences are referred to as the 'dark figure' of crime.

Crimes may not appear in official figures for many reasons (police mistrust, fear of reprisals, police recording rules). Farrington and Dowds (1985) found Nottinghamshire police were far more likely to record thefts under £10 than other counties, hence a 'spike' in their figures.

This suggests that police priorities may distort official figures.

One strength is victim surveys are thought to have a greater degree of accuracy.

Surveys include crimes not reported to police (e.g. 2006/7 official statistics showed a 2% drop in crime compared to a 3% *increase* reported by victim surveys).

But victim surveys rely on respondents accurately recalling crimes. They may misremember a crime as happening in the current year because the trauma is still fresh in their mind.

This means that inaccurate victim recall may distort the crime figures.

Neil thought no one would miss the office stapler. Unfortunately for him, the company was based in Nottinghamshire – he was arrested and sentenced to life imprisonment the following day.

The main strength of offender surveys is the insight they provide.

They gather information on how many people are responsible for certain offences (e.g. burglaries are committed by a small number of people who commit many crimes).

But despite anonymity, the offenders' responses may be unreliable – they conceal serious crimes or even exaggerate the numbers (e.g. out of bravado).

In addition, the sampling technique may mean that 'middle-class' crimes such as corporate crime and fraud are under-represented.

REVISION BOOSTER

You have just over a minute to spend writing for each mark – but make sure you give that time to the short-answer questions. It's probably easier to boost your mark on these rather than on essay questions.

A further limitation is the politics of measuring crimes.

Political parties use some measures rather than others. Opposition parties use crime rates that make the government look bad. The party in power uses rates that show crime is falling.

Crime statistics in the UK are compiled by a supposedly objective body – the Office of National Statistics (ONS), but questions about their **validity** are still often raised.

This questions the extent to which figures on crime can be trusted.

KNOWLEDGE CHECK

1. Distinguish between victim surveys and offender surveys as ways of measuring crime.
   (3 marks)

2. Forced marriage has been illegal in the UK since 2014. Homosexuality is not a crime in the UK now, but it was before 1967. It still is in some countries.

   Explain **two** problems in defining crime. In your answer refer to the examples given above. *(4 marks)*

3. Briefly evaluate official statistics as a way of measuring crime. *(4 marks)*

4. Outline and evaluate **at least two** ways of measuring crime.
   (16 marks)

A further strength could be a multidisciplinary approach.

Each method has issues in terms of reliability and validity of the data they produce. So all crime figures should be carefully scrutinised and interpreted with caution.

Researchers advocate a multidisciplinary approach when measuring crime – a combination of all available methods provides the best insight into the true extent of offending.

If all measures point to the same pattern, this increases the validity of the findings.

Offender profiling: The top-down approach

Spec spotlight

Offender profiling: the top-down approach, including organised and disorganised types of offender.

Fido claimed it was a case of 'mistaken identity' but he fitted the profile perfectly: small, four legs, black around the eye, furry. The game was up.

REVISION BOOSTER

An application (AO2) question might ask you to explain how a description of an offender matches the organised/disorganised profile. A good response would be to use some of the features described here – link them to the stimulus material in the question.

The top-down approach

Offender profiling: Aims to narrow the list of suspects.	The main aim of offender profiling is to narrow the field of enquiry and the list of likely suspects.
	Professional profilers are employed to work alongside the police especially in high-profile murder cases.
	The scene and evidence are analysed to generate hypotheses about the probable characteristics of the offender (e.g. age, background, occupation, etc.).
Top-down approach: Match crime/offender to pre-existing templates.	The pre-existing template was developed by the FBI.
	Murderers or rapists are classified in one of two categories (organised and disorganised) based on this evidence. This then informs the investigation.
Organised and disorganised types based on offender 'ways of working'.	The organised and disorganised distinction is based on the idea that serious offenders have certain signature 'ways of working'.
	These generally correlate with a particular set of social and psychological characteristics that relate to the individual.
Organised: targets victim, controlled, higher IQ.	Organised offenders are characterised by:
	• Evidence of planning the crime – victim is deliberately targeted and the killer/rapist may have a 'type' of victim.
	• High degree of control during the crime and little evidence left behind at the scene.
	• Above-average IQ – in a skilled/professional job.
	• Usually married and may even have children.
Disorganised: Impulsive, lower IQ.	Disorganised offenders are characterised by:
	• Little evidence of planning, suggesting the offence may have been spontaneous.
	• The crime scene reflects the impulsive nature of the act – body still at the scene and the crime shows little control on the part of the offender.
	• Below-average IQ – may be in unskilled work or unemployed.
	• A history of failed relationships and living alone, possible history of sexual dysfunction.
FBI profile construction: Data, classification, reconstruction, profile generation.	There are four main stages in the construction of an FBI profile:
	1. Data assimilation – review of the evidence (photographs, pathology reports, etc.).
	2. Crime scene classification – organised or disorganised.
	3. Crime reconstruction – generation of hypotheses about the behaviour and events.
	4. Profile generation – generation of hypotheses about the offender (e.g. background, physical characteristics, etc.).

One limitation of top-down profiling is it only applies to particular crimes.

Top-down profiling is best suited to crime scenes that reveal important details about the suspect, (e.g. rape, arson, murder and sadistic torture).

Common offences (e.g. burglary, destruction of property) do not lend themselves to profiling because the crime reveals little about the offender.

This means that, at best, it is a limited approach to identifying a criminal.

Bernard regretted painting his garden fence red before attempting to nick his neighbour's curtains.

A further limitation is this approach is based on outdated models of personality.

The typology classification system is based on the assumption that offenders' patterns of behaviour and motivations are consistent across situations and contexts.

Alison *et al.* (2002) argue this is based on outdated personality models that see behaviour as driven by dispositional traits rather than by constantly changing external factors.

This means that the top-down approach may have poor **validity** when it comes to identifying possible suspects and/or predicting their next move.

Apply it

A criminal profiler becomes national news when a serial killer is caught. The police used the profile he composed to make an arrest. The profiler is interviewed on BBC News and is asked to explain the secret of his success. He says he uses the top-down approach. The interviewer doesn't understand, so asks him to explain what that means and why it was successful.

Outline what the profiler might say in response to the interviewer.

Another limitation is little support for the idea of the 'disorganised offender'.

Canter *et al.* (2004) used *smallest space analysis* of 100 murders in the US. Each case was examined against 39 characteristics typical of organised and disorganised killers.

The findings showed evidence of a distinct organised type but not a disorganised type – which undermines the whole classification system.

Despite this, the organised/disorganised distinction is still used as a model for professional profilers in the US and has widespread support.

Another limitation is that the classification system is too simplistic.

Behaviours describing organised/disorganised offenders are not mutually exclusive (e.g. Godwin 2002 asks: how would police investigators classify a killer with high intelligence who commits a spontaneous murder?).

So there are more detailed typologies. Holmes (1989) suggests four types of serial killer: visionary, mission, hedonistic, power/ control. Keppel and Walter (1999) suggest we focus on motivations of killers rather than 'types'.

The conflicting typology versions and approaches suggest that classification systems for criminals may be too simplistic.

KNOWLEDGE CHECK

1. In relation to offender profiling, distinguish between organised and disorganised types of offender. *(4 marks)*

2. Outline the top-down approach to offender profiling. *(6 marks)*

3. Briefly evaluate **one** approach to offender profiling. *(4 marks)*

4. Octavia is a criminal profiler investigating the scene of a murder. There is very little physical evidence, but she notices there are indications that the murderer was organised and controlling. She believes she can use this information to construct a profile.

   Discuss the top-down approach to offender profiling. Refer in your answer to Octavia's experience. *(16 marks)*

A final limitation is the way the typology approach was developed.

Interviews were used with 36 killers in the US (25 serial killers, 11 single or double murderers) – a small, unrepresentative sample on which to base a typology system that may have a significant influence on the nature of the police investigation.

Canter has argued that it is not sensible to rely on self-report data with convicted killers when constructing a classification system.

This methodological criticism of the way the approach was developed questions the validity of the top-down approach as a whole.

Offender profiling: The bottom-up approach

Spec spotlight

Offender profiling: the bottom-up approach, including investigative psychology; geographical profiling.

Heston liked to dress up and pretend to be a forensic psychologist whilst doing his gardening late at night.

Apply it

A criminal profiler who specialises in the bottom-up approach has been asked by the police to construct a profile of an offender believed to be responsible for a series of rapes and sexual assaults. The profiler notices that the crimes were committed in an area with a radius of about three miles. Two women have also been killed just outside this area, but the police do not know if this is the same offender. The profiler notices that all of the crimes show signs of a very controlling attacker.

a. Explain how the profiler might use the bottom-up approach to construct her profile.

b. What might the profiler include in the profile?

Bottom-up or top-down

Both are based on crime-scene data. The difference is that the top-down approach uses the data to generate the profile and, from then on, the investigator fits the profile to the crime scene. In the bottom-up version the investigator always starts again at the bottom and generates a profile.

Investigative psychology

Bottom-up approach: Offender profile emerges based on the data.	Unlike the US top-down approach, the British bottom-up model does not begin with fixed typologies. Instead, the profile is 'data-driven' and emerges as the investigator rigorously scrutinises the details of a particular offence.
	The aim is to generate a picture of the offenders' characteristics, routines and background through analysis of the evidence.
Statistical analysis of crime-scene evidence.	Statistical procedures detect patterns of behaviour that are likely to occur (or coexist) across crime scenes.
	This is done to develop a statistical 'database' which then acts as a baseline for comparison.
	Features of an offence can be matched against this database to suggest potentially important details about the offender, their personal history, family background, etc.
Analysis based on psychological concepts: *Interpersonal coherence*.	A central concept is interpersonal coherence – the way an offender behaves at the scene (including how they 'interact' with the victim) may reflect their behaviour in everyday situations (e.g. controlling, apologetic, etc.); i.e. their behaviour 'hangs together' (has coherence).
	This might tell the police something about how the offender relates to women (for example) more generally.

Geographical profiling

Inferences about the offender *based on location*.	The locations of crime scenes are used to infer the likely home or operational base of an offender – known as *crime mapping*.
	Location can also be used alongside psychological theory to create hypotheses about the offender and their *modus operandi* (habitual way of working).
Marauder and *commuter* types of offender.	The assumption is that serial offenders restrict their 'work' to areas they are familiar with. Canter and Larkin (1993) proposed two models of offender behaviour:
	1. The *marauder* – operates close to their home base.
	2. The *commuter* – likely to have travelled a distance away from their usual residence when committing a crime.
Circle theory uses offending locations.	Canter and Larkin suggest that the pattern of offending locations is likely to form a circle around the offender's usual residence, and this becomes more apparent the more offences there are.
	The offender's spatial decision-making can provide insight into the nature of the offence (planned or opportunistic, mode of transport, employment status, etc.).

Offender profiling: The bottom-up approach

One strength is that evidence supports investigative psychology.

Canter and Heritage (1990) did a content analysis of 66 sexual assault cases using *smallest space analysis*. Several characteristics were commonly identified in most cases (e.g. use of impersonal language, lack of reaction to the victim).

This can lead to an understanding of how an offender's behaviour may change over a series of offences, or in establishing whether two or more offences were committed by the same person.

This supports the usefulness of investigative psychology because it shows how statistical techniques can be applied.

The burglar's mistake was to leave gigantic red inflatable symbols in the gardens of each of the houses he robbed. An elementary error.

A further strength is that evidence also supports geographical profiling.

Lundrigan and Canter (2001) collated information from 120 murder cases involving serial killers in the US. Smallest space analysis revealed spatial consistency in the behaviour of the killers.

The location of each body disposal site was plotted and a 'centre of gravity' identified; offender's base was invariably in the centre of the pattern. The effect was more noticeable for 'marauders' (offenders travelling short distances).

This supports Canter's claim that spatial information can be a key factor in determining the base of an offender.

REVISION BOOSTER

You can help the clarity of your evaluation hugely by doing what we've done here – provide introductory 'signposts' at the start of an evaluative paragraph. It keeps you on the path of evaluation and it tells the examiner what you are doing – it's a way of saying 'I'm *using* this evidence, not just describing it.'

Another strength is the approach has a scientific basis.

Canter argues the bottom-up approach is more objective and scientific than top-down (more psychological theory and evidence, less speculation and fewer 'hunches').

Investigators can use geographical, biographical and psychological data to quickly produce data to assist in the investigation.

Investigative psychology has also expanded to include areas like suspect interviewing and examination of material presented in court – this supports its use in the judicial process.

A final strength is the wider application of the approach.

The bottom-up approach can be applied to a wider range of offences compared to the top-down approach.

Techniques (e.g. smallest space analysis, principle of spatial consistency) can be used in the investigation of crimes from burglary/theft to murder/rape.

This means that the bottom-up approach is more valuable than the top-down approach as an investigative technique.

KNOWLEDGE CHECK

1. In relation to offender profiling, explain what is meant by the 'top-down' and the 'bottom-up' approaches. *(2 marks + 2 marks)*

2. Outline research into geographical profiling. *(6 marks)*

3. Briefly evaluate investigative psychology in relation to offender profiling. *(4 marks)*

4. Outline and evaluate the bottom-up approach to offender profiling. In your answer, refer to investigative psychology **and** geographical profiling. *(16 marks)*

One limitation is that there are mixed results for profiling.

Despite many successes of the bottom-up approach, there have been significant failures and studies examining its effectiveness have found mixed results.

Copson (1995) surveyed 48 police forces – advice provided by a profiler was judged 'useful' in 83% of cases, but led to accurate identification of an offender in just 3% of cases.

This evidence questions the effectiveness of the bottom-up approach.

Biological explanations: Atavistic form

Spec spotlight

Biological explanations of offending behaviour: an historical approach (atavistic form).

Lombroso argued that primitive offenders cannot adjust to civilised society – although this lad's doing his best.

Funny word, atavistic

Here's a dictionary definition of the term atavistic: 'Relating to or characterised by reversion to something ancient or ancestral.' That's where the idea of 'criminal features' being an evolutionary throwback comes from.

Apply it

Cordelia and Regan are discussing the forensic topics they've been doing in psychology. Cordelia says, 'The criminals in those mugshots you see on telly always look well dodgy.' Regan replies, 'I know quite a few people who have gone to prison and none of them look like that.'

What features might Cordelia be referring to when she uses the term 'well dodgy'? Explain why Regan makes a valid point about these features.

Atavistic form	
Lombroso's *historical approach* laid foundations of profiling.	Cesare Lombroso (1876) was an Italian physician.
	He proposed that criminals were 'genetic throwbacks' – a primitive sub-species who were biologically different from non-criminals. This is the 'atavistic form'.
	His theory of the atavistic form, though now discredited, laid the foundation for modern offender profiling.
Offenders lack *evolutionary development*.	Offenders were seen by Lombroso as lacking **evolutionary** development.
	Their savage and untamed nature meant that they would find it impossible to adjust to civilised society and would inevitably turn to crime.
	Therefore Lombroso saw criminal behaviour as an innate tendency and thus was proposing a new perspective (for his time) that the criminal was not at fault. In this way his ideas were revolutionary.
Atavistic features biologically determined.	Lombroso argued the criminal sub-type could be identified as being in possession of physiological 'markers'.
	These 'atavistic' characteristics are **biologically determined**.
	These characteristics are mainly features of the head and face that make criminals physically different from the rest of us.
Cranial and other physical and emotional features.	In terms of characteristics of the skull (cranium), the atavistic form included:
	• A narrow, sloping brow.
	• A strong prominent jaw.
	• High cheekbones.
	• Facial asymmetry.
	Other physical features included dark skin and existence of extra toes, nipple or fingers.
	Besides physical traits, Lombroso suggested there were other aspects of the atavistic form including insensitivity to pain, use of criminal slang, tattoos and unemployment.
Different types of criminals have different physical characteristics.	Lombroso also suggested that particular physiological 'markers' were linked to particular types of crime.
	For example, murderers were described as having bloodshot eyes, curly hair and long ears.
	Sexual deviants were described as having glinting eyes with swollen and fleshy lips.
Lombroso's research found 40% of criminal acts accounted for by atavistic characteristics.	Lombroso meticulously examined the facial and cranial features of 383 dead criminals and 3839 living ones.
	From this research he proposed the atavistic form.
	He concluded that 40% of criminal acts could be accounted for by people with atavistic characteristics.

One strength of Lombroso's research is its large contribution to criminology.

Lombroso has been hailed as the 'father of modern criminology' (Hollin 1989) and credited as shifting emphasis in research away from moralistic (e.g. 'weak-minded') discourse to scientific discourse (e.g. evolution and genetics).

Also, in trying to describe how particular types of people are likely to commit particular types of crime, Lombroso's theory heralded the beginning of criminal profiling.

In this way he made a major contribution to the science of criminology.

One limitation is the racial undertones of Lombroso's work.

Many of the features that Lombroso identifies as criminal and atavistic, such as curly hair and dark skin, are most likely to be found among people of African descent.

Similarly, his description of the atavistic form being as 'uncivilised, primitive, savage' would lend support to the eugenic philosophies of the time (i.e. that certain groups should not be allowed to breed).

Lombroso's intention is unclear, but there is little doubt that these racial undertones are an uncomfortable and controversial legacy which overshadows his work.

Lombroso, known to researchers in the field as the 'father of modern criminology', and known to his mum as 'our Ces'.

A further limitation is the contradictory evidence for the atavistic form.

Goring (1913) compared 3000 criminals and 3000 non-criminals and concluded there was no evidence that offenders are a distinct group with unusual physical characteristics.

But he did suggest that many people who commit crime have a lower-than-average IQ – this offers some limited support for the idea of a criminal sub-species.

However, this evidence does question the key element of his theory that criminals are different in terms of their *appearance*.

Another limitation is the poor control in Lombroso's research.

Unlike Goring, Lombroso did not compare his criminal sample with a non-criminal **control group**. Had he done so, the significant differences in atavistic form may have disappeared.

Lombroso's research also failed to account for other important variables. Many of the criminals he studied had a history of psychological disorders which may have acted as **confounding variables**.

Therefore, the evidence on which the atavistic form is based has serious flaws.

A final limitation is that causation is a problem in Lombroso's theory.

Even if there are criminals who have atavistic elements in their facial appearance, this does not necessarily mean this is the *cause* of their offending.

Facial and cranial differences may be influenced by other factors (e.g. poverty or poor diet) rather than being an indication of delayed evolutionary development.

Although, in fairness to Lombroso, in his later work he acknowledged that criminals could be made as well as born.

REVISION BOOSTER

Write a very brief essay plan for each possible essay and then practise writing the essay in full from this. Time yourself – 20 minutes for a 16-mark essay.

KNOWLEDGE CHECK

1. In relation to biological explanations of offending behaviour, explain what is meant by the term 'atavistic form'. *(3 marks)*
2. Outline atavistic form as a biological explanation of offending behaviour. *(6 marks)*
3. Evaluate an historical approach to explaining offending behaviour. *(6 marks)*
4. Modern explanations of offending behaviour grew out of an historical approach which focused on facial characteristics. But this approach seems very primitive by today's standards.

   With reference to the above statement, discuss **one** biological explanation of offending behaviour. *(16 marks)*

Biological explanations: Genetic and neural explanations

Spec spotlight

Biological explanations of offending behaviour: genetics and neural explanations.

'I'm warning you Warren, stop copying my outfits or I'll chase you with this massive pipe.' It was just another typical day in the staffroom.

Twin and adoption studies

Both of these are quasi-experiments where the independent variable is genetic or environmental similarity (for example, an adoptive parent shares environment with a child and the biological parent shares genetics). The dependent variable is similarity in offending behaviour.

Apply it

Hermione and Yakira are discussing their friend Ziv who has been caught by the police for several driving offences including driving without a licence or insurance and speeding. He also resisted arrest and hit a police officer. Hermione comments that she always knew Ziv would get into trouble one day because, well you only have to look at his dad. And he's got a twin brother who's just the same. Yakira agrees and adds, 'Yes, and Ziv was always doing things without thinking about them first. I wondered if he had something wrong with his brain.'

Explain the issues raised in this conversation using your knowledge of neural **and** genetic explanations for offending behaviour.

Genetic explanations

Twin and adoption studies suggest genes predispose offenders to crime.	Lange (1930) studied 13 **MZ** and 17 **DZ twins** where one of the twins in each pair spent time in prison. Ten of the MZ twins had a co-twin who was also in prison but this was only true for two of the DZ twins. Crowe (1972) found that adopted children who had a biological parent with a criminal record had a 50% greater risk of a criminal record by the age of 18. But adopted children whose mother didn't have a criminal record only had a 5% risk.
Candidate genes: MAOA and CDH13.	A genetic analysis of 900 offenders by Tiihonen *et al.* (2014) revealed two genes that may be associated with violent crime: • The MAOA gene controls **serotonin** and **dopamine** and is linked to aggressive behaviour. • CDH13 is linked to substance abuse and ADHD. This high-risk combination led to individuals being 13 times more likely to have a history of violent disorder.
Diathesis-stress model.	If genes have an influence on offending, this influence is likely to be at least partly moderated by environmental factors. A tendency to criminal behaviour may come about through a combination of: • Genetic predisposition (diathesis). • A biological or psychological stressor or 'trigger' (e.g. criminal role models or dysfunctional upbringing).

Neural explanations

Antisocial personality disorder (APD).	There may be neural differences in the brains of criminals and non-criminals. For example, APD is associated with a lack of empathy and is suffered by many convicted criminals.
Less activity in *prefrontal cortex* = less emotional regulation.	Raine *et al.* (2000) found an 11% reduction in the volume of grey matter in the prefrontal cortex of people with APD compared to controls. This is the part of the brain that regulates emotional behaviour.
Mirror neurons (empathy) may not always be turned on.	Keysers (2011) found that only when criminals were *asked* to empathise did they show an empathy reaction (controlled by mirror neurons in the brain). This suggests APD individuals do experience empathy, but may have a neural 'switch' that turns on and off. In a normally-functioning brain the empathy switch is permanently on.

AO3
Evaluation

Biological explanations: Genetic and neural explanations

One limitation is the methodological problems with twin studies of criminality.

Lange's research was poorly controlled (e.g. judgements of whether twin pairs were MZ or DZ based on appearance not DNA testing).

Also, most twins are reared in the same environment – so **concordance rates** may be due to shared learning experiences rather than genetics.

Methodological issues such as **confounding variables** mean twin studies of criminality may lack **validity**.

One strength is the support for a diathesis-stress model of crime.

Mednick *et al.* (1984) studied 13,000 Danish adoptees and criminality (**operationalised** as having at least one court conviction which was checked against police records).

When neither biological nor adoptive parents had convictions, the percentage of adoptees that had a conviction was 13.5%. This rose to 20% when *either* of the biological parents did, and 24.5% when *both* adoptive parents *and* biological parents did.

These data suggest that both genetic inheritance and environment influence criminality – supporting the diathesis-stress model of crime.

Crime runs in families.

A further limitation is methodological problems with adoption studies.

Adoption studies are complicated by the fact that many children experience late adoption. So these children spent time with their biological parents before adoption.

In addition, lots of adoptees maintain contact with their biological parents.

Both of these points make it difficult to assess the environmental (nurture as well as nature) impact the biological parents might have had.

Another limitation is that these explanations are biologically reductionist.

Criminality is complex; explanations that reduce offending behaviour to a genetic or neural level ignore higher level explanations. Crime runs in families but so do poverty, deprivation and mental illness.

This makes it difficult to disentangle the effects of genes and neural influences from other factors.

This indicates that genetic and neural explanations in isolation are too simplistic.

A final limitation is that these explanations are also biologically determinist.

The notion of a 'criminal gene' presents a dilemma. The legal system is based on the premise that criminals have personal and moral responsibility for their crimes.

Only in extreme cases (e.g. diagnosis of mental illness) can someone claim that they were not acting entirely of their own **free will**.

This raises ethical questions about what society does with people who are suspected of carrying criminal genes and who therefore have a limited choice.

REVISION BOOSTER

The concordance rate for identical twins is not 100% – so what? Students often jump on this figure as proof that a behaviour is not completely genetically inherited. This is true, but not very interesting. A much more sophisticated evaluation recognises offending behaviour is not completely genetic, but it is partly – so the important question is: 'To what *extent* is it genetic?'

KNOWLEDGE CHECK

1. Outline research into the genetic explanation of offending behaviour. *(6 marks)*

2. Briefly outline **two** biological explanations of offending behaviour. *(6 marks)*

3. Evaluate the neural explanation of offending behaviour. *(6 marks)*

4. Discuss genetic **and/or** neural explanations of offending behaviour. Refer to research evidence in your answer. *(16 marks)*

Psychological explanations: Eysenck's theory

Psychological explanations of offending behaviour: Eysenck's theory of the criminal personality.

Who says air guitar doesn't make you look cool? Er, most of this guy's audience actually.

Personality

People differ in the way they think, feel and act. The sum total of such individual differences is their personality.

Joss is a prison psychologist who frequently runs therapy groups as part of his job. He has noticed that some of the more violent prisoners have quite a lot in common. They are reckless, unpredictable and often cruel. They don't seem to understand how others feel. But they are also different in some ways. Some are quiet and shy, others outgoing and impulsive. Some seem quite stable but others are insecure and anxious.

Use Eysenck's theory of the criminal personality to explain why the prisoners are similar in some ways, but different in others.

Eysenck's theory of the criminal personality

Three *personality dimensions*.	Eysenck (1947) proposed that personality could be represented along three dimensions: • Introversion–extraversion (E). • Neuroticism–stability (N). • Psychoticism–socialisation (P). The dimensions combine to form a variety of personality characteristics or types.
Innate, biological basis for personality types.	Eysenck suggested personality types are innate and based on the nervous system we inherit. Extraverts have an underactive nervous system which means they seek excitement and stimulation and engage in risk-taking. Neurotic individuals have a high level of reactivity in the **sympathetic nervous system** – they respond quickly to situations of threat (fight-or-flight). This means they tend to be nervous, jumpy and over-anxious so their behaviour is difficult to predict. Psychotic individuals are suggested to have higher levels of **testosterone** – they are cold, unemotional and prone to aggression.
Criminal personality = neurotic extravert + high psychoticism.	The criminal personality type is a combination: • Neurotics are unstable and therefore prone to overreact to situations of threat. • Extraverts seek more arousal and thus engage in dangerous activities. • Psychotics are aggressive and lacking empathy.
Criminal behaviour is concerned with *immediate gratification*.	Eysenck saw criminal behaviour as developmentally immature in that it is selfish and concerned with immediate gratification. Criminals are impatient and cannot wait for things – so they are more likely to act antisocially.
High E and high N scorers lack ability to learn (be *conditioned*).	In the process of socialisation children are taught to become more able to delay gratification and more socially orientated. Eysenck believed that people with high E and N scores had nervous systems that made it difficult for them to learn (be conditioned). As a result, they are less likely to learn anxiety responses to antisocial impulses.
Personality can be measured using the *EPI*.	The notion that personality can be measured is central to Eysenck's theory. He developed the *Eysenck Personality Inventory* (EPI), a psychological test that locates respondents along the E and N dimensions to determine their personality type. A later scale was introduced to measure psychoticism.

One strength is the evidence supporting Eysenck's theory.

Eysenck and Eysenck (1977) compared EPI scores of 2070 male prisoners with a **control group** of 2422 non-criminal males. Prisoners scored higher on P, E and N, supporting predictions of the theory.

However, Farrington et al.'s (1982) review of studies showed offenders scored high on P but not on E or N. Also, little evidence of consistent differences in **EEGs** (used to measure cortical arousal) between extraverts and introverts.

This casts doubt on the physiological basis of Eysenck's theory.

Eysenck – as in Eysenck Personality Inventory. How much of a coincidence is that?!

One limitation is the idea that there is one single criminal type.

Moffitt (1993) proposed several distinct types of adult male offender based on the timing of the first offence, and how long offending persists.

Eysenck's theory is out of step with modern personality theories. Digman's (1990) *five factor model* suggests three additional dimensions of openness, agreeableness and conscientiousness.

This suggests that many different types of criminal may exist because E and N are not the only factors that contribute.

REVISION BOOSTER

In a 16-mark essay you don't have to write everything on this spread. What is here is actually more than 1000 words!! For a 16-mark essay you probably only have time to write 500 words – but don't cut down the elaboration of the AO3 points. Better to do four elaborated points rather than five briefer ones.

A further limitation is cultural bias.

Bartol and Holanchock (1979) studied Hispanic and African-American offenders in a New York maximum security prison, dividing them into six groups based on criminal history and offence.

All six groups were less extravert than a non-criminal **control group**. Bartol and Holanchock suggested this was because the sample was a different cultural group from that investigated by Eysenck.

This questions the **generalisability** of the criminal personality.

KNOWLEDGE CHECK

1. Outline Eysenck's theory of the criminal personality.
   (6 marks)

2. Describe **one** study related to Eysenck's theory of the criminal personality. In your answer include information on what the researcher(s) did and what was found. *(6 marks)*

Another limitation is the mismeasurement of personality.

Eysenck's theory assumes it is possible to measure personality. However, critics argue we cannot reduce personality type to a 'score' from the EPI.

Some even suggest there is no such thing as personality as a stable entity. We adopt different personalities in different contexts (Mischel 1988).

This undermines the concept of a stable and measurable criminal personality.

3. Evaluate **one** psychological explanation of offending behaviour. *(6 marks)*

4. Cruz is outwardly charming, friendly and outgoing. But he is also unfeeling, selfish, anxious and tense. He is currently in prison for serious assault.

   Outline and evaluate Eysenck's theory of the criminal personality. Refer to Cruz in your answer. *(16 marks)*

Another strength is that the theory fits other biological approaches.

The theory recognises personality may have a genetic basis. Raine suggested **APD** due to brain structure (see page 210). Eysenck linked it to nervous system activity.

Because of its biological basis, Eysenck's theory does suffer from some of the same limitations of genetic and neural explanations.

Therefore, Eysenck's theory could be criticised as **biologically reductionist** and **determinist**.

Psychological explanations: Cognitive explanations

Spec spotlight

Psychological explanations of offending behaviour: cognitive explanations; level of moral reasoning and cognitive distortions, including hostile attribution bias and minimalisation.

Kohlberg's stages

Level I Preconventional
- Punishment orientation
- Instrumental/personal gain

Level II Conventional
- Good boy/girl orientation
- Maintenance of social order

Level III Postconventional
- Individual rights
- Morality of conscience

One of Kohlberg's moral dilemmas – should Heinz steal the drug to save his wife? 57 varieties of possible response.

Winona is interviewing offenders as part of her doctorate thesis. She is interested in the language offenders use to describe their crimes. She notices that many of them talk about even serious crimes like anyone else would talk about their jobs. The offenders often refuse to accept that they have caused their victims any harm. Winona has also shown the offenders several images of everyday situations involving people. The images are all neutral, but most of the offenders interpret them as hostile or aggressive.

Use your knowledge of the cognitive explanation of offending behaviour to explain Winona's findings.

Level of moral reasoning

Stages of moral development.	Kohlberg proposed that people's decisions and judgements about right and wrong can be identified in his stage theory of moral development.
	The higher the stage the more sophisticated the reasoning.
Criminals at *preconventional* level.	Kohlberg *et al.* (1973) used a moral dilemma technique and found criminal offenders tend to be at the preconventional level – non-criminals progress to the conventional level and beyond.
	Preconventional level is characterised by:
	• A need to avoid punishment and gain rewards.
	• Less mature, childlike reasoning.
	Offenders may commit crime if they can get away with it or gain rewards (e.g. money, respect).
Offenders more *egocentric* and show less sympathy.	Research shows that offenders are often self-centred (egocentric) and display poorer social perspective-taking skills (Chandler 1973).
	Individuals who reason at a higher level tend to sympathise more and exhibit behaviours such as honesty, generosity and non-violence.

Cognitive distortions

Faulty and biased thinking helps criminals justify behaviour.	**Cognitive** distortions are errors or biases in people's information processing system characterised by faulty thinking.
	We all occasionally exhibit faulty thinking, but research shows this is a much more typical way for criminals to interpret their behaviour and justify their actions.
Hostile attribution bias Ambiguous situations judged as threatening.	Schönenberg and Justye (2014) found violent offenders were more likely than non-offenders to perceive ambiguous facial expressions as angry and hostile.
	Offenders misread non-aggressive cues (e.g. being 'looked at') and this can trigger a disproportionate and violent response.
Minimalisation Downplaying the significance of the crime.	Minimalisation reduces a person's sense of guilt.
	For example, burglars may describe themselves as 'doing a job' or 'supporting my family' as a way of minimising the seriousness of their actions and their sense of guilt.
	This is particularly likely in sex offenders – Pollock and Hashmall (1991) found 35% of a sample of child molesters argued the crime they had committed was non-sexual (e.g. 'being affectionate') and 36% stated the victim consented.

One strength is the evidence supporting levels of moral reasoning.

Palmer and Hollin (1998) used a scale of 11 moral dilemma-related questions – offenders showed less mature moral reasoning than a non-offending **control group**.

This finding is in line with Kohlberg's prediction. Blackburn (1993) argues delinquents may show poor moral development due to a lack of role playing in childhood.

This suggests that role playing opportunities should be provided in order to develop moral reasoning.

Offenders show less mature reasoning than non-offenders. That's certainly the case with 'Billy the Hood' (pictured above), the scourge of the local nursery.

One limitation is that there may be better theories of moral reasoning.

Gibbs's (1979) revised version of Kohlberg's theory has *mature* (guided by conscience) and *immature* (guided by reward and avoidance of punishment) reasoning – similar to Kohlberg's preconventional and conventional stages.

Gibbs argued that Kohlberg's postconventional level should be abandoned because it was culturally biased (towards Western culture) and did not represent a 'natural' maturational stage of cognitive development.

Gibbs's view is supported by Piaget's theory of moral development, which suggests that child-like (criminal) reasoning is egocentric and gives way to empathy as children get older.

Another strength is applications of cognitive distortions research.

Understanding cognitive distortions helps treat criminal behaviour (e.g. **CBT** helps offenders to 'face up' to their behaviour with a less distorted view of their actions).

Studies suggest reducing denial and minimalisation in therapy is correlated with reduced reoffending risk. Acceptance of one's crimes is a key feature of anger management.

This cognitive explanation is therefore supported by the evidence that it is linked to effective rehabilitation techniques.

REVISION BOOSTER

You will know a lot about the cognitive approach by now. So you need to avoid writing about it in a generic way. Use specific cognitive concepts (levels of moral reasoning, distortions) and *shape* them to the topic in the question. How do they link to offending behaviour? A good way to make sure you stick to the point is to use relevant evidence and examples.

A further limitation relates to individual differences in levels of moral reasoning.

Thornton and Reid (1982) found those committing crimes for financial gain (robbery) were more likely to show preconventional reasoning than those committing impulsive crimes (e.g. assault).

Preconventional reasoning was also associated with offenders who believed they could evade punishment.

This suggests that the emphasis placed on moral reasoning as an explanation of criminality may be misplaced.

KNOWLEDGE CHECK

1. In relation to cognitive explanations of offending behaviour, explain what is meant by the terms 'hostile attribution bias' and 'minimalisation'.
   (3 marks + 3 marks)
2. Outline level of moral reasoning as a cognitive explanation of offending behaviour. *(6 marks)*
3. Briefly evaluate cognitive distortions as an explanation of offending behaviour.
   (4 marks)
4. Discuss **one or more** cognitive explanations of offending behaviour. *(16 marks)*

Another limitation is cognitive explanations are descriptive, not explanatory.

While the cognitive approach may be good at describing the criminal mind, it is rather less successful when it comes to explaining it.

Cognitive explanations are 'after the fact' theories – useful when predicting offending but they give us little insight into why the offender committed the crime in the first place.

This questions whether cognitive explanations provide us with the underlying cause of criminal behaviour.

Psychological explanations: Differential association

Spec spotlight

Psychological explanations of offending behaviour: differential association theory.

Pro-crime versus anti-crime. Whoever comes out on top will tip the scales towards offending or non-offending.

Apply it

Two psychology teachers decided to perform an unscientific 'experiment'. They both asked their students the same question: 'What would you do if you had to get hold of a lot of money quickly?' Eden's students from inner-city Liverpool mostly replied, 'Sell drugs.' Thelma's students from suburban Guildford mostly said, 'Credit card fraud.'

(Based on a true story)

Explain how the differential association theory could explain these responses.

REVISION BOOSTER

Write a very brief essay plan for each possible essay and then practise writing the essay in full from these. Time yourself – 20 minutes for a 16-mark essay.

Differential association theory

A set of *scientific principles* to explain offending.	Sutherland (1924) attempted to develop a set of scientific principles that could explain all types of offending. He believed there were clear cause and effect links between the backgrounds of people who become criminals and those who do not. Social experiences should clearly predict criminal behaviour. His theory was designed to ignore race, class or ethnic background.
Crime is learned through interactions with significant others.	Offending behaviour is acquired through the process of learning. Learning occurs through interactions with significant others that the child associates with, such as family and peer group. 'Differential' association refers to the degree to which a person associates with individuals – they spend time with some people more than others, most especially the 'significant others'. Criminality arises from two factors: • Learned attitudes towards crime. • Learning of specific criminal acts.
Crime occurs if exposure to *pro-crime values* outweighs anti-crime values.	When a person is socialised into a group they will be exposed to certain values and attitudes. This includes values and attitudes toward the law – some of these will be pro-crime, some will be anti-crime. Sutherland argues that if the number of pro-criminal attitudes the person comes to acquire outweighs the number of anti-crime attitudes, they will go on to offend.
We can make a *mathematical prediction* about committing crime.	Differential association theory proposes that it should be possible to mathematically predict how likely it is that an individual will commit crime. The prediction is based on our knowledge of the frequency, intensity and duration of an individual's exposure to deviant and non-deviant norms and values.
Both criminal *techniques and attitudes* are learned.	In addition to being exposed to pro-criminal attitudes, the would-be offender may also learn particular techniques for committing crime. For example, how to break into someone's house through a locked window or how to disable a car stereo before stealing it.
Reoffending may be due to *socialisation in prison*.	Sutherland's theory can account for why so many convicts released from prison go on to reoffend. It is reasonable to assume that whilst inside prison inmates will be exposed to pro-criminal attitudes and also learn specific techniques of offending from more experienced criminals which they can put into practice upon their release.

One strength of differential association theory is its explanatory power.

The theory can account for crime in all sectors of society. Sutherland recognised some crimes (e.g. burglary) are clustered in working-class communities, but others are prevalent in affluent sections of society.

Sutherland was particularly interested in corporate crime and how this may be a feature of middle-class social groups who share deviant norms and values.

It is a strength of this theory that it can help our understanding of different types of crimes.

Just use the front door like everyone else. What? Oh you're a burglar – ah, makes sense. Anyway carry on, sorry to disturb.

A further strength was Sutherland's overall contribution to criminology.

Sutherland moved the emphasis away from early biological accounts of crime (e.g. Lombroso's atavistic theory) and from those that pointed to individual weakness or immorality.

Differential association theory draws attention to the fact that dysfunctional social circumstances and environments may be more to blame for criminality than dysfunctional people.

This approach is more desirable than others because it offers a more realistic solution to the problem of crime instead of eugenics (the biological solution) or punishment (the morality solution).

REVISION BOOSTER

Have you checked out our revision advice on pages 4 to 9?

One limitation is the difficulty of testing the theory.

Despite Sutherland's promise to provide a scientific and mathematical framework for predicting offending behaviour it has proved difficult to test.

It is unclear how we can measure the numbers of pro- or anti-criminal attitudes a person is exposed to – so how can we know at what point criminality is triggered?

The theory does not provide a satisfactory solution to these issues, undermining its scientific credibility.

KNOWLEDGE CHECK

1. Outline differential association theory as an explanation of offending behaviour. *(6 marks)*

2. Describe **one** study related to the differential association theory of offending behaviour. *(4 marks)*

3. Briefly evaluate differential association theory **and one other** psychological explanation of offending behaviour. *(6 marks)*

4. A politician is explaining how criminals all come from a social underclass living in working-class and inner-city areas. A psychologist points out that most frauds and many driving offences are committed by middle-class people.

   Outline and evaluate **two or more** psychological explanations of offending behaviour. Refer to the politician's and psychologist's remarks in your answer. *(16 marks)*

A further limitation is that there are alternative explanations.

Sutherland suggested family attitudes are crucial in determining whether an individual turns to crime – supported by studies showing that criminal behaviour runs in families.

However, evidence that criminality runs in families could also be explained by a genetic influence, rather than by environmental or nurture influences.

This makes it hard to draw any conclusions from data about crime running in families.

Another limitation is this may be an overly determinist explanation.

Not everyone exposed to criminal influences commits crime. Differential association theory may stereotype people from impoverished backgrounds as 'unavoidably criminal'.

The theory suggests exposure to pro-criminal values is enough to produce offending in those who are exposed and ignores the fact that people may *choose* not to offend despite such influences.

Ultimately, this indicates that differential association theory may be **environmentally determinist**.

Psychological explanations: Psychodynamic explanations

Spec spotlight

Psychological explanations of offending behaviour: psychodynamic explanations.

Hopefully Rory's dad is a huge baseball fan. Hopefully.

REVISION BOOSTER

Maternal deprivation is not a named term in this part of the specification. But it could help you to add detail to your answer on the psychodynamic explanation. On the other hand, you might already have enough detail for 6 marks after writing about inadequate superegos. LESS IS MORE – writing about fewer things gives you the opportunity to demonstrate your detailed understanding.

Apply it

Tyler saw his father very rarely when he was growing up. This is because his dad was in and out of prison. When he was at home, Tyler's dad was what his mum called a 'bad influence', telling Tyler all about his criminal exploits and making it sound fun. When he eventually went back into prison, Tyler always felt guilty, as if it was his fault.

a. Use your knowledge of **one** psychodynamic explanation of offending behaviour to explain whether or not Tyler is likely to become an offender himself.

b. Based on an alternative psychodynamic explanation, construct a different scenario (like the one above) involving Tyler.

Psychodynamic explanations of offending

An *inadequate superego* can lead to immoral behaviour.	Freud's psychoanalytic theory is an example of the **psychodynamic** approach. He proposed that the superego is guided by the *morality principle* and leads to feelings of guilt for wrongdoing and feelings of pride for moral behaviour.
	Blackburn (1993) argued that if the superego is somehow inadequate then the id (governed by the *pleasure principle*) is given 'free rein' and is not properly controlled – an uncontrolled id means that criminal behaviour is inevitable.
	There are three types of 'inadequate' superego: weak, deviant or over-harsh.
Weak superego Absence of same-sex parent.	During the *phallic stage* the superego is formed in response to the *Oedipus complex*.
	If the same-sex parent is absent during this stage the child cannot internalise a fully-formed superego as there is no opportunity for identification.
	This would make criminal behaviour more likely.
Deviant superego Child internalises deviant values.	The child internalises the same-sex parent's moral attitudes to form their superego.
	If these internalised moral attitudes are deviant this would lead to a deviant superego and to offending behaviour later in life.
	For instance, a boy who is raised by a criminal father is likely to learn that wrongdoing is acceptable and will not associate guilt with wrongdoing.
Over-harsh superego Criminal acts satisfy need for punishment.	An excessively punitive or overly harsh superego means the individual is crippled by guilt and anxiety – the superego has strict rules and is unforgiving.
	This may (unconsciously) drive the individual to perform criminal acts in order to satisfy the superego's overwhelming need for punishment.
Loss of attachment leads to *affectionless psychopathy*.	Bowlby (1944) argued that a warm, continuous relationship with a mother-figure was crucial to future relationships, well-being and development.
	A loss of attachment in infancy (maternal deprivation) could lead to affectionless psychopathy (lack of empathy and guilt) and increased likelihood of delinquency.
44 juvenile thieves study supports Bowlby's maternal deprivation hypothesis.	Bowlby (1944) supported his claims with his investigation of 44 juvenile thieves. He found that 14 of the thieves showed signs of affectionless psychopathy – 12 of these had experienced prolonged separation from their mothers in infancy.
	In a **control group**, only two had experienced prolonged separation (maternal deprivation).
	Bowlby concluded that the effects of maternal deprivation had caused affectionless psychopathy and delinquent behaviour among juvenile thieves.

One limitation of psychodynamic theory is gender bias.

Psychodynamic theory assumes girls develop a weaker superego than boys – this is because girls do not experience the castration anxiety associated with the Oedipus complex so have less need to identify with their mothers.

This should mean females are more prone to criminal behaviour. This is simply not supported by evidence from prison populations.

This highlights a serious flaw in the psychodynamic explanations of offending behaviour.

Freud suggested that little boys develop a stronger superego and are therefore more moral than little girls. I have to say, I have my doubts...

A further limitation is contradictory evidence for the explanation.

There is little evidence that children raised without a same-sex parent are less law-abiding as adults – contradicting Blackburn's weak superego argument.

Similarly, if children raised by deviant parents go on to commit crime themselves, this could be due to the influence of genetics or socialisation, rather than a deviant superego.

It is also implausible that criminality reflects an unconscious desire for punishment – offenders go to great lengths to conceal their actions to avoid punishment.

Another limitation is the lack of falsifiability in psychodynamic explanations.

The many unconscious concepts within Freudian theory mean that applications to crime are not open to empirical testing.

In the absence of supporting evidence, arguments such as the inadequate superego can only be judged on their face value rather than their scientific worth.

For this reason, psychodynamic explanations are regarded as pseudoscientific ('fake' science) and contribute little to our understanding of crime.

Another limitation is problems with Bowlby's research.

Bowlby has been accused of **researcher bias** (e.g. in the 44 thieves study) because his expectations may have influenced the responses of his interviewees.

Furthermore Koluchová (1976) found deprivation effects are not inevitable. Some cases of very severe deprivation have had good outcomes provided a child has good aftercare.

This undermines the evidence used to support the psychodynamic explanations.

A final limitation concerns causality.

Lewis (1954) analysed data from interviews with 500 young people and found that maternal deprivation was a poor predictor of future offending behaviour.

Even if there was a link between maternal deprivation and crime, this does not necessarily indicate a causal link. Genetics and differential association theory are both alternative explanations.

Any **correlation** found between maternal deprivation and criminality cannot be said to have found a causal link between the two variables.

KNOWLEDGE CHECK

1. Outline psychodynamic explanations of offending behaviour. *(6 marks)*

2. Briefly outline the psychodynamic explanation **and one other** psychological explanation of offending behaviour. *(6 marks)*

3. Briefly evaluate **two** psychological explanations of offending behaviour. *(6 marks)*

4. Ashton is at secondary school and has always had a reputation for being distant and unfriendly. He can be very cruel to others but never seems to feel any guilt. He never expresses warmth or positive emotion towards others. Everyone knows Ashton is a frequent shoplifter.

   Outline and evaluate **one or more** psychodynamic explanation(s) of offending behaviour. Refer to Ashton's behaviour in your answer. *(16 marks)*

Spec spotlight

Dealing with offending behaviour: the aims of custodial sentencing and the psychological effects of custodial sentencing. Recidivism.

Tim kept bringing the family back to Butlin's every year. He had to, he was the reigning 'knobbly knees' champion.

Apply it

A newspaper website runs an article on the use of prisons as punishment for crime. Two researchers present their arguments for and against. One claims that the problem of recidivism shows that prisons do not work. The other researcher points out that prison acts as a deterrent, putting others off committing crimes. Both researchers make other arguments as well as these.

a. Briefly develop the **two** main arguments presented here.

b. Outline some of the other arguments the two researchers might present.

Aims of custodial sentencing

Deterrence Putting people off committing crime.	Custodial sentencing involves a convicted offender spending time in prison, hospital or young offender's institute. Deterrence is based on conditioning principles (punishment): • The unpleasant experience of prison is designed to put the individual off repeating the same crime again (*individual deterrence*). • It also aims to send a message to members of society that crime will not be tolerated (*general deterrence*).
Incapacitation Protect the public by removing criminals.	Ensures that the offender is taken out of society which protects the public from further offending. The need for incapacitation depends on the severity of the crime (e.g. society needs more protection from serial murderers compared to people who do not pay council tax).
Retribution Revenge against the offender.	Society enacting revenge by making the offender suffer. Level of suffering should be proportionate to the severity of the crime.
Rehabilitation Reform the offender.	Reform of the offender (i.e. he or she learns new attitudes and values and stops being a criminal). Prison should provide an opportunity to develop skills, access addiction treatments and reflect on crime.

Psychological effects of custodial sentencing

Stress, depression, institutionalisation and prisonisation.	Several psychological effects are associated with prison time: 1. Stress and depression: suicide rates and self-harm are higher in prison than in the general population. 2. Institutionalisation: inability to function outside of prison having adapted to the norms and routines of prison life. 3. Prisonisation: behaviours unacceptable outside prison are encouraged via socialisation into an 'inmate code'.

Recidivism

57% of UK offenders reoffend within a year.	Recidivism refers to reoffending. Rates vary according to the type of offence committed. UK and US recidivism rates are amongst the highest in the world. Rates are lower in Norway where there is more emphasis on rehabilitation. But some criticise the Norwegian model as 'soft'.

One limitation is the psychological effects of custodial sentencing.

Bartol (1995) suggested prison can be 'brutal and devastating'. Suicide rates among offenders are about 15 times higher than in the general population. Young single men in the first 24 hours of confinement are most at risk.

In addition, the Prison Reform Trust (2014) found that 24% of women and 15% of men reported symptoms of psychosis.

This suggests that custodial sentencing is far from effective in rehabilitating the individual, particularly those who are vulnerable.

One limitation of custodial sentencing is the effect of individual differences.

Prison time is damaging for many but we cannot assume all offenders react in the same ways. Different prisons have different regimes, so experiences vary.

Length of sentence, reason for incarceration and previous prison experience are likely to affect reactions. Some offenders may also have pre-existing vulnerabilities.

Therefore, it is very difficult to make general conclusions that apply to every prisoner and every prison.

One strength of custodial sentencing may be the opportunity for rehabilitation.

The rehabilitation model argues offenders may become better people in prison and less likely to reoffend – many prisoners do access education, training and anger management schemes.

This suggests prison could be a worthwhile experience assuming offenders are able to access these programmes. But evidence of long-term benefits from prison schemes is inconclusive.

The potential benefits of rehabilitation are a strength, but the lack of evidence undermines this argument.

Another limitation is that prisons can become 'universities for crime'.

Alongside the legitimate skills that offenders may acquire during their time in prison, they may also undergo a more dubious 'education'.

Differential association theory suggests time spent with hardened criminals may give younger inmates the chance to learn 'tricks of the trade' from experienced offenders.

This may undermine attempts to rehabilitate prisoners, making reoffending more likely.

A further limitation is that there are alternatives to custodial sentencing.

Davies and Raymond (2000), in a review of custodial sentencing, concluded that government ministers often exaggerate the benefits of prison in a bid to appear tough on crime.

The researchers suggest prison does little to rehabilitate offenders or deter others. Alternatives (e.g. community service or restorative justice) allow employment and family contact to be maintained.

The difficulty for politicians, however, is that even just proposing these alternatives is seen as being 'soft' on crime.

Victor Hugo. Wise words, Victor.

REVISION BOOSTER

Consider the three things relevant to this topic that you could specifically be asked to write about – the aims of custodial sentencing, its psychological effects or recidivism (or a combination of these). When terms are named in the specification you can't afford to pick and choose in your revision.

KNOWLEDGE CHECK

1. Briefly outline **one** way of dealing with offending behaviour. *(4 marks)*
2. Outline research into recidivism. *(6 marks)*
3. Evaluate research into the aims **and** psychological effects of custodial sentencing. *(6 marks)*
4. Since Dagny arrived in prison four months ago, she has self-harmed several times and attempted suicide once. She is no longer shocked by what goes on in the prison and has forgotten how to do things for herself.

   Discuss some of the psychological effects of custodial sentencing. Refer to Dagny's experience in your answer. *(16 marks)*

Spec spotlight

Dealing with offending behaviour: behaviour modification in custody.

Dennis's long-term escape plan was finally coming to fruition. He'd saved up 50,000 tokens during his 25-year stretch and could now exchange them for the light aircraft he'd set his heart on. In a matter of hours he'd be flying out of the prison grounds forever.

Apply it

A campaigning British newspaper has discovered that prisoners are being rewarded inside prisons, and is outraged. The article describes how prisoners are given tokens which in themselves are not worth anything. But they are furious that prisoners (some of them inside for terrible crimes) can swap the tokens for real things. Some prisoners get free cigarettes, others have extra visits from their parents. How long, the paper asks, before they are getting caviar, roast swan and 'other', unspecified, benefits?

Reading the article, you quickly realise it is nonsense. Write a reply dealing with the points raised above, using psychological evidence.

Behaviour modification in custody

Behaviourist approach – undesirable behaviours can be unlearned.	The **behaviourist** approach proposes that behaviour is learned – it should be possible to unlearn behaviour using the same principles. Behaviour modification programmes are designed with the aim of reinforcing obedient behaviour whilst punishing disobedience in the hope that it dies out (becomes extinct).
Token economy: Tokens given to reinforce desirable behaviours.	Token economy systems are managed by prison staff to modify the behaviour of inmates. Based on **operant conditioning** – desirable inmate behaviours are rewarded (reinforced) with tokens. Desirable behaviours might include avoiding conflict, being quiet in the cell, following rules and so on.
Tokens can be exchanged.	Tokens are not rewarding in themselves but rewarding because they can be exchanged for something desirable. The subsequent reward will vary according to the institution, but may include exchanging tokens for a phone call to a loved one, time in the gym or exercise yard, extra cigarettes or food.
Tokens are *secondary reinforcers* and may be removed for disobedience (punishment).	The rewards such as phone calls to loved ones or food are *primary reinforcers*. Tokens are *secondary reinforcers* because they derive their value from their association with a primary reinforcer. Behaviours and rewards would be made clear to the prisoners in advance. It would also be clear that disobedience may result in tokens and rewards being removed.
Desirable behaviours are broken down into *increments*.	When designing a behaviour modification programme: • The desirable behaviour is identified (e.g. avoiding confrontation). • It is broken down into small steps (called increments). • A baseline measure is established (i.e. a way of objectively identifying whether the offender is displaying the required behaviour). For example, a desirable behaviour (being polite to prison staff) is broken down into a set of behaviours (not raising voice, having conversation with a guard, etc.). Each day the prison staff rate prisoners on politeness and then a decision is made about what would count as achieving that goal (e.g. two guards give a rating of four or more stars).
Prison staff must *selectively* reinforce the identified behaviours.	All of those that come into contact with offenders must follow the same regime of selective reinforcement. So if the prison staff decide to give tokens for a tidy room then they all must do this consistently and not give tokens if the prisoner's room doesn't meet the standard.

One strength of behaviour modification is that it is easy to implement.

Behaviour modification does not need specialist professionals as other treatments do (e.g. anger management). It is also cost-effective and easy to follow once the programme is designed.

But its use depends on a consistent approach from prison staff. Bassett and Blanchard (1977) found any benefits were lost after inconsistent staff application, lack of training or high staff turnover.

Therefore, although behaviour modification is easy to implement, there are still factors that can undermine its effectiveness.

Behaviour modification has been accused of being dehumanising and manipulative. Tell you what, we'll call it quits if you give me that chocolate.

One limitation is that there is little rehabilitative value.

Blackburn (1993) argued that positive changes in prison may quickly be lost when the offender is released. Token economy works well inside prison but progress is unlikely to be maintained outside.

This may be because law-abiding behaviour is not always reinforced on the outside, or the rewards the offender receives from breaking the law (e.g. group status) may be more powerful.

So token economy systems are limited in their value.

A further limitation is the ethical issues raised.

The conditions of behaviour modification are regarded as manipulative and dehumanising by some. Participation is often obligatory for offenders rather than optional.

An offender who decides not to comply with the scheme loses 'privileges' (e.g. contact with loved ones) through withdrawal of tokens and this is ethically questionable.

This questions the morality and fairness of using token economy systems.

Another limitation is that learning is only superficial.

Behaviour modification encourages passive learning and focuses on surface behaviours. In contrast, anger management is much more active and reflective.

Offenders can simply play along with the token economy system to access rewards but this leads to little change in their overall principles.

This means it is not useful in the long term and individuals quickly regress back to their former behaviour.

KNOWLEDGE CHECK

1. In relation to dealing with offending behaviour, explain what is meant by 'behaviour modification in custody'. *(3 marks)*

2. Describe **one** study that has investigated behaviour modification in custody. Refer to what the researcher(s) did and what was found. *(6 marks)*

3. Evaluate behaviour modification in custody as a way of dealing with offending behaviour. *(6 marks)*

4. Describe and evaluate **two** ways of dealing with offending behaviour. *(16 marks)*

A further strength is that individually tailored programmes can be effective.

Field *et al.* (2004) examined a token economy programme for young people with behavioural problems. It was generally effective, but a number of young people did not respond.

These youths were later placed on a special programme where the rewards were more frequent and immediate – and the results were more positive.

This suggests that effectiveness can be maximised when the rewards, and frequency of rewards, suit each individual.

Dealing with offending behaviour: Anger management

Spec spotlight

Dealing with offending behaviour:
anger management.

*Someone else bitterly regretting their
rash choice of 'alternative' wallpaper
(see page 178).*

Apply it

A school decides that a good way
to tackle bullying is to run an anger
management programme. Clarissa
is one of the first to benefit. She
explains how frustrated she feels
most of the time. She can feel
anger welling up inside whenever
she believes people are not
respecting her. She sees people being
disrespectful all the time, and thinks
of it as a challenge to be confronted.
This is when she lashes out – because
she feels threatened. Being aggressive
makes her believe she is doing
something about the situation.

Describe the stages Clarissa will go
through in the anger management
programme and how each one
would address her problems.

Anger management with offenders

Cognition *triggers emotions* that trigger aggression.	Novaco (1975) suggests that **cognitive** factors trigger the emotional arousal that comes before aggressive acts.
	Novaco's argument is that, in some people, anger is quick to surface in situations they perceive to be threatening or anxiety-inducing.
	Becoming angry is then reinforced by the individual's feeling of control in that situation.
CBT: Teach individuals to recognise anger + skills to deal with it.	Anger management programmes are a form of **cognitive behaviour therapy** (**CBT**).
	The individual is taught to:
	• Recognise the *cognitive* factors that trigger their anger and loss of control.
	• Develop *behavioural* techniques that bring about conflict-resolution without the need for violence.
Stage 1: *Cognitive preparation* Reflect on the past.	This stage requires the offender to reflect on past experience – they learn to identify triggers to anger and the ways their interpretation of events may be irrational.
	For instance, the offender may view someone looking at them as confrontation. In redefining the situation as non-threatening, the therapist is attempting to break what may be an automatic response for the offender.
Stage 2: *Skill acquisition* Techniques to deal with anger.	In this stage offenders are introduced to a range of techniques and skills to help them deal with anger-provoking situations.
	Techniques may be:
	• Cognitive: positive self-talk to promote calmness.
	• Behavioural: assertiveness training to communicate more effectively.
	• Physiological: methods of relaxation and/or meditation.
Stage 3: *Application practice* Role play.	In this stage offenders are given the opportunity to practise their skills in a carefully monitored environment.
	For example, role play between the offender and therapist may involve re-enacting scenarios that led to anger and violence in the past.
	Successful negotiation of the role play would be met with positive reinforcement by the therapist.
Positive outcomes with *young offenders*.	Keen *et al.* (2000) studied the progress of young offenders between 17 and 21 who took part in an anger management programme – eight two-hour sessions.
	Initially there were difficulties with the offenders forgetting their diaries and not taking it seriously.
	By the end offenders generally reported increased awareness of their anger and capacity for self-control.

One strength of anger management is that it is an eclectic approach.

Anger management works on different levels. Cognitive preparation identifies precursors to anger (stage 1). The behavioural perspective develops self-management techniques (stage 2).

Also, a social approach is adopted when offenders are required to demonstrate what they have learned during role play (stage 3).

This multidisciplinary approach acknowledges that offending is a complex social and psychological activity.

Morris's anger was not alleviated by being forced to wear an orange jumpsuit for the rest of the day.

Another strength is that anger management tries to tackle causes.

Rather than focusing on superficial surface behaviour (as in the case of behaviour modification), anger management addresses the thought processes underlying offending behaviour.

Anger management may give offenders new insight into the causes of their criminality enabling them to self-discover ways of managing themselves outside of prison.

As such, it is more likely than behaviour modification to lead to permanent behaviour change and lower rates of recidivism.

One limitation is evidence for long-term effectiveness.

Blackburn (1993) claimed that follow-up studies tended to show that anger management has a definite short-term effect, but there is little evidence it reduces recidivism in the long-term.

This may be because the application phase of treatment still relies heavily on artificial role play which may not properly reflect all the possible real-life anger triggers.

This questions the effectiveness of anger management programmes.

A further limitation is that anger may not be the cause of offending.

Theories of anger often assume a straightforward causal relationship between anger and offending. However, this assumption may be false.

Loza and Loza-Fanous (1999) found no differences in levels of anger between offenders classed as violent or non-violent.

This suggests that anger management programmes may be misguided or even damaging if they provide offenders with justification for their behaviour.

Another limitation is the expense and commitment required.

Anger management programmes are expensive to run as they require trained specialists used to dealing with violent offenders. Many prisons cannot fund these programmes.

In addition, the success of anger management is often based on the commitment of those who participate. This may be a problem if prisoners are uncooperative.

These issues limit the effectiveness of the programmes.

KNOWLEDGE CHECK

1. Explain the difference between anger management and behaviour modification in custody as ways of dealing with offending behaviour. *(4 marks)*

2. Outline **two** ways of dealing with offending behaviour. *(6 marks)*

3. Briefly evaluate anger management as a way of dealing with offending behaviour. *(4 marks)*

4. Discuss anger management as a way of dealing with offending behaviour. *(16 marks)*

Dealing with offending behaviour: Restorative justice

Spec spotlight

Dealing with offending behaviour: restorative justice programmes.

The teacher looked regretfully at Lydia's one-word 'essay' held in the palms of her hands. If that was an essay...

Apply it

Drew was robbed in the street and suffered some injuries that had to be treated in hospital. The police eventually caught the offender, who was tried and convicted and is serving a prison sentence. Drew was visited several times by Dolores, from Victim Support. Dolores asked Drew if he would like to participate in a restorative justice programme with his attacker. Drew didn't know what that meant, so he asked Dolores to explain what would be involved.

Imagine you are Dolores. What would you tell Drew about the process of restorative justice he could expect to go through?

Restorative justice programmes

Crime against individual rather than crime against state.	Historically, a person convicted of a criminal offence would have been regarded as committing a crime against the state. In contrast restorative justice programmes switch the emphasis from the need of the state (to enforce the law) to the needs of the victim (to come to terms with the crime and move on).
Victim takes active role. Offender sees consequences of actions.	Victims are encouraged to take an active role in the processes. Offenders are required to take responsibility and face up to what they have done. A supervised meeting between the two parties is arranged and managed by a trained mediator.
A *healing* process.	Braithwaite (2004) suggests: 'crime hurts, justice should heal'. Restorative justice (RJ) is a process of managed collaboration between offender and victim based on the principles of healing and empowerment. The victim is given the opportunity to explain how the incident affected them (including emotional distress) – an important part of the rehabilitative process.
Key features shared.	RJ programmes share key features: 1. Focus on acceptance of responsibility and positive change, less emphasis on punishment. 2. Non-courtroom setting where offenders voluntarily choose to meet face-to-face with victim (survivor). 3. Active rather than passive involvement of all parties. 4. Focus on positive outcomes for both survivors and offenders.
Some variations.	Not all RJ programmes involve face-to-face contact between offender and victim. Occasionally, the offender may make some financial restitution to the victim to compensate for the physical or psychological damage done. May be an 'add-on' to community service or as an incentive which may lead to the reduction of an existing sentence. The offender may fix any physical damage themselves (e.g. in the case of a burglary).
RJC establishes the standards.	The Restorative Justice Council (RJC) is an independent body. Role is to establish clear standards for the use of restorative justice and to support victims and specialist professionals. It advocates the use of restorative justice in schools, hospitals, prisons, etc.

One of the strengths is the diversity of RJ programmes.

There is flexibility in the way RJ programmes can be used (unlike custodial sentencing) and RJ covers a wide range of possible applications (prisons, schools, etc.).

This is positive in the sense that schemes can be adapted and tailored to the needs of the individual situation.

However, this does not prevent difficulties in terms of drawing conclusions about the effectiveness of the approach.

One limitation is the reliance on the offender showing remorse.

The success of RJ programmes may hinge on the extent to which the offender feels remorse for their actions. Some offenders may 'sign up' to avoid prison or for a reduced sentence.

The victim themselves may have an ulterior motive – to seek revenge or retribution of their own.

This means that RJ programmes may not lead to positive outcomes where the participants themselves do not have the best of intentions.

STOP DOMESTIC VIOLENCE

In all seriousness.

Another limitation is that RJ may not always be cost-effective.

Shapland *et al.* (2007) concluded after a seven-year project that every £1 spent on RJ programmes would save the criminal justice system £8 through reduced offending (but other estimates are much more conservative).

However, it requires the input of a skilled and experienced individual to act as a mediator to prevent serious conflict. These people are hard to come by so are expensive. Also, programmes have high dropout rates as the victim and/or offender may 'lose their nerve'.

This means that, in practice, it may not always be the best and most cost-effective solution.

A further limitation is the feminist critique of RJ programmes.

Feminist commentators take issue with the widespread use of RJ. The charity Women's Aid has called for a legislative ban on its use in domestic violence cases.

They are concerned about the power imbalance in the relationship between abuser and abused, and the fact that the wider community, which should be supportive, often resorts to blaming the victim.

This questions the suitability of RJ programmes for certain types of offence.

KNOWLEDGE CHECK

1. Distinguish between restorative justice and anger management as ways of dealing with offending behaviour. *(4 marks)*

2. Describe **one** study that has investigated restorative justice as a way of dealing with offending behaviour. *(6 marks)*

3. Evaluate restorative justice as a way of dealing with offending behaviour. *(6 marks)*

4. Discuss restorative justice **and one other** way of dealing with offending behaviour. Refer to research evidence in your answer. *(16 marks)*

A final limitation is that RJ programmes are seen as a 'soft option'.

RJ may reduce recidivism rates and is cheaper than running overcrowded prisons, but it often does not receive public support.

Programmes are often regarded as soft options, a view echoed by politicians keen to convince voters they are 'tough on crime'.

So despite their effectiveness, the political will to use RJ is not always there.

Describing addiction

Spec spotlight

Describing addiction: physical and psychological dependence, tolerance and withdrawal syndrome.

Go on, you know you want one... Saying no to a cigarette (or three) is not easy when you are addicted.

Apply it

Jess plays online poker on most days. She enjoys the excitement and it distracts her from her day-to-day troubles. But over the past few weeks Jess has been playing more often and she doesn't get the same thrill out if it that she used to. She also gets very anxious and angry when she can't get online or something else stops her from playing.

Explain Jess's behaviour in terms of the concepts on these pages.

KNOWLEDGE CHECK

1. Explain what is meant by the term 'addiction'. Use an example in your answer. **(3 marks)**
2. In terms of addiction, distinguish between physical **and** psychological dependence. **(3 marks)**
3. In relation to addiction, explain what is meant by the terms 'tolerance' **and** 'withdrawal syndrome'. **(2 marks + 2 marks)**

Physical and psychological dependence

Physical dependence results in withdrawal syndrome.	Physical dependence is said to have occurred when a withdrawal syndrome is produced by stopping the drug. It's only possible to establish for certain that someone is physically dependent on a substance when: • They abstain from it. • Withdrawal symptoms are apparent.
Psychological dependence is the compulsion to continue.	Psychological dependence refers to the compulsion to experience the effects of a drug for: • An increase in pleasure, or • A reduction of discomfort. Psychological dependence leads to the drug/behaviour becoming a habit, despite the harmful consequences.

Tolerance

Greater doses needed for same effect.	Tolerance occurs when an individual's response to a drug is reduced. This means they need even greater doses to produce the same effect on behaviour. Tolerance is caused by repeated exposure to a drug.
Cross-tolerance is when tolerance of one drug reduces sensitivity to another.	A special instance of tolerance is cross-tolerance. Developing tolerance to one type of drug can reduce sensitivity to another type. For example, people who have developed a tolerance to the sleep-inducing effects of alcohol need higher doses of anaesthetic in surgery.

Withdrawal syndrome

Symptoms that develop *after* abstinence.	A withdrawal syndrome is a collection of symptoms associated with abstaining from a drug or reducing its use. Symptoms are usually the opposite of ones created by the drug. For example, withdrawal of nicotine leads to irritability, anxiety.
Indicates *physical dependence.*	Withdrawal symptoms indicate that a physical dependence on the drug has been developed. Symptoms are experienced whenever the drug is not available. Motivation for taking the drug partly stems from the avoidance of these symptoms.

As we have a blank page, here is a little extra for those of you who do addiction.

A word search. How many addiction-related words can you spot in the word search? You should find 35 of them. The answers are below for those who can't bear it.

You should really be revising.

```
I X V D C B S S Q C Q W F B O S R R F B Z E U F P
V G P B I J N L T C N Y M K E E A J Z E N U I F P
H Q E D U O H C J R T A H V Y X T X J O F O M X S
S T M Q E Q X T O I E G S G I P L R D G K W P E O
A D X Z R S H S L C G S Z H N E J A F O D J U V R
D Q A R D E E A M F B J S G H C H S O W H I L Y D
V J Q K P B N N T O O T K Y H T J C S M Y T S F Y
P L C Z N O Z B S O K I I X E A Y O E I U A I B H
F G N D S G B H I I L I W M Z N X F N D E I V C G
Y C W R F V N K Y M T E N I J C B V S B H N I L T
A V E R S I O N T S P I R G T Y W K I G U G T B K
G P I V G R W O G Y A B S A O H S H T B E M Y G T
W M R M M W D U L X K C M A N Z D U I K N N K C O
T W S R I G R I Z N P K T W T C R R S N X X T F K
G I Y K H D M L C U B K C Y X I E O A Z V J L Q S
Q G J R K A V G T N G C C R O J O D T W T T F R R
R B R Y F K D T M Z P A C I Q T L N I E A W A U Z
D E P E N D E N C E C S T V A K H J O K Z L P T X
T Q T J N S E R E I N F O R C E M E N T M E L R E
W P D F P A G H F E G Z L R I N A L T R E X O N E
R W G A Y V J F H M O R X Q O D P R R G E A P U D
C X L B R D E V R I B Y P S V F N F M W U R V G K
L E Q X L F N Z N R D Y V R L P K D K A Q V O B M
R S N W L B N E I R V D N W A M P R O C H A S K A
H Z X E V E T R U A Y A T U J N Z Z C D L R L I N
F D S X Q T D A E T S D I P W P T C B G J C V G G
G S O R P Y T C G I R J W W B W U A S A I O C K N
B D W Y S P R C R O B O X K W W X N G D V Y G Z G
I I D O M Y P W I N Y V N Y S L T F B O O U E D C
C Q R M M U I Z F A J E G S N I C O T I N E S V D
U K E R I S A Q F L S R I J H L S A V N N I S C L
Z N I C E O Q P I R S L I D D V S S I I R T S X N
P Q N V M O X H T L W A I F K S R Y M P D Y R T F
H Y F F V O Z N H L Z P T I L H F A K B X B E K K
U G O I A Q D M S U R D G V U H P G E N E S W T V
W A R D H E W C O V E R T W P O L O Z B L P A L A
U N C S P R O G B Z F K X D D Z W N I E E Q R Y U
J V E K P R F T J Y X G E S J I U I D C Z Q D O O
M J R B H Y P E E R S R X M B D I S S B M I Y Q P
B A B M T E J O G A M B L I N G H T Y S U M R I N
```

Answers

withdrawal, tolerance, dependence, stress, peers, family, genes, APD, impulsivity, personality, desensitisation, nicotine, drugs, dopamine, reward, smoking, reinforcement, reinforcer, gambling, expectancy, relapse, Griffiths, irrational, self-efficacy, agonist, antagonist, naltrexone, covert, NRT, methadone, sensitisation, aversion, CBT, TPB, Ajzen, Prochaska

Risk factors in the development of addictions

Spec spotlight

Risk factors in the development of addiction, including genetic vulnerability, stress, personality, family influences and peers.

Apply it

Damien experienced considerable trauma during his upbringing. His parents gave him a lot of independence to set his own rules about his behaviour. Damien's family moved to a different part of the country and he joined a college where he met a group of people who seemed interesting and exciting. They appeared to be able to get hold of alcohol whenever they wanted and drank a lot.

Use your knowledge of risk factors in the development of addiction to explain Damien's vulnerability to developing an addiction.

Impulsivity – a key component of APD.

REVISION BOOSTER

Genetic vulnerability, stress, personality, family influences and peers are all named key words on the specification for this topic. Be prepared to define them all. It's very unlikely you'll get an essay question on one of these alone. Answering a general question on 'risk factors' means you can describe any of the factors here – but for 6 marks just two or three of them is probably enough. Remember – less is more!

Risk factors in the development of addictions

Genetic vulnerability	Genes are not inevitable causes of addiction on their own but may explain why some people become dependent and others do not.
Low D2 receptors CYP2A6 enzyme	Possible direct genetic mechanisms: • **Dopamine**: low numbers of D2 receptors inherited; people compensate by engaging in addictive behaviour. • Nicotine metabolised by CYP2A6 enzyme – people are *less* likely to smoke if enzyme is *not* fully functioning because nicotine levels are higher.
Stress Childhood trauma	Epstein *et al.* (1998) found a strong **correlation** between incidence of childhood rape and adult alcohol addiction, but only for women with **PTSD** – stress increases vulnerability.
Sensitive period	Early experiences of distress damage the brain during a 'sensitive period' – creates a vulnerability to addiction in adolescence (Andersen and Teicher 2008).
Personality Hostility	No 'addictive personality' but *some* traits (e.g. hostility) linked.
APD and impulsivity	**Antisocial personality disorder** (APD) strongly correlated with addiction-related behaviour and begins in early adolescence. Key component is impulsivity: risk-taking, a lack of planning and a preference for immediate gratification. Ivanov *et al.* (2008) suggest that impulsivity and addiction may share a genetic and neurological basis.
Family influences Perceived parental approval	Parents may approve: Livingston *et al.* (2010) found when parents allowed their children to drink alcohol at home in their final school year, their children were more likely to drink excessively at college the next year. Parents may simply not care about their child's behaviour.
Exposure	Exposure: adolescents are more likely to start using alcohol where it is an everyday feature of family life or where there is a history of alcohol addiction.
Peers Rule-breaking norms	Peer behaviours do not have to specifically concern drugs. Instead a group norm that favours rule-breaking generally can be influential.
Attitudes and opportunity	O'Connell *et al.* (2009) suggest there are three major elements to peer influence for alcohol addiction: • Attitudes about drinking are influenced by associating with peers who use alcohol. • Peers provide more opportunities to use alcohol. • Individuals overestimate how much their peers are drinking and attempt to keep up with the perceived norm.

One strength is that there is research support for genetic vulnerability.

Kendler *et al.* (2012) used data from the National Swedish Adoption Study. At least one biological parent had an addiction.

Those with a biological parent with addiction had a greater risk of developing addiction (8.6%) compared to those with no addicted biological parent (4.2%).

This is strong evidence for the role of genetic vulnerability as an important risk factor, and it is supported by other research.

A further strength is that genes may help to explain indirect effects.

Self-control and the ability to regulate emotions may well be at least partly genetically determined.

A young person with less self-control may be less able to succeed in school leading to negative attitudes, disruptive behaviour and low achievement.

They may gravitate to friends with similar characteristics, leading ultimately to involvement in drugs. Genetic vulnerability is therefore a significant risk factor.

Stress is correlated with, but not necessarily the cause of, addiction.

REVISION BOOSTER

It really pays to practise writing 16-mark essays with your book shut and timing yourself – about 20 minutes for a 16-mark essay. Don't think it will magically come right on the day – test yourself.

One limitation in looking at risk factors is that they all interact.

Mayes and Suchman (2006) point out that different combinations of risk factors partly determine the nature and severity of an addiction.

Furthermore genetic, stress, personality, family and peer influences can be *protective* – i.e. make addiction less likely (e.g. less impulsive personality).

Understanding that there are many 'pathways' to addiction is a more realistic approach to addiction than a focus on single factors.

Another limitation is with cause and effect.

Many studies have shown a strong correlation between stressful experiences and addiction behaviours.

Indeed, many addictions create higher levels of stress because of their negative effects on relationships and finances.

Because risk factors and addiction co-relate, it makes it very difficult to separate the effects of one upon the other.

KNOWLEDGE CHECK

1. Explain how both family influences **and** peers can be risk factors in the development of addiction.
   (6 marks)

2. With reference to addiction, explain what is meant by 'genetic vulnerability'. *(3 marks)*

3. Briefly evaluate genetic vulnerability **and** stress as risk factors in the development of addiction. *(6 marks)*

4. Tim comes from a family of alcohol addicts. Kim believes she is the 'sort of person' who gambles. Jim smokes because he is having a tough time.

   With reference to these experiences, **and/or** using other examples, discuss risk factors in the development of addiction. *(16 marks)*

One strength in this area is the real-life applications.

Hawkins *et al.* (1992) believe that if we understand the risk factors we can identify those at risk and intervene.

For example, Tobler *et al.* (2000) created a peer-pressure resistance training programme to help prevent young people taking up smoking.

This suggests that a focus on risk factors can have useful and beneficial results.

Explanations for nicotine addiction: Brain neurochemistry

Spec spotlight

Explanations for nicotine addiction: brain neurochemistry, including the role of dopamine.

Frontal cortex
Mesocortical pathway
Nucleus accumbens
Mesolimbic pathway
Ventral tegmental area (nicotinic receptors)

The desensitisation hypothesis

Nicotine stimulates nicotinic receptors primarily located in the ventral tegmental area (VTA) of the brain. This causes dopamine to be transmitted along the mesolimbic and mesocortical pathways to the nucleus accumbens and the frontal cortex (yellow lines). Dopamine is then released into the frontal cortex (blue arrows) creating rewarding effects.

Addiction is then explained by the nicotine regulation model.

The desensitisation hypothesis

The role of *nAChRs*.	Dani and Heinemann's (1996) hypothesis focuses on the neurotransmitter **dopamine**. Some neurons that produce dopamine are in the ventral tegmental area (VTA) of the brain. These neurons have acetylcholine (ACh) receptors that also respond to nicotine – these receptors are called nicotinic receptors (nAChRs).
Desensitisation caused by nicotine.	When nicotine binds to a nAChR: 1. The neuron is stimulated and produces dopamine. 2. The receptors shut down within milliseconds and cannot respond to neurotransmitters = *desensitisation* of the neuron (no longer responds) leading to *downregulation* (fewer active neurons available).
Effect of *dopamine*.	When the neurotransmitter dopamine is released from the VTA it is transmitted along the: • Mesolimbic pathway to the *nucleus accumbens* to be released in the frontal cortex. • Mesocortical pathway to be released in the frontal cortex. The dopamine system creates a sense of reward and pleasure (e.g. reduced anxiety, mild euphoria, increased alertness). This is now associated with intake of nicotine.

The nicotine regulation model

Resensitisation of neurons leads to upregulation.	When smokers go without nicotine for a prolonged period (e.g. when asleep), nicotine disappears from the body. nAChRs become functional again, so neurons *resensitise* and more become available (*upregulation*).
Upregulation leads to withdrawal symptoms.	Because more nAChRs are available but not stimulated, the smoker experiences acute withdrawal syndrome (e.g. anxiety). Meanwhile nAChRs are at their most sensitive, which is why smokers describe the first cigarette of the day as the most pleasurable – it reactivates the dopamine reward system (as outlined above). This explains how dependence to nicotine is maintained – the smoker is motivated to avoid unpleasant withdrawal symptoms.
Chronic desensitisation increases tolerance.	Persistent desensitisation of nAChRs through repeated smoking leads to a permanent decrease in the number of active receptors – requiring more nicotine for the same effects. In other words tolerance develops.

Apply it

Karen is a clinical psychologist who runs a 'quit smoking' group. She discusses with her clients their experiences of smoking. She has found that most people are well aware of the health risks of smoking, but they carry on as if they cannot help it. Almost all of her clients particularly enjoy the first cigarette of the day each morning. They also report needing to smoke more and more to get the same effects.

Using your knowledge of brain neurochemistry, explain Karen's clients' experiences of nicotine addiction.

One strength is that there is supporting research evidence.

McEvoy *et al.* (1995) studied smoking behaviour in patients with schizophrenia, some of whom were taking *haloperidol*, a dopamine antagonist drug treatment for schizophrenia.

Haloperidol treatment increased smoking in this sample of participants. It appears that this was a form of self-medication, an attempt to achieve the nicotine 'hit' by increasing dopamine release.

There is also more direct evidence for the importance of the dopamine reward system in brain imaging studies (Ray *et al.* 2008).

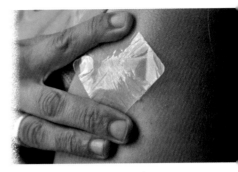

Nicotine replacement patches are used to help people overcome addiction.

A further strength is the development of real-life applications.

A greater understanding of neurochemistry has led to the development of treatments such as nicotine replacement therapy (NRT) in the form of patches and inhalers.

But the practical benefits of understanding go beyond nicotine addiction. Some diseases have high co-morbidity rates with nicotine use (e.g. depression, alcoholism).

This raises the prospect of further research leading to greater advances in treatments for these co-morbid disorders.

One limitation of neurochemical explanations is they only consider dopamine.

An explanation of nicotine addiction that considers only the role of dopamine is limited because there are many other neuro-mechanisms involved.

The current picture shows a vastly complex interaction of several systems such as **GABA** and **serotonin** pathways, and endogenous opioids.

So although dopamine is central to nicotine addiction neurochemistry, we have to understand how it interacts with these other systems.

A further limitation is that neurochemical explanations are reductionist.

Neurochemical explanations explain addiction at the most basic level of the activity of neurotransmitter molecules, rather than at 'higher' levels (e.g. social and psychological influences).

Only around 50% of people who **experiment** with smoking become dependent. Choi *et al.* (2003) found that most adolescents who become dependent had peers who smoked or felt they were underachieving at school.

It could therefore be argued that crucial psychological factors are in danger of being ignored by focusing on brain neurochemistry.

A final limitation concerns individual differences.

Shiffman *et al.* (1995) studied 'chippers', people who regularly smoke for long periods but who do not become dependent. Even those who smoked an average of five per day did not show withdrawal symptoms.

It is suggested that non-chemical factors protect some people from addiction. Such people smoke because of **modelling** and learning and their motivation has nothing to do with nicotine.

This questions the emphasis placed on exclusively **biological approaches** to understanding addiction to smoking.

Explanations for nicotine addiction: Learning theory

Spec spotlight

Explanations for nicotine addiction: learning theory as applied to smoking behaviour, including reference to cue reactivity.

Lighters can be secondary reinforcers.

Janice socialises with a group of friends who all smoke, and she herself has smoked since she was a teenager. Janice and her friends all say they would love to give up, but the hardest part is when they go out together. Seeing her friends in the bar or restaurant with drinks or food seems to trigger her desire for a cigarette.

Use your knowledge of learning theory to explain Janice's nicotine addiction.

Classical conditioning

UCS unconditioned stimulus
UCR unconditioned response
NS   neutral stimulus
CS   conditioned stimulus
CR   conditioned response

Before conditioning:
UCS produces UCR

During conditioning:
NS associated with UCS and becomes CS

After conditioning:
CS produces CR

Operant conditioning

Positive reinforcement – mild euphoria.	If the consequence of a behaviour is rewarding to an individual, then that behaviour is more likely to occur again. Smoking can create feelings of mild euphoria which positively reinforce the smoking behaviour.
Mild euphoria caused by the **dopamine** *system.*	Nicotine is a powerful reinforcer because of its physiological effects on the dopamine reward system in the *mesolimbic pathway.* Nicotine stimulates the release of dopamine which produces the feeling of mild euphoria.
Negative reinforcement – avoid withdrawal symptoms.	Cessation of nicotine use can lead to an acute withdrawal syndrome including such symptoms as disturbed sleep, agitation, poor concentration and mood disturbances. Therefore addiction is maintained because smoking another cigarette is negatively reinforcing – it stops the unpleasant stimulus (withdrawal symptoms).

Classical conditioning

Smoking is a *primary reinforcer* as it is intrinsically rewarding.	Smoking is intrinsically rewarding (not learned). It doesn't have to be learned because of the biologically-determined effects of nicotine on the dopamine reward system. The pleasure created by nicotine reinforces the behaviour so the individual is more likely to smoke again.
Secondary reinforcers include pubs, friends, lighters, smells, etc.	Any other stimuli present at the same time as (or just before) smoking (and intake of nicotine) become associated with the pleasurable effect of smoking (i.e. **classical conditioning** has taken place). These stimuli become secondary reinforcers (rewarding in their own right). Certain environments (e.g. pubs) and certain people or objects (e.g. a lighter) create a sense of anticipation and pleasure and thus become secondary reinforcers. Even the seemingly harsh feeling of smoke hitting the back of the throat can become a secondary reinforcer because it is associated with the pleasurable impact of nicotine.
Cue reactivity: Cravings are triggered by cues related to smoking.	The secondary reinforcers also act as cues, because their presence produces a similar response to nicotine itself. This is called cue reactivity and is indicated by three main elements: 1. Self-reported desire to smoke. 2. Physiological signs of reactivity to a cue (e.g. heart rate). 3. Objective behavioural indicators when cue is present (e.g. how many 'draws' are taken on the cigarette).

One strength is support from non-human animal studies.

Levin *et al.* (2010) gave rats the choice of self-administering doses of nicotine or water by licking one of two water spouts (one with nicotine).

The rats licked the nicotine water spout significantly more often. This behaviour increased in frequency with every subsequent training session.

The effects of nicotine positively reinforce nicotine self-administration in rats, suggesting a similar mechanism in humans.

Levin et al.'s rats self-administered nicotine through water bottles.

Another strength is research support for cue reactivity.

Carter and Tiffany's (1999) **meta-analysis** included measures of self-reported craving and physiological arousal in dependent and non-dependent smokers, following exposure to smoking-related cues.

The researchers found that dependent smokers reacted strongly to cues (e.g. lighters), reporting high levels of craving and demonstrating higher levels of physiological arousal.

The findings were consistent with the predictions of cue reactivity theory and therefore support the theory.

A further strength is the real-life application of the theory.

Aversion therapy works on the basis of counterconditioning nicotine addiction by associating the pleasurable effects of smoking with an aversive stimulus such as a painful electric shock.

Smith (1988) found that 52% of participants who gave themselves electric shocks whenever they engaged in smoking-related behaviours were still abstaining after a year.

Such effective applications of learning theory have measurable and significant practical benefits in terms of reducing NHS spending and improving health.

A final strength is that gender differences can also be explained.

Carpenter *et al.* (2014) suggest females struggle to give up smoking because they are more sensitive to smoking-related cues, making relapse more likely.

The concept of **self-efficacy** would suggest that female smokers have less confidence in their ability to give up smoking and this undermines their attempts.

Self-efficacy is learned which means that gender differences can be explained in terms of learning, thus supporting this approach.

One limitation is it cannot explain why some people do not become addicted.

Even though positive reinforcement is a strong explanation, not everyone who **experiments** with smoking becomes dependent.

Many adolescents smoke cigarettes occasionally, but few are dependent to the extent that they experience withdrawal symptoms.

This is a challenge for any theory seeking to explain addiction; there are likely to be several causes of smoking behaviour.

REVISION BOOSTER

At A level you can be required to write 16-mark essays. This is split between AO1 and AO3 in a ratio of 6:10. Therefore you're aiming to write 10 marks' worth of evaluation (AO3), which can usually be provided by four or five evaluative points. But these must be thorough (that is, well-elaborated) and ideally show some evidence of 'discussion' (e.g. considering contrasting views).

KNOWLEDGE CHECK

1. In relation to nicotine addiction, explain what is meant by 'cue reactivity'.
   (3 marks)
2. Outline learning theory as applied to smoking behaviour. Refer to cue reactivity in your answer.
   (6 marks)
3. Describe **one** study of learning theory as applied to smoking behaviour. In your answer explain what the researcher(s) did and what was found. *(6 marks)*
4. Describe and evaluate **two** explanations for nicotine addiction. *(16 marks)*

Explanations for gambling addiction: Learning theory

Spec spotlight

Explanations for gambling addiction: learning theory as applied to gambling, including reference to partial and variable reinforcement.

Watching others winning may be the starting point of an addiction. Not something that happens very often if you're a Leeds United fan.

Apply it

Tina started playing the National Lottery a few months ago. She won £10 just on her third go. Before long she was playing every week and won another £50 after five weeks. It took another 11 weeks before she won anything else, and since then…nothing yet. But Tina knows that you have to be 'in it to win it', so she is going to carry on playing the Lottery each week because she knows it's just a matter of time before she wins again.

Using your knowledge of learning explanations, explain Tina's gambling behaviour.

REVISION BOOSTER

Always think 'less is more' – writing about fewer things gives you the opportunity to demonstrate your detailed understanding. For 6 AO1 marks we have given you six points but you may need to do fewer to ensure sufficient detail.

Learning theory of gambling addiction

Vicarious reinforcement can be the start of an addiction.	One way in which people begin gambling is through seeing others being rewarded for gambling (e.g. seeing someone else enjoying money and sometimes winning money). Vicarious reinforcement can also be through newspaper articles reporting big wins (e.g. on the National Lottery).
Direct reinforcement can be positive or negative.	Positive reinforcement comes from a direct gain (e.g. winning money), and from the 'buzz' that accompanies a gamble (which is exciting). Negative reinforcement occurs because gambling can offer a distraction from aversive stimuli (e.g. the anxieties of everyday life).
Partial reinforcement more effective than continuous.	Skinner's research with rats found that continuous reinforcement schedules do not lead to persistent behaviour change. Once the rewards stop, the behaviour quickly disappears (called *extinction*). A partial reinforcement schedule leads to more persistent behaviour change. When only some bets are rewarded there is an unpredictability about which gambles will pay off, which is enough to maintain the gambling.
Variable reinforcement schedule is the most effective.	A variable (ratio) reinforcement schedule is a partial reinforcement schedule where the intervals between rewards vary. This kind of reinforcement schedule is highly unpredictable. For example, a slot machine might pay out after an *average* of 25 spins, but not on *every* 25th spin. The first payout might be on the 11th spin, then the 21st, then the 38th, etc.
Variable reinforcement is *very resistant to extinction*.	Whilst it takes longer for learning to be established if the reinforcement schedule is variable, once it is established it is more resistant to extinction. The gambler learns that they will not win with every gamble, but they will eventually win if they persist (and then the gambling is reinforced). This explains why some people continue to gamble despite big losses.
Cue reactivity explains how associated stimuli can trigger gambling.	In the course of their gambling, an individual will experience many secondary reinforcers – things they associate with the exciting arousal experienced through gambling. For example, the atmosphere of the betting shop, the colour of lottery scratch cards, TV horse-racing channels can all cue the arousal that the gambler craves. These low-level reminders are difficult to avoid. These cues can both maintain gambling and cause its reinstatement after a period of abstinence.

One strength of the learning theory explanation is research support.

Dickerson (1979) found high-frequency gamblers in natural settings were more likely than low-frequency gamblers to place bets in the last two minutes before a race.

These gamblers may delay betting to prolong the rewarding excitement (e.g. the tension they get from the radio commentary heard in the betting shop).

This is evidence for the role of positive reinforcement on gambling behaviour in frequent gamblers in a more 'real-life' setting than a psychology lab.

If these bets were very last minute, it is possible they were placed by high frequency gamblers.

One limitation is the lack of explanatory power.

Learning theory explains some types of gambling better than others. Fruit machine gambling is dependent on chance and rewards are *temporally contiguous* (no delay between the bet and the outcome).

In contrast, gambling games like poker require an element of skill and there is greater delay between the bet and knowing the outcome; this is more difficult to explain in terms of conditioning.

Therefore, learning theory lacks explanatory power because it does not provide a general explanation of all gambling addiction.

Another limitation is individual differences.

Griffiths and Delfabbro (2001) argue that people do not respond in the same ways to conditioning even when using identical stimuli.

Some people gamble to relax, some to be aroused. Some people stop gambling and never relapse but some are more vulnerable to cues.

These observations are difficult to explain for learning theory without invoking **cognitive** features of addiction such as distortions in thinking.

A further limitation is learning theory doesn't explain all aspects of gambling.

Gambling addiction is multifaceted. Psychologists have tried to use learning theory to understand the cycle of gambling addiction from initiation, through maintenance to cessation and relapse.

Conditioning processes may be less important at some points. Brown (1987), for example, suggests learning theory can explain the persistence of gambling behaviour but not its start.

This means that it is not a complete explanation for the cycle of gambling behaviour.

Another strength is learning theory explains failure to stop gambling.

Some people see continued gambling as a moral failure – the person wants to stop but lacks willpower. This can be explained by learning theory because learning occurs in the absence of active decisions.

Thus learning theory is an effective explanation of a common phenomenon – how gamblers fail to stop gambling whilst at the same time being determined to do so.

Their conscious desire to give up conflicts with the motivational forces acquired through conditioning that drive them to continue gambling.

REVISION BOOSTER

Students like to write essays with a beginning, middle and end. It's tempting to 'set the scene' by defining addiction but that won't get you any marks. Focus on the middle. Endings also generally fail to be creditworthy because they are not much more of a summary of what has already been said.

KNOWLEDGE CHECK

1. In terms of learning theory as applied to gambling, distinguish between partial and variable reinforcement. *(3 marks)*

2. Outline learning theory as applied to gambling. Refer to partial **and** variable reinforcement in your answer. *(6 marks)*

3. Identify and briefly evaluate **one** explanation for gambling. *(5 marks)*

4. Gamblers often report that the enjoyment they get from their addiction comes from the environment in which they gamble, such as the noises and flashing lights of slot machine arcades.

   With reference to this experience, outline and evaluate learning theory as applied to gambling. *(16 marks)*

Explanations for gambling addiction: Cognitive theory

Spec spotlight

Explanations for gambling addiction: cognitive theory as applied to gambling, including reference to cognitive bias.

Gambling addicts often believe they are especially lucky.

Apply it

Josh has played poker just about every day for several years. He has won some money, but lost a lot more. He has 'noticed' that he is more likely to win (he thinks) when he wears his lucky underpants. Also, as long as the cards are dealt in just the 'right' way, Josh's current losing streak is bound to come to an end. His next win is just around the corner.

How can cognitive biases explain Josh's gambling behaviour?

REVISION BOOSTER

There may be exam questions that specifically ask for a description of a relevant study. It makes sense to give some information about the procedures and some about the findings – in fact such questions may ask for this.

Cognitive theory of gambling behaviour

Expectancy theory – expected benefits outweigh costs.	We all have expectations about the future benefit and costs of our behaviour. If people expect the benefits of gambling to outweigh the costs, then addiction becomes more likely. This sounds like a conscious decision but it is not. This is because memory and attention processes do not operate in a rational and logical manner.
Cognitive biases – selective processing of information.	The cause of gambling addiction lies in the fact that addicts hold beliefs about gambling that are irrational (i.e. cognitive biases). Such cognitions may involve attention and/or memory processes – addiction occurs and is maintained due to the selective attention to and memory of gambling-related information.
Four different categories of cognitive bias.	Rickwood *et al.* (2010) categorised them thus: 1. Skill and judgement – gambling addicts have an illusion of control and overestimate their skill against chance. 2. Personal traits/ritual behaviours – addicts believe they are especially lucky or engage in superstitious behaviour. 3. Selective recall – gamblers remember their wins but ignore/forget their losses. 4. Faulty perceptions – gamblers have distorted views of chance (e.g. belief that a losing streak cannot last).
Relapse occurs due to a lack of **self-efficacy**.	Self-efficacy refers to the belief we have in our own competence to achieve a desired outcome. An individual resumes gambling because he/she does not believe they are capable of giving it up. The relapse then reinforces their lack of self-efficacy, 'I told you I couldn't give it up.'

Key study: Griffiths (1994) Cognitive biases

Procedure	The study used the 'thinking aloud' method (a form of introspection) to investigate differences between regular slot machine gamblers and occasional users. Content analysis was used to classify their utterances into rational or irrational. Interviews were also used to explore participants' perceptions of the skill required to win.
Findings	Regular gamblers made almost six times as many irrational verbalisations (e.g. 'The machine likes me') compared to occasional gamblers (14% v 2.5%). Regular gamblers were also prone to *illusion of control* (e.g. 'I'm going to bluff this machine') and overestimated the skill required to win.

One strength is the evidence supporting the cognitive theory.

Michalczuk *et al.* (2011) compared addicted gamblers with a non-gambling **control group**. The addicted gamblers had significantly higher levels of gambling-related cognitive distortions.

They were also more impulsive and were more likely to prefer immediate rewards, even if the rewards were smaller than those they could gain if they waited.

These findings support the view that there is a strong cognitive component to gambling addiction.

Feeling you can control the dice – a form of cognitive distortion.

Another strength is that cognitive theory can explain automatic behaviour.

McCusker and Gettings (1997) asked participants to complete a modified Stroop procedure. Participants had to pay attention to ink colour while ignoring word meanings.

Gamblers took longer to do this compared to a control group when gambling words were shown. This suggests gamblers have an automatic cognitive bias to pay attention to such information.

This supports the view of the cognitive explanation that many cognitive biases influence addiction and operate without us even being aware we have them.

One limitation is the existence of individual differences.

Burger and Smith (1985) found that people with high levels of control motivation (wished to have control over their lives) were more likely to believe they could influence chance-determined situations.

It may be that such people are attracted to certain types of gambling where they (wrongly) believe their 'skill' can make a difference, such as choosing lottery numbers.

Such individual differences in personality mean that cognitive biases alone cannot explain all gambling.

A further strength is the development of real-life applications.

Many aspects of gambling are related to distorted thinking (e.g. gambler's fallacy or the significance gamblers put on a near miss). This means **CBT** could be useful.

Clark (2010) suggests that cognitive distortions probably have an underlying cause in brain neurochemistry, raising the prospect of drug treatment.

So cognitive theories are stimulating beneficial research into both biological and psychological treatments.

Another limitation relates to methodological issues.

Many research studies into cognitive distortions in gambling access the thinking processes of gamblers through self-report methods such as introspection.

Dickerson and O'Connor (2006) state that what people say in gambling situations may not be representative of deeply-held beliefs.

This is a serious problem for the **validity** of the research and therefore the theory which is based on that evidence.

REVISION BOOSTER

What's the Number One route to evaluating an explanation or concept? The answer is – THINK LINK. You've probably noticed that the evaluation sections of this Revision Guide are chock-full of research studies. You need to make sure you use them effectively by LINKING the study back to the point you were trying to make.

KNOWLEDGE CHECK

1. In relation to cognitive theory as applied to gambling, explain what is meant by 'cognitive bias'. Use an example in your answer.
   (4 marks)

2. Outline cognitive theory as applied to gambling. Refer to cognitive bias in your answer.
   (6 marks)

3. Briefly evaluate **two** explanations for gambling addiction. *(3 marks + 3 marks)*

4. Discuss cognitive theory as applied to gambling. Refer to **one** other explanation for gambling in your answer.
   (16 marks)

Reducing addiction: Drug therapy

Spec spotlight

Reducing addiction: drug therapy.

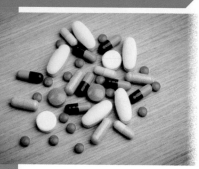

Are drugs the answer to reducing addiction?

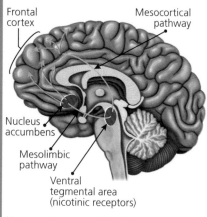

Frontal cortex

Mesocortical pathway

Nucleus accumbens

Mesolimbic pathway

Ventral tegmental area (nicotinic receptors)

You may have seen this diagram before (on page 232) but here it is again – the mesocortical pathway is mentioned on the right.

Apply it

Miah has been desperate to give up smoking ever since she and her boyfriend decided to start a family. She understands the dangers to her and her unborn child's health. She knows that there is no way she can continue to smoke heavily when she is pregnant. She has absolutely decided to give up but she fears that she might not have the 'willpower'.

Explain how drug therapy could help Miah. Refer to why it would be particularly suitable for her.

Drug therapy for addiction

Aversive drugs pair addictive stimuli with unpleasant consequences.	The main effect of aversive drugs is to pair the behaviour with unpleasant consequences such as vomiting (**classical conditioning**).
	For example, *disulfiram* is a drug therapy that creates the effects of a severe hangover just minutes after alcohol is drunk.
	The idea is that the addict will associate the alcohol with these unpleasant effects rather than the ones they enjoy.
Agonists replace addictive drug by producing a similar effect.	Agonists bind to the neuron receptors and activate them.
	This produces a similar effect to the addictive drug and controls the withdrawal effects.
	For example, *methadone* is used to treat heroin addiction but has fewer harmful side effects than heroin itself.
Antagonists block the effects of the addictive drug.	Antagonists treat addiction by binding to the receptor sites and blocking them.
	Therefore the drug of dependence cannot produce its usual addictive effects.
	For example, *naltrexone* is used to treat heroin addiction.
Smoking: *NRT* helps to avoid withdrawal symptoms.	Nicotine replacement therapy (NRT) comes in the forms of gum, inhalers and patches to deliver nicotine in a less harmful fashion.
	Dosage can be reduced over time, decreasing the aversiveness of withdrawal symptoms.
	NRT operates neurochemically by:
	1. Binding to nicotinic acetylcholine receptors in the mesolimbic pathway of the brain.
	2. Stimulating the release of dopamine in the *nucleus accumbens*, just as it does in cigarette smoking.
Gambling: *opioid antagonists* reduce release of dopamine.	Gambling addiction taps into the same dopamine reward system as heroin, nicotine, etc.
	Therefore the same drugs used to treat heroin are used with gamblers.
	Opioid antagonists (such as *naltrexone*) dampen the cravings to gamble by:
	1. Enhancing the release of neurotransmitter **GABA** in the mesolimbic pathway, which…
	2. Reduces the release of **dopamine** in the nucleus accumbens, which…
	3. Reduces the craving to gamble.
Drugs not officially approved for gambling addiction.	Despite the research there is not yet a drug that is thought good enough to be officially approved.
	Even if *naltrexone* was prescribed for gambling addiction, people probably wouldn't use it because of the unpleasant side effects.

One strength of drug therapy is the research support.

Stead et al. (2012) concluded that NRT is more effective in helping smokers quit than either **placebo** or no treatment. NRT users were up to 70% more likely to have still abstained from smoking after six months.

Research also indicates two extra benefits of NRT: it is safer than cigarette smoking because it eliminates the harmful effects of tobacco smoke, and it does not appear to foster dependence.

This shows that NRT is a useful treatment.

One limitation is the side effects of drug therapy.

Common side effects are sleep disturbances, dizziness and headaches. In relation to gambling, the dose of *naltrexone* required leads to side effects worse than would be the case when using it to treat opiate addiction.

Such side effects mean there is a risk that the patient will discontinue the therapy, especially when they have also lost the pleasurable effects of the addiction.

The risk of side effects should be carefully weighed up against the benefits of the drug therapy and psychological therapies such as covert sensitisation (see next page).

NRT helps many smokers break their addiction.

A further limitation is that drug therapy requires motivation.

Drug therapy is often seen as more convenient than making changes to thought processes but it requires compliance and people with addictions may be too disorganised to take medicine regularly.

Drug therapy is therefore probably best suited to a relatively small subset of addicts who are extremely motivated and who are not leading chaotic lifestyles.

This means, paradoxically, that drug therapy is not effective for everyone despite its perceived convenience.

REVISION BOOSTER

Write a very brief essay plan for each possible essay and then practise writing the essay in full from this. Time yourself – 20 minutes for a 16-mark essay.

Another strength is the removal of addiction stigma.

Drug therapy encourages a growing perception that drug addiction is a medical problem. Research is rapidly revealing the neurochemical and genetic basis of addiction.

This is changing the view that addiction is a form of psychological or moral failure. Addiction therefore becomes less stigmatised as more people accept that it may not be the addict's 'fault'.

This is a strength because in turn it could encourage more addicts to seek treatment.

KNOWLEDGE CHECK

1. Identify and discuss **one** drug therapy for reducing addiction. *(5 marks)*

2. Outline drug therapy as a way of reducing addiction. *(6 marks)*

3. Using evidence, evaluate drug therapy as a way of reducing addiction. *(6 marks)*

4. Some psychologists believe that the most effective way to treat addiction is to address the biological factors underlying the addiction, such as brain biochemistry.

   With reference to this argument, describe and evaluate drug therapy as a way of reducing addiction. *(16 marks)*

One limitation is that there are individual differences.

Drugs do not work in the same way for everyone and genetic variations between people have a significant impact on the treatment success.

For example, alcoholics with one gene variant respond more readily to *naltrexone* treatment than those with a different version of the gene.

As Chung et al. (2012) point out, drug treatments need to become more tailored to individual genetic profiles if they are to be more effective.

Reducing addiction: Behavioural interventions

Spec spotlight

Reducing addiction: behavioural interventions, including aversion therapy and covert sensitisation.

Classical conditioning

UCS unconditioned stimulus
UCR unconditioned response
NS neutral stimulus
CS conditioned stimulus
CR conditioned response

Before conditioning:
UCS produces UCR

During conditioning:
NS associated with UCS and becomes CS

After conditioning:
CS produces CR

Aversion therapy could include imagining uncomfortable images while smoking.

REVISION BOOSTER

In an exam everyone feels some measure of anxiety – when you are anxious, you forget those things which are not well learned or well practised. So practise, practise, practise.

Behavioural interventions for addiction

Aversion therapy associates the addiction with unpleasant consequences.	Aversion therapy is a behavioural intervention based on **classical conditioning**. According to learning theory, an addiction can develop through repeated associations between a drug and the pleasurable state of arousal caused by it. It follows that the addiction can be reduced by associating the drug with an unpleasant state (counterconditioning).
Disulfiram used to associate alcohol with severe nausea.	Aversion therapy has been used in treating alcoholism. The client is given a drug such as *disulfiram* (UCS) which causes a person drinking alcohol to experience an instant hangover with severe nausea and vomiting (UCR). The client learns to associate the alcohol (NS and then CS) with the unpleasant symptoms (CR) and the fear of the symptoms can prevent the client from drinking.
Electric shocks used to associate gambling with pain.	Electric shocks have been used in place of drugs for behavioural addictions such as gambling. The gambler selects phrases that relate to their gambling behaviour and others that do not (e.g. 'Went straight home'). They read out each phrase and whenever a gambling-related phrase is read (NS and then CS) they receive a two-second electric shock which is painful (UCR and then CR) but not too bad.

Covert sensitisation

Imagined not real.	Traditional aversion therapy has been largely superseded by covert sensitisation. This is a type of aversion therapy, but *in vitro* rather than *in vivo*, in that the unpleasant stimulus is imagined rather than actually experienced.
Nicotine: therapist asks client to vividly imagine vomiting.	Patients with nicotine addiction are first encouraged to relax, then conjure up a vivid image of themselves smoking a cigarette (CS), followed by the most unpleasant consequences (CR) such as vomiting (including graphic details of smells, sights, etc.). The association formed (classical conditioning) should reduce smoking behaviour.
Technique may involve imagining snakes or faeces.	The client imagines being forced to smoke a cigarette covered in faeces (or other aversive stimuli chosen by them). Towards the end of the session, the client imagines turning away from cigarettes and experiencing the resulting feelings of relief.

AO3 Evaluation

One limitation is that aversion studies suffer from methodological problems.

Hajek and Stead (2001) reviewed 25 studies of aversion therapy for nicotine addiction, claiming it impossible to judge effectiveness because the studies suffered from errors.

In most studies 'blind' procedures were not used, so the researchers who evaluated the outcomes of the studies knew which participants received therapy or **placebo**.

Such inbuilt biases generally make therapy appear more effective than it actually is, which challenges the **validity** of the findings.

Another limitation of aversion therapy is treatment adherence issues.

Given the unpleasant nature of the treatment, many patients and research participants avoid the stimuli and drop out of treatment before it is completed.

It is therefore difficult to judge overall effectiveness as there may be a pattern to which patients and participants drop out – leaving those who are willing to be conditioned.

If this is the case, then research is probably overoptimistic about the efficacy of aversion therapy.

Perhaps he is imagining this cigarette covered in faeces?

A further limitation of aversion therapy is short-term effectiveness.

McConaghy et al. (1983) found that aversion therapy was more effective in reducing gambling behaviour after one month than after one year.

In a long-term follow-up, it was found that aversion therapy was no more effective than a placebo and covert sensitisation was more beneficial.

This suggests that any benefits of aversion therapy seem to be mostly short-term and that there is no long-term effectiveness.

A final limitation of aversion therapy is the ethical issues.

Inflicting nausea and pain can be seen as unethical and patients could lose their dignity by vomiting in social situations.

Covert sensitisation is often preferred as it does not induce vomiting or other self-shaming behaviours, allowing patients to retain their dignity and self-esteem.

This means that the limitations of aversion therapy can also be seen as a strength of covert sensitisation.

A strength of covert sensitisation is research support.

McConaghy et al. (1983) found that after one year gambling addicts who had received covert sensitisation were much more likely (90%) to have reduced their gambling activity than those who received aversion therapy (30%).

The participants also reported experiencing fewer and less intense gambling cravings than the aversion-treated participants.

This is one of many studies suggesting covert sensitisation is a highly promising treatment for addiction to alcohol, nicotine and gambling.

Apply it

Abby has an addiction to alcohol. She has tried a number of (unsuccessful) treatments but her doctor suggests she might benefit from a therapy that makes her vomit. Abby finds it hard to believe this could work, so she has turned to you, her friend, for some advice because she knows you are a psychology student.

What type of therapy is Abby concerned about? Explain what you would tell her about the effectiveness of this therapy.

KNOWLEDGE CHECK

1. Distinguish between aversion therapy and covert sensitisation as behavioural interventions for reducing addiction. *(3 marks)*

2. Outline aversion therapy as a behavioural intervention for reducing addiction. *(6 marks)*

3. Evaluate aversion therapy as a behavioural intervention for reducing addiction. *(6 marks)*

4. Discuss **two** behavioural interventions for reducing addiction. *(16 marks)*

Reducing addiction: Cognitive behaviour therapy

Spec spotlight

Reducing addiction: cognitive behaviour therapy.

Refusing alcohol with a minimum amount of fuss would be a part of the social skills training element of CBT.

Adrian has been referred to a clinical psychologist for cognitive behaviour therapy to treat his addiction to high-stakes gambling machines. He feels compelled almost against his will to start playing on these machines. He has to go into betting shops where the machines are, he can't help it. Unfortunately, because Adrian gambles when he feels happy and also when he feels depressed, he is gambling a lot of the time and losing huge amounts of money.

Explain what Adrian would expect from cognitive behaviour therapy, and how effective it could be in helping him.

Cognitive behaviour therapy for addiction

CBT aims to tackle *distorted thinking* and develop coping behaviours.

Cognitive behaviour therapy (CBT) has two key elements:

1. **Cognitive**: identify, tackle and replace cognitive distortions that underlie the addiction (functional analysis).

2. **Behaviourist**: skills-training helps the client develop coping behaviours to avoid the high-risk situations that trigger the addiction-related behaviour.

---

1. *Cognitive = functional analysis*

Therapist deals with distorted cognitions.

CBT starts with the client and therapist together identifying the high-risk situations that lead to the client's drug use or gambling.

The therapist reflects on what the client is thinking before, during and after such a situation.

The therapist's role in the relationship is to challenge the client's cognitive distortions.

This process of functional analysis continues throughout the treatment, not just at the beginning of the therapy.

---

2. *Behaviourist = skills training*

Replacing poor coping behaviours.

People seeking treatment for addiction may have a huge range of problems but only one way of dealing with them – their drug of choice.

CBT helps to replace this strategy with more constructive ones by developing new skills.

Developing new skills

Cognitive restructuring confronts and challenges faulty beliefs.

For example, a gambler may hold faulty beliefs about probability, randomness and control in gambling.

In the initial education phase, the therapist may give the client information about how to challenge these faulty beliefs.

Specific skills are taught (e.g. to deal with anger).

CBT focuses on the wider aspects of the client's life related to the addiction.

For example, in the case of a lack of skills to cope with situations that trigger alcohol use:

- Anger may trigger addictive behaviour, and anger management training may be appropriate.

- Interpersonal conflicts may trigger addictive behaviour, and may be dealt with through assertiveness training.

Social skills training (SST) can help with social anxiety.

Most clients can benefit from developing skills that allow them to cope with anxiety in social situations (e.g. trying not to drink alcohol at a wedding).

SST helps the client to refuse alcohol in order to avoid embarrassment (e.g. making eye contact and being firm).

The therapist and client may model coping strategies using role play.

One strength of CBT is the research support.

Petry *et al.* (2006) found that gamblers assigned to a treatment condition (Gamblers Anonymous meetings + CBT) were gambling less than a **control group** (GA meetings only) 12 months later.

An important feature of this study is that the participants were **randomly allocated** to the CBT group or the control group, and there were no significant differences in the extent of their gambling at the start.

Therefore, the findings are strong evidence that CBT is effective in treating gambling addiction, from a methodologically-sound study.

Gamblers Anonymous groups plus CBT are effective.

One limitation, however, is a lack of long-term gains.

Cowlishaw *et al.* (2012) found CBT has definite beneficial effects for up to three months after treatment. However, after 9–12 months, there were no significant differences between CBT and control groups.

In addition, the researchers also concluded that the studies they reviewed were of such poor methodological quality that they probably overestimated the efficacy of treatment with CBT.

Therefore, CBT may be effective in reducing gambling behaviour, but the 'durability of therapeutic gain' is unclear.

A further limitation is a lack of treatment adherence.

Cuijpers *et al.* (2008) indicate that the drop-out rates in CBT treatment groups can be up to five times greater than for other forms of therapy.

Even when clients continue in treatment, their commitment to homework and attendance wanes. Clients often seek CBT during a life crisis and give up once the crisis ends.

Lack of treatment adherence suggests that CBT may not be an effective long-term treatment strategy because clients see it as too challenging.

A strength of CBT is relapse prevention.

CBT incorporates the likelihood of relapse into treatment, viewing it as a further opportunity for learning and cognitive restructuring.

Relapse, rather than being seen as a failure, may be seen as an inevitable part of the addict's life, but acceptable as long as improvement continues.

CBT's effectiveness at preventing relapse is a strength of the therapy.

A limitation of CBT is that it is difficult to know which elements work.

CBT uses a variety of techniques to reduce addictions and can now be delivered in many ways (e.g. online and with telephone support). This allows CBT to be tailored to the individual.

However, this flexibility and variety of use means it is difficult for researchers to identify which elements of CBT are most useful in reducing addiction because there is no standard treatment.

So, whilst CBT's flexibility is a strength of the therapy, it also makes it difficult to draw conclusions about its efficacy.

Applying the theory of planned behaviour

Spec spotlight

The application of the following theory of behaviour change to addictive behaviour – the theory of planned behaviour.

Recovering addicts need more than the best of intentions.

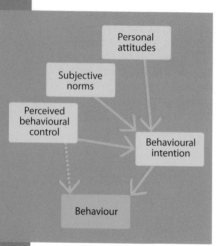

The theory of planned behaviour can be applied to gambling addiction. Intention to stop gambling is central, but does it really determine whether someone gives up?

REVISION BOOSTER

Have you checked out our revision advice on pages 4 to 9?

Theory of planned behaviour applied to addiction

Intention to change must be deliberate and linked to three key influences.	Ajzen's (1985; 1991) theory of planned behaviour (TPB) suggests that changes in addictive behaviour depend on exercising self-control and deliberate behaviours. Central to the model is a person's *intention* to change. Subsequent behaviour can be predicted from a person's intentions. These intentions arise from three key influences: 1. Personal attitudes towards the addiction. 2. Subjective norms: perception of what others think. 3. Perceived behavioural control: beliefs about ability to quit.
1. *Personal attitudes*: Favourable and unfavourable.	'Personal attitudes' refers to the entire collection of the addicted person's attitudes towards their addiction. The addict's overall attitude is formed from weighing up the balance of favourable and unfavourable attitudes. For example, 'it gives me a thrill', 'it's an escape' versus 'I lose more money than I win', 'it makes me feel anxious'.
2. *Subjective norms*: What is 'normal'?	Ideas of 'normality' are based on what key people in the addict's life believe to be 'normal' behaviour. For example, in the case of gambling: Do others gamble? How much? What views have they expressed about it? If the addict concludes that others are unhappy about their gambling, this would make them less likely to *intend* to gamble.
It is about *perception*.	The most influential aspect of subjective norms is the person's *perception* of whether the people closest to them approve or disapprove of their gambling. For example, parents may express favourable attitudes towards something in general (e.g. getting drunk) but disapprove of their own children doing it. Nevertheless the *perception* is that they approve.
3. *Perceived behavioural control*: **Self-efficacy**.	Perceived behavioural control is about how much control we think we have over our behaviour. This is called *self-efficacy*. For example, does the addicted gambler believe they are capable of giving up gambling? This may be related to their perception of resources available to them (e.g. support, time, skill, determination).
Direct and indirect	According to the TPB, perceived behavioural control has two possible effects: 1. It can influence behaviour directly: the greater the perceived control, the longer and harder the addict will try to stop. 2. It can influence intentions to behave: the stronger the self-efficacy, the stronger the intention to stop the gambling.

One strength is that there is some research support.

Hagger et al. (2011) found that the TPB's three factors all predicted an intention to limit drinking. Intentions were also found to influence *actual* alcohol consumption after one and three months.

However, the time periods between intention and behaviour were relatively short. Also, the theory was not able to predict behaviour related to all addictions (e.g. binge drinking).

Therefore, the success of TPB may depend on the addiction that is being studied.

One limitation is that it does not explain the intention-behaviour gap.

Miller and Howell (2005) found strong support for the element of TPB that predicts gambling *intentions* from attitudes, norms and perceived behavioural control in underage teenagers.

However, the model did not predict the occurrence of actual gambling behaviour. Psychologists now question whether TPB is an effective model of behaviour change.

If the theory can't predict behaviour change, it is difficult to create drug-related interventions that bridge the gap between intention to reduce the behaviours and the actual behaviours themselves.

Another limitation is the prediction of long-term changes.

McEachan et al. (2011) conducted a **meta-analysis** of 237 studies and found that the strength of **correlation** between intention and behaviour varied according to the length of time between the two.

Intention to stop drinking, for example, may be a good predictor of giving up, but only if the time between intention and behaviour is short (i.e. less than five weeks). If the time span was longer then intention was not a good predictor.

This may help to explain why the research evidence for the TPB is mixed. Therefore the TPB cannot be accepted as an entirely **valid** explanation of addictive behaviour.

A further limitation is methodological issues.

The TPB is based on measurement of attitudes, norms and perceived behavioural control which are subject to **social desirability**.

Also correlational studies do not allow us to conclude that drug-related intentions cause drug-related behaviours. It may even be that behaviours influence our attitudes.

If the evidence on which the TPB is based is flawed, this affects the validity of the theory.

A final limitation is that TPB assumes behaviour is rational.

The TPB explanation of drug-related behaviours is limited because it emphasises rational reasoning in decision-making.

It has difficulty in accounting for less rational factors such as emotions, **cognitive** biases and past experiences.

Therefore, the TPB lacks explanatory power for the different ways that people think about their behaviour.

Apply it

Holly uses cannabis every day and it is affecting her studies at college. A friend has told her what the long-term effects could be, and there is a real danger that Holly could fail all her exams. She has finally realised that she needs to quit or at least reduce her use – she is enthusiastic about doing this, and believes she has the right motivation. Holly thinks that the time is now.

How could the theory of planned behaviour explain Holly's behaviour and the chances of her changing it?

REVISION BOOSTER

Evidence is key in psychology. But whether it's description (AO1) or evaluation (AO3) depends on how you use it. Are you outlining what the evidence is? Are you describing the procedures and findings of a study? That's AO1. Are you explaining what the evidence tells us about, say, a theory or concept? Are you linking the findings of the study to the theory? That's AO3. But you need to make this clear to the examiner.

KNOWLEDGE CHECK

1. Identify and explain **one** element of the theory of planned behaviour in relation to addictive behaviour. *(3 marks)*
2. Outline the theory of planned behaviour as it applies to addictive behaviour. *(6 marks)*
3. Briefly evaluate the theory of planned behaviour as it applies to addictive behaviour. *(4 marks)*
4. Simon has been discussing with his friends who study psychology that he would like to quit smoking. His friends describe the theory of planned behaviour to him and use it to explain how he could quit.

   Discuss the theory of planned behaviour as it applies to addictive behaviour. Relate your discussion to Simon's situation. *(16 marks)*

Application of Prochaska's model to addictive behaviour

Spec spotlight

The application of the following theory of behaviour change to addictive behaviour – Prochaska's six-stage model of behaviour change.

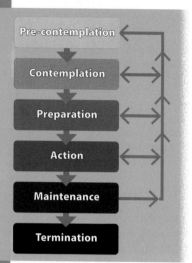

Prochaska's six-stage model.

Kayla believes that she will always be an alcoholic, but she hasn't had a drink for several years. To finally get to this point in her life where she has managed to stay away from drinking, she first had to recognise that she had reached 'rock bottom', that she needed to change, that it would be hard and she would frequently 'fall off the wagon' and relapse. Each time she did, Kayla picked herself back up and stayed away from alcohol until the next time.

Describe Kayla's experience in terms of the stages of Prochaska's model of behaviour change.

Prochaska's six-stage model of behaviour change

Each stage represents differences in readiness to change.	Prochaska and DiClemente (1983) suggest a six-stage model in which overcoming addiction is a cyclical process. Some stages may be reached in order but there is also some backtracking or even missing out of stages. The model is based on two insights about behavioural change: 1. People differ in how ready they are to change. 2. The usefulness of a treatment intervention depends on the stage the person has reached.
Stage 1: Pre-contemplation: 'Ignorance is bliss'.	People in this stage are not thinking about changing their addiction-related behaviour within the next six months. This could be due to *denial* ('I don't have a problem') or *demotivation* ('I have tried before but had no success, so why bother'). *Intervention* should focus on helping the addicted person to consider the need for change.
Stage 2: Contemplation: 'Sitting on the fence'.	Someone at this stage is thinking about making a change to their behaviour in the next six months. They are aware of both the benefits of change and the costs. *Intervention* should focus on helping the person see that the pros outweigh the cons and help them reach a decision to change.
Stage 3: Preparation: 'OK, I'm ready for this'.	Now the individual believes that the benefits are greater than the costs and has decided to make a change within the next month. However, they have not decided how to do this. *Intervention* is support in constructing a plan (e.g. to see a drugs counsellor, to ring a helpline, to see a GP).
Stage 4: Action: 'Let's do this'.	People at this stage have done something to change their addictive behaviour in the last six months. For example, they may be having **cognitive** treatment or have done something less formal such as remove alcohol from the house. *Intervention* should focus on coping skills needed to quit.
Stage 5: Maintenance: 'Stay on track'.	The person has maintained some behavioural change (e.g. stopped gambling) for more than six months. *Intervention* should focus on relapse prevention by encouraging application of coping skills and offering support.
Stage 6: Termination: Abstinence becomes automatic.	At this stage abstinence is automatic and the person no longer returns to addictive behaviours to cope with anxiety, stress, loneliness and so on. *Intervention* is not required at this stage but it may not be possible or realistic for everyone to reach this point.

A strength is that this model recognises the nature of addictive behaviour.

Traditional theories have considered recovery from addiction as an 'all-or-nothing' event. However, the six-stage model stresses a dynamic and continuing process and the importance of time.

This is why the model proposes that behavioural change occurs through six stages of varying duration for each person and that these stages may not be linear.

Therefore, a strength of the model is that it recognises that changing addictive behaviours is a dynamic process.

A limitation is the contradictory research.

Taylor *et al.* (2006) reviewed available evidence and concluded that stage-based approaches are no more effective than alternatives in treating nicotine addiction.

West (2005) is brutal in his assessment of the six-stage model. He concluded that, 'The problems with the model are so serious ... it should be discarded'.

So despite optimistic claims made for the model, the overall research picture is negative.

A further limitation is the arbitrary nature of the stages.

Sutton (2001) points out that if an individual plans to stop smoking in 30 days' time they are in the preparation stage, but in the contemplation stage if they plan to give up in 31 days' time.

Bandura (1997) claims that the first two stages are not even qualitatively different, because the only difference between them is quantitative (how much a person wants to change).

These criticisms challenge the usefulness of the model. Kraft *et al.* (1999) have even suggested that the stages 2–5 should be grouped together.

A strength of the model is the attitude to relapse.

DiClemente *et al.* (2004) suggest that 'relapse is the rule rather than the exception'. The model does not view relapse as a failure, but as an inevitable part of the dynamic process of behaviour change.

The model takes relapse seriously and does not underestimate its potential to blow change off course. Changes to behaviour require several attempts to reach the maintenance or termination stages.

Therefore, it could be said that this model is more realistic and sympathetic in its assessment of behaviour change than other models.

A final limitation is the model's lack of predictive validity.

Most research on the model tries to show that the different stages are associated with addiction-related or treatment-seeking behaviours.

However, this research has produced mixed findings which suggests the model is not a good predictor of who is likely to make changes.

This limits the usefulness of the model and questions the underlying **validity**.

Relapse

is a part of Recovery

Recognising this is a key element of Prochaska's model.

Mnemonic time

The specification includes Prochaska's stages – six of them. That's quite a few, but you should be able to name them all. Create a mnemonic to help you. Make a sentence out of words beginning with the initial letters of each stage:

PC – C – P – A – M – T.

In an essay you won't have time to describe all six in detail so practise an outline version for 200 words maximum.

KNOWLEDGE CHECK

1. Briefly explain **two** theories of behaviour change as applied to addictive behaviour. *(4 marks)*

2. Outline Prochaska's six-stage model of behaviour change as it applies to addictive behaviour. Use examples in your answer. *(6 marks)*

3. Briefly evaluate Prochaska's six-stage model of behaviour change as it applies to addictive behaviour. *(4 marks)*

4. Discuss Prochaska's six-stage model of behaviour change as it applies to addictive behaviour. Refer to evidence in your answer. *(16 marks)*

Glossary

adaptive Any physical or psychological characteristic that enhances an individual's survival and reproduction, and is thus likely to be naturally selected. Such characteristics are passed on to future generations. This is an evolutionary explanation. **18, 19, 41, 74, 89, 136, 137, 148, 157, 186, 188, 189, 196**

androcentric bias Male-centred; when 'normal' behaviour is judged according to a male standard (meaning that female behaviour is often seen as 'abnormal' or 'deficient' by comparison). **103, 157**

antisocial personality disorder A mental health condition where a person has a repeated pattern of manipulating other people or violating the rights of others. Often leads to crimes against people. **198, 210, 213, 230**

APD See antisocial personality disorder.

autonomic nervous system (ANS) Transmits information to and from internal bodily organs. It is 'autonomic' as the system operates involuntarily (i.e. it is automatic). It has two main divisions: the sympathetic and parasympathetic nervous systems. **26, 60, 156, 166, 182**

behaviourist A way of explaining behaviour in terms of what is observable and in terms of learning. **8, 9, 10, 12, 13, 14, 15, 16, 17, 24, 25, 60, 62, 64, 66, 222, 244**

biological approach A perspective that emphasises the importance of physical processes in the body such as genetic inheritance and neural function. **4, 9, 10, 11, 15, 18, 19, 25, 60, 95, 99, 105, 127, 134, 141, 151, 193, 213**

biological determinism The belief that behaviour is caused by biological (genetic, hormonal, evolutionary) influences that we cannot control. **60, 63, 208, 211, 213**

biological reductionism A form of reductionism which attempts to explain social and psychological phenomena at a lower biological level (in terms of the actions of gene, hormones, etc.). **64, 65, 211**

case study A research method that involves a detailed study of a single individual, institution or event. Case studies provide a rich record of human experience but are hard to generalise from. **11, 21, 31, 38, 39, 46, 47, 66, 67, 102**

CBT A method for treating mental disorders and other conditions based on both cognitive and behavioural techniques. From the cognitive viewpoint the therapy aims to deal with thinking, such as challenging negative thoughts. The therapy also includes behavioural techniques. **24, 132, 133, 134, 135, 149, 215, 224, 229, 239, 244, 245**

classical conditioning Learning by association. Occurs when two stimuli are repeatedly paired together – an unconditioned (unlearned) stimulus (UCS) and a new 'neutral' stimulus (NS). The neutral stimulus eventually produces the same response that was first produced by the unlearned stimulus alone. **12, 15, 132, 136, 138, 139, 146, 234, 240, 242**

cognitive Refers to the process of thinking – knowing, perceiving, believing. **6, 8, 10, 11, 13, 14, 15, 16, 17, 18, 24, 25, 31, 33, 36, 43, 46, 61, 64, 66, 80, 95, 98, 99, 100, 101, 104, 108, 109, 110, 111, 112, 113, 114, 115, 116, 117, 118, 119, 121, 122, 128, 129, 130, 132, 133, 148, 149, 152, 154, 155, 157, 174, 178, 192, 200, 201, 214, 215, 224, 225, 237, 238, 239, 244, 245, 247, 248**

cognitive behaviour therapy See CBT.

collectivist A group of people who place more value on the 'collective' rather than on the individual, and on interdependence rather than on independence. The opposite is true of individualist culture. **23, 59, 73, 81, 85, 89, 165, 198**

concordance rates A measure of similarity (usually expressed as a percentage) between two individuals or sets of individuals on a given trait. **18, 62, 63, 109, 142, 143, 150, 151, 184, 211**

confederate An individual in a study who is not a real participant and who has been instructed how to behave by the researcher. **183, 190, 195, 200, 201**

confounding variable (CV) Any variable, other than the independent variable (IV), that may have affected the dependent variable (DV) so we cannot be sure of the true source of changes to the DV. Confounding variables vary systematically with the IV. **19, 39, 41, 43, 63, 143, 165, 167, 199, 209, 211**

control condition The condition in a repeated measures design that provides a baseline measure of behaviour without the experimental treatment (independent variable). **120, 191, 195**

control group In an experiment with an independent groups design, a group of participants who receive no treatment. Their behaviour acts as a baseline against which the effect of the independent variable (IV) may be measured. **32, 49, 115, 119, 120, 129, 133, 135, 148, 153, 155, 158, 169, 177, 181, 190, 196, 209, 213, 215, 218, 239, 245**

correlation A mathematical technique in which a researcher investigates an association between two variables, called co-variables. Correlational studies are studies which have used a correlational analysis. **44, 45, 48, 49, 50, 51, 53, 73, 75, 80, 83, 89, 97, 106, 107, 119, 126, 127, 153, 160, 161, 162, 163, 164, 166, 182, 183, 189, 195, 198, 199, 219, 230, 231, 247**

criterion validity A means of assessing validity by considering the extent to which people who do well on a particular test also do well on other things that you would expect to be associated with the particular test. **125**

cultural bias Refers to a tendency to ignore cultural differences and interpret all phenomena through the 'lens' of one's own culture. **23, 58, 59, 107, 125, 213**

de-individuation A psychological state in which an individual loses their personal identity and takes on the identity of the social group when, for example, in a crowd or wearing a uniform. The result may be to free the individual from the constraints of social norms. **65, 86, 194, 195**

demand characteristics Any cue from the researcher or from the research situation that may be interpreted by participants as revealing the purpose of the investigation. This may lead to a participant changing their behaviour within the research situation. **15, 59**

determinism The view that an individual's behaviour is shaped or controlled by internal or external forces rather than an individual's will to do something. **15, 17, 19, 21, 24, 25, 60, 61, 217**

diathesis-stress model An interactionist approach to explaining behaviour. For example, schizophrenia is explained as the result of both an underlying vulnerability (diathesis) and a trigger, both of which are necessary for the onset of schizophrenia. In early versions of the model, vulnerability was genetic and triggers were psychological. Nowadays both genes and trauma are seen as diatheses, and stress can be psychological or biological in nature. **25, 62, 65, 129, 134, 135, 143, 147, 184, 210, 211**

disinhibited (disinhibition) Normal social constraints against certain behaviours can be weakened by environmental triggers. These behaviours then appear temporarily socially acceptable and therefore more likely. **86, 150, 152, 153, 154, 155, 200, 201**

dopamine A neurotransmitter that generally has an excitatory effect and is associated with the sensation of pleasure. Unusually high levels are associated with schizophrenia and unusually low levels are associated with Parkinson's disease. **9, 29, 126, 127, 129, 130, 131, 134, 142, 143, 150, 151, 210, 229, 230, 231, 232, 233, 234, 240**

DSM The Diagnostic and Statistical Manual of Mental Disorders is a classification system of mental disorders published by the American Psychiatric Association. It contains typical symptoms of each disorder and guidelines for clinicians to make a diagnosis. The most recent version is DSM-5. **108, 124, 125, 148**

DZ twins (dizygotic) Non-identical twins formed from two fertilised eggs (or zygotes). **18, 62, 108, 126, 142, 143, 151, 184, 210, 211**

EEG Electroencephalograph. A method of detecting activity in the living brain, electrodes are attached to a person's scalp to record general levels of electrical activity. **6, 10, 36, 37, 40, 176, 213**

environmental determinism The belief that behaviour is caused by aspects of our physical or social world that we cannot control, such as rewards/punishments from other people determining our future behaviour (learning theory). **13, 60, 61, 63, 217**

environmental reductionism The attempt to explain all behaviour in terms of stimulus-response links that have been learned through experience. **64, 65**

evolutionary An account of the changes in species over millions of years. Genetic characteristics that enhance survival and reproduction are naturally selected. These characteristics are passed on to the next generation. Animals without such characteristics are less successful at reproduction and thus are not selected. **18, 19, 41, 64, 70, 71, 74, 75, 122, 123, 136, 137, 178, 188, 189, 208, 209**

experiment Involves the manipulation of an independent variable (IV) to measure the effect on the dependent variable (DV). Experiments may be laboratory, field, natural or quasi. **4, 9, 10, 12, 13, 15, 35, 44, 46, 48, 49, 50, 54, 55, 60, 65, 155, 174, 182, 185, 198, 199, 210, 216, 233, 235**

experimental condition The condition in a repeated measures design containing the independent variable (IV) as distinct from the control condition. **15, 120**

external validity The degree to which a research finding can be generalised to, for example, other settings (ecological validity), other groups of people (population validity) and over time (temporal validity). **17, 159**

extraneous variable (EV) Any variable, other than the independent variable (IV), that *may* have an effect on the dependent variable (DV) if it is not controlled. EVs include CVs but also include 'nuisance variables' that do not vary systematically with the IV. Such nuisance variables should not confound the results of research. **4, 60**

face validity A basic form of validity in which a measure is scrutinised to determine whether it appears to measure what it is supposed to measure – for instance, does a test of anxiety look like it measures anxiety? **49, 61**

fMRI Functional magnetic resonance imaging. A method used to scan brain activity while a person is performing a task. It enables researchers to detect those regions of the brain that are rich in oxygen and thus are active. **10, 19, 36, 37, 123, 182**

free will The notion that humans can make choices and are not determined by biological or external forces. **13, 15, 17, 21, 22, 25, 60, 61, 211**

GABA Gamma-aminobutyric acid, a neurotransmitter that inhibits the activity of neurons in most areas of the brain. **143, 172, 233, 240**

gender bias When considering human behaviour, bias is a tendency to treat one individual or group in a different way from others. In the context of gender bias, psychological research or theory may offer a view that does not justifiably represent the experience and behaviour of men or women (usually women). **4, 56, 57, 124, 125, 145, 219**

generalisation In relation to research findings, the extent to which findings and conclusions from a particular investigation can be broadly applied to the wider population. This is made less likely if the sample of participants is unrepresentative of the wider population. **35, 39, 43, 44, 49, 55, 67, 73, 97, 109, 141, 165, 183, 187, 213**

hard determinism Implies that free will is not possible as our behaviour is always caused by internal or external events beyond our control. **60, 61, 63**

holism An argument or theory which proposes that it only makes sense to study a whole system rather than its constituent parts (which is the reductionist approach). **9, 23, 25, 30, 31, 64, 65**

humanistic approach/ psychology An approach to understanding behaviour that emphasises the importance of subjective experience and each person's capacity for self-determination. **4, 9, 11, 22, 23, 25, 60, 64, 66**

ICD The International Classification of Disorders published by the World Health Organisation. The most recent version (1993) is number 10. ICD is used in the UK and Europe whereas DSM is American. **124, 125**

individualist A group of people who value the rights and interests of the individual. This results in a concern for independence and self-assertiveness. People tend to live in small families unlike collectivist societies. This is typical of Western cultures, in contrast to many non-Western cultures that tend to be collectivist. **23, 59, 73, 81, 85, 89, 165, 198**

informed consent An ethical issue and an ethical guideline in psychological research whereby participants must be given comprehensive information concerning the nature and purpose of the research and their role in it, in order for them to make an informed decision about whether to participate. **37**

longitudinal Research conducted over a long period of time – months or years. **46, 81, 119, 198, 199**

meta-analysis 'Research about research', refers to the process of combining results from a number of studies on a particular topic to provide an overall view. This may involve a qualitative review of conclusions and/or a quantitative analysis of the results producing an effect size. **44, 75, 151, 175, 184, 185, 191, 198, 235, 247**

modelling From the observer's perspective modelling is imitating the behaviour of a role model. From the role model's perspective, modelling is the precise demonstration of a specific behaviour that may be imitated by an observer. **14, 15, 24, 104, 105, 146, 147, 193, 233**

MZ twins (monozygotic) Identical twins formed from one fertilised egg (or zygote). They have exactly the same genes. **18, 62, 63, 108, 109, 126, 142, 143, 150, 151, 184, 210, 211**

natural experiment An experiment where the change in the independent variable (IV) is not brought about by the researcher but would have happened even if the researcher had not been there. The researcher records the effect on the dependent variable (DV). **164, 165**

nature–nurture debate The question of whether behaviour is determined more by nature (inherited and genetic factors) or nurture (all influences after conception, i.e. experience). **18, 19, 24, 62, 63, 97, 107, 109**

oestrogen The primary female hormone, playing an important role in the menstrual cycle and reproductive system. **40, 94, 95, 178**

operant conditioning A form of learning in which behaviour is shaped and maintained by its consequences. Possible consequences of behaviour include positive reinforcement, negative reinforcement or punishment. **12, 13, 15, 132, 138, 146, 176, 192, 222, 234**

operationalise Clearly defining variables in terms of how they can be measured. **48, 49, 65, 79, 211**

oxytocin A hormone which causes contraction of the uterus during labour and stimulates lactation. It is linked to the 'tend and befriend' stress response. **56, 94, 95, 178, 179**

parasympathetic nervous system A division of the autonomic nervous system (ANS) which controls the relaxed state (rest and digest), conserving resources and promoting digestion and metabolism. The parasympathetic nervous system works in opposition to the sympathetic nervous system. One or the other system is active at any time. **26, 27, 156**

placebo A treatment that should have no effect on the behaviour being studied; it contains no active ingredient. Therefore it can be used to separate out the effects of the independent variable (IV) from any effects caused merely by receiving any treatment. **41, 95, 131, 173, 177, 183, 241, 243**

predictive validity A means of assessing the validity or trueness of a psychological test (or explanation) by correlating the results of the test with some later example of the behaviour that is being tested. If the test result is positively correlated with the later behaviour this confirms the validity of the test. **249**

psychodynamic An approach to understanding behaviour that describes the different forces (dynamics), most of which are unconscious, that operate on the mind and direct human behaviour and experience. Freud's psychoanalytic theory is the best known example of the psychodynamic approach. **7, 11, 20, 21, 25, 66, 95, 102, 103, 105, 128, 144, 190, 218, 219**

PTSD (post-traumatic stress disorder) A disabling reaction to stress following a traumatic event. The response does not always appear immediately after the event. The reactions are long-lasting, and include: reliving the event recurrently in flashbacks and dreams; emotional numbness; and general anxiety which may result in lack of concentration. **230**

publication bias The tendency for some kinds of research to be published rather than other types. For example, academic journals may prefer not to publish research that is counter to established principles or research with negative results. **198, 199**

random allocation An attempt to control for participant variables in an independent groups design which ensures that each participant has the same chance of being in one condition as any other. **133, 135, 153, 165, 197, 199, 245**

randomised controlled trial An independent groups design where participants are randomly allocated to conditions and one condition acts as a control. Often used to test medical treatments. **173**

reductionism The belief that human behaviour is best explained by breaking it down into smaller constituent parts. **4, 9, 17, 23, 24, 25, 64, 65, 233**

replicate Repeating an investigation under the same conditions in order to test the validity and reliability of its findings. **8, 10, 13, 43, 54, 58, 77, 123, 141, 157, 169**

researcher bias The effect that a researcher's expectations have on participants and thus on the results of an experiment or any study. **46, 219**

schema A mental framework of beliefs and expectations that influence cognitive processing. Schema contain our understanding of an object, person or idea. Schema become increasingly complex during development as we acquire more information about each object or idea. **16, 17, 24, 100, 101, 108, 109, 110, 111, 112**

self-efficacy One's confidence in being able to do something. Such confidence generates expectations and these act as self-fulfilling prophecies. **165, 192, 193, 235, 238, 246**

serotonin A neurotransmitter found in the central nervous system. Low levels have been linked to many different behaviours and physiological processes, including aggression, eating disorders and depression. **18, 29, 40, 64, 130, 142, 143, 150, 151, 182, 183, 184, 185, 210, 233**

social desirability bias A tendency for respondents to answer questions in such a way that presents themselves in a better light, i.e. they appear kinder, more intelligent, more attractive, etc. **49, 89, 247**

social learning theory (SLT) A way of explaining behaviour that includes both direct and indirect reinforcement, combining learning theory with the role of cognitive factors. **13, 14, 15, 24, 25, 61, 95, 99, 100, 104, 105, 138, 139, 146, 147, 192, 193**

soft determinism The concept that there are constraints on our behaviour but within these limitations we are free to make choices. **17, 24, 60, 61**

somatic nervous system (SNS) Transmits information from receptor cells in the sense organs to the central nervous system (CNS). It also receives information from the CNS that directs muscles to act. **26**

Glossary

standardised (procedures, instructions, conditions) Using exactly the same formalised procedures, instructions and conditions for all participants in a research study.   **10, 11, 35, 37, 48, 49, 54, 67**

sympathetic nervous system A division of the autonomic nervous system (ANS) which activates internal organs for vigorous activities and emergencies, such as the fight or flight response. It consists of nerves that control, for example, increased heart rate and breathing, and decreased digestive activity. The sympathetic branch works in opposition to the parasympathetic branch of the ANS.   **26, 172, 200, 212**

temporal validity The extent to which findings from a research study can be generalised to other historical times and eras. A form of external validity.   **49, 77, 93**

testosterone A hormone produced mainly by the testes in males, but it also occurs in females. It is associated with the development of secondary sexual characteristics in males (e.g. body hair), and has also been implicated in aggression and dominance behaviours.   **15, 60, 94, 95, 178, 182, 183, 212**

validity Refers to whether an observed effect is a genuine one.   **8, 13, 17, 23, 35, 41, 46, 47, 49, 55, 57, 59, 61, 65, 67, 68, 75, 77, 79, 81, 83, 87, 89, 91, 93, 99, 101, 103, 107, 111, 113, 115, 117, 121, 124, 125, 129, 141, 143, 147, 149, 151, 153, 155, 157, 159, 161, 163, 165, 167, 169, 171, 179, 181, 183, 185, 187, 189, 191, 193, 197, 199, 201, 203, 205, 208, 211, 239, 243, 247**

p.11, p.16, p.26, p.34 (bottom), p.90 (bottom), p.91 (bottom), p.96 (both), p.116 (bottom), p.120 (bottom), p.126, p.130, p.152 (bottom), p.166, p.182, p.186 (bottom), p.232, p.240 (bottom), p.246 (bottom), p.248 © Illuminate Publishing

p.13 © Craig Swanson www.perspicuity.com

p.31 Barking Dog Art

p.3 and p.256 Stars Aha-Soft / Shutterstock.com; p.5 marekuliasz / Shutterstock.com; Aleksova / Shutterstock.com; Sashkin / Shutterstock.com; p.6 Kuklos / Shutterstock.com; p.7 ostill / Shutterstock.com; p.10 CYCLONEPROJECT / Shutterstock.com; p.12 WilleeCole Photography / Shutterstock.com; p.14 Evgeny Atamanenko / Shutterstock.com; p.17 Lukiyanova Natalia / frenta / Shutterstock.com; p.18 Katrina Elena / Shutterstock.com; p.19 kiss / Shutterstock.com; p.20 RACOBOVT / Shutterstock.com; p.21 ehmi nanthis / Shutterstock.com; p.22 Joseph Sohm / Shutterstock.com; p.23 Jane0606 / Shutterstock.com; p.24 arda savasciogullari / Shutterstock.com; p.25 gielmichal / Shutterstock.com; p.27 Mike Baldwin / Cornered ; p.28 Fotolia ; p.29 joshya / Shutterstock.com; p.30 Alila Medical Media / Shutterstock.com; p.32 Ocskay Bence / Shutterstock.com; p.33 martan / Shutterstock.com; p.34 (top) Chad Zuber / Shutterstock.com; p.35 Oksana Telesheva / Shutterstock.com; p.36 Daisy Daisy / Shutterstock.com; p.37 Oleg Senkov / Shutterstock.com; p.38 yomogi1 / Shutterstock.com; p.39 jadimages / Shutterstock.com; p.40 Albina Glisic / Shutterstock.com; p.41 Image Point Fr / Shutterstock.com; p.42 fotofeel / Shutterstock.com; p.43 Javier Brosch / Shutterstock.com; p.44 Fabrik Bilder / Shutterstock.com; p.45 A. and I. Kruk / Shutterstock.com; p.46 / Shutterstock.com; p.47 eteimaging / Shutterstock.com; p.48 Tony Campbell / Shutterstock.com; p.49 VICHAILAO / Shutterstock.com; p.50 kurhan / Shutterstock.com; p.51 studiovin / Shutterstock.com; p.53 JONGSUK / Shutterstock.com; p.54 124706830 / Shutterstock.com; p.55 alphaspirit / Shutterstock.com; p.56 Lightspring / Shutterstock.com; p.57 Aleutie / Shutterstock.com; p.58 Evannovostro / Shutterstock.com; p.59 Ilike / Shutterstock.com; p.60 Dmitry Guzhanin / Shutterstock.com; p.61 (top) wavebreakmedia / Shutterstock.com; p.61 (bottom) vkilikov / Shutterstock.com; p.62 LeventeGyori / Shutterstock.com; p.63 herjua / Shutterstock.com; p.64 aaltair / Shutterstock.com; p.65 NEIL ROY JOHNSON / Shutterstock.com; p.66 Andrey_Kuzmin / Shutterstock.com; p.67 Kichigin / Shutterstock.com; p.68 Paul Vasarhelyi / Shutterstock.com; p.69 AndreAnita / Shutterstock.com; p.70 gpointstudio / Shutterstock.com; p.71 pathdoc / Shutterstock.com; p.72 Ollyy / Shutterstock.com; p.73 Maros Bauer / Shutterstock.com; p.74 Flashon Studio / Shutterstock.com; p.75 Halfpoint / Shutterstock.com; p.76 beeboys / Shutterstock.com; p.77 MAD_Production / Shutterstock.com; p.78 BlueSkyImage / Shutterstock.com; p.79 Di Studio / Shutterstock.com; p.80 docstockmedia / Shutterstock.com; p.81 Yanush868 / Shutterstock.com; p.82 Ekaterina Pokrovsky / Shutterstock.com; p.83 Jack Frog / Shutterstock.com; p.84 g-stockstudio / Shutterstock.com; p.85 DNF Style / Shutterstock.com; p.86 Syda Productions / Shutterstock.com; p.87 Mila Supinskaya Glashchenko / Shutterstock.com; p.88 mooinblack / Shutterstock.com; p.89 Featureflash Photo Agency / Shutterstock.com; p.90 (top) FMStox / Shutterstock.com; p.91 (top) Monkey Business Images / Shutterstock.com; p.92 Tinxi / Shutterstock.com; p.93 Mai Groves / Shutterstock.com; p.94 Knorre / Shutterstock.com; p.95 Zerbor / Shutterstock.com; p.98 Fred Ho / Shutterstock.com; p.99 zlikovec / Shutterstock.com; p.100 dotshock / Shutterstock.com; p.101 Hugo Felix / Shutterstock.com; p.102 Oksana Kuzmina / Shutterstock.com; p.103 Antonio Guillem / Shutterstock.com; p.104 InnervisionArt / Shutterstock.com; p.105 Videologia / Shutterstock.com; p.106 Jamie Hooper / Shutterstock.com; p.107 Stuart Miles / Shutterstock.com; p.108 racorn / Shutterstock.com; p.109 TheModernCanvas / Shutterstock.com; p.110 AJP / Shutterstock.com; p.111 Andi Berger / Shutterstock.com; p.112 Purino / Shutterstock.com; p.113 Kidsada Manchinda / Shutterstock.com; p.114 Kokliang / Shutterstock.com; p.115 Boris Bulychev / Shutterstock.com; p.116 (top) gualtiero boffi / Shutterstock.com; p.117 fizkes / Shutterstock.com; p.118 jeafish Ping / Shutterstock.com; p.119 Monkey Business Images / Shutterstock.com; p.120 (top) Tomasz Trojanowski / Shutterstock.com; p.121 Dean Drobot / Shutterstock.com; p.122 George Rudy / Shutterstock.com; p.123 mayakova / Shutterstock.com; p.124 alphaspirit / Shutterstock.com; p.125 Antonio Guillem / Shutterstock.com; p.127 AkeSak /

Shutterstock.com; p.128 Sangoiri / Shutterstock.com; p.129 Luis Molinero / Shutterstock.com; p.131 Gwoeii / Shutterstock.com; p.132 SpeedKingz / Shutterstock.com; p.133 bluezace / Shutterstock.com; p.134 Joshua Resnick / Shutterstock.com; p.135 ostill / Shutterstock.com; p.136 Photographee.eu / Shutterstock.com; p.137 Lopolo / Shutterstock.com; p.138 Nagy-Bagoly Arpad / Shutterstock.com; p.139 Monkey Business Images / Shutterstock.com; p.140; stefan3andrei / Shutterstock.com; p.141 Cathy Keifer / Shutterstock.com; p.142 Phovoir / Shutterstock.com; p.143 Ermolaev Alexander / Shutterstock.com; p.144 Iakov Filimonov / Shutterstock.com; p.145 Lisa F. Young / Shutterstock.com; p.146 Featureflash Photo Agency / Shutterstock.com; p.147 Keith Homan / Shutterstock.com; p.148 Photographee.eu / Shutterstock.com; p.149 wavebreakmedia / Shutterstock.com; p.150 Kletr / Shutterstock.com; p.151 LuckyStep / Shutterstock.com; p.152 (top) Vlue / Shutterstock.com; p.153 Duplass / Shutterstock.com; p.154 Lamberrto / Shutterstock.com; p.155 VGstockstudio / Shutterstock.com; p.156 Cartoonresource / Shutterstock.com; p.157 Sam72 / Shutterstock.com; p.158 altafulla / Shutterstock.com; p.159 Anelina / Shutterstock.com; p.160 Anton Havelaar / Shutterstock.com; p.161 Tyler Olson / Shutterstock.com; p.162 Thinglass / Shutterstock.com; p.163 DJTaylor / Shutterstock.com; p.164 Iakov Filimonov / Shutterstock.com; p.165 g-stockstudio / Shutterstock.com; p.167 Minerva Studio / Shutterstock.com; p.168 (top) Mooshny / Shutterstock.com; p.168 (bottom) wavebreakmedia / Shutterstock.com; p.170 Brocreative / Shutterstock.com; p.171 tomertu / Shutterstock.com; p.172 iofoto / Shutterstock.com; p.173 Image Point Fr / Shutterstock.com; p.174 wavebreakmedia / Shutterstock.com; p.175 Luis Molinero / Shutterstock.com; p.176 J. McPhail / Shutterstock.com; p.177 Andrey_Popov / Shutterstock.com; p.178 Peshkova / Shutterstock.com; p.179 Rawpixel.com / Shutterstock.com; p.180 michaeljung / Shutterstock.com; p.181 Paul Looyen / Shutterstock.com; p.183 SFIO CRACHO / Shutterstock.com; p.184 Dimj / Shutterstock.com; p.185 marcovarro / Shutterstock.com; p.186 (top) Shaiith / Shutterstock.com; p.187 Monkey Business Images / Shutterstock.com; p.188 Dusan Petkovic / Shutterstock.com; p.189 William Perugini / Shutterstock.com; p.190 pathdoc / Shutterstock.com; p.191 Catalin Petolea / Shutterstock.com; p.192 Shutterstock / SpeedKingz; p.193 wavebreakmedia / Shutterstock.com; p.194 Alexander_P / Shutterstock.com; p.195 (top) 1000 Words / Shutterstock.com; p.195 (bottom) natrot / Shutterstock.com; p.196 Lightspring / Shutterstock.com; p.197 Nejron Photo / Shutterstock.com; p.198 Ekaterina_Minaeva / Shutterstock.com; p.199 Bojan656 / Shutterstock.com; p.200 antos777 / Shutterstock.com; p.201 Aleksei Semjonov / Shutterstock.com; p.202 sebra / Shutterstock.com; p.203 Orange Line Media / Shutterstock.com; p.204 Javier Brosch / Shutterstock.com; p.205 Opachevsky Irina / Shutterstock.com; p.206 Couperfield / Shutterstock.com; p.207 pingebat / Shutterstock.com; p.208 Zemler / Shutterstock.com; p.210 Chandler McGrew / Shutterstock.com; p.211 Monkey Business Images / Shutterstock.com; p.212 CREATISTA / Shutterstock.com; p.213 Sirswindon at English Wikipedia; p.214 Lucky Business / Shutterstock.com; p.215 marina shinkarchuk / Shutterstock.com; p.216 En min Shen / Shutterstock.com; p.217 sdecoret / Shutterstock.com; p.218 Eugene Partyzan / Shutterstock.com; p.219 Brian A Jackson / Shutterstock.com; p.220 Fer Gregory / Shutterstock.com; p.221 chekart / Shutterstock.com; p.222 TaraPatta / Shutterstock.com; p.223 chrisdorney / Shutterstock.com; p.224 Carlos Caetano / Shutterstock.com; p.225 bikeriderlondon / Shutterstock.com; p.226 StepanPopov / Shutterstock.com; p.227 WindVector / Shutterstock.com; p.228 wk1003mike / Shutterstock.com; p.229 iQoncept / Shutterstock.com; p.230 M-SUR / Shutterstock.com; p.231 Maridav / Shutterstock.com; p.233 Meryll / Shutterstock.com; p.234 moj0j0 / Shutterstock.com; p.235 Tony Wear / Shutterstock.com; p.236 nd3000 / Shutterstock.com; p.237 Icatnews / Shutterstock.com; p.238 Enrique Pellejer / Shutterstock.com; p.239 Photostriker / Shutterstock.com; p.240 (top) Dima Sobko / Shutterstock.com; p.241 Kjpargeter / Shutterstock.com; p.242 ra2studio / Shutterstock.com; p.243 Sabphoto / Shutterstock.com; p.244 Shcherbakov Ilya / Shutterstock.com; p.245 Photographee.eu / Shutterstock.com; p.246 (top) Constantin Stanciu / Shutterstock.com; p.249 Marie Appert / Shutterstock.com

Revision Guide

+

Revision App

=

An unbeatable combination for revision!

Have your cake and eat it when you combine this **Revision Guide** with its companion *Revision App*. The app content mirrors the guide but the app has special features and is ideal for revision on the go.

- Flash cards summarise all the essential knowledge
- Drill deeper for more detailed revision notes as well as exam advice
- Quizzes and challenges test and reinforce knowledge and understanding
- Web links take you to useful web pages and films
- Exam-style questions help you study and practise for the exams
- Definitions for key terms can be accessed as you read the content

Read this guide when you are at home and then consolidate your knowledge with the app when you are on the move.

Boost your revision into the stratosphere. Download the Year 1 & AS and Year 2 apps from the Apple and Android App Stores NOW!

Visit: www.illuminatepublishing.com/psychapp for links to the app stores.

Year 1 & AS Revision Guide and App also available!